T0310195

Praise for *Getting Multi-Channel Distribution Right*

"Despite their prevalence and importance to firms, multi-channel distribution systems remain poorly understood. This book provides an original and much-needed framework for examining such distribution arrangements. It does a masterful job of blending academic research, both classic and emerging, with cutting-edge industry examples and case studies. The book is packed with original insights; in particular I found the discussion of performance metrics to be outstanding. It will be an invaluable resource to a number of audiences, including academics, marketing and sales practitioners, and regulators. Professors Ailawadi and Farris clearly got multi-channel distribution right."

Jan Heide
Professor, University of Wisconsin School of Business

"The digital revolution has fundamentally changed the way that distribution channels work. Along with the opportunities to reach consumers through many different routes comes much greater potential for conflict between manufacturers, retailers, and the other intermediaries in the marketplace today. The insights, frameworks, and in-depth case examples in Getting Multi-Channel Distribution Right effectively separate the signal from the noise. The book is comprehensive and timely, and also an enjoyable read. You'll find yourself referring to it often as you navigate your physical and digital distribution channels."

Barbara Kahn
Professor, Wharton School, Author of *The Shopping Revolution*

"Every marketer should read *Getting Multi-Channel Distribution Right* and have it on their bookshelf. Distribution is arguably the most fundamental dimension of marketing, yet mysterious because few have exposure to the business-to-business "blocking and tackling" which undergirds distribution partnerships. This book is a gift from two researchers, experienced with distribution practice, who are responsible for the marketing literature's richest distribution insights. Kusum Ailawadi and Paul Farris move us from designing a distribution channel from a small set of well understood components to assembling a channel ecosystem with business models that did not even exist a decade ago. In this accessible presentation of modern routes-to-market, they guide suppliers through the triple objective of expanding distribution in the different channels where consumers search for or buy their products, while reducing conflict among channel members and preserving the equity of their brands."

Leigh McAlister
Professor, McCombs School of Business, UT Austin

More Praise for *Getting Multi-Channel Distribution Right*

"A lot is written about omnichannel retail, and rightly so. But if you are a supplier, you need to figure out how to choose and manage the multiple *independent* channels, both physical and online, through which you sell your products. That is the challenge Professors Ailawadi and Farris tackle in this timely and thoughtful book. With up-to-date metrics and frameworks applied to live case studies, they pull together a physical and online distribution strategy toolkit unlike any other available today. If you are a supplier looking to bring your route-to-market in line with how consumers shop today, or if you are a retailer, e-tailer, or other intermediary operating in that value chain, or if you are managing a digitally native vertical brand, or if you train any of these aforementioned executives, then this book is an essential read."

Das Narayandas
Professor and Senior Associate Dean, Harvard Business School

"This book addresses a pressing need in marketing today: the challenge of expanding into and managing multiple channels of distribution. Experienced marketers as well as those new to marketing channels will discover how classic frameworks must be expanded and adapted to manage digital as well as brick and mortar distribution systems. The authors deftly integrate metrics with strategic issues such as understanding consumers' search loyalty, the application and preservation of power, the limits of the direct-to-consumer channel, and policies that achieve the right physical and digital coverage while keeping conflict manageable. The value of the metrics and strategic frameworks is vividly illustrated in cases and examples that span both digital and physical products."

John Quelch
Vice Provost, University of Miami and Dean, Miami Herbert Business School

"As P&G's former CEO A.G. Lafley said distribution is the "first moment of truth." If you fail in getting the product to the customer and getting the right support and appeal at the point of purchase, you fail. Ailawadi and Farris provide a *comprehensive* coverage of multi-channel marketing and its evolution in today's world. With the advent of e-commerce, m-commerce, what Jim Lecinski, Google's former VP of Customer Solutions has called the "zero moment of truth," and new forms of distribution, a re-boot of how we think

More Praise for *Getting Multi-Channel Distribution Right*

about distribution is essential. Few aspects of marketing, if any, have changed more over the last couple of decades than distribution. With real life case examples, Ailawadi and Farris make the issues come alive. They have nailed how to manage your distribution strategy."

David Reibstein
Professor, Wharton School, Coauthor of *Marketing Metrics*

"Ailawadi and Farris draw on their extensive consulting and academic experience to provide a compelling account of multi-channel distribution. The book skillfully blends academic insights with relevant examples and provides actionable frameworks and metrics. A must-read for manufacturers and retailers that want to thrive in the multi-channel environment."

Jan-Benedict Steenkamp
Professor, Kenan-Flagler School UNC Chapel Hill, Co-author of *Retail Disruptors*

"Digital disruption and the resulting need to manage distribution and demand across channels are critical issues for the leading corporations sponsoring the Marketing Science Institute. But as Professors Ailawadi and Farris note, "getting multi-channel distribution right is about much more than going digital." Beyond a focus on *omni*-channel—offering customers a "seamless" experience across touchpoints—the authors demonstrate the equally important need to optimize *multi*-channel relationships between upstream suppliers and downstream channel partners. Combining rigor and practical relevance, this book provides managers with clear strategic frameworks for implementing multi-channel distribution."

Earl Taylor
Chief Knowledge Officer, Marketing Science Institute

"Multi-channel distribution is the most important, complex challenge facing manufacturers today. Kusum and Paul explain it using recent examples in plain English. Most importantly, they show how to make realistic solutions work in practice. *Getting Multi-Channel Distribution Right* is the clearest and most useful book in its category."

Kenneth Wilbur
Professor, Rady School of Management, UC San Diego

Getting Multi-Channel Distribution Right

Getting Multi-Channel Distribution Right

Kusum L. Ailawadi
Paul W. Farris

WILEY

Published by John Wiley & Sons, Inc., Hoboken, New Jersey.
Published simultaneously in Canada.

For general information on our other products and services or for technical support, please contact our Customer Care Department within the United States at (800) 762–2974, outside the United States at (317) 572–3993, or fax (317) 572–4002.

Wiley publishes in a variety of print and electronic formats and by print-on-demand. Some material included with standard print versions of this book may not be included in e-books or in print-on-demand. If this book refers to media such as a CD or DVD that is not included in the version you purchased, you may download this material at http://booksupport.wiley.com. For more information about Wiley products, visit www.wiley.com.

Library of Congress Cataloging-in-Publication Data:

Names: Ailawadi, Kusum L., author. | Farris, Paul W., author.
Title: Getting multi-channel distribution right / Kusum L. Ailawadi, Paul W. Farris.
Description: First edition. | Hoboken, New Jersey : John Wiley & Sons, 2020. | Includes index.
Identifiers: LCCN 2019056782 (print) | LCCN 2019056783 (ebook) | ISBN 9781119632887 (hardback) | ISBN 9781119632900 (adobe pdf) | ISBN 9781119632917 (epub)
Subjects: LCSH: Marketing channels.
Classification: LCC HF5415.129 .A45 2020 (print) | LCC HF5415.129 (ebook) | DDC 658.8/7—dc23
LC record available at https://lccn.loc.gov/2019056782
LC ebook record available at https://lccn.loc.gov/2019056783

Cover Design: Wiley
Cover Images: Top view of an infinity © Sahacha Nilkumhang/Getty Images, Binary code © nadla/Getty Images

Printed in the United States of America

V10018058_031820

We dedicate this book to our parents,
Nirmal and Raj Kumar Ailawadi
Frances and Paul Farris

Contents

About the Authors

Kusum L. Ailawadi is the Charles Jordan 1911 TU'12 Professor of Marketing at the Tuck School of Business at Dartmouth College. She received her BSc (Honors) and MBA degrees from Delhi University and the Indian Institute of Management-Bangalore, respectively, and her PhD from the University of Virginia. She has been on the faculty at Tuck since 1993 and currently serves as the chair of the marketing department.

Professor Ailawadi's research expertise is in managing the partnership and the power balance between suppliers and their distribution channel members. She has published extensively in the major marketing journals on topics such as the manifestation of brand equity in marketplace performance; the impact of promotions and private label brands on the performance of manufacturers and retailers; and consumer, competitor, and channel response to major marketing policy changes. Her work has won accolades and awards from the *Journal of Marketing, Journal of Marketing Research, Journal of Retailing*, and *Marketing Science* for best contributions to marketing theory and the practice of marketing research, for best collaboration between academics and practitioners, for overall best papers, and for long-term impact. She has also written on these topics for practitioner audiences in publications like the *Harvard Business Review, Wall Street Journal, Forbes*, and *Advertising Age's CMO Forum*. She teaches a highly subscribed and highly regarded MBA course on multi-channel distribution and consults on these topics.

Professor Ailawadi is the president-elect of the INFORMS Society for Marketing Science and an academic trustee of the Marketing Science Institute and of AiMark. MSI and AiMark are organizations in the United States and Europe, respectively, that bring together academics, senior practitioners, and data providers to facilitate research and idea exchange. She is currently an associate editor for three major marketing journals—*Journal of Marketing, Journal of Marketing Research*, and *Marketing Science*—and has served on the editorial boards of several others.

Paul W. Farris is the Emeritus Landmark Communications Professor of Business at the University of Virginia's Darden Graduate School of Business Administration. His doctorate is from the Harvard Business School, where he taught before his appointment at the University of Virginia. His MBA is from the University of Washington and his undergraduate degree is from the University of Missouri. He has also served in in the U.S. Army, worked in marketing management for UNILEVER, Germany, and in account management for the LINTAS advertising agency.

Professor Farris has published twelve books and over eighty articles. He has co-authored award-winning articles on distribution and marketing metrics, retailer power, dynamics of marketing strategy, and marketing budgeting. He is a current or past member of the editorial boards for the *Journal of Marketing*, the *Journal of Retailing*, *Journal of Advertising Research*, *Marketing: A Journal of Research and Management*, the *International Journal of Advertising*, and also served as an academic trustee of the Marketing Science Institute. *Marketing Metrics: 50+ Metrics Every Executive Should Master*, now in the fourth edition, was selected by *Strategy + Business*, as "2006 Marketing Book of the Year." His 2015 co-authored paper on clarifying marketing ROI was the Marketing Science Institute's most frequently downloaded paper.

Professor Farris has consulted for many international companies, including Google, Apple, Kroger, Best Buy, and Procter & Gamble. He has provided expert witness testimony in a number of lawsuits involving marketing and distribution practices. Professor Farris has also served as a director on the boards of six companies, including retailers, manufacturers, and distributors.

Acknowledgments

Over the past many years, the two of us have worked on a number of research articles, industry assignments, case studies, and teaching materials related to the measurement and management of distribution channel performance. Some of this work was together and much was with other colleagues from industry and academia. For this book, the challenge that we set ourselves was to quilt together our own and others' writing and our experiences interacting with executives from a variety of companies and distill what we believe thoughtful managers would find useful.

Jim Weber, president and CEO of Brooks Running, shared details of the revival of the Brooks brand and the company's strategy and has been so generous with his insights and his time in meetings and conversations over almost a decade. Jim, we appreciate it more than we can say!

Jesse LaFlamme, CEO, and Paul Turbeville, Vice President of Marketing, at Pete and Gerry's Organic Eggs offered an inside look at their distribution expansion and their data and patiently answered all of our many questions. Robert McDowell, Chief Commercial Officer of Choice Hotels, made time, multiple times, to discuss the travel industry with us and give us his insights. Michael Campbell, CEO of Leather Italia, allowed us to tell the story of his company's early years. You all have made this book possible.

Many other friends from industry made time for conversations and interviews – Elyse Kane, Jamie Russo, Doug Laue, Aniruddh Pandit, Erik Kiewiet de Jonge, Sarah Searls, James Black, Bill Bean, Charlene Eisenberg, Rick Paschal, Jim Lecinski, and Jim Walker. The nuggets of information and insight you shared have been so helpful.

Our colleagues Erv Shames, Scott Neslin, and David Mills read the first few chapters and provided both encouragement and critiques in equal measure, for which we could not be more grateful. Bill Branch and Leandro Guissoni helped us with hard-to-get data for several examples. The very same was true of Walt Salmon, late Professor at the Harvard Business School and world famous retailing expert. His encouragement helped one of us get a research foothold in distribution. Leigh McAlister, John Quelch, Earl Taylor, Elyse Kane, Jan Heide, Robert Spekman, JB Steenkamp, Raj Venkatesan, and Sandy Jap gave us the psychological boost we needed to cross the finish line.

Diksha Gautham, Kesav Vasudevan, Georgios Mexis, Rong Guo, Bob Burnham, Ajay Kumar, and especially Anne Givens, helped with industry background research and the data compilation for several charts. Anne, thank you so much for your patient help through the many iterations of some of the Figures. Jeanne Levine helped us navigate the process of selecting our publisher.

Kirk Kardashian worked tirelessly with us to edit the chapters more than once, asking us questions along the way that helped us make our points clearer and our writing crisper. Kirk, thank you for always meeting the deadlines we imposed, for the fun pictures and news pieces you often sent us, and for your valuable editing.

We owe thanks to our respective schools, the Tuck School at Dartmouth and the Darden School at UVA, for supporting and appreciating our research through the years and for providing the intellectual environment without which we would not have been able to embark on this endeavor. Our students have motivated and shaped this book with their class discussions and projects, and with their questions over the years. A special thanks to the students in Kusum's Multi-Channel Route-to-Market course who served as a test market for early versions of many chapters and were instrumental in making improvements.

It is a lot easier to start a book than it is to finish one. Our spouses, Anand Natrajan and Kate Farris, have not only tolerated us being on Skype and on the phone on evenings, nights, and weekends for longer than we care to admit but have also been our biggest supporters. What would we do without their love and their patience?

The research and writing have been rewarding, and often even fun! In the same way that we enjoy working together and learning from each other, we hope readers of this book will find their time well spent.

Preface

We have written this book to provide guidance on how a supplier can manage the multiple distribution channels—physical and digital, independent and company-owned—through which its products reach end consumers today. Multi-channel distribution is sometimes conflated with omni-channel marketing but the two are very different. Omni-channel is primarily a retail concept. It represents efforts by a retailer to integrate its different touchpoints with consumers so that the consumer's overall experience with the retailer is "seamless." A consumer might want to get advice from a salesperson in the retailer's brick-and-mortar store, order a particular color and size for same- or next-day delivery on the retailer's app, and perhaps exchange or return part of the order back in the store. The retailer, who owns all of these interfaces, tries to coordinate the whole series of transactions and the relationship with the consumer—the same as you would experience if you were conversing with a friend in person, over email, on the phone, or by text. The memories, the relationship, and the flow of topics of conversation all remain uninterrupted. Omni-channel is harder to execute than it appears at the surface, and most retailers are still struggling to perfect it.

Now consider an upstream supplier who sells its product line to and through different types of retailers (even if it also has a direct-to-consumer retail operation). The retailers are independent firms that compete with one another, and the supplier does not have ownership control over them. Can the supplier create a seamless omni-channel experience for consumers across all those retailers? Browsing at one retailer, purchases at another retailer, returns at a third? Most likely not. Should the supplier even make that an objective? The same products, the same services, the same prices everywhere? In some instances, perhaps. In many others, probably not. The supplier's perspective, certainly by necessity and often by choice, is one of multiple channels and multiple channel partners. Of course, the supplier's multi-channel distribution is driven by where, why, and how consumer segments shop, and it requires coordination. But the coordination is focused on the supplier's various independent channels as it strives to optimize market coverage and selling effort while minimizing conflicts among channel partners. Satisfying the requirements of omni-channel resellers needs to be part of a supplier's toolkit, but that is only one of many important considerations in multi-channel distribution.

Consider Brooks Running, a company we will come back to frequently in this book. As a performance running shoe manufacturer, it wants to meet runners where they search and where they buy, so it distributes its full product line through multiple channels, from specialty running stores to omni-channel general sporting goods chains and some pure-play online retailers, and it has its own direct digital channel. Companies like Brooks must develop a set of metrics by which to measure distribution coverage and channel partner efforts and consider whether they should reward some channels for being used as showrooms, even if purchases, especially repeat ones, are made elsewhere. In contrast, many other suppliers don't want to sell the same products at the same prices in all channels, especially online. Burberry decided to sell a few products through Amazon.com in exchange for Amazon's cooperation in weeding out unauthorized sellers but it keeps most of its product line for its own stores and for selected retail partners. In both cases the goals are the same—to reduce channel conflict and preserve the equity of their flagship brands while still having sufficient distribution coverage—even if the approaches are different.

The web and mobile have occupied center stage in most descriptions of how distribution channels are evolving, but this is far from the whole story. Even companies that were "born digital" have discovered that they need to be present in, if not master, traditional distribution channels. Walmart-owned clothing marketer Bonobos not only has its own web and brick-and-mortar "guide shops" but is also using independent retailer Nordstrom. Jessica Alba founded the Honest Company as an e-commerce business (proclaiming that supermarkets are not where consumers should have to shop for diapers, detergents, and the like) but the company is now working hard to get its products on the shelf in the grocery channel. Like brands that are rooted in physical distribution and are now navigating digital channels, these suppliers too must figure out which channels they need to be in and why, how much coverage is right, and how to attain and keep it.

Technology and the prospect of greater profits have encouraged more suppliers who traditionally relied on third-party channels not just to open up but increasingly emphasize the direct-to-consumer route. Nike has clearly stated its goal of accelerating its direct-to-consumer business and becoming "more personal at scale." Competing with their customers creates the obvious but difficult problem of channel conflict. But, in addition, some suppliers find they need other middlemen to provide special services or must invest in those services themselves, while also having to expand their product line and marketing budgets to attract consumer traffic to the direct channel. Hotel companies like Hilton and Choice Hotels have invested heavily in loyalty programs and advertising campaigns, but they also need meta-search platforms like TripAdvisor to route traffic to Brand.com. Meanwhile, the Marriott-Starwood merger was motivated at least partly by wanting the scale to build up the direct channel. So was AT&T's acquisition of Time Warner. These companies must (a) consider the full set of costs, not just the benefits of going direct, (b) ensure that the consumer still receives all the services she expects along the path-to-purchase and beyond, and (c) figure out the long-term strategic role of their independent and direct channels.

The consequences of many of these multi-channel distribution decisions are hard to foresee. With the plethora of choices available today, it is even more important to select and organize channels in a way that delivers the experience shoppers demand, while generating the volume and margins for everyone in the channel that are needed to sustain the business. Keeping the breadth and depth of distribution in line with the evolving nature and location of demand is not only a question of having a clear strategy, but also one of careful measurement and monitoring. Along with distribution channels, product lines, pricing, and channel incentives also trend toward more complexity. Wishing it could be simpler does not make it so. Instead, we believe that managers must accept the challenge of managing the increasing channel complexity with clear objectives, good frameworks, and the right metrics. Our goal with this book is to help managers, MBA students who will soon step into those roles, and the professors who train them, meet that challenge.

—Kusum L. Ailawadi and Paul W. Farris

CHAPTER 1

Distribution Channels Today

1.1 INTRODUCTION

Marketers today must develop well-informed strategies for managing their distribution channels during times of significant change. Those strategies will include anticipating, minimizing, and addressing the channel conflict inevitably wrought by change. This book is about how firms can select metrics, design strategies, and implement policies that free them to adapt to the rapidly evolving landscape that combines physical and digital routes-to-market.

Our book is primarily intended for marketers and those who train them, but marketers aren't the only ones paying attention to channel dynamics. Economists, regulators, and social psychologists are also interested in how distribution channels affect competition, efficiency, and consumer welfare. They want to understand the marketing challenges of distribution channels, the causes and consequences of channel conflict, and the approaches to managing that conflict. So, while our writing is rooted in marketing, we also incorporate these other perspectives.

What is a distribution channel? By its simplest definition, it is the chain of distributors, retailers, and other intermediaries through which a supplier's product reaches end consumers, implying a unidirectional movement of goods along one route, from the point of production to the point of consumption.[1] Even simple distribution channels are delicate systems, where suppliers and their independent resellers struggle to balance a cooperative partnership against a desire for a bigger share of the total profit available in the channel. The partners need to cooperate in ways that create value for consumers, appropriate some of that value in the form of profit for the channel, and share the profit in a way that sustains the partnership.

Modern, mainly digital, technology has complicated that partnership. These days, firms must employ a multitude of distribution channels—sometimes complementary, but almost always competing—in a way that satisfies consumers' needs for products, services, and information. What a unidirectional, one-route perspective can easily miss is the variety of interactions and conflicts among firms in the ecosystem, because each firm performs some functions and tries to appropriate some of the value created.

Conflict and power go together in any relationship between interdependent entities. The (mis)use of power can exacerbate conflict, but a channel member's power position also determines the strategies it can use to appropriate value and manage conflict. Accumulating channel power and exercising it wisely is a key to surviving and prospering in periods of change. In the words of Professor Raymond Corey of the Harvard Business School, marketers must learn "to use power without using it up."

The sources of power, and the ways to exercise it, have been complicated by recent technological, market, and legal developments. Distribution practices that were developed and refined over years have become vulnerable. Some challenges are easy to recognize (should digital books be priced the same as paper copies in book stores?) and others are more nuanced (how does resale price maintenance affect trade promotions?). Some are fundamentally new and require different thinking (how can we measure and manage distribution coverage online or assess the power of a channel member that operates a multisided platform?), while others are simply different manifestations of enduring channel issues (double marginalization,

---

[1]Throughout the book, we will use the term "consumers" to designate purchasers who are typically end users, meaning that they do not resell the product or incorporate it into other products for resale. Of course, products purchased by someone may be used or consumed by others (e.g., members of the same household or business). We avoid calling them "customers" because, at least in the consumer packaged goods industry, retailers are referred to as customers.

free riding, and the tug between intra- and inter-brand competition). Throughout the book, we try to distinguish what is new from what is not. The former needs fresh thinking and emerging solutions. The latter has a history with important lessons that marketers ignore at their peril.

Technology has also blurred the distinction between distribution channels and communication channels, especially since some of the new digital distribution channels mainly satisfy consumers' need for information rather than directly sell the products and services (consider Trip Advisor and Trivago for hotels, for example). A purely consumer-centric view might suggest that any sources of products or information that the consumer seeks out or is exposed to would qualify as "channels." By that definition, search engines, blogs, and social media would be "channels."

The consumer is certainly at the center of it all, but our perspective in this book is firmly rooted in firms that sell through independent distribution channels. Our view is that, for an entity to be viewed as a distribution channel, it must perform, and be paid for, at least some of the functions involved in the sale of a particular product along the route to market from a clear upstream supplier to a clear downstream reseller or end customer. So, DoubleClick is a distribution channel for firms that sell advertising, but it is not a distribution channel for the product being advertised. A wine brand's sales may be affected by what an influential wine blog writes about it, but the blog is not a distribution channel. Drawing this line between distribution and communication channels is useful to guide the strategies of marketers and it delineates the scope of the issues we tackle in this book. Of course, it is not a bright line and one can easily see how it might blur. For example, what if the blog has a link to the wine brand's site and gets paid to route demand to the wine marketer? Such an "affiliate" arrangement would make the blog a distribution partner.

Most frequently, we take the perspective of suppliers selling through independent resellers (distributors, retailers, aggregators, marketplaces, and other middlemen), but this requires analyzing the viewpoints of the middlemen too. Other disciplines, notably operations and strategy, refer to these middlemen as members of a "supply chain" or "value chain." So, what's the difference between supply chains, value chains, and distribution channels?

Our view is that the distinction is largely in perspective and emphasis. The terms "upstream" and "downstream" are used to describe those firms that are closer to the production versus the consumption "end" of the channel, and we will do that too. This kind of thinking can subconsciously imbue the upstream firm with more responsibility, power, or authority. Our counterparts in manufacturing and operations take the perspective of a "downstream" firm—often a manufacturer looking backwards at its raw material and component suppliers.

Those in the strategy and economics domains refer to the "value chain" as the entire collection of firms and activities in producing and delivering a product or service with an emphasis on the "value added" (not too far from margins) at each stage. Value chains therefore include a firm's backward supply chain and forward distribution channels in addition to its own value-adding operations. Where relevant, we adopt some approaches from these other disciplines to enrich our understanding of how channels work and how they can become more efficient.

1.2 WHAT IS NEW: RADICAL CHANGES IN THE NAVIGATION OF DISTRIBUTION CHANNELS

The sustainability of channel partnerships is a goal that businesses value highly. Pricing, marketing communications, and even products are quite often easier to change than distribution-channel relationships. Frequently, businesses are built around serving end-consumer markets through a specific set of immediate customer-distribution channels. For example, automobile manufacturers have learned to market through their dealers, major soft drink manufacturers Coke and PepsiCo through their bottling networks, and Avon and Natura through their independent consultants. Learning to serve these channel customers along with end consumers is a critical competency. Channel affiliations are also often personal relationships, even friendships, that go well beyond golf games once a year. That's why a channel partnership is not often severed, and only happens after some serious soul searching (or its commercial equivalent).

Often, growth necessitates expanding into new channel relationships while maintaining existing ones. Retailers add more suppliers and categories while also opening more stores and expanding into new markets. Manufacturers add more retailers, expanding to service new geographic markets. They also add new types of retail formats that service additional market segments. Although these types of expansions are sure to bring "growing pains," businesses today are encountering challenges far beyond normal growing pains. That is why, even though channel management is a well-worn topic in marketing, we believe it is worth a new look now.

We see four general areas of change in the economy that call for a renewed study of the management of multiple routes-to-market. To some degree, all four areas have been affected by digital technologies.

1.2.1 Changing Business Models

The first set of changes relates to new business models for distribution that derive from technology. Firms based on these new business models are inserting themselves into traditional routes-to-market, bringing corresponding opportunities for suppliers to gain or lose strategic advantage by managing or mismanaging their distribution channels.

When products are digitized, the marginal costs of manufacturing and distribution may approach zero though the fixed costs remain high, making pricing challenging. Witness the difficulty of pricing and monetizing digital distribution of books, news, streamed music, and video. Variety that was expensive in a purely brick-and-mortar world may be much cheaper to offer but organizing and presenting that variety in a meaningful way and pricing it appropriately is more important.

Another technology tradeoff: the Internet and mobile technology allow shoppers to search for the best price without moving from their desks or the aisle in a store, but the online world is increasingly tailored and targeted. Marketers can use information about consumers in real time to tailor offers to each consumer—through different products, presentations, messages, and prices—often without consumers even realizing it.

More than 50 years ago, Wroe Alderson, one of marketing's preeminent scholars, captured the nature of distribution channels when he wrote, "economic progress has consisted largely of finding more efficient ways of matching heterogeneous supply with heterogeneous demand."[i] The web and mobile are wonderfully efficient at facilitating that matching, so companies are disintermediating (a fancy word for cutting out the middleman) channel members and going direct to consumers.

At the same time, though, new business models have emerged primarily by unbundling the functions that used to be provided by traditional channels. Along with the traditional channel members in the physical world of bricks (top half of the figure), Figure 1.1 shows new intermediaries in the virtual world of clicks (bottom half of figure). Some new middlemen deal in the flow of information rather than the flow of physical products. They present information

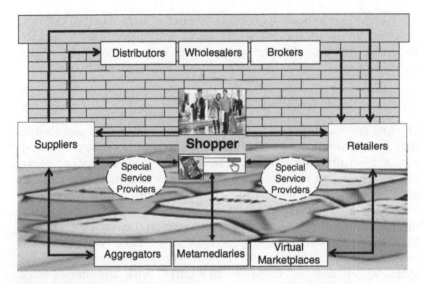

Figure 1.1 Physical and digital distribution in today's channel ecosystem.

on multiple options to consumers who can comparison shop and then be seamlessly routed elsewhere for making a purchase. Some new middlemen are digital versions of physical malls or retailers. Many of them are platforms, such as Etsy's marketplace or TripAdvisor's meta-search site, that have two or more sets of customers with interdependent demand. The value that one set of customers (e.g., suppliers) derives from the platform depends upon the demand from the other set of customers (e.g., consumers). It is worth noting that many of these new platforms are thriving, while classic two-sided markets like newspapers and shopping malls are struggling to survive. Other new middlemen are special service providers who perform narrow but important functions like delivery or payment processing or reverse logistics.

1.2.2 Omni-Channel Retailing

The second change is the relentless pressure for resellers to become omni-channel, as a consumer may become aware of a product in a brick-and-mortar store or catalog, check reviews and compare prices on the website, make a purchase on the mobile app, and pick it up (and perhaps return part of it) in the store. When retailers intend to serve customers in one channel but they end up buying from another channel, marketers used to refer to it as "leakage" or customers "escaping," implying a failure of strategy or tactics. Instead, the concept of omni-channel embraces the inevitability of needing physical, online, and mobile arms, and of managing one's social presence to serve their best customers better. Omni-channel strategies focus on integrating activities within and across channels to correspond to how consumers shop.

In the face of omni-channel efforts by their downstream resellers, suppliers have to adjust their own channel management practices. They must decide which, if any, of their brands and product lines they prefer to distribute in a multi-channel rather than omni-channel way, for example, by making different brands or product lines available through different channel partners. And, for others, they need to weave together, manage, and reward a combination of many types of channels to match how consumers want to search, buy, and return. Managing omni-channel distribution is like recruiting and coaching a team of players with different roles and skills. Linemen rarely make touchdowns, but they protect the players who do. So, if some channels increasingly get used as showrooms while purchases get made elsewhere, the showrooms need to be rewarded. Becoming omni-channel is not easy for retailers.[2] It's even harder for suppliers to build a team, integrating not within one organization but across many independent ones.

1.2.3 Data

The third change relates to the type of data that technology has made available, some owned by suppliers, some by their channel partners, and some (actually, a lot!) by third parties. The data are coming in at an accelerating pace of data volume, timeliness, and richness. Figure 1.2 shows some of the changes in data availability that are directly relevant to the management of distribution channels.

The bar code scanner, and more powerful, cheaper, and smaller computers, took us from tracking quarterly shipments and inventories to knowing daily store movement of individual SKUs; from self-reported diaries to scanner and home-scan panels; and from counting loyalty points to capturing and using detailed purchase data from program members. Then came computer cookies, click-stream data on what consumers do in the virtual world, followed

---

[2] We recommend a good look at the 2015 special issue of the *Journal of Retailing,* co-edited by Peter Verhoef, P.K. Kannan, and Jeff Inman.

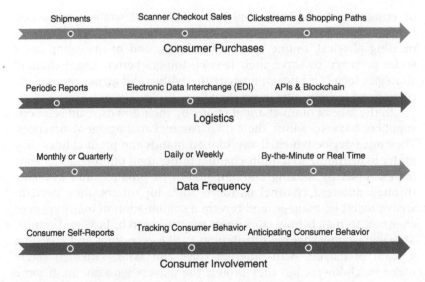

Figure 1.2 The progression of data available in the channel, 1970–2018.

by mobile IDs and GPS technology that allow us to also pinpoint where consumers are in the physical world. Mobile technology lets the consumer compare retail prices in real time and order instantly from whichever channel she chooses. But it has also reestablished the importance of physical location, redefined convenience and in-store visibility, and increased the reach, in both space and time, of savvy marketers. Avi Goldfarb wrote, "the internet killed distance; mobile brought it back,"[ii] and David Bell, after documenting several ways in which physical location influences online behavior, argued: "location is still everything."[iii]

Although the integration of offline and online data is not nearly seamless yet, we are farther along than we were even a couple of years ago. Sophisticated software and the ability to analyze big and not-so-big data now allow us to profile consumers, anticipate what they will buy next, and tailor not just prices but assortment, presentation, and messaging in real time. We used to think of artificial intelligence in the context of autonomous cars and robots, but platforms like Amazon and Alibaba are using AI to predict what consumers might be interested in and to offer them more precise search results and recommendations for products and content.[iv] They are in a uniquely advantageous position to integrate information about consumers from a whole range of activities, including product search, purchases, payments, social media activity, and newsfeed and other content consumption—a near-omniscience that no single supplier or retailer can match.

Other technologies, such as RFIDs, QR codes, and now Blockchain, make it possible to track information up and down the distribution value chain, ranging from the source of our Chicken McNuggets, to the conditions a product was exposed to during transportation, to the shopping path a consumer takes in a store, to whether the item she buys came from a regular shelf or a special display. Sensors in malls and stores track shoppers' movements, building flowcharts of their shopping paths and heat maps of the areas and products they spend more time with, enabling marketers to make improvements in store layout, employee deployment, and more, in real time.

All of these are making more data available faster to evaluate programs and decisions and, as Google's ex-VP of Consumer Solutions Jim Lecinski likes to say, "data beats opinion." Which parties in the channel ecosystem have what data, how effectively they use the data, and how much of it they share with their partners, is impacting power positions, negotiations, and all terms of trade, ranging from product assortment and shelf placement to logistics and pricing.

1.2.4 Regulation

The final set of changes consists of legal and regulatory shifts. Channel practices that used to be illegal per se are now under the more lenient *rule of reason* (only prohibiting actions that unreasonably restrain trade). Most notable is Minimum Resale Price Maintenance (minimum RPM), which came under the rule of reason with the 2007 U.S. Supreme Court's decision in Leegin Creative Leather Products, Inc. v. PSKS, Inc.[3] At the same time as RPM opportunities have increased, however, some promotional practices such as loyalty discounts and bundled discounts have come under increased scrutiny for their exclusionary and predatory potential.[v]

The variation in regulations across geographic regions—not just different countries but also different states within the U.S.—makes it more challenging for both suppliers and their channel members

_____

[3]However, minimum RPM remains in flux: Maryland passed its own law in 2009 enacting the illegality per se of minimum RPM, and other states, such as California, New York, and Kansas, took the position that the Supreme Court decision does not affect their own state laws. As a result, suppliers did not rush to take advantage of the opportunities for price control. But that may change as they continue to grapple with showrooming and price erosion online.

to manage distribution. Uber faces varying degrees of regulatory opposition state by state and country by country in its bid to be treated as a digital service and not a transportation service. Tesla fights similar battles against individual state franchise laws in its efforts to sell cars directly to consumers in the U.S.

According to some economists, the tenets of economic theory used in antitrust have to be modified for multi-sided platform businesses. The most commonly cited example is pricing below marginal cost: it's traditionally viewed with suspicion by competition authorities, but can be fully consistent with efficiency for a platform, who may price below marginal cost for one set of customers because it can reap the benefits from increased demand by another set of customers. For example, Open Table charges restaurants for bookings made on its site but doesn't charge consumers anything, even giving them reward points that can be redeemed at restaurants in the Open Table system. The nature of interdependent demand can be asymmetric or competition can have different effects on two sides of a platform, potentially reducing prices on one side and increasing them on the other.[vi] But there are several other aspects to the economics of platforms, and antitrust perspectives are still in flux.[vii]

New business models also pose challenges as regulators figure out what functions the new intermediaries perform and how they should be viewed. For example, it's unclear whether Uber's drivers should be treated as independent contractors or employees—a question that will have major implications for its profitability. In a related vein, it may be unclear whether some new intermediaries, such as travel aggregator Booking.com, are independent distributors or agents—an important distinction when it comes to antitrust regulations.

As new and different intermediary models evolve, the services that the intermediaries provide, the costs and risks they incur, and the ways in which they are compensated, are becoming increasingly important, not just from a channel management perspective, but from a legal and antitrust perspective as well.

1.3 THE ROAD AHEAD

This book is about developing, executing, and adapting distribution strategy, and managing channel conflict and power in the new channel ecosystem. Our goal is to provide an analytically grounded and metrics-based approach to channel management in a time of change. How will we get there? Well, before we can manage something, we need to have a clear mental model of how it works. So, we use Part I of the book (Chapters 2–6) to introduce an organizing framework for how suppliers work together with their channel partners; impart a clear understanding of the fundamental causes of conflict in today's channels; lay out a map of the intermediaries in the new channel ecosystem and their functions; and explain the sources, indicators, and outcomes of power in the channel. Part II (Chapters 7–12) is devoted to the metrics, tools, and frameworks that can help a supplier select the right type and intensity of physical and online distribution coverage. In Part III (Chapters 13–16) we discuss the strategies related to product line, channel pricing, and promotional incentives that can be used, in the lingo of economists, to "coordinate" the channel and manage ongoing conflict.

ENDNOTES

i. Alderson, W. (1957). *Marketing Behavior and Executive Action*. Homewood, Ill: Richard D. Irwin Publishers, p. 195.

ii. Goldfarb, A. (2013). The Internet Killed Distance, Mobile Brought it Back. *MIT Technology Review* 117 (1): 62–63.

iii. Bell, D. (2015). *Location Is (Still) Everything*. Amazon.

iv. Wei, H. (2017). E-Commerce Shoppers Embrace Smart Apps (4 December), *China Daily*.

v. Federal Trade Commission (2014). FTC Issues Opinion and Final Order Finding McWane, Inc. Unlawfully Maintained Its Monopoly in Domestic Pipe Fittings by Excluding Competitors. Press release (6 February).

vi. Federal Trade Commission (2009). Policy Roundtable on Two-Sided Markets (4 June).

vii. Here are a couple of recent reviews and perspectives: Evans, D. S., and Schmalensee, R. (2015). The antitrust analysis of multisided platform businesses. In: *The Oxford Handbook of International Antitrust Economics*, vol. 1 (eds. R. D. Blair and D. D. Sokol), 404–449. Oxford: Oxford University Press.

viii. Katz, M. (2019). Platform Economics and Antitrust Enforcement: A Little Knowledge is a Dangerous Thing. *Journal of Economics and Management Strategy* 28: 138–152.

ix. Melamed, D.A. and Nicolas, P. (2019). The Misguided Assault on the Consumer Welfare Standard in the Age of Platform Markets. *Review of Industrial Organization* 54 (4): 741–774.

PART **I**

THE BEDROCK OF CHANNEL FUNCTIONS, POWER, AND CONFLICT

CHAPTER 2

Push, Pull, and Total Channel Performance

2.1 INTRODUCTION

Suppliers use independent resellers and other channel partners because they would not be able to effectively or efficiently perform all the functions needed by consumers in a fully vertically integrated system. Yet, they must work together if their individual efforts are to generate sustainable revenue and profit for the system.

A fundamental concept in channel management is the separation of marketing efforts and effects into "push" and "pull." Suppliers' "pull" marketing efforts are aimed directly at creating demand among consumers, while their "push" marketing efforts focus on convincing independent resellers to stock and promote the product to consumers. We believe that these two complementary concepts are absolutely essential to understanding marketing in general and channel management in particular. As marketers, we are accustomed to using these terms in everyday conversations and writing. However, operations and supply chain professionals also use the same two words, but with somewhat different meanings. More recently, digital advertisers have adopted them too, and almost reversed the "original" marketing definitions.[1] These other usages of push and pull do not require the presence of a reseller, whereas marketing's usage is almost entirely applicable only to marketing systems that rely on resellers. In both those settings, there is also a negative connotation to "push" that doesn't exist in the marketing universe. Business cuts across many functions, and clear communication within and among these functions is critical. So, let your audience and co-workers know what you mean by push and pull.

2.2 AN ORGANIZING FRAMEWORK ILLUSTRATED WITH NATURA'S DISTRIBUTION CHANNEL

2.2.1 Push

Natura Cosmetics is a Brazilian beauty and personal care company that was ranked in 2015 by Brand Finance as the 14th most valuable beauty brand in the world. The company sells a wide variety of beauty and personal care products through one of the world's largest distribution networks of independent beauty "consultants." The consultants purchase Natura products from the company and sell them to consumers. While some of these consultants deal exclusively with Natura products, quite a few also represent other cosmetics brands. The company's marketing efforts are organized around a number of promotions, including temporary price discounts, brochures and catalogs featuring certain products, and other selling aids that they provide to the beauty consultants. Most of these can be understood as "push marketing inputs" aimed at recruiting, engaging, and supporting Natura consultants. Making it easy for consumers to find Natura consultants is one intended result of those inputs. The immediate downstream effects of these reseller push efforts are (1) a greater quantity of Natura beauty consultants and (2) their selling activity to generate consumer sales that can be described, respectively, as the breadth and depth of "reseller push."

---

[1] In supply chain, a push approach refers to pushing inventory through from suppliers to channel members based on demand forecasts so that the channel takes most of the inventory risk, while a pull approach refers to the channel member pulling inventory from the supplier with "at-once orders" based on actual demand. Digital marketers call all the advertising and promotion aimed at a target audience through traditional media "push" or "outbound marketing" and place under "pull" the search advertising, retargeting, and so on that place a product in the path-to-purchase of consumers when they are actively looking for it.

2.2.2 Pull

Natura also employs mass media advertising to promote the company's products to consumers in what would be described as "pull marketing inputs." Some of the advertising emphasizes the company's use of natural ingredients in its products, and its concern for the environment and for preserving Brazil's natural beauty. Other advertising themes include creating awareness of the brand, introducing new product lines, and promoting the role of the beauty consultants. Over time, Natura has created awareness and preference among many consumers for the brand and its specific products, something that is referred to as "consumer pull." This "consumer pull" makes it easier for the consultants to sell Natura products, increases their efficiency and profitability, and makes it easier to recruit new consultants. But the consultants too have created "consumer pull" for Natura products by educating consumers about the Natura product line, suggesting products that would work for specific consumers, and encouraging consumers to try the brand.

The downstream "consumer pull" and "reseller push" work together and reinforce each other to generate consumer purchases and profit for the whole system, which is shared between Natura and its independent beauty consultants. In recent years, Natura has expanded into new channels, including its own direct-to-consumer website, Natura-sponsored web pages for independent consultants, the drug store channel, and physical Natura-branded stores, and it has acquired the Body Shop as well as Avon, making its multi-channel distribution system a lot more complex, with many more "types" of distribution breadth.

2.2.3 Supplier Inputs, Downstream Effects, and Channel Performance

Figure 2.1 puts the Natura push and pull system into a more general, though still abbreviated, organizing framework.[i] We ask the reader to review this figure before reading further. Note that the framework distinguishes between the upstream supplier's marketing "inputs" and the downstream effects (intended or unintended) on resellers and consumers. Suppliers' marketing inputs are largely under their own direct control, while the effects that these inputs generate among consumers and resellers are not. Of course, the ultimate aim of these marketing inputs is to create sales and profits that are shared between suppliers and resellers. But there are some important concepts and metrics that

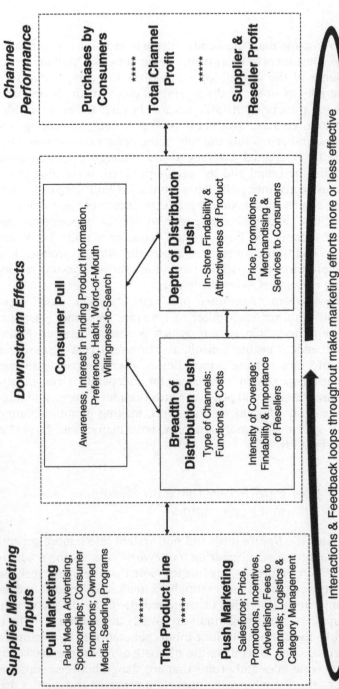

Figure 2.1 Push, pull, and channel performance.

18

describe intervening consumer and reseller behaviors. These are also shown in the figure and, as we will see throughout the book, they can help formulate strategy, diagnose problems, and assess the effectiveness of decisions and spending.

We want to make four observations about our framework at this point. First, the classification of marketing *inputs* into push and pull can sometimes appear to be arbitrary, though most designations are widely accepted. Trade promotions, listing fees, and other channel incentives are almost always viewed as push. Traditional mass media and digital advertising (referred to as "paid media"), marketing programs via the supplier's own website, apps, blogs, and social media (referred to as "owned media"), and promotions aimed at consumers are generally designated as pull marketing (although, as we mentioned earlier, digital marketers refer to mass media as pushing themselves into the consumers' life). Package design and funds for cooperative advertising (which are provided by suppliers to support reseller advertising either online or in traditional media) are examples of marketing efforts that might reasonably be classified as either or both. In many (probably most) consumer product companies, there are "marketing" departments that have more responsibility for pull programs and "sales" organizations that are charged with implementing and sometimes designing push programs.

Second, both push and pull *effects* are always required for sales to consumers. Pull effects include consumers' interest in finding information about the supplier's products, their preference and willingness to search for the products, and their word-of-mouth—offline as well as online (referred to as "earned" media). Push effects include the decision by different resellers to stock the supplier's products and to merchandise and support them in their stores. Even if the consumer's willingness to purchase is primarily generated by the reseller at the point of purchase, some pull is required for a voluntary transaction between consumer and reseller. The same goes for push effects. Without at least some reseller support, even if that is only agreeing to list products for sale and place orders with the supplier, consumers cannot buy a product even if the supplier's pull marketing inputs have created strong preference for it. Marketers can differ widely on the relative extent to which they rely on pull and push marketing inputs, but putting together the most effective, profitable, and sustainable mix of pull and push effects is one of the important challenges in channel management.

The third point is that distribution breadth includes both the *types* of different channels the supplier uses and the extent of their *coverage*. At Natura, for example, this manifests as a large network of beauty consultants and a wide range of physical and online retail channels. The types of channels expand with new consumer segments, changing needs along consumers' path-to-purchase, under competitive pressure, and as technology enables new business models. They differ, amongst other things, in the functions they perform, and therefore the costs they incur. The intensity of coverage refers to the ease with which the consumer can find a store or website that stocks the supplier's products.

This findability increases as a supplier adds more channel partners. But it also increases as existing channel partners become more important—for example because they expand their customer base by increasing their product assortment, the number of physical outlets, or their own advertising. Which brings us to our last point. Figure 2.1 takes the perspective of the supplier selling through independent channel members, and its marketing inputs and effects. But channel members also expend their own marketing efforts to attract consumers to their own physical and virtual stores. We will integrate that into the discussion and framework in later chapters.

2.3 PUSH-PULL INPUTS AND DOWNSTREAM EFFECTS IN PEPSICO'S CHANNEL

Figure 2.1 depicts only one middleman (the reseller) between the supplier and the consumer, and Natura's consultant channel fits that structure. But most suppliers have longer distribution channels, so the marketing inputs and downstream effects cascade through each level of the channel. PepsiCo's beverage business, for example, has a longer channel of distribution than does Natura. Pepsi's beverages are manufactured and distributed by what are mainly independent bottlers. In addition to manufacturing, the bottlers, who are Pepsi franchisees, employ large numbers of sales and delivery people who convince retailers to carry, merchandise, and promote the company's beverages and work to ensure that the retail outlets are adequately stocked. Retail outlets include grocery stores and supercenters, convenience stores and kiosks, restaurants and other food service outlets, vending machines, and hotel mini-bars, among others. Depending on the type of outlet, beverages are sold in a variety of package forms for immediate or take-home consumption.

Pepsi and its bottler franchisees comprise what some might term a quasi-vertically integrated system (we will have more to say about franchise systems in Chapter 4). For now, note that PepsiCo's own push marketing inputs are aimed at recruiting good bottlers and supporting them. But the bottlers' salesforce and logistics organizations are the heart of the system's push efforts aimed at retailers. This push marketing is an essential part of the company's success.

PepsiCo's pull marketing inputs are most easily recognized as mass media advertising on television and billboards, major sponsorships, and digital advertising. These might generate consumer pull by making new consumers aware of Pepsi products, reinforcing the preferences of those consumers who have already experienced the products, reminding them that a Pepsi might taste good right now, and/or introducing new packages and products. What might not be as immediately recognized as creating consumer pull are the bottlers' trucks that serve as mobile billboards, the package that makes the product easy to recognize, the point-of-purchase coolers and signage that invite the consumer to try a cold Pepsi or remind her to stock-up, and the vending machines that are painted with the Pepsi blue, which is easy to distinguish from those wearing the Coke red. The awareness, preference, habit, and loyalty (often difficult to distinguish from habit) that constitute "consumer pull" result from the combined and mutually reinforcing effects of wide availability, easy findability in the store, affordable selling prices, preference for the product taste, and the pleasurable associations generated by advertising.

2.4 PUSH AND PULL FOR SERVICES AND DIGITAL CHANNELS

The framework is just as applicable to services and digital products as to products, and it spans digital channels of distribution just as it does physical channels. Choice Hotels is one of the world's largest lodging companies, with more than 6,800 hotel properties spanning multiple brands, mostly in the economy and mid-scale segments of the market. Examples of Choice brands are Econolodge and Quality Inn at the economy end of the market, the more mid-scale Sleep Inn and Comfort Inn, and Cambria at the somewhat upscale end. Like most other large hotel chains, Choice is a franchisor. Franchisees pay the company a variety of fees in return for the right to own and/or operate a hotel under one of the Choice Hotels brands. These include, for example, upfront fixed fees, an ongoing royalty as a percentage of revenues, marketing fees to cover advertising, other marketing, and the "Choice Privileges" loyalty program costs, system fees to cover maintenance of a central reservation system, and other such costs.

The distribution channel for Choice, and other travel companies in the lodging and airline businesses, is a little different than our previous two examples. These companies deal with two sets of parties in their distribution channel. One is the franchisees who own and/or operate their hotel properties, and the other party is the various independent travel agents and other intermediaries through which travelers (business and leisure) may make their bookings. Let's just focus on the leisure travelers for now. The independent distribution channels to reach this segment include travel agents like Booking.com or Expedia .com, meta-search sites like Kayak and TripAdvisor, search engines like Google, and any Global Distribution Systems (GDS) that the company might use to feed room inventory and pricing information to these channel partners. In addition, of course, there are multiple direct channels. A traveler might visit the company's own "brand.com" website (e.g., Choicehotels.com), call its central reservation number, or call an individual property to make a direct booking.

Choice's pull marketing inputs include its customer loyalty program and various types of advertising, both traditional media and online and mobile search advertising. These are executed by the company but paid for by its franchisees via the marketing fees. As we will discuss in a later chapter, hotel companies, including Choice, are expanding their pull marketing inputs in the hope of switching more travelers from independent distribution channels to direct booking.

The company aims different push marketing inputs at franchisees and independent distribution channel partners. It supports franchisees in various ways such as through training programs, property management software, and construction design services. Other hotel companies also make similar push efforts to support their franchisees. Accor, for example, has a one-stop-shop website and app called MAX that allows franchisees to easily access information, reports, services, and more with the goal of improving both the performance of the franchisees' properties and their relationship with Accor. The push marketing inputs that Choice, Accor, and other hotel companies aim at independent distribution channel partners include listing and advertising fees to make their properties more visible on the websites of the channel partners. These too are paid for by franchisees.

The downstream effects of these push and pull marketing inputs work the same way as in our other examples. Reseller breadth refers to the number and variety of different channels who list Choice Hotel properties and how easy they are for the traveler to find, and depth refers to how visible and attractive the Choice listings are within their sites. Revenues generated from travelers get shared between Choice Hotels, the franchisees, and any independent channel members involved in the booking.

2.5 BENEFICIAL AND HARMFUL FEEDBACK LOOPS IN THE PUSH-PULL SYSTEM

The push-pull framework is simple to describe at a general, abstract level; in practice, keeping the system in balance is anything but simple. A critical aspect of balancing the system is to recognize—and whenever possible, manage—the interactions and feedback between the various moving parts. Interactions refer to the idea that the effects of different marketing inputs can be greater than the sum of their separate effects. Feedback generally occurs as second-order effects, with a delay (often a substantial delay), and it is driven by the actions and reactions of all the players in the system—the supplier, resellers, consumers, and of course, competitors.

An example of beneficial feedback is the increased willingness of retailers to stock and promote a product that enjoys strong prefer-ence among consumers and exhibits growing sales. Another is the increased likelihood of consumers to amplify the effectiveness of the supplier's marketing inputs with their own word-of-mouth. A third is the ability of wide availability, visible in-store displays and other point-of-purchase advertising to create consumer awareness and preference for the brand and build habit.

Undesirable second-order effects between the breadth and depth of reseller push can occur if too many resellers or too many different types of channels compete on selling prices, reducing their profit margins and leading some resellers to reduce shelf space or drop the product entirely. To illustrate both the value of positive feedback loops and the pitfalls of negative ones, we describe one of each type in some detail in the next two Figures.[2] We caution that the figures look complicated, at least at first glance, but that is because feedback loops are not simple. Marketers cannot manage distribution without a good understanding of the potential sources of feedback. So, let's start with Figure 2.2. The flow goes from left to right in the top half of the figure and back again in the lower half.

If all goes well, the supplier balances its push and pull marketing of a great product so that the downstream consumer pull and distribution push effects are able to reinforce one another. The consequence is a distribution channel in which resellers face enough competition to be

---

[2]Feedback loops enjoy such popularity in the description of "business models" that one *Harvard Business Review* editor, Gardiner Morse, accuses many authors of adding "crap circles" to their presentations and figures whether or not they apply! We are mindful of that criticism and caution that each link in these loops should be deliberately considered.

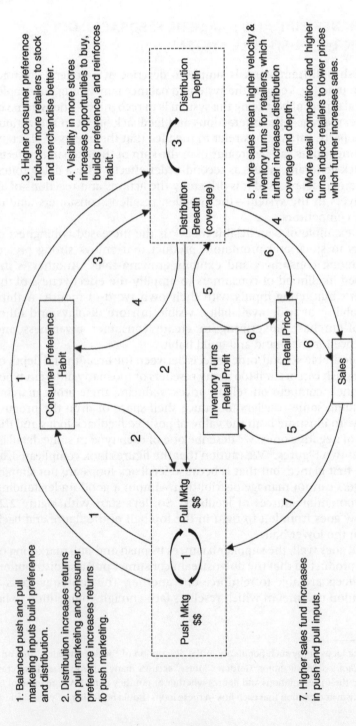

1. Balanced push and pull marketing inputs build preference and distribution.

2. Distribution increases returns on pull marketing and consumer preference increases returns to push marketing.

3. Higher consumer preference induces more retailers to stock and merchandise better.

4. Visibility in more stores increases opportunities to buy, builds preference, and reinforces habit.

5. More sales mean higher velocity & inventory turns for retailers, which further increases distribution coverage and depth.

6. More retail competition and higher turns induce retailers to lower prices which further increases sales.

7. Higher sales fund increases in push and pull inputs.

Consumer Preference Habit

Distribution Breadth (coverage)

Distribution Depth

Inventory Turns Retail Profit

Retail Price

Sales

Pull Mktg $$

Push Mktg $$

Figure 2.2 A series of beneficial feedback loops to be nurtured.

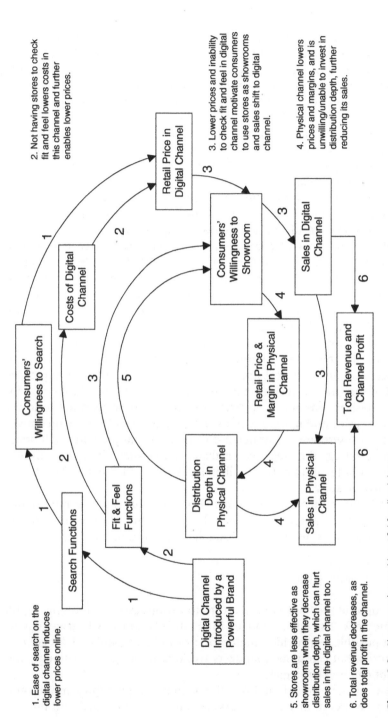

Figure 2.3 Showrooming and harmful feedback loops.

1. Ease of search on the digital channel induces lower prices online.

2. Not having stores to check fit and feel lowers costs in this channel and further enables lower prices.

3. Lower prices and inability to check fit and feel in digital channel motivate consumers to use stores as showrooms and sales shift to digital channel.

4. Physical channel lowers prices and margins, and is unwilling/unable to invest in distribution depth, further reducing its sales.

5. Stores are less effective as showrooms when they decrease distribution depth, which can hurt sales in the digital channel too.

6. Total revenue decreases, as does total profit in the channel.

motivated to price and merchandise the supplier's product attractively, and enough demand to make their efforts worthwhile. But this fine balance can't last forever. So it becomes more important to identify when and how such a virtuous cycle can become a vicious cycle. If there is too much emphasis on expanding distribution breadth, and not enough emphasis on ensuring that there is adequate demand to sustain the channel partners, then sales velocity (which is simply sales per point of distribution) can start to decrease, hurting the profitability of the resellers and their ability and willingness to invest in distribution depth.

Figure 2.3 describes how the expansion of distribution breadth through a new type of channel—in this illustration a digital channel—can result in a downward spiral if it is not managed well. Not all types of channels are created equal when it comes to the functions they can perform efficiently and effectively. The endless aisles of virtual stores mean that consumers can get pretty much anything they want, and the effortless search (at least relative to physical stores) means they are willing to search for it. And, since they also have the lower fixed costs, virtual stores will be motivated to charge lower prices. But, not being able to touch, feel, and try a product in the digital channel means that consumers will want to check it out in a physical store, at least in categories that are expensive and where fit and feel are important. This makes conditions ripe for the physical channel to be "showroomed" and be tempted to lower its own price and margin. Unless the supplier puts in place incentives for the showroomed channel and/or policies that prevent retail prices from eroding, the negative feedback loops may drag the physical channel, and ultimately the digital channel and the supplier, into a downward spiral.

We hope these two examples begin to illustrate the importance of recognizing potential feedback loops and the need to nurture the beneficial loops, while minimizing damage from the harmful ones.

2.6 CONCLUSION

Throughout the book we will return to various aspects of this push-pull framework. The devil is indeed in the details, so we will strive, whenever possible, to provide suitable metrics and tools, and look for general patterns that can guide managers working to design, implement, and adapt channel strategies.

A mental model of how the system of push-pull inputs and effects works in any given market underlies the explicit and implicit agreements reached by channel partners. But even a carefully planned and constructed arrangement between channel partners is subject to ever-evolving consumer behavior, economic circumstances, technologies, and regulations. There will be plenty of opportunities for dissatisfaction and misunderstandings to emerge. Suppliers and resellers will disagree, among other things, about whether: (1) there was enough pull and push effort; (2) there are too many or too few types of channels and too many or too few resellers within each; (3) resellers are working hard enough to increase the depth of distribution; (4) the feedback loop from reseller push to consumer pull is more or less important than the reverse; (5) consumers are truly loyal to the supplier or care more about their relationship with the channel member; (6) both parties are working to maximize total revenues and profit; and (7) the profit is being split equitably between them. We trace such disagreements back to some root causes in the next chapter.

ENDNOTE

i. The joint effect of push and pull on market share was originally described and modeled in Farris, P., Olver, J., and de Kluyver, C. (1989). The Relationship Between Distribution and Market Share. *Marketing Science* 8 (2): 107–128.

CHAPTER 3

Root Causes of Channel Conflict

3.1 INTRODUCTION

*There are two basic problems confronting the cooperating
firms making up a trade channel. One is that of getting
the job done and the other is that of dividing the returns
among the several participants.*

—Wroe Alderson

Channel conflict is a broad term that marketers use to describe a
situation in which one or more channel members are unhappy about
the state of the mutual relationship. Usually they are unhappy because
they believe they are not being treated "fairly"—meaning they are not
being adequately rewarded, respected, or appreciated for their efforts
and investments in the relationship. A series of actions and reactions
can escalate the conflict.

Downstream resellers typically complain that they are not earning enough because (1) supplier prices are too high; (2) suppliers
make insufficient investments in consumer pull; (3) suppliers'
products are slow-selling; or (4) they are faced with too many, too
aggressive, or free-riding competitors. Furthermore, resellers can be

dissatisfied with manufacturers' inability or unwillingness to finance inventories, supply timely and complete shipments, and support their omni-channel logistics.

At the other end of the chain, upstream suppliers may be irritated that resellers: (1) raise resale prices too high to generate adequate sales volume, or reduce them so much that it hurts the brand's image; (2) refuse to stock the full line, delist some products, or refuse to carry new ones; (3) push other products, including private labels; (4) are unwilling to perform promotion requirements or invest in services for their products; or (5) make slow payments or unauthorized deductions from invoices.

Upstream suppliers have many avenues to discipline or punish downstream resellers. They can: (1) withhold important products; (2) tie supply of products in high demand to other, less popular products; (3) charge higher prices or cut promotional allowances; (4) impose restrictions on selling areas or advertised prices; (5) authorize additional resellers; or (6) move downstream to sell to end consumers themselves. For resellers, the next step up might be threats to drop the entire product line or launching lawsuits to compel changes or seek damages.

With such a broad definition of channel conflict, it is reasonable to ask whether conflict is just a natural result of economic transactions between two parties. In our view, it is. But some conflicts will be situational and can be eliminated with careful analysis and negotiation while many other conflicts are due to the inherent differences in the perspectives of channel members and can only be managed. Like salt, a little channel conflict is good. Without some conflict (e.g., resulting from competition among resellers), many upstream suppliers believe that they don't have enough market coverage and/or that their channel partners may be too "comfortable" (e.g., being compensated too generously for the functions they are performing). But too much conflict is difficult to fix. You can't "unsalt" the soup!

EXAMPLES OF CHANNEL CONFLICT IN INCREASING ORDER OF SEVERITY

Amazon says it will suppress the "Buy Box" if a third-party seller's Buy Box–winning offer is above the list price. Sellers are upset because, without Buy Box, shoppers may think they have no inventory available.

7-Eleven's franchisees complain that the company takes an increasingly bigger cut of their profits, wants them to carry private-label products even if they don't sell well, and forces them to use company-approved suppliers even if those suppliers cannot guarantee the best prices.

DirectTV parent AT&T considers not renewing its exclusive rights to the NFL's Sunday Ticket Package because the price tag is too high.

Amazon delays shipment of Hachette books and blocks preorders of new titles in dispute during contract negotiation. Amazon wants lower wholesale prices for e-books to shore up its own margin.

The two largest movie theater chains refuse to sell tickets for Disney's *Iron Man 3* online because Disney wants too high a share of box-office revenue.

Walgreen Co. offers additional services to patients to help manage medication and wants prescription-benefit manager Express Scripts to reimburse at a higher rate. Express Scripts refuses and Walgreen Co. threatens to leave the network. A similar tussle occurs between Walmart and CVS Caremark.

Taylor Swift pulls her music from digital streaming service Spotify after Spotify refuses to make her music available only to paid subscribers and not to users of the free ad-supported tier. She later threatens to pull her album from Apple Music to protest Apple Music's three-month free trials.

United Airlines announces it will withdraw its flights from Expedia's sites, saying they no longer provide enough value given the cost.

Molson Coors sues SABMiller for terminating a licensing agreement by which Molson distributed Miller beer in Canada. SABMiller says Molson did not sufficiently grow Miller sales in Canada.

Uber drivers file a class-action suit alleging that classification as independent contractors, not as employees, results in lower wages and lack of benefits such as minimum wage, overtime, and expense reimbursement.

DISH Network sues Disney, claiming that Disney favored other distributors in contracts and because it is forced to buy a bundle of ESPN channels, including ESPN Classic, which only 0.5% of consumers watch.

Ohio Art tries to raise its price and Walmart kicks them out. Ohio Art redesigns product to reduce costs but encounters quality problems. It is unclear whether consumers were even concerned about price.

3.1.1 Examples of Channel Conflict

We have tried to sort the examples of conflict in the boxed insert in increasing order of severity from top to bottom. When it comes to legal action, marketers are wise to take Justice William Rehnquist's advice that "bringing parties who must remain in a continuing relationship into the adversarial atmosphere of a courtroom" can permanently damage what many refer to as a partnership.[i] Moreover, a single public disagreement can snowball if other channel partners feel encouraged to dig in their heels too. For example, Taylor Swift's 2014 decision to pull her music off the music-streaming service Spotify spurred others to think about whether music and video streaming services are financially viable if supported only by advertising.[ii]

All of these conflicts emerge even though channel members frequently and fervently refer to their relationship as a "partnership." Of course, the partnership is not only an economic arrangement of convenience; it's often a legal relationship too, defined by carefully crafted statements of mutual responsibilities. Still, because the partnership is between independent entities, each with their own goals and incentives, with neither having direct ownership or control of the other, there is a need to "coordinate" the channel. Channel coordination is the global concept that refers to policies that exploit the synergies while avoiding the inefficiencies and frictions that can accompany non–vertically integrated channels. But you can't effectively coordinate the channel without understanding the root causes of conflict.

3.1.2 Myopia and Four Root Causes of Conflict that Strain the Partnership

As these examples illustrate, discontent can span many issues, but we believe they exist under the single, broad heading of myopia. Since Ted Levitt's famous 1960 article on marketing myopia, published by the *Harvard Business Review*, many types of managerial myopia have been written about in the business literature. In our context of a channel, myopia is when firms make decisions solely in their own self-interest without considering the effect of those decisions on the health of the channel as a whole, or when they make decisions focused on the short term without considering the longer-term ramifications. One or more partners in the channel may act myopically, or one partner may simply perceive that the other is acting myopically, but in the channel, as in many other contexts, perception becomes reality. In the channel, myopia is usually manifested in pricing and selling effort, the extent of distribution coverage, the division of work and pay between channel members, and when adapting to change. The rest of this chapter will explore these four myopia-induced root causes of conflict while underscoring "what is new?" for the channel ecosystem of today.

3.2 UNCOORDINATED PRICING AND SELLING EFFORT

As separate entities, different members of the channel will have their own ideas of what is required for them to be productive and profitable. Left uncoordinated, this leads to the age-old economic inefficiency of double marginalization (DM), wherein each party chooses its selling price to maximize its own profit, not the total channel profit. It's called double marginalization because when both the supplier and the reseller have some power to set their own price and margin, the final price to the consumer is higher and quantity sold is lower due to the "double margin"—the supplier's and the reseller's. This is in contrast to the "single margin" that would occur if the supplier were vertically integrated and sold directly to the consumer. Pricing is just one aspect in which channel coordination is needed. The provision of adequate levels of marketing and other channel functions is just as critical, as is the need to share data that would improve the ability of all the members along the route to market to do their jobs effectively.

3.2.1 Double, Triple, and Quadruple Marginalization

DM is most prevalent when both the upstream company (e.g., the supplier) and the downstream company (e.g., a retailer) have some degree of pricing power. Pricing power simply means that they have some latitude for changing price without seeing volume disappear entirely or explode beyond their capability to supply.[1] DM occurs when both the upstream and downstream channel members set prices to maximize their own profits without taking into consideration how the other channel member(s) will be affected. The result is that consumers can pay higher prices and are generally worse off. Manufacturers suffer lower output (sales) and the combined profits of manufacturers and retailers are lower than what a coordinated system would generate.

For example, Sto Corp manufactures and sells high-tech exterior and interior coatings for buildings. Some of the coatings work with continuous insulation, some work to reduce interior odors and pollutants, and one uses the "lotus effect" to clean itself with rainwater. Sto Corp only sells these coatings to selected distributors in several geographical markets, and the distributors do not stock or sell directly

---

[1] Suppliers sometimes inappropriately say that they "give" the channel a margin. Resellers understandably are more likely to say that they "earn" a certain margin or set prices in order to yield a particular margin.

competing products. Such exclusive or selective distribution is used by suppliers to motivate resellers to invest in the training and selling effort the product requires. But, depending on the degree of competition (and differentiation) faced by distributors, this situation may be ripe for the DM problem. A distributor may simply harvest the demand for Sto's products in its territory, while charging prices that are too high, not investing enough in inventory, spending too little on selling effort, or a combination of all three. Sto Corp will find that the market is not being developed at a satisfactory rate. Since competition among resellers constrains their ability to raise prices and reduce selling effort, DM is apt to be more of a problem in cases like this where distribution is exclusive or selective.

One of the more colorful illustrations of the concept of DM is in the history of the Rhine River toll castles that were erected along the more vulnerable passages to exact tolls from barge owners engaged in river commerce.[2] Each toll castle owner charged high tolls in an attempt to maximize his own take. Without some coordination, there was the danger that traffic could be brought to a standstill and everyone involved would be worse off than if they had arranged a system to charge reasonable tolls and share the revenue.

Economists use a series of equations or graphs to demonstrate these effects, and a quick Google search will uncover many lecture notes with graphs of price-quantity relationships. However, spreadsheet calculations are the lingua franca for businesspeople, and that is what we will use to illustrate the problem.

In the simplified example of Figure 3.1, which we developed in an article we wrote for the *Sloan Management Review,* the table on the left shows the demand function—how many bottles of table wine are sold at different retail prices.[iii] The manufacturer's variable cost is $2.50. The manufacturer sells through a retailer, who incurs a cost of $0.50 per bottle for stocking and selling. So, the total variable costs in the channel are $3.00 per bottle and fixed costs are irrelevant. The "sweet spot" for total channel profits is a $6 retail price. At that retail price, there will be $333 for the retailer and manufacturer to share (111 units sold times $3 channel profit per unit). Selling at a higher or lower retail price will sacrifice this total profit, as the smaller sizes of the total channel profit pie on the right show. If the retail price was $6 and the manufacturer's selling price were $4, the two would each earn

---

[2] We first heard this analogy when it was used by an economics professor, F.M. Scherer, at a conference honoring the work of another economist, Robert Steiner.

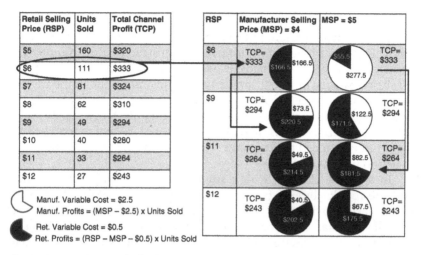

Retail Selling Price (RSP)	Units Sold	Total Channel Profit (TCP)
$5	160	$320
$6	111	$333
$7	81	$324
$8	62	$310
$9	49	$294
$10	40	$280
$11	33	$264
$12	27	$243

Manuf. Variable Cost = $2.5
Manuf. Profits = (MSP − $2.5) x Units Sold

Ret. Variable Cost = $0.5
Ret. Profits = (RSP − MSP − $0.5) x Units Sold

Figure 3.1 Double marginalization.

$166.50. Once the manufacturer fixes their own selling price, how-ever, the retailer has an opportunity to earn more by raising the retail price. If this happens, the manufacturer will lose more profits than the retailer gains.

As you can see from the right side of the figure, if the manufacturer charges $4, the retailer will want to charge a price of $9 instead of $6. In that case, the retailer makes $220.50 and the manufacturer's profits drop from $166.50 to $73.50. Of course, the manufacturer might now raise its price to $5, setting off another round of price increases by the retailer and moving them both further from the combination of prices that would leave manufacturer, retailer, and consumer better off.

The same idea applies to functions that must be performed to gen-erate sales: the selling effort made by downstream resellers is lower than what's optimal for the total channel profit pie.[iv] And so is the willingness to share data.[3]

Where several independent levels exist in the distribution chain, DM can become triple or even quadruple marginalization. Ohio Art, a marketer of toys (one of which is the iconic Etch A Sketch), had

---

[3]While blockchain technology makes it feasible for various parties to contribute and use data on a single so-called "distributed ledger" without having to worry about data integrity, it doesn't change the fact that independent channel partners are unwilling to share data that they may see as a source of leverage even if the channel as a whole would do better with sharing than without.

one of the longer distribution chains that we have encountered. The company is headquartered in Bryan, Ohio, and negotiated the exclusive U.S. rights to market an innovative construction toy, Nanoblock, owned by a Japanese company, Kawada Co., Ltd. Nanoblock was manufactured by yet a different company in mainland China. In the United States, Ohio Art sold Nanoblock through manufacturer representatives and agents to toy stores throughout the country. Each of these five separate organizations set its own price and earned its own margin before the product reached the consumer, so there was the potential for price to be too high at each level.

In a simple channel with a supplier selling through one reseller and the reseller buying from a single supplier, the DM problem was much easier to identify. It showed up as higher prices and lower overall sales than the supplier would like. But pricing in today's retail environment evolves through a series of negotiations and promotional programs spread over time, and has become much more complicated and difficult to monitor. Especially when multiple levels in the channel are involved, the pass-through of promotional allowances and incentives becomes less transparent. In such cases, DM can occur in subtler ways when wholesalers and retailers accumulate upstream promotional payments and don't pass them through to consumers in the form of promotions and price reductions. In the pharmaceutical industry, for example, drug companies habitually post high list prices and then offer rebates on those prices to middlemen like pharmacy benefit managers (PBMs), who process prescriptions for insurers and negotiate with drug companies for lower prices. PBMs have been coming under attack for their potential role in rising drug prices because they pocket some portion of those rebates.[4]

The point is that the DM problem may be more prevalent than managers realize. Competition among resellers alleviates it somewhat but doesn't eliminate it. Although systems of promotional allowances are increasingly needed to coordinate the channel, they can be dauntingly complex to administer. Even those who have the best intentions can find that accounting for promotional allowances that are increasingly conditional on performance can make it difficult to estimate the most basic channel metric: contribution margin. When the intention is to obfuscate channel margins, you can imagine what might be possible. U.S. Food Services was a distributor of food products serving mainly

---

[4]Responding to such criticism, the CEO of CVS Health was quoted in the *Wall Street Journal* (August 9, 2018) as saying that about 3% of its 2018 earnings were expected to come from rebates that the company retains.

commercial food operations, such as restaurants and cafeterias, and promising prices that were "cost plus" an agreed-upon margin. U.S. Food Services' contract also allowed them to retain and similarly process promotion payments that manufacturers and upstream vendors might offer. Downstream customers sued U.S. Foodservices, claiming that it had created a wholly owned middleman in the form of "shell companies," performing few or no services of economic value. The main purpose of this additional middleman, it was successfully argued, was to increase the margin accruing to U.S. Food Services, to the detriment of downstream customers.[v]

3.2.2 Loss Leaders Have Their Own Problems

DM represents one extreme in the breakdown of effective pricing. As you might guess, the other extreme also causes problems: when resellers, faced with intense competition, cut their own prices and margins too far. It is quite common for resellers to sell leading national brands at prices that yield lower percentage (and sometimes dollar) margins for them than do less-well-known brands and private labels.[vi] Figure 3.2 shows a stylized example of this pattern.

This inverse relationship between manufacturer and retailer margins is quite common, but often not recognized by either marketers or economists, so it is useful to give the reader a deeper appreciation of why it occurs.

	Leading Brand	Secondary Brand	Private Label
Retail Selling Price	$1.00	$0.90	$0.80
Retail Margin (%)	10%	20%	30%
Retail Margin ($)	$0.10	$0.18	$0.24
Manuf. Selling Price	$0.90	$0.72	$0.56
Manuf. Cost of Goods	$0.50	$0.50	$0.50
Manuf. Margin ($)	$0.40	$0.22	$0.06

Figure 3.2 Inverse relationship between retailer and manufacturer margins: a stylized example.

First, it is likely that the Leading Brand (think Heinz ketchup, Tide detergent, etc.) sets the price ceiling for other brands that do not have the same strong demand and consumer loyalty. Without the same level or intensity of demand, adequate sales volume for secondary brands can often only be generated by setting prices below the leader's. So we believe it is more accurate to say that the Secondary Brand sells at a discount to the Leading Brand, even though it is common marketing parlance to say that the Leading Brand sells at or "commands" a price premium.

Second, retailers set retail prices in order to earn margins that are consistent with each brand's role in their strategy, consumer willingness to pay and search, the competition faced by the retailer, and the costs incurred. Since Leading Brands are stocked by many other retailers, are visible indicators of the store's overall price levels, are more likely to take the consumer to a competing store for a better price, and typically sell at faster rates per unit of shelf space or inventory, it is not surprising that retailer margins on the Leading Brands are usually lower. Further, the retailers have some latitude in selecting *which* Secondary Brand might go on the shelf. (Should grocery stores' second national brand of ketchup be Hunt's or Del Monte?) The ability to choose among many may put the retailer in a position to negotiate lower wholesale prices or higher promotion payments from the Secondary Brand. The same is true, but to a greater degree, for Private Labels, whether they are sourced from dedicated private label manufacturers or national brand manufacturers. After all, since it is "harder" for the retailer to sell the Secondary Brands and Private Labels, why not be sure that the margins justify the effort?

In Figure 3.3, we show the unit and percentage margins that one U.S. packaged goods retailer we have worked with earns on Leading and Secondary Brands in a variety of product categories. This pattern appears to be a wonderful situation for the Leading Brand. A 10% price difference from the Secondary Brand at retail equates to a 20% difference in manufacturer price and a 45% difference in manufacturer unit margin. As long as the Leading Brand continues to invest a little of the additional margin in marketing and R&D, what could go wrong?

In the consumer packaged goods (CPG) industry, it is certainly the case that brand marketers worry more about retailers pricing their products too high, not too low. This is also an industry where so-called "loss leader pricing" by retailers may be sustainable because a retailer can make up a low or even negative margin on one product with larger margins on the other items bought by the consumer who was attracted to the store by the "loss leader." But even in this industry, low prices can go too far. A few years ago, the CEO of a large CPG company confided

	Unit Retail Margin		% Retail Margin	
	Leading Brand	Secondary Brand	Leading Brand	Secondary Brand
Pain Relievers	0.84	1.41	17%	28%
Toothpaste	0.11	0.68	5%	27%
Baby Formula	1.26	1.47	14%	14%
Laundry Cleaners	−0.89	0.41	−16%	17%
Salty Snacks	0.25	0.76	19%	42%
Soup	0.08	0.41	7%	25%
Chips	0.25	0.24	19%	23%

Figure 3.3 A major U.S. retailer's margins on leading and secondary brands.

to one of us that one of his main marketing worries was that his biggest retail customer didn't earn enough money on his company's products. He was concerned that the low margins on his national brands would make the retailer shift merchandising emphasis to selling other, higher-margin brands and their own private labels. He was also worried that the extreme discounting would cause other retailers to drop his brands, reduce their shelf space, or cut the number of SKUs.

For CPG products, which are mainly sold in self-service stores, at least in developed markets, extreme discounting can be problematic, but not nearly as worrisome as it is for products that rely heavily on resellers to explain and persuade consumers of the value and benefits of product features. Home furnishings, expensive consumer electronics, automobile tires, and large household appliances are examples of product categories in which the purchases are so infrequent that consumers often seek assistance from salespeople to finalize their choice of what to buy. Training/compensating effective salespeople, convenient locations, and attractive retail displays are just some of the expenses that retailers incur in order to provide the kind of presale services that consumers need to feel comfortable making a decision to buy a particular brand and model.

For suppliers of brands that have strong consumer loyalty and too-low retail margins, the problem is that full-service retailers may cut critical services and erode brand loyalty, or turn to "bait-and-switch" practices. These tactics typically involve "baiting" consumers by advertising the well-known brand at attractive prices in order to bring them into their store and then "switching" them to brands with higher margins at the point of purchase.

Some of these tactics, such as intentionally limiting supply of the advertised brands below expected demand, are illegal. Others, such as using in-store signage that points to the stark price comparison between national brands and private labels, may be tolerated by some suppliers and not by others. American Express, for example, prohibits merchants from posting signage or offering discounts to consumers that encourage consumers to use other credit cards that charge lower merchant fees.[5] Some suppliers employ mystery shopper services with hidden cameras in bags and purses in an attempt to monitor retailer behavior. But policing reseller behavior is not easy. And, of course, the most extreme reseller behavior is to simply abandon the brand or the product category.

3.3 OVER- AND UNDER-DISTRIBUTION

The problem of uncoordinated pricing and selling effort always exists, but it is exacerbated by companies over- or under-distributing their products and services. Too much distribution coverage can induce resellers to cut important services in order to afford lower prices than the store down the street or their competitors on a price comparison app. In the worst case, as discussed, resellers may use the low prices to attract consumers and switch them to other, higher-margin products. Too little distribution can lead resellers to exploit their "monopoly" position through higher prices and lower levels of selling investment.[vii]

3.3.1 Under-Distribution

The costs of under-distributing a product or service are easy to recognize. In the short term, marketers are apt to worry much more about under-distribution than about over-distribution. It isn't just that DM becomes more likely. They are also concerned about the consequences of lost sales and the opportunity that is created for competitors to enter when products are not widely distributed enough to allow the reseller supply to meet customer demand. Every time someone orders a Pepsi, only to be told that the restaurant offers Coke, Pepsi loses a sale. Worse

---

[5] As we noted in Chapter 1, the U.S. Supreme Court in 2018 ruled that the AmEx policy was not anticompetitive when viewed in the context of its two-sided market.

than a single lost sale, a previously loyal customer might not only give up asking but get in the habit of drinking Coke. This is not only true for fast-moving consumer goods, but for expensive durables as well. Those in the market for a new car might consider test-driving a new Lexus, but are likely to balk if they discover that, as is the case in Charlottesville, Virginia, there is no local dealer and they have to drive 75 miles to Richmond to obtain warranty service or repairs.

After the introduction of innovative new products that spark the emergence of new product categories—for example, energy drinks, e-cigarettes, or even distinct product segments within established categories (Greek yogurt, bottled tea)—there is a rush to fill store shelves to take advantage of growing demand. The product innovators are well aware that competitors will be hanging on their coattails. Those arriving late to the game may find that the shelves are full and entry is foreclosed, or at least very expensive and risky. Slotting allowances may be required by retailers to discontinue products that are already on the shelf and make room for new ones. The cost of paying for that shelf space may bleed funds from marketing programs that would otherwise fuel demand, and overall risk is higher.

Red Bull is an example of a brand that established the category of energy drinks. It successfully managed the transition from a highly selective distribution strategy that reached influencers in several key market segments to the current intensive distribution that includes multiple refrigerators in many large grocery stores, and a nearly ubiquitous hotel minibar presence. That original selective-distribution strategy was critical to building interest and an element of exclusivity and mystery about the product that, in turn, drove word of mouth. The exclusivity also motivated the retail stores, bars, and other outlets that did get to carry the product to prominently feature and display it. Of course, the downside was that outlets who could not obtain Red Bull were eager to take on Monster, Rock Star, or one of the many other brands that followed Red Bull into the energy drink category.

Under-distribution is not only a problem for growing brands and categories. Brands that find themselves in what otherwise might be temporary downturns in demand for their products risk losing distribution, and that loss can turn into a downward spiral. Once a substantial amount of distribution coverage is lost, the brand will often find that national or even regional marketing programs designed to boost demand are no longer as productive. That can lead to cutting funding for advertising and product development, reinforcing the downward slide. We have heard from marketing-analytics teams at more than one CPG company that a new product that doesn't get 70% All Commodity

Volume (ACV) within three months is doomed to failure and a product whose distribution falls to 30% ACV is dead.[6]

3.3.2 Over-Distribution

The pressure for growth and to stay ahead of competition can easily tempt companies to expand distribution too rapidly and too much. This is especially true if they fear that competitive offerings will occupy scarce shelf space and be hard to dislodge. Growing sales by growing distribution is often the fastest way to growth—the distribution elasticity of demand is as much as ten times higher than advertising elasticity, for example.[viii] But it can easily lead companies to overshoot their marks. Consider the case of Stainmaster in the boxed insert.

STAINMASTER: A STELLAR PUSH-PULL PROGRAM UNRAVELED BY OVER-DISTRIBUTION

The story of Dupont Stainmaster is a cautionary tale about over-distribution. Seeking to capitalize on the serendipitous discovery of stain resistance in an inexpensive chemical, Dupont introduced Stainmaster branded nylon for carpet in 1986.

In the context of the residential carpeting market of the 1980s, DuPont's marketing strategy of differentiating its stain-resistant nylon fiber and branding carpets made from it as "DuPont Stainmaster" was widely saluted as brilliant. The company invested heavily in both push and pull marketing, installing equipment at certified mills, training mill personnel, providing point-of-purchase demonstrations that permitted retail salespeople to show the stain resistance to shoppers, providing a warranty supported by a 1-800 number, and producing award-winning consumer advertising campaigns.

All of this was paid for by charging mills an initial 25% price premium per pound of nylon and only selling to mills that produced plush, high-quality carpets, ensuring that more pounds of nylon were sold per square yard of carpet. Consumers gladly paid more for the enhanced stain protection and peace of mind, so DuPont enjoyed high margins. Mills and retailers participated in the revived market and higher prices, at least for a little while.

But the mills lost their influence. Before Stainmaster, consumers looked for mill brands as a gauge of quality, but Stainmaster relegated mills to the background. Few cared much if

---

[6]%ACV is a commonly used measure of distribution coverage, especially in CPG. Instead of just counting the percentage of resellers in the market who stock the product, it weights them by their total sales. We will discuss this and other distribution metrics in detail in Chapter 7.

the "Stainmaster" carpet was made by Burlington, Shaw, Mohawk, or any other licensed mill.

As competitors introduced their own stain-protection systems and quoted lower prices for the nylon to mills, DuPont reduced their own price to mills and allowed more and more mills to make Stainmaster carpets. It was an effort to reap more market share as the reward for revitalizing the carpeting market. Price competition reemerged at the retail level, and price comparisons among retailers were now easier for consumers: They'd ask, "What's your price on Stainmaster?"

As the Stainmaster brand became stronger and more widely available, retailers competed more fiercely on prices (see Figure 3.4) and lowered their own margins. The retail price pressure fell back on the mills, too, who started producing lighter-weight Stainmaster carpet to afford the lower prices and also looked to do more business with DuPont's competitors. Mills such as Shaw and Mohawk consolidated and even backward-integrated into making fiber, wanting to become big enough to have some countervailing power against DuPont.

Figure 3.4 Intense retail price competition on Stainmaster.

DuPont scrambled to regain control of its brand and its distribution system with brand extensions, exclusive retailers, and such, which we will return to in Chapter 8.

Our main point here is that excessive distribution coverage can lead to severe retail price competition, which erodes margins for everyone, and can send reseller support and brand equity spiraling downwards.

Over-distribution may also be an unintended consequence when forecasting demand is hard. Consider, for example, the classic case of a grass-seed supplier. The company noticed that each spring, because of the unpredictability of weather, football games, and golf tee times, it was difficult to know when (which Saturday?) local demand for grass seed would peak. Since grass seed is bulky, hard to store, and not a high-dollar item, stores were reluctant to build up advance inventories sufficient to meet uncertain demand. Hordes of suburban gardeners would often be inspired at about the same time to visit hardware and garden stores in search of seed to replenish their lawns. Those getting up a little later often found the first store "sold out." Quite a few would not be deterred, visiting one store after another looking for seed. Each store justifiably thought they could have sold seed to each of those suburban consumers if they had it in stock and that feedback traveled back to the grass seed company. Based on that overly rosy forecast of sales, when the company decided to offer retailers inventory on "consignment" only to be paid for when sold, they found retailers happy to take them up on the offer. The company also encouraged their sales force to place as much seed inventory as they could with as many retailers as they could. By the time fall rolled around, there was a record amount of unsold inventory on retail floors and little prospect of selling it in the coming winter months.

3.3.3 Competing with Your Customers

A particular version of what downstream channel members view as over-distribution occurs when suppliers start selling directly to consumers or to the next reseller in the chain, thus "competing with their customers." As we said in Chapter 1, the Internet has made it much easier for suppliers to go directly to the end user, so there has been an exponential growth in the number of suppliers who compete with their customers.

In the travel industry, for example, our colleague Erv Shames, who is a board member at Choice Hotels, notes that "there is a pitched battle to capture where the consumer books her travel." Hotels use "lowest rate" guarantees and extra loyalty points to incentivize travelers to book directly with them, because commissions to online aggregators such as Expedia or Booking.com cut directly into hotels' margins, and it is easy to lose bookings to the tens of competing options the aggregators show to competitors. The aggregators, for their part, are concerned about becoming "billboards" where travelers search but don't book, and are offering loyalty points and bundled deals of their own.

Even CPG companies are trying a hand at direct-to-consumer subscription businesses: After arch rival Unilever bought the Dollar Shave Club, P&G launched Tide Wash Club and Colgate Palmolive took a stake in a New York City start-up named Hubble, with whom it is expected to start a subscription service for Colgate products.

Other companies try to reassure their customers that they do not plan to compete with them. For example, the merger of online meta-mediaries Zillow and Trulia in the real estate industry caused real estate agents to worry about the possibility that the merged giant will get into the business of selling real estate, although the companies claimed they have no intention of doing so. As Spencer Rascoff, the CEO of Zillow, said at the announcement of the merger plan, "We sell ads, not houses."[ix] Similarly, Devin Wenig, CEO of the stand-alone eBay after its split from PayPal, told the *Wall Street Journal* about standing up to Amazon.com in e-commerce, "There is a big difference between eBay and Amazon and it goes to the heart of the business model: we don't compete with merchants."[x]

3.3.4 Unauthorized Distribution

Another specific version of over-distribution occurs when products find their way into channels and outlets that are not authorized to sell them. Authorized resellers are unhappy because the lower prices at which unauthorized outlets generally sell take revenue away from them. Suppliers are unhappy because the image of their brands is sullied by the association with unauthorized channels and the lowering of price points. Unauthorized distribution, or gray markets, are often a consequence of the arbitrage opportunity created by price differentials across markets. An unauthorized party may buy the product from an authorized reseller in the lower-priced market, incur the cost of transporting and selling it at below-market price in a higher-priced market, and still come out well ahead because the differential in prices across the markets is large enough. And, because an unauthorized reseller can reach more consumers faster on the Internet, the incidence of this problem as well as the severity of its effects are greater than ever before.

In cross-border gray markets, the arbitrage opportunity may be due to exchange rate variations, other reasons for prices to be different, or because the supplier does not (yet) have authorized resellers in a market. Since the product first has to have come from an authorized source, one or more authorized resellers or the supplier are likely either actively engaging in the practice or are looking the other way.

Within a market, the arbitrage opportunity may be because authorized channels are saddled with excess inventory and want to get rid of it. The excess inventory may be due to poor sales forecasting or overbuying by resellers on trade promotion deals. The overbuying may be unintentional if the reseller, and indeed the supplier, expected to sell more than they actually did. Or it may be intentional: sometimes large resellers exploit suppliers' ill-conceived quantity discounts to buy up large quantities and make an extra buck by diverting them to unauthorized channels. Supplier response to such unauthorized distribution can range all the way from "stop it at any cost" to "so what, it is working for us." Some luxury product manufacturers would rather destroy excess inventory than have it get into unauthorized discount channels—Burberry got some notoriety, for example, when they reportedly destroyed more than $300 million in excess inventory in 2017. One supplier we know realized that their largest authorized resellers were buying extra stock on quantity discount and diverting it to an unauthorized channel. But the supplier got so used to the revenue that came through the unauthorized channel that they didn't have the will to curtail the practice.

3.4 DIVISION OF WORK AND PAY: WHO SOLD THAT?

Whether it is a roll of wallpaper, a box of detergent, an auto insurance policy, or television programming, there is always an issue of dividing credit (and compensation) for the sale. Was it the quality and branding of the supplier's products, its advertising, and other consumer marketing that built consumer-based brand equity and made the sale? Or was it the channel's push in presenting and explaining the product's virtues at the right time and place? Of course, it was a combination of both that made the sale. Still, there is a natural tendency to attribute positive results to one's own actions and negative ones to others or to uncontrollable factors—psychologists call it self-attribution bias. In channels, that is especially so because it is easier to observe your own efforts than those of your partner.

The questions of who's responsible for a sale, and what margin they deserve, are not limited to separating channel push and consumer pull. The margins earned by the different channels need to be consistent with the functions they perform. And seemingly mundane functions, such as delivery and returns, have big effects on costs and margins.

3.4.1 The Case of Leather Italia: Functions Performed and Margin Earned

Leather Italia USA (LI) is a high-end leather-furniture company. It was founded by Michael Campbell and began operations in 1996.

Campbell had a long history and expertise in leather-tannery work and aimed to offer the highest-quality leather furniture at prices previously unmatched in the industry.

According to Campbell, by 2009, LI was regarded as a national brand name and had partnered with many of the finest retail-furniture stores in the U.S. Sourcing leather from as far as Australia, and contracting manufacturing from multiple sources in China, the company was positioned to grow its distribution network and sales well into the future. It had received some prestigious awards and been recognized by many organizations including *Furniture Today* and several top-100 retail chains. By 2011, it had multiple warehouse facilities, employed approximately 35 people in the corporate office, and had more than 40 independent sales representatives. Sales had grown to nearly $30 million a year and the company was profitable.

The company produced and marketed four main products: sofas, loveseats, chairs, and ottomans. Each of the products was produced in a variety of styles, colors, and types of leather in order to offer consumers a coordinated group of furniture. The items that consumers ordered from a furniture store were produced to LI's specifications and with LI-sourced leathers by LI's Chinese partner. Container loads of these products were shipped to the furniture store's warehouse. Once a container was shipped, the item was deemed to have been sold to the retailer. Because the furniture store clients were generally a good credit risk, Campbell could factor their receivables at a high percentage of face value.[7]

The process by which consumers bought LI's products from retail-furniture stores was roughly this: the consumer would browse the furniture collection in stores, consult with salespeople, negotiate price and delivery, and then pay by check or credit card. The product would be scheduled for delivery to the consumer's home or office. When the furniture store received the items at its warehouse, it would unpack the pieces and check them for damages incurred in shipment. On occasion, minor repairs or cleaning were done by the warehouse before delivery. The final step was delivery by the furniture store's employees, accompanied by a request for the consumer to sign a receipt acknowledging that the item was what they ordered and in good condition.

---

[7]Factoring is a financial transaction in which a business sells its accounts receivable to a third party like a bank (called a factor) at a discount. The factor then collects payment on those invoices from the business's customers.

All told, the retailers took responsibility for exhibiting the furniture, taking orders, delivering items, and handling any returns, and earned margins that were between 40% and 50% of the retail selling price.

In 2011, Costco approached LI. The retailer was interested in selling LI's products on its website. The Costco deal required substantial changes in the way LI had done business with its other retailers but also had the promise of substantial volume growth. LI developed a product line for Costco that would only be available as a four-piece group and, although it was the same general style as what LI sold through furniture stores, it was constructed from different leather and sourced from a different factory. This lowered costs so that the product could hit a price point to generate higher sales volumes. LI also took responsibility for delivery and returns.

The new arrangement resulted in very different price points and margin structures, as you can see in Figure 3.5, which shows the prices and margins for the "Aspen" group of furniture sold through retail-furniture stores and the "Mauro" group sold through Costco .com. The responsibility for delivery drastically reduced LI's margin, bringing it from $683 for sales through furniture stores to $367 for sales through Costco.com. But Costco, which famously limits its own margins on selling price to 15% or less, charged prices that resulted in a margin of only $264 for Costco, compared to the furniture store's $1,790.[xi] How can this be? Presumably because Costco passed on almost all of the typical retail functions and financial risks to LI. This

Prices and Margins	"Aspen" Group Sold through Furniture Stores	"Mauro" Group Sold through Costco.com
Retail Selling Price	$3,896	$2,299
Leather Italia Selling Price	$2,106	$2,035
Landed Cost	$1,423	$1,218
Leather Italia Margin before Delivery	$ 683	$ 817
Delivery Cost	----	$ 450
Leather Italia Margin after Delivery	$ 683	$ 367
Retailer Margin	$1,790	$ 264

Figure 3.5 Different margins for different channels and functions.

enabled the products sold through Costco to hit attractive retail price points. The hope at LI was that high volume would make these low margins worthwhile for both parties. And that hope became reality as revenue through Costco grew rapidly, bringing in more than $15 million during 2012. So far so good, but stay tuned for the end of the story in Chapter 6.

3.4.2 Free Riding on Showrooms, Webrooms, and Billboards

The division of work and pay is often even more complicated than the LI example illustrates because of the many independent channels that play a role in the "journey" consumers undertake when searching for, evaluating, and buying products. When a dedicated runner sees an advertisement for a new running shoe model in *Runner's World* magazine, that might make her just a little more likely to think it is time to get a new pair of shoes. Going online for more information, she might visit a couple of retailer sites and the brand's own website, which might suggest nearby stores that stock the product. Visiting a local shop, looking over the display, talking to the salesperson, and trying on a pair, she might decide that it is the shoe she wants and buy it there. If she logs 15 to 20 miles per week, even a well-constructed, high-quality shoe may need replacing in a few months. At that point, she might buy the same model online, perhaps ordering it in a different color. Indeed, the next few purchases might be what marketers call a "rebuy" with not a lot of consideration going into the product choice. It is easy to see that attributing even the first and especially subsequent sales to pull versus push and to particular channel partners will not be easy.

Even before the advent of the Internet, consumers elected to browse in one store and buy elsewhere. That "elsewhere" might be a retailer that has elected to cut expenses and prices and free ride on the services provided by full-service and full-price competitors. Think warehouse outlets for carpeting and furniture, and 1-800 stores for wallpaper. The U.S. residential-wallpaper market provides a window into the potential effects of free riding over a long time frame. Many industry participants believe that the inability or unwillingness of wallpaper manufacturers to control free riding contributed to the decline of that industry.

Today's versions of free-riding have different labels. It is called showrooming when consumers browse and check out products in a store, then check prices online and buy there. And it is called webrooming or ROBO when the reverse happens—research online and buy in store. The travel industry refers to billboarding—when the traveler becomes aware of options by visiting an online travel agent site but then books directly with the hotel or airline.

 FREE RIDING AND THE DEMISE OF WALLPAPER

In the 1970s, the retail-wallpaper industry was dominated by independent stores that flourished in the residential-construction boom following World War II. Compared to painting, hanging wallpaper is more time consuming and requires very specialized skills. Once applied, it is not easily removed, so errors are expensive. Consumers, wanting to get it right the first time, welcomed the opportunity to browse in stores that stocked as many as 1,000 separate manufacturer catalogs, wherein the variety of colors and designs reached into the tens of thousands. Many stores hired design consultants to help consumers find their way through the extensive offerings. Once the selection was made, the retailer ordered the specific brand and pattern of wallpaper from a distributor, asking the consumer to return in a few days to pick it up.

This delivery delay, plus the fact that wallpaper is high in value, lightweight, and easy to ship, made the wallpaper industry particularly vulnerable to free riding. They may not rival the Internet as a technological innovation, but 1-800 numbers encouraged some dealers to vastly expand their market simply by advertising huge discounts. Once the pattern was selected at a traditional brick-and-mortar store, consumers could easily order from 1-800 dealers. An increasing share of wallpaper was shipped through 1-800 dealers that had discounts as high as 80%.

Traditional dealers faced other threats to their once-thriving industry, including the advent of big-box stores such as Lowe's and changes in decorating tastes. But even if 1-800 dealers were not the sole or even the main reason for the decline, traditional dealers blamed manufacturers for not controlling them. Manufacturer attempts to reduce free riding with drop-shipping charges and other strategies were frustrated by lawsuits that cost time and money and pitted them against some of their highest-volume customers.

Traditional dealers began to advertise discounts of their own and funded these discounts by cutting back on the services such as the number of books they stocked and the design consultants they employed. So without the full-service dealers to generate customer demand for specific products, the 1-800 dealers also began to exit. As one author writes, "Sure, people still put up wallpaper, and there are many interesting designers currently working in the form, but try this little experiment: What images does the phrase '1950s wallpaper' conjure in your mind? *Tiny flowers on a light green ground.* OK, how about '1970s wallpaper'? *Overlapping brown oblongs with rounded corners.* Now try this: '1990s wallpaper.' Drawing a blank?"

3.5 ADAPTING TO CHANGE: WHERE DOES THE FUTURE LIE?

As companies grow, they look for new market segments and new ways to increase penetration of existing segments. They introduce new products that require different functions from channel members. And in an age of relationship marketing, firms are eager to develop direct contact with consumers. They may perceive existing channel members as reluctant or unable to make the necessary investments, so they seek to develop new partnerships. Existing partners are made nervous by efforts to "go around them"; these channel members may think of themselves as the customer, but the upstream marketer views them as a vehicle to reach the real customer. Past investments in pushing the brand are sunk costs and ancient history to the upstream marketer, but the intermediary sees it differently. They made their investments and early commitments to support the brand with the expectation of enduring loyalty. All of this is complicated by the social network of personal relationships that support the economic relationships. So, changing channel strategy, or even adding channels, is a decision that companies must make and execute carefully and deliberately, even if they may not have a lot of time to make the changes.

Upstream suppliers develop channel strategies to address consumer needs given existing channel alternatives, technological possibilities, and legal constraints. They settle on a configuration that satisfies these requirements in an efficient manner. As the environment changes, the pressure for channel changes may increase. New consumer segments emerge and the basis for competition changes along with consumer needs. New technologies enable new digital distribution models, and we hear the most about those. Yet, those who began with digital distribution find that they also need traditional distribution channels in order to grow. Honest Company, founded by actress Jessica Alba in 2011, began as a direct-to-consumer subscription business selling safe baby and personal care products. It became a Unicorn (a term that the tech industry applies to privately held start-ups that reach a valuation of $1 billion). To continue to grow, however, Honest realized that it also needed a strong presence in brick-and-mortar stores and has been trying to grow physical distribution in addition to its online presence under CEO Nick Vlahos, who is a veteran of the CPG industry.

Questions abound, whether you are a digital native or one that grew up on physical distribution. Which are the channels of the future? Which consumer needs will be met by which channel? What functions will each channel perform? Is the value added consistent with the cost of the channel? Who will flock to the new channels? Who will migrate with a little encouragement? Who will never buy from them? Will one channel serve to acquire customers for the other? Will one channel be rewarded for continuing to perform its functions even if the consumer makes their final purchase in a different channel?

Even with answers to these questions, implementing changes in the face of channel conflict is usually not easy. Some suppliers may plunge right in. A cosmetic company selling to the youth market has taken its products off the shelf at brick-and-mortar stores and intends to use teen sleepovers and other Tupperware-like parties together with social media to reach its target market.[xii] But, many others may adopt bandages, work-arounds, and temporary fixes instead of fundamental changes, as they assess which channels to bet on for the future. If existing resellers fear that they may be marginalized, their reactions can be exaggerated. Why invest in supporting a brand when you might soon be undersold in a big-box discount outlet or online?

The challenge of transitioning from one channel structure to another is akin to what the late Professor Ray Corey of Harvard Business School called the "Monkey Law of Business." Just as the fabled monkey, traveling through the jungle, swinging through the trees, needs to have a firm grasp on the next vine before he lets go of the last one, businesses desperately want to be firmly established with new channels before they abandon the old ones. Of course, there is a certain amount of momentum required for both traveling monkeys and evolving channel strategies. Almost every business finds it difficult to adapt to new channels at the fast pace of commerce today. Finding the strategy and speed for transitioning from the current structure to the one envisioned is one of the most important tasks that marketers face. Risk will never be eliminated, but clear-eyed and systematic assessment of the ability of new channel structures to perform critical functions will go a long way toward motivating and smoothing the needed changes.

3.6 CONCLUSION

"Old wine in new bottles" is a phrase frequently used to discount the possibility of real and significant change. Although we have laid out the enduring underlying causes of channel conflict in this chapter, our intent is not to minimize the effects that digitization, e-commerce, and m-commerce are having on distribution strategy. Rather, our purpose is to show that as marketers move to build new routes to market, the consequences of uncoordinated channels, over-distribution and under-distribution, and failure to recognize the functions required and compensate the channels that perform those functions, are likely to be become more severe.

Although every textbook lists the basic functions to be performed in a channel, many of those functions are being digitized, unbundled, monetized, cost reduced, and shifted among channel members in ever-changing fashions. This makes it much harder to keep track of who is performing what functions, how effectively they are performing them, and how they are and should be compensated. It also takes even more control out of the hands of upstream marketers and their traditional channels as new intermediaries route consumers toward or away from products at the very moment when they are ready to search and buy. So, we devote the next chapter to describing the main players in today's channel ecosystem and the functions they perform, again distinguishing the enduring from the new.

 ## Summary

- Some conflict is inevitable in a channel. The new digitally enabled channel ecosystem may exacerbate that conflict, but the root sources of channel conflict are enduring.

- Both suppliers and their independent resellers may be unable or unwilling to formulate strategies from the perspective of the entire channel. This can manifest in retail prices that are either too high from the perspective of upstream marketers (because of "double marginalization") or too low for downstream resellers to earn enough margin. It can also result in selling effort that falls short of what would maximize the total channel profit pie.

- Margin problems and lack of selling effort are exacerbated by over- or under-distribution, but getting it "just right" requires a clear strategy, metrics, and especially discipline that may be missing when most needed.

- Competing with one's customers by opening up a direct-to-consumer channel is one of the more contentious forms of what downstream channel partners view as over-distribution.

- So is unauthorized distribution, which can occur any time there is excess inventory or a price differential between markets or channels or individual resellers. Whether intentional or unintended, whether attributable to the supplier or an authorized reseller or both, the friction it creates in the channel is significant.

- Many disputes can be traced to the division of work and pay. They occur when the total profit pie is not divided among channel members with an eye to sustaining critical services needed by the end consumer.

(Continued)

(Continued)

▪ Changes in technology and consumer behavior have enabled new intermediaries that free ride on the efforts of others, or prove that some services are no longer needed, or simply perform a narrower set of functions. Differentiating between these and paying for, and only for, needed functions is becoming more difficult.

▪ In the face of these changes, businesses will struggle to neither get too far ahead nor fall too far behind the most important market shifts. Even getting it "just right" will produce conflict from established channels.

ENDNOTES

i. Rehnquist, W. (1978). The Adversary Society. Keynote Address of the Third Annual Baron de Hirsch Meyer Lecture Series, 33 *U. Miami L. Rev.* 1.

ii. Pfanner, E., and Mochizuki, T. (2014). Doubts Spread at Sony About Music Streaming. *Wall Street Journal* (19 November), p. B6.

iii. Ailawadi, K., Farris, P., and Shames, E. (1999). Trade Promotion: Essential to Selling Through Resellers. *Sloan Management Review* 41 (1): 83–92.

iv. See, for example, Tsay, A., and Agrawal, N. (2000). Channel dynamics under price and service competition. *Manufacturing & Service Operations Management* 2 (4): 372–391.

v. Allen, B., Farris, P., Mills, D., and Sack, R. (2011). Vendor Incentives: Out of the Shadows and Into the Sunlight. *CPA Journal* June: 6–15.

vi. Steiner, R. (1978). A Dual Stage Approach to the Effects of Brand Advertising on Competition and Price. In: *Marketing and the Public Interest* (ed. John F. Cady), 78–105. Cambridge, MA: Marketing Science Institute. Farris, P. and Albion, M. (1987). Manufacturer Advertising and Retail Gross Margins. *Advances in Marketing and Public Policy* 1: 107–136. Farris, P. (1981). Advertising's Link With Retail Price Competition. *Harvard Business Review* 59 (1): 40–44. Steiner, R. (1993). The Inverse Association Between the Margins of Manufacturers and Retailers. *Review of Industrial Organization* 8: 717–740. Lal, R., and Narasimhan, C. (1996), "The Inverse Relationship Between Manufacturer and Retailer Margins: A Theory," *Marketing Science* 15 (2): 132–151.

vii. Vinhas, S., and Heide, J. (2015). Forms of Competition and Outcomes in Dual Distribution Channels: The Distributor's Perspective. *Marketing Science* 34 (1): 164–175. Here, the authors report that even end customer satisfaction, at least as perceived by resellers, is higher at a medium level of distribution where intra-brand competition is neither too high nor too low.

viii. Please see: Ataman, B., van Heerde, H., and Mela, C. (2010). The Long-term Effect of Marketing Strategy on Brand Sales. *Journal of Marketing Research* 47 (5): 866–882. Datta, H., Ailawadi, K. and van Heerde, H. (2017). How Well Does Consumer-Based

Brand Equity Align with Sales-Based Brand Equity and Marketing-Mix Response? *Journal of Marketing* 81 (3): 1–20.

ix. Light, J. (2014). In Zillow-Trulia Deal, Making Room for Brokers. *Wall Street Journal* (28 July), p. B1.

x. Bensinger, G. (2014). Soon to Be Single, eBay Gets Back to Shopping. *Wall Street Journal* (19 November), p. B7.

xi. Logan, L., and Beyman, M. (2012). Costco: Breaking All the Retail Rules. CNBC Business News (25 April), www.cnbc.com/id/47175492 (accessed December 2017).

xii. Loten, A. (2014). Move Over Avon Lady, the Tweens Are Here. *Wall Street Journal* (20 June).

CHAPTER 4

Middlemen in Today's Channel Ecosystem and Their Functions

4.1 INTRODUCTION

The basic justification for the existence of middlemen is that they can simplify and streamline the process of connecting suppliers with consumers, as Figure 4.1 depicts. But search engines and their historical precursors, the Yellow Pages, also connect suppliers with consumers, so what value do middlemen in the distribution channel really offer? In the popular imagination, they are gatekeepers that control access to products and drive up their price, so "Cut out the middleman!" is a familiar refrain. Curiously enough, it is sounded even by middlemen themselves, as you can see in the sign in the figure, which was displayed at a Trader Joe's store.[1]

---

[1]The picture was taken in a New Jersey store on June 25, 2018, by Kirk Kardashian, who helped us with the editing of this book. Presumably, Trader Joe's is touting its direct sourcing of the mostly private label products it sells versus national brand manufacturers' products.

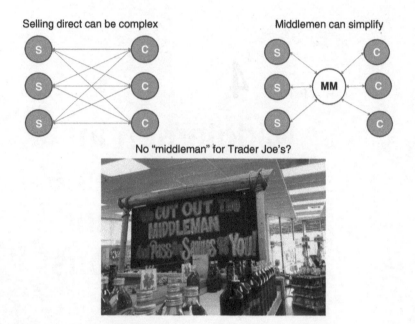

Figure 4.1 Long live the middleman?

Upstream suppliers have long had the option of selling direct to their end customers. Historically, some of the better known direct-marketing organizations were encyclopedia publishers, the Fuller Brush Company, and cosmetics companies such as Avon. Today, most suppliers are using the web to build relationships directly with consumers, and often to transact with them. But they can't do it all themselves. The name of the person who first said, "You can do away with the middleman, but you can't do away with the middleman's functions," has been lost to history. It is a shame, because that phrase has been repeated in slightly altered forms so many times that the originator deserves some credit.

In this chapter, we dig a little deeper into the services that middlemen in the distribution channel provide. For the most part, these intermediaries exist because they perform valuable functions for suppliers or for consumers, and often for both.[2] Put simply, they add value by

---

[2]The existence of intermediaries between sellers and buyers may sometimes become enshrined through legal requirements or institutional powers long after the original purposes are no longer valid. Automobile distribution is a prime example in the United States, to which we will return in later chapters.

making products, services, and information available in a form and at a time, place, and price that suppliers and consumers need. Of course, today's channels are a lot more varied than they used to be, as the reader will recall from Chapter 1.

Figure 4.2 fleshes out contemporary intermediaries and their sources of revenue in a little more detail. The top panel lists channels

Type of Business	Examples	Typical Revenue Model
Largely Brick-and-Mortar Intermediaries		
Wholesalers, Distributors	C&S Wholesalers, DPG Distributors, Sysco	Margin on sales
Retailers, Value-Added Resellers	Walmart, Best Buy, Verizon Wireless	Margin on sales, VA revenue
Buying Cooperatives	CCA Global, Wakefern Food Corp.	Member fee, margin on sales, VA revenue
Independent Sales Associates	Avon Ladies	Commission or margin on sales and sometimes on recruitment
Manufacturers Reps, Brokers, Agents	Acosta Grocery Brokers, Independent Insurance Agents	Commission on sales
Franchisees	Marriott, McDonald's, Coca-Cola Bottlers, Eggland's Best	Margin on sales
Largely Digital Intermediaries		
E-tailers	Amazon, Birchbox, Stitchfix	Margin on sales
Aggregators	Expedia, Booking, RoomKey, Uber, Truecar	Commission on sales, advertising, listing fee, member fee
Metamediaries	Zillow, Edmunds, Kayak, TripAdvisor	Listing fee, commission on clicks/leads, advertising
Online Marketplaces	Amazon Marketplace, Taobao, Etsy	Commission on sales, advertising, listing fee
Special Support Service Providers		
Affiliates	Affiliates of Amazon or Expedia	Commission on sales or clicks
Delivery Service	UPS, Shoprunner, Google Shopping Express, Instacart	Fee per delivery, membership fee
Payment Processors	PayPal, Square, Apple Pay, AliPay	Transaction fee
eCommerce / Reverse Logistics Service	Radial, Returns Management Inc.	Fees for services
Other Special Services	Pillow, Carnow	Subscription fee, commission on sales

Figure 4.2 Intermediaries in the channel ecosystem and their sources of revenue.

that operate in the traditional brick-and-mortar world and handle physical products. Intermediaries in the second panel have arisen in the online world. Some are virtual analogs of retail stores and malls, while others only sell information about products to consumers, and information about the flow of consumers to upstream suppliers. Those in the third panel are not, in our view, distribution channels in their own right. However, they play an important role in the channel ecosystem by providing specific support services that enable channels, especially digital ones, to complete transactions with consumers.

The functions that channel intermediaries perform in bringing together supply and demand are typically represented as a generic "laundry list" that we have broken out in a little more detail in Figure 4.3. As in the previous figure, the top panel contains traditional intermediaries that operate in the physical world, and we start with what they do.

4.2 BRICK-AND-MORTAR INTERMEDIARIES

Wholesalers and Distributors: Wholesalers buy products in bulk from suppliers and sell and deliver them to several different retailers, thus aggregating purchases on the "buy" side (bringing many shoppers together under one roof) and breaking bulk on the "sell" side (selling and delivering products in individual sizes to consumers instead of shipping large truckloads to middlemen). They take title to goods and services, negotiate deals with suppliers, and set their own selling prices. Some act as "rack jobbers" who maintain in-store inventories at retail outlets and bill the retailer as the inventories are replenished. Distributors are much like wholesalers, but they typically serve a subset of suppliers with whom they have close relationships. They are actively involved in selling and promoting the suppliers' products to retailers. Some distributors, such as those in produce and frozen food, specialize in specific products and the storage and transportation they require.

Both wholesalers and distributors usually take some form of inventory and payment risk. If goods spoil, go out of fashion, or don't sell at all, they usually incur a cost penalty, even if upstream suppliers are enlisted to help offset those risks. Customer credit risk can also be significant for wholesalers and distributors.

As large retailers increasingly do business directly with suppliers, wholesalers have become most in danger of being cut out of the channel ecosystem. Many have responded by expanding the functions they provide. For example, C&S Wholesale Grocers, the largest wholesaler

Figure 4.3 Functions in the channel ecosystem.

Intermediary ↓ / Function →	Inventory Management & Ownership		Product Assortment		Demand Aggregation		Pricing & Selling		Payments		Fulfillment & Returns			
	Warehousing & Breaking Bulk	Inventory Ownership & Risk	Multi-Brand Assortment	Multi-Category Assortment	Locational Convenience	Routing Demand to Sellers	Pricing	Persuasion & Selling	Financing & Credit	Payment Processing	Delivery	Installation, Value Added Services	Returns	Reverse Logistics
Largely Brick & Mortar Intermediaries														
Distributors	●	●	●	●	●	●	●	●	●	●	●	●	●	◐
Wholesalers	●	●	●	●	●	●	●	●	●	●	●	◐	●	◐
Retailers & Value Added Resellers	●	●	●	●	●	●	◐	●	●	●	◐	●	◐	●
Buying Cooperatives	○	○	●	●	◐	●	●	●	◐	●	◐	●	◐	●
Independent Sales Associates	●	◐	◐	○	●	●	○	●	○	●	●	○	●	○
Manuf. Reps, Brokers, Agents	◐	○	◐	◐	●	●	○	●	○	●	●	○	◐	○
Franchisees	◐	◐	○	○	●	●	●	●	●	●	●	○	○	◐
Largely Digital Intermediaries														
Aggregators	○	○	●	◐	●	●	◐	◐	○	●	◐	◐	◐	○
Metamediaries	○	○	●	◐	●	●	◐	◐	○	○	○	○	◐	○
Online Marketplaces	○	○	●	●	●	●	◐	◐	◐	◐	◐	○	◐	○
Special Support Service Providers														
Affiliates	○	○	○	○	●	●	○	◐	○	○	○	○	○	○
Delivery Providers	○	○	○	○	●	○	○	○	○	○	●	◐	●	○
Payment Processors	○	○	○	○	◐	○	○	○	○	●	○	○	○	○
eCommerce Providers	◐	○	○	○	●	○	○	○	◐	◐	◐	◐	●	●
Reverse Logistics Providers	○	○	○	○	○	○	○	○	◐	◐	◐	◐	●	●

How Frequently Function Performed: ○ Rarely or Never   ◐ Sometimes   ● Almost Always in the U.S. grocery industry as of this writing, has invested heavily in warehouse automation and autonomous bots to generate logistical efficiencies for its supplier and retailer clients. In addition, it owns and licenses some private-label brands, and provides back-office accounting and front-end pricing, merchandising, and category management services to retailers.[i]

Retailers and Value-Added Resellers: These businesses typically sell to end consumers, but some—such as Costco, Sam's Club, and Staples—may also sell to smaller retailers and other businesses. Brick-and-mortar retailers perform most of the functions listed in Figure 4.3, but credit and debit cards have made financing risk less relevant. Also, the density of their stores has made locational convenience an important benefit, together with one-stop shopping. Since consumers typically came to their physical locations to shop, delivery was not a large part of their responsibility. But that is changing in the era of omni-channel, where consumers want to order and take delivery of products at home, even if they come from a local store. Value-added resellers (VARs) buy a product from suppliers or distributors and add value to it in some way, often changing its form. Wireless service providers, for example, combine their software and services with hardware from suppliers to provide complete solutions to end users.

Buying Cooperatives: These cooperatives evolved as groups of small retailers who wished to combine their buying power in order to negotiate better terms from suppliers and achieve economies of warehousing, purchasing, and delivery.[3] For instance, Wakefern Food Corp. is the largest retailer-owned cooperative in the U.S. It has responsibility for buying, warehousing, and transporting products for its members, who independently own and run grocery stores under the ShopRite name. As with wholesalers, we are seeing a broadening of services offered by cooperatives to their member retailers. Many, like Wakefern and CCA Global, provide a wide range of services, such as buying, private-label design and sourcing, payroll and training, and promotional design and merchandising. Cooperatives often share their earnings with the membership as dividends.

Independent Sales Associates: These individuals sell the supplier's products to end users in their community. In many cases, they make an investment in registration by purchasing a "starter kit," undergoing

---

[3]There are also "seller cooperatives" whose members join forces to collectively sell their produce to branded manufacturers. Examples are the Sunkist orange grower and Land O'Lakes dairy cooperatives.

training, carrying an inventory, having house parties, and other activities. They buy products on a wholesale discount and make a profit by selling it at retail price. In other cases, the associates place end-customer orders with the supplier and earn a commission for obtaining and delivering the order. Often, this channel is "multilevel" in that sales associates not only sell products to end users but also recruit other sales agents and get paid for recruitment and/or for the sales made by those they recruited.[4] Some well-known examples of companies who use this channel are Avon, Mary Kay Cosmetics, and Herbalife.

Interestingly, this channel is reinventing itself as associates sell products online to their social communities. For instance, Chloe & Isabel is a "social retail brand" that uses independent sales associates to sell its jewelry online. The associates create their own "boutiques" of the company's products online and sell to people in their social network, earning a commission of approximately 30% on their sales.[ii] Willa, a cosmetics and skin care product maker, recruits its teen and tween customers to host Tupperware-party-style get-togethers at places where they hang out with their friends. Invitations often go out in text messages and the young sales associates earn 25% of sales, plus other freebies and incentives.

Manufacturer Representatives, Brokers, and Agents: These intermediaries act as representatives of the supplier and perform many of the channel functions listed in Figure 4.3. Importantly, though, they do not take product ownership or incur inventory risk, and they operate on an "agency pricing" model. That means they have little pricing authority, usually earning commissions on prices to consumers that are set by the suppliers. In the insurance industry, independent insurance agents represent several insurance companies, while captive agents may only represent a single company. Food brokers typically represent a number of noncompeting companies: they work on commission and provide sales and merchandising services. In many industries, brokers are associated with one-time transactions, such as buying and selling yachts or oil tankers. Other brokers, such as those in the food industry, may represent clients for many years.

Franchisees: Franchisees buy the right to use the franchisor's trademark or brand name and distribute its products or services, and are required to adhere to the product or service standards specified by

---

[4]Some companies relying on this channel have come under criticism for being "pyramid schemes" in which sales associates earn money not so much for selling products as for recruiting other associates.

the brand owner. There are two main types: "traditional product" and "business format" franchisees. Franchisees in both types make a significant start-up investment and operate the business, earning revenues from sales of products and/or services. The better-known product franchisees are probably soft drink bottlers, who buy concentrate from franchisors like the Coca-Cola Company, produce finished beverages, and are responsible for managing distribution to retailers. But there are also others like Eggland's Best egg producers, who supply eggs under the Eggland's Best brand name in local markets around the country.

The most well-known business format franchise operations are in the hotel and restaurant industries, but they also exist in many other services—for example, H&R Block tax services or SuperCuts hair salons. Business format franchisees pay ongoing royalties, which are typically a percentage of revenue, as well as advertising fees. In operating the business, the franchisee must adhere closely to the terms of the franchise agreement, which typically lays out in detail the standardized products, services, logos, designs, and employee uniforms required by the franchisor. Sometimes, franchisees agree to purchase supplies only from certain vendors or from the franchisor itself.

Franchisee numbers are increasing as restaurant chains like TGI Fridays, Burger King, and Applebee's sell their company-owned restaurants to franchisees, reducing their own capital investments and ensuring a predictable revenue stream in the form of royalties and fees. A speed bump came along in 2014 when the (then Democratic-controlled) National Labor Relations Board, responding to complaints that McDonald's and its franchisees violated labor laws, determined that a franchisor could be treated as a joint employer with its franchisees in worker complaints.[iii] This ruling was counter to the long-standing general rule that franchisees are legally independent from franchisors for labor relations. After three years of litigation, McDonald's settled the labor board case in 2018 without admitting wrongdoing, but the judge rejected the settlement. The issue continues to be closely watched under the current NLRB because the outcome will significantly affect franchisee-based businesses.

4.3 NEW DIGITAL INTERMEDIARIES

These new channels are largely a result of the Internet and e-commerce. E-tailers, of course, are retailers in the virtual world, Amazon 1P and Wayfair being prime examples. Many of them are value-added resellers. For example, Stitchfix curates apparel, sending the consumer a monthly box of items handpicked by a personal stylist to fit the consumer's tastes.

But many other digitally based businesses, such as metamediaries and online marketplaces, don't take ownership of products, and they perform only a few of the product-related functions that a traditional channel is responsible for. Instead, they are two-sided or multisided platforms that facilitate transactions between potential suppliers and customers, generally "re-intermediating" or adding another level to existing channels. Sellers, who are on one side of the platform, only find the platform valuable if it has enough consumers on the other side, and vice versa.

Aggregators: Aggregators collect information about multiple competing products and present it to consumers who are searching for it. Travel-related websites are probably the best-known examples of aggregators. Most, like Expedia.com and Booking.com. make bookings themselves and are paid a commission from the hotels and airlines. In an interesting development, some suppliers who compete with one another have tried to cooperate to create their own aggregator sites with the goal of wresting control (and revenue) back from independent aggregators. An example is "RoomKey" which was launched by seven leading hotel companies including Marriott, Choice Hotels, and Hilton. Consumers can search for rooms on the site and the individual hotels manage the booking process. RoomKey charged its member companies lower fees to list their offers than other online travel aggregators like Expedia or Orbitz. The challenge for this and other such sites is to invest in pull marketing and to build awareness and draw traffic despite the smaller set of booking options they are able to offer.

It is interesting to consider whether these aggregators should be viewed as agents. Technically, they don't take inventory risks. But Expedia and Booking can lose hotel partners if there are not enough bookings and lose travelers if there is a shortage of rooms. Also, while they negotiate a commission on the rates agreed upon with hotels, they are able to determine pricing of travel bundles (including, for example, flight, car, and hotel) for consumers and offer "member only" loyalty points. So, they don't follow "agency pricing" in the strict sense of the word.

Metamediaries: The term "metamediary" derives from "infomediary," which was defined in 1997 as a firm that collects personal information from consumers and sells it to businesses, on behalf of consumers, to help businesses target advertisements and special offers.[iv] Today, however, the term "infomediary" is more commonly used for information intermediaries that do the reverse: collect information about different types of products and present it to consumers who are searching for it. They generate revenue from subscriptions, advertising, or listing fees, and often also get paid for the leads they generate for sellers. Examples are BizRate.com for all types of products, Zillow.com for real estate, Edmunds.com for automobiles, and Kayak.com for travel. These firms and others like them are called metamediaries or meta-search sites because they are organized around a major category, service, or life event. They provide product-related information and easy price comparisons that are valued by the consumer, but they generally don't execute actual transactions. The payments they receive from the marketer side of their platform subsidize the information and comparison shopping convenience they provide to the consumer side. Separating information from persuasion is not easy and, perhaps, may be impossible. Nevertheless, infomediaries and metamediaries purport to be neutral in presenting or describing alternatives for consumers to consider. Of course, the advertising and listing fees mean some options are ranked higher and presented in more prominent positions.

Online Marketplaces: An online marketplace is the virtual analog to a mall. It is a site that hosts many merchants, providing consumers with easy access to a much wider range of products than any single retailer—even Amazon—can offer by itself. It typically charges fees for setup and monthly listings as well as a commission on individual sales. The largest of these are Amazon's third-party (3P) marketplace and Alibaba's TaoBao and TMall, but there are also several smaller, specialized marketplaces. For example, Etsy.com is a marketplace that specializes in arts and crafts, handmade goods, and collectibles. It charges a nominal amount to list an item and takes a percentage of the sale as its commission.

Amidst the enthusiasm surrounding marketplaces, business professors Andrei Hagiu and Julian Wright offer a cautionary note with some advice about when it makes sense for an intermediary to operate closer to the "retailer" end of the spectrum rather than the "marketplace" end.[v] For example, they point out that operating as a retailer makes more sense for high-demand products with potential scale economies, for products that shoppers like to buy together, in cases where control over the consumer experience is particularly important. They also point out that sometimes an intermediary that will ultimately become a marketplace will start off as a retailer (Amazon, for example) and vice versa (Zappos, for example).

Summary: As digitization continues to enable some channel functions to be bundled and others unbundled, more channel classifications will emerge and others will continue to morph and blur into one other.

As the *Wall Street Journal* observed, Alibaba, the Chinese e-commerce giant, "is a mix of Amazon, eBay and PayPal, with a dash of Google thrown in."[vi] TripAdvisor tried to go from being a metamediary to also becoming an aggregator with its Instant Booking initiative, which, as we will discuss in Chapter 12, has not been particularly successful.

4.4 SUPPORT SERVICE PROVIDERS

The growth of digital channels has spawned firms that take on narrow support functions to enable suppliers and their intermediaries to target consumers and/or complete transactions with them. As we said earlier, we distinguish these from distribution channel members, although the line separating them is not a bright one. Affiliates, for example, may exist in a gray area between channel intermediaries and support service providers.

Affiliates: Affiliates are websites that enable a seller to reach consumers wherever they may be surfing on the web, by cross-linking across e-commerce sites. An affiliate simply provides click-through to the seller on its own site. In return, the affiliate obtains financial incentives from the seller that are usually in a pay-for-performance model—if an affiliate does not generate sales, it represents no cost to the seller. Many blogs and websites link to books and other products on Amazon.com, for example, and they earn a commission on sales that result from the click-throughs.

Delivery and White Glove Services: As purchases of all types of goods grow online, demand for delivery services has increased exponentially. Many suppliers and retailers use traditional delivery companies like FedEx, UPS, and the U.S. Postal Service. Suppliers whose products require additional assembly and installation often turn to white glove services. Many other innovative delivery services have sprung up. eBay Now promises one-hour delivery of orders placed online. For a $5 fee and $25 minimum order, eBay Now's "valets," who are couriers traveling by foot, bicycle, or car, pick up the item from a partner retailer and deliver it to the consumer. Shoprunner helps other retailers compete with Amazon Prime. Consumers who shop online can pay an annual fee to become Shoprunner members and get free two-day shipping and returns on all purchases from the many online sellers who partner with Shoprunner. Google Shopping Express is an amalgam of the Amazon Prime, eBay Now, and Shoprunner models: shoppers go to the Google Shopping Express website to buy products from partner retailers. Deliveries are made in Google-branded Priuses or trucks for a small shipping cost, or shipping is free if the order is substantial (generally $35 or more). Roadie is a crowd-sourced delivery start-up whose same-day delivery service, called "on-the-way," uses an app to tap into drivers who are already on the road.

Payment Processors and Other Special Service Providers: Suppliers and retailers struggle with providing the same security and quality of services online that consumers expect in face-to-face transactions. An array of special service providers rushed in to fill this need: secure payment processors like PayPal, AliPay, Square, and Google Wallet; style and fit advisors like Keaton Row, Trunk Club, and Fits.me; and other service providers like Breeze, which leased cars to Uber drivers for a weekly fee, and Pillow, a rental and property management service for property owners who want to make their properties available for short-term rentals on Airbnb or elsewhere.[vii] As a sign of the importance of these services, PayPal—which was originally owned by eBay and viewed by many analysts as eBay's "crown jewel"—was spun off as a separate company to compete more nimbly and flexibly in the payment space. Alipay, which was originally launched by Alibaba as an escrow service for consumers on its marketplaces so that they would not have to pay for a product until they actually received it, has become central to an increasingly cashless society in China. The value of the service to Alibaba is not just in the transaction fees it earns but in the treasure trove of customer data it collects.

Styling and other advisory services also have the potential to add value by decreasing the returns for online merchants. Business professors Santiago Gallino and Antonio Moreno demonstrated this in a randomized field experiment they conducted in partnership with a major online clothing retailer. They found that consumers who had access to a virtual fitting tool not only purchased more items at a higher average price, they also visited the e-tailer more often and had a significantly lower product return rate.[viii]

The narrow functions that these businesses provide come with correspondingly narrow margins, so the long-term viability of many of them is unclear, especially as stand-alone entities. As a stand-alone payment processing company, Square racked up losses even though more than a million merchants used its square-shaped credit card reader, which is attachable to mobile phones and tablets. In order to turn a profit, Square had to increase merchant fees and add other financial services, ending up looking more like a bank than a simple payment processing company. Meanwhile, the styling advisor Keaton Row has shut down, and so has Breeze. Nordstrom purchased Trunk Club for $350 million but wrote down more than half of that value two years later.

E-commerce and Reverse Logistics Providers: As traditional retailers have raced to build their digital capabilities and become omni-channel, many of them outsource part or all of their e-commerce operations. For years, Amazon managed Target's e-commerce business. Specialized e-commerce firms like Radial provide a full suite of services, from order and inventory management to payment processing, fulfilment, and post-purchase customer service. Some, like software and technology company Narvar Inc., manage online orders and returns for companies and are brokering deals for their clients to use brick-and-mortar stores of retailers like Walgreens and Nordstrom for order pickup and/or returns. Others, like Returns Management Inc., focus on returns and reverse logistics, functions that are becoming increasingly important as companies try to limit losses from returns and strive for sustainability in their businesses. Reverse logistics encompasses a host of activities, including returns, recycling, refurbishing, upgrading, and reuse. In emerging markets, financial necessity has long created a large though informal economy for resale and reuse of all kinds of durable products. Today, the function is becoming more mainstream as firms try to participate in a "circular economy" that retains and reuses more of its increasingly scarce resources.[ix]

4.5 WHAT'S DIFFERENT ABOUT TODAY'S CHANNEL FUNCTIONS

Are traditional distribution functions changing? A look at the list of functions at the top of Figure 4.2 shows that, by and large, the answer is no. But the cost and importance of many functions is changing rapidly with digitization. The new business models that have emerged make it necessary to think carefully about who is performing which functions, how the nature of those functions is shifting, and how each channel member is (or should be) compensated.

4.5.1 The Critical Nature of Delivery and Returns

Delivery and returns have become more important and also more expensive as consumers move their shopping online. These are some of the least exciting functions for marketers, but they can make or break businesses. Amazon is far ahead of others in delivery but it continues to invest in ways to make delivery faster and less expensive. The company has added distribution centers to reduce delivery time, and rents space from many different businesses (convenience stores, coffee shops, parking garages, among others) for its lockers.

One of the benefits from its acquisition of Whole Foods is the quantum increase in its number of delivery (and return) points. It is also doing a few things that might have sounded outlandish just a short time ago: predicting and preparing an order for delivery before the order is actually placed, using drones for delivery, starting its own cargo airline called Prime Air, and helping people start their own small businesses delivering Amazon packages in Amazon-branded vehicles and uniforms. At the same time, the company is reducing shipping costs by modifying its algorithms to ship multiple items together and working with suppliers to reduce product packaging.[5]

Omni-channel retailers are searching for ways to reduce delivery costs by taking advantage of their stores. Retailers like Walmart encourage consumers to order online and pick up in store, allowing those who are unable or unwilling to pay by credit card to pay cash in the store, and even advertising lower prices for store pickup. Research shows that such options may reduce the number of orders placed online, but that is more than offset by the increased revenue generated by consumers who do order online and then buy additional items in the store when they go to pick up their order.[x]

You might think the surge in deliveries from e-commerce has been an unmitigated boon to traditional delivery businesses, but they've had their own growing pains. UPS, for instance, is struggling to manage the strains that online holiday shopping puts on its network; it's left with unused investments in some years and suffers from falling short in others.[xi] And whether Amazon's delivery business has been a boon or a drag on the U.S. Post Office is very much a topic of discussion. In an interesting article, Timothy Laseter, a managing director at PwC-Strategy&, and his colleagues propose the idea of a "last mile exchange" where sellers, consumers, and transportation service providers might come together to share order management, inventory, and delivery resource data on a digital platform, and deliveries would be algorithmically optimized and bid on.[xii]

For e-commerce marketers, getting deliveries right is only part of the challenge; managing returns is just as important. By some accounts, one third of apparel ordered online is returned compared to only 8% for apparel bought in physical stores, and processing an online return costs twice as much as a return to a physical store.[xiii] We have heard

---

[5]The rush by developers to build warehouses that can enable retailers to deliver faster is creating a real estate boom, though it remains to be seen whether that will sustain for long (*Wall Street Journal*, January 23, 2019, "Retailer Warehouses Get Taller, More Sophisticated," p. B7).

the CMO of one major omni-channel retailer cite return rates as high as 70%. Strict return policies make sense for some categories, such as designer clothes whose one-time use for special events may invite consumer abuse. Many retailers attach very visible tags to such apparel and will only accept a return if the tag has not been removed. Most of us have also seen the notices inside product packages that implore us to call the manufacturer and not return the item to the retailer. A phone call to a 1-800 number and knowledgeable consumer advice can reduce the costs of returns.[xiv] In fact, online fit and style consultants like Fitsme.com (now owned by Rakuten) sell themselves to marketers by claiming to reduce return costs.

In general, though, generous return policies are a necessary part of doing business online for many categories and consumers. They put consumers at ease, which makes them more likely to buy on impulse, though that impulse buying also increases returns. Some researchers report that the increase in sales from such impulse purchases can exceed the increase in returns[xv] while others find that the increased purchases resulting from promotional offers of "free shipping" are returned at a high enough rate that the impact of the promotion on profits is actually negative.[xvi] Many retailers, including Amazon, are trying to deal with the problem of excessive returns by using a scoring system to identify customers whose return behavior makes them not worth retaining and cutting them off. Some of them use third-party firms like Retail Equation to police returns.

4.5.2 Increasingly Targeted Selling and Peer Persuasion

Another function that is seeing tremendous change is selling and persuasion. The theme here is tailoring the consumer experience. Curating the product assortment, merchandising it, and dynamically adjusting pricing: these activities can be performed better, faster, and potentially less expensively in digital environments. In the brick-and-mortar world, retailers spend substantial sums on merchandising—the art of arranging the display of products and signage to best suit consumer preferences and encourage buying. Consider the effort that goes into window displays for major department stores, and how (in)frequently these are changed to reflect the seasons and new offerings. Now consider how Nordstrom emails its customers with daily, tailored offerings and a different landing page depending on what element in the email the customer clicks.

The science of merchandising is surely undergoing one of the biggest changes retailing will see. As distribution moves to the web there is less excuse for being told that a certain shoe size is out of stock (why even show me that model if it is not in my size?). Staying current on a product's price-value ratio has always been essential. The speed at which price changes can be made online, and compared by consumers, means that it is more important to have systems that monitor competitive prices, respond dynamically, and assess the effectiveness of that response. Marketers also need ways to communicate value in real time or else the lowest price may win. Faster shipping, consumer reviews, automatic replenishment, and generous return policies are just some of the ways that suppliers and their retail partners might gain an edge on lower-priced competitors. Chat boxes and chatbots provide digital communications that may be even more relevant with respect to timing. And yet, in a bit of back-to-the-future, retailers like Best Buy and Amazon are sending well-trained sales people, paid a salary and not commission, into consumers' homes to understand their needs and recommend products and services to fit them.[xvii]

In the midst of all of this, tech giants play a selling and persuasion role far beyond the reach of most marketers, and are coming under increased regulatory scrutiny for how they display search results, and which brands and sellers rank higher. On the one hand, they portray their businesses as neutral platforms, but on the other hand, they are being accused of loading the dice in favor of some sellers over others. In 2017, the EU levied a fine of $2.7 billion on Google for favoring its own comparison shopping service in its search engine results.

And finally, we would be remiss in not noting the growing power of consumer reviews and endorsements. They are expected and increasingly relied upon more than the advertising and other selling efforts of marketers, and, if they are not available, prospective customers will wonder why.

4.5.3 Location Means More, Not Less

In physical retail, the saying goes, it's all about "location, location, location." Traditionally, channel members have placed outlets in the vicinity of widely dispersed consumers, making locational convenience one of the most important functions they provided, together with one-stop and comparison-shopping. But today, marketers are expected to be "available" at exactly the right time and place (when the consumer is solving a problem), with the relevant information that helps the consumer find a solution.

Similarly, the nature of first impressions is changing. Procter & Gamble called the consumer's encounter with its products on the retail shelf the "first moment of truth"—the best chance to make a sale.

Now there is the "zero moment of truth" (a term made famous by Google's ex–Vice President of Sales, Jim Lecinski), which is the consumer's first online search for a product. Moreover, the "first moment of truth" is often returning shoppers to the "zero moment" as they use their smart phones to locate products and compare prices while shopping in a store. So, locational convenience today has at least three different aspects. One is easy access to a physical store or showroom where the consumer can see and compare physical products; another is easy access online, whether it is through a great app or through the top rank in voice search or through a prime location on the Search Engine Results Page (SERP) from Google or Amazon or TripAdvisor, or wherever the consumer searches online; and the third is the ability to receive relevant information and offers online and on mobile depending on the consumer's physical location.[6]

Having a convenient physical location is a challenge for both brick-and-mortar and digital channels. Physical retailers close more and more of their doors almost every day, and the suppliers who relied on their locational convenience (from cosmetics makers like Estee Lauder to performance running shoe manufacturers like Brooks) must find ways to fill these distribution holes. In the meantime, digitally native suppliers like Warby Parker and Bonobos are opening showrooms to encourage try-ons.

The second locational convenience—easy online access—is an illustration of how the lines between advertising and distribution are blurring online. We know a high rank on the SERP is noticed and clicked on more by consumers, and this position effect is even stronger on the mobile Internet.[xviii] Researchers pointed to the "golden triangle" in the upper left corner of the SERP as prime location, but that space, and everything above the fold, is now taken entirely by sponsored search and product listing ads—at least on Google, which changes its SERP layout. And it is not just keyword search but also image and voice search that suppliers must try to stay on top of. Of course, as more product searches are begun on sites like Amazon (as many as 58% by some statistics) instead of on Google, online location convenience puts increasing pressure on brands to be available there as well.

The third convenience—location-specific offers on mobile— is an area where we are seeing a lot of experimentation. Walmart's app,

---

[6]We refer the interested reader to David Bell's book titled *Location is (Still) Everything* for a nice discussion of all the ways in which location in the physical world ties in with behavior in the virtual world.

which steers consumers to where products are located in a physical store and notifies them of nearby special promotions, is an example of how the mobile online world is changing the brick-and-mortar in-store experience. Geo-based promotional offers sent by sellers in the vicinity of a consumer's mobile location are another example. Indeed, increasing mobile-influenced offline sales may be a bigger priority for some retailers than increasing online sales. With mobile-based offers, as with all promotional deals, the key will be to ensure that the sales they bring are incremental; that is, the discounts are not just for purchases that would have been made anyway.

4.5.4 Agglomeration Is Alive and Well

In the world of bricks-and-mortar retail, agglomeration, or the propensity for retailers who sell the same product category to locate close to one another, is an age-old concept. Consumers like one-stop shopping, which spawned large supermarkets, department stores, and supercenters. But, for many high-ticket products, they also want to comparison-shop and they don't like traveling to multiple stores over long distances to do so. What might be considered competing stores can ensure traffic. That is why "auto miles," where dealers sell competing car brands on a long strip of road, are so prevalent, and why dollar stores often choose to locate near Walmart stores.[xix] It is also why single-product stores are so uncommon. They may be single brand but multi-product (think Brooks Brothers or Body Shop) or multi-brand and multi-product (think most retailers), but they are always multi-something.

One might think that agglomeration is irrelevant on the geographically unbounded web, where search is supposedly costless. But that is far from the case. Brand websites account for a very small portion of total online sales in the U.S., where most of the top 10 players are retailers, with number 1 Amazon capturing almost 50% of all online sales. The reason is simple. Most consumers don't want to visit multiple websites to do their shopping, just like they don't want to spend a lot of time traveling to multiple stores. But they do want the benefits of comparison-shopping. Agglomeration is the raison d'être for online marketplaces, meta-search sites, and aggregators.

4.6 CONCLUSION

It should be clear from this chapter that in most cases it is not practical for a supplier to rely solely on a vertically integrated distribution channel. Why? Because it is unable to optimally provide all the functions that consumers value. Primary among these is bulk-breaking, locational convenience, and the aggregation of supply for consumers who like one-stop shopping across multiple product categories and comparison-shopping across multiple brands within a category. But, as we have discussed, there is an array of choices when it comes to choosing distribution partners, and there is generally a trade-off between control and coverage (and perhaps cost). Figure 4.4 shows where the physical and digital channel intermediaries we have discussed exist along the spectrum from high to low control. We will illustrate how suppliers navigate these trade-offs in Chapters 10, 11, and 12.

No matter how carefully those trade-offs are made, there will always be some conflict between the parties, as Chapters 2 and 3 made clear. Recognizing the root causes of conflict and the need for change in distribution policies, and having a clear vision of who should do what in one's channel ecosystem, which is what we have done so far, are first steps. But implementing change and coordination requires an understanding of power structures, and the awareness that companies (even those in the same industry) may attempt to resolve similar conflicts quite differently, depending on their relative power positions and the sources of power that got them there. So, that's what we tackle next.

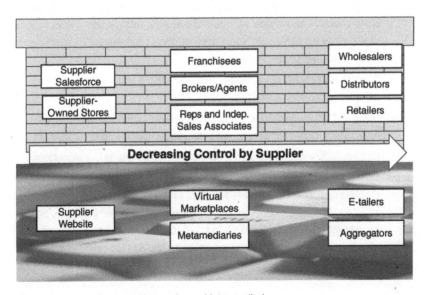

Figure 4.4 Supplier control over channel intermediaries.

Summary

■ Whether in the physical or digital world, middlemen offer the same value proposition they always have: they make products, services, and information available in a form and at a time, place, and price that suppliers and consumers need.

■ The specific functions to be performed fall under six major categories related to inventory management, product assortment, demand aggregation, pricing and selling, payments, and fulfillment and returns.

■ Brick-and-mortar intermediaries include wholesalers, distributors, retailers, independent sales associates, manufacturers' reps, brokers, agents, and franchisees, and most of them perform the full gamut of channel functions.

■ Largely digital intermediaries include e-tailers, aggregators, metamediaries, and online marketplaces. The most important functions that many of them provide are wide product assortment in one place and demand aggregation, often without taking on inventory risk.

■ Agents are unique as intermediaries in that they do not take ownership of product and therefore don't incur inventory risk, nor do they typically have pricing authority.

■ Some digital intermediaries, such as aggregators in the travel industry, act like agents in some ways but not in others, and the distinction can be important when it comes to regulation.

■ The growth of digital channels has spawned firms that unbundle and take on narrow support functions for suppliers and intermediaries alike. These include affiliates who route traffic to supplier or intermediary websites, delivery and reverse logistic service providers, and payment processors.

■ When the products and services themselves cannot be digitized, managing deliveries and returns has become critical to success.

■ Selling and persuasion today is all about using data and current location, not just the home address, to tailor and make the experience more relevant to individual consumers.

■ Location, both physical and digital, is more important than ever, as is agglomeration, which refers to the co-location of competing sellers of the same product category.

■ Suppliers must almost always trade off control for coverage. In the brick-and-mortar world, they have more control over agents, manufacturers' reps, and franchisees than over wholesalers, distributors, and retailers. In the digital world they have more control when they work with metamediaries and online marketplaces than with e-tailers and aggregators.

ENDNOTES

i. Wheelan, R. (2016). A Grocery Baron and His Robots: Rick Cohen pitches autonomous bots in a business slow to automate. *Wall Street Journal* (21 September).

ii. Loten, A. (2014). Chloe & Isabel Crafts Its Own Sales Model. *Wall Street Journal* (18 July).

iii. Jargon, J (2014). McDonald's Ruling sets Ominous Tone for Franchisers. *Wall Street Journal* (29 July).

iv. Hagel, J., and Rayport, J. (1997). The Coming Battle for Customer Information. *Harvard Business Review* (January–February).

v. Hagiu, A., and Wright, J. (2013). Do You Really Want to Be an eBay? *Harvard Business Review* (March).

vi. Osawa, J. (2014). Meet Alibaba: China's Mix of Amazon, eBay, and PayPal. *Wall Street Journal* (17 March), p. B1.

vii. Wells, C. (2015). 'Piggybackers' Hitch Themselves to Airbnb, Uber. *Wall Street Journal* (19 February), p. B5.

viii. Gallino, S., and Moreno, A. (2018). The Value of Fit Information in Online Retail: Evidence from a Randomized Field Experiment. *Manufacturing & Service Operations Management* 20 (4): 601–800.

ix. *McKinsey Quarterly* (2014). Moving toward a circular economy (February).

x. Gallino, S., and Moreno-Garcia, A. (2014). Integration of Online and Offline Channels in Retail: The Impact of Sharing Reliable Inventory Availability Information. *Management Science* 60 (6): 1351–1616.

xi. Stevens, L., and Bensinger, G. (2015). Amazon Seeks to Ease Ties with UPS. *Wall Street Journal* (22 December), p. A1.

xii. Laseter, T., Tipping, A., and Duiven, F (2018). The Rise of the Last-Mile Exchange. *Strategy + Business* (30 July). www.strategy-business.com/article/The-Rise-of-the-Last-Mile-Exchange?rssid=all_updates&gko=7cf43 (accessed January 2019).

xiii. Ryan, C. (2018). A Consumer Slump Threatens European Online Retailers. *Wall Street Journal* (21 December), p. B12.

xiv. Timberlake, C. (2013). Don't Even Think About Returning That Dress. *Business Week* (26 September) at www.businessweek.com/articles/2013-09-26/return-fraud-clothing-and-electronics-retailers-fight-back (accessed January 2018).

xv. Padmanabhan, V., and Png, I. (1995). Return Policies: Make Money by Making Good. *Sloan Management Review* (15 October). Petersen, J. and Kumar, V. (2015). Perceived Risk, Product Returns, and Optimal Resource Allocation: Evidence from a Field Experiment. *Journal of Marketing Research* 52 (2).

xvi. Shehu, E., Papies, D., and Neslin, S. (2016). Free Shipping and Product Returns. Tuck School of Business Working Paper No. 2864019.

xvii. Safdar, J., and Stevens, L. (2017). Gadget Sellers Make House Calls. *Wall Street Journal* (29 August).

xviii. Ghose, A., Goldfarb, A., and Han, S. (2012). How Is the Mobile Internet Different? Search Costs and Local Activities. *Information Systems Research* (20 December).

xix. Thomas, B. (2012). Dollar Stores Take On Wal-Mart, And Are Starting To Win. *Forbes* (16 April) at www.forbes.com/sites/investor/2012/04/16/dollar-stores-take-on-wal-mart-and-are-starting-to-win/ (accessed December 2017).

CHAPTER 5

The Sources and Indicators of Power in the Channel

5.1 INTRODUCTION

Marketing plans which are conceived only in terms of money, goods, and their physical movement are doomed to fail. A marketing plan must be executed through sales organizations, distribution channels, and other organized behavior systems which can only be understood as power structures.

—Wroe Alderson

As we explained in Chapter 3, channel conflict is inevitable as suppliers and their resellers act in their own self-interest. Usually, these independent parties have no formal authority over one another, but they do have a strong incentive to try to find cooperative, mutually beneficial solutions. When managers seek to resolve or manage channel conflict, they must appreciate not only the different perspectives of the channel members, but also their different power positions. Indeed, it may be the appearance of conflict that first causes them to assess their relative power in the relationship. But what constitutes power in channel relationships?

Many academics view channel power through the lenses of social psychology and organizational theory, focusing on resource dependence and the so-called bases of power, distinguishing between exercised and unexercised power, and examining the consequences for different facets of the health of the channel. Economists who specialize in industrial organization and antitrust are often concerned with the extent of a firm's market power over competitors, the manifestation of that power in the firm's "horizontal" conduct vis-à-vis competitors, its "vertical" conduct vis-à-vis distribution channel partners, and the profit and consumer welfare outcomes of that conduct. Marketing professionals operate at the interface of these fields, differentiating their brands, building routes to market, and designing channel policies to successfully reach end consumers and earn their loyalty. It is the accumulation and judicious exercise of power through these activities, we assert, that determines the performance of various parties in the channel and reinforces or diminishes their future freedom of action.

Figure 5.1 charts the territory we will cover in this chapter and the next one. In this chapter, we'll look at the sources of power and its indicators from the perspective of social psychologists and economists

Figure 5.1 Perspectives on power in the distribution channel.

and hopefully convince the reader of why those perspectives are important for practicing marketers. And in Chapter 6, we'll take on the challenge of applying but still preserving one's power in a channel relationship.

5.2 POWER IN THE CHANNEL AND ITS SOURCES

5.2.1 How Social Psychologists and Economists Think about Power

Social psychologists think of power in mutually dependent relationships as control over other parties. In the context of a distribution channel, where each party has its own goals and perspectives, the more powerful partner can make the less powerful partner act in a way the latter would not otherwise choose. Of course, mutual dependence means that one party's power is offset by some countervailing power of the other, even if the balance of power tips toward one party at a given time.[i]

For example, Priceline Group and Expedia became behemoths in the online travel agent (OTA) channel after a spate of acquisitions in over a decade. By 2015, Priceline Group had 60% of OTA bookings in Europe, and Expedia had 75% in the U.S. In contrast, the hotel industry is highly fragmented. Sixty percent of hotels in Europe are independent and only 16% of rooms belonged to the top five hotel companies as of 2015.[ii] The U.S. hotel market is more concentrated, but even so, the top five companies accounted for no more than 50% of rooms around the same time. As a result, these OTAs have been able to negotiate very attractive terms in their negotiations with hotels. In addition to being able to command commissions of 15–30%, their contracts included "rate parity" and "last room available" clauses. These clauses meant that hotels could not offer lower prices on their own brand.com (e.g. Marriott.com) websites or elsewhere, nor could they hold back from the OTA any rooms that were available on brand.com or elsewhere. However, large well-known hotel chains are in a somewhat stronger negotiating position than smaller chains and independent hotels. And, the last couple of years have seen that position get even stronger. Marriott, Hilton, Choice Hotels, and others have invested in consumer pull through their direct-booking advertising campaigns and loyalty programs. Marriott has even more leverage after its merger with Starwood. The threat of having such a large hotel company part ways with them gives OTAs much greater pause because that may significantly reduce the attractiveness of the assortment that OTAs offer to travelers. OTA commissions paid by large hotel companies have been falling, down to less than 15% by some accounts.

In economics, a firm's market power refers to its ability to behave persistently in a manner that differs from the behavior that a competitive market would enforce. Narrower definitions of market power refer to a seller firm's ability to price higher and produce less than in a competitive market, or to a buyer firm's ability to force sellers to sell at a price lower than would emerge in a competitive buyer market.[1] The ability to choose a price is itself an indication of some power. Indeed, economists use the labels "price taker" for firms in competitive markets and "price setter" for those with some market power.

Again, an example will help. Ohio Art, the marketer of the classic toy Etch A Sketch that we introduced in Chapter 3, depended on a few large retailers for the majority of its sales. A few years ago, Ohio Art approached Walmart with the need to increase prices to cover higher costs of production. Walmart rejected the price increase and suggested that any price above a certain point would be unacceptable. When Ohio Art insisted that the price increase was needed, the retailer didn't test consumer response to higher prices—it just dropped Etch A Sketch from its shelves. Ohio Art was forced to confront the fact that, in this market, it was a price taker, not a setter. With a large percentage of its sales eliminated, the company believed it had little choice but to source the product overseas to cut costs. It learned the skills required to manage the logistics of overseas production, lowered prices, and got back into Walmart's good graces (and, more importantly, onto its shelves).

The economic concept of market power is in a horizontal context—between competing firms at the same level of the distribution channel. Yet that power is generally exercised in a vertical context—in transactions between firms at different levels of the channel. As an example, witness the merger and acquisition activity in the pay TV industry in the past few years. In Comcast's attempted acquisition of Time Warner Cable in 2014, it was not just horizontal competitors such as DirecTV and Dish Network that were worried. Upstream TV-network owners worried that the merged company would pay less to carry their programming. Downstream online video services worried that the merged company would charge more for broadband use. [iii] There were similar concerns about the 21st Century Fox bid for Time Warner, which was later withdrawn. David Bank, an

---

[1] This is the same problem of setting prices too high and outputs (sales) too low associated with the phenomenon of double marginalization, discussed in Chapter 3.

analyst at RBC Capital Markets, was quoted in the *Wall Street Journal* as saying, "If I control more of the market, you are going to find it harder to live without me, and that way when I come to negotiate, I'm in a better position."[iv] In 2018, the Justice Department (unsuccessfully) sued to block AT&T's merger with Time Warner, ostensibly because of similar worries. And in 2019, an important motivation for CBS and Viacom to reunite after they were split up in 2006 was to have greater leverage in the negotiation of carriage fees with pay TV distributors.

Of course, if one channel partner is already operating efficiently in a competitive market with no "excess" profit margins, it will not be possible for the other partner to extract concessions. This is the economic equivalent of the impossibility of getting blood from a turnip. Walmart may have a great deal of power, but it can't further reduce the already competitive purchase price from dedicated private-label suppliers that operate with little or no market power in their horizontal market.[2] For example, when we last checked, Cotts, one of the largest manufacturers of private-label beverages, earned a gross margin of approximately 12%, compared with Coke's 60%. Similarly, even powerful suppliers can't extract much more from grocery retailers because of the strong horizontal competition those retailers face, at least in the United States.

5.2.2 Sources of Power in the Distribution Channel

For years, when we asked executives about the source of Walmart's power, the first answer was always the same: market share (i.e., Walmart's unmatched access to the all-important end consumer). Once a supplier sees a fourth to a third of their sales go through Walmart, walking away may not be a realistic option. In this view of power, managers and economists are on the same page. One of the first things that economists look at in assessing market power is the firm's market share. Defining the relevant market in which to assess market share is important (and challenging) and CPG executives would name not only Walmart but also Kroger, Walgreens, and convenience-store chains as players with significant share and power in certain regions of the U.S. market or in specific product categories.

---

[2] Of course, the story might be different when private labels are supplied by manufacturers of national brands who can bring some of their market power to bear on private-label negotiations and can also use the additional volume to lower their costs.

Executives also noted sales growth and/or business models that show prospects for future growth. This seems to be how CPG manufacturers view Amazon today. Amazon is far from a small player, but online still accounts for a fairly small percentage of CPG sales. And yet, the prospects for growth mean that many manufacturers are paying much more attention to Amazon than its current share of total CPG sales might warrant.

But this begs the question: what drives market share and growth? Marketers and economists alike believe that market power can be gained through effective differentiation, "real" differences with superior products or services, as well as "perceived" ones with brand or store image. If this is combined with the will and ability to fund further innovation that promises to reinforce differentiation and brand equity—well, that's even better. Once a supplier's brand becomes a vehicle for introducing and distributing new products quickly and less expensively than competitors, the supplier may have more incentive to invest in R&D and innovation. But resellers differentiate themselves too. A retail brand becomes a means for bringing in the most desirable suppliers, good prices, and trade deals, building up private label products, and enabling further investments in services, logistics, and consumer insights.

In a similar vein, organizational theorists point to asymmetric control of valued resources as the source of power. The greater the value to a channel member of resources controlled by a supplier, and the lower the availability of those resources from other suppliers, the more dependent the channel member is on the supplier, and the more powerful the supplier is. Some examples of those resources include physical infrastructure, intellectual capital and knowhow, scale that lowers costs, supplier or retailer brand equity, and customer data.[3]

So the sources of power are simple, at least in theory: create a high-quality and differentiated product or service and market it effectively through pull and push marketing inputs. To build a powerhouse brand, grow sales rapidly, and continue the stream of innovation and maintain differentiation. While you are at it, be sure that your costs are lower than competitors', and collect a ton of customer data to guide your investment in the most effective resources. Of course, if

---

[3]Not only are data and the ability to mine it an increasingly important source of power, they form the revenue backbone for many new digital intermediaries, as we described in Chapter 4. The power of data is also evident in the fact that competition authorities are beginning to scrutinize its ability to enable firms like Google and Amazon to disadvantage or exclude competitors from the market.

we could tell you exactly how to *do* all of those things, we would be building the next Apple or Amazon instead of writing this book. But even if we can't tell you how to create the next successful business, we will—to paraphrase Supreme Court Justice Potter Stewart's much-regretted statement about pornography—lay claim to being able to recognize the sources of power when we see them.

5.3 CONSUMER SEARCH LOYALTY: THE ULTIMATE SOURCE OF POWER

Ultimately, potential sources of channel power must be judged by their ability to win the loyalty of consumers. That loyalty (along with confidence in its existence) determines who needs whom the most in a distribution partnership and who can afford to walk away from the negotiating table. That is what we depict in the middle of Figure 5.2. Even Walmart's (and now Amazon's) logistical expertise and low-cost structure only build power because they translate into lower prices, broader assortment, and fast fulfillment. Those qualities lead to consumer loyalty, which gives these firms market power over their competitors and bargaining power over their suppliers. The growth and profit outcomes from that power can create positive feedback (the forward and reverse arrows in Figure 5.2) because there is more to invest in differentiation and cost reduction. The ultimate prize for both manufacturers and their resellers is the consumer and her loyalty—and

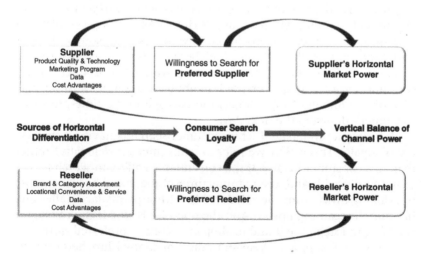

Figure 5.2 Consumer search loyalty: the ultimate source of channel power.

they have to depend on one another to get it. Neither one can go it alone, but both want to own the consumer's heart, mind, and wallet to safeguard their investments and maximize their share of the total channel-profit pie.[v]

5.3.1 Loyalty to the Brand or to the Channel?

Each party pursues consumers' loyalty in its own way. Suppliers use the quality of their products, protected by patents, trademarks, and trade secrets, and supported by pull marketing activities. Because of the importance of what consumers experience at the point-of-purchase—the "first moment of truth"—they must also rely on push marketing and the efforts of reseller (recall the push-pull framework from Chapter 2). And resellers, who have the advantage of being consumer facing and physically accessible (in the brick-and-mortar world), use the functions we described in Chapter 4 to build channel loyalty—their assortment of products, usually from several suppliers in several categories and their own private label, together with their own marketing, point of sale, and after-sales service. Both parties also do their best to leverage any cost advantages and insights from the data they collect or can buy about consumer preferences and behavior.

Is the consumer more loyal to the brand or to the channel? Years ago, A. J. O'Reilly, who was CEO of H. J. Heinz, said that his acid test of loyalty was whether the consumer, intending to buy Heinz ketchup and finding it to be out of stock, would walk out of the store to buy it elsewhere or switch brands. Conversely, will a consumer go out of their way to shop at their favorite store even if it is not easy to get to or might not stock all of their preferred brands? The "favorite" might be Walmart because its low prices means financially strapped consumers *have* to shop there, or it might be Trader Joe's because its exclusive assortment of almost entirely Trader Joe's branded private-label products makes consumers *want* to shop there, or it might be Amazon because a single click or a command to Alexa gets the package to the time-pressured consumer's doorstep the next day.

It is easy to understand why consumer search behavior is the acid test of loyalty. This is why we refer to "consumer *search* loyalty" rather than just consumer loyalty. If the consumer is willing to search for his or her preferred brand, the manufacturer of the brand has less to lose by walking away from the relationship with a particular retailer and has more bargaining power. And the opposite is true if the consumer is willing to forego the brand to shop at his or her preferred store.

Consider Spam, a 75-year-old brand of canned luncheon meats. Walmart took it off the shelf but had to bring it back to satisfy the small but highly loyal and vocal customer base that Spam serves. Losing Spam sales is one thing, but losing all the shopping baskets of consumers who are loyal to Spam is quite another. Or consider DirecTV's unease over the high price tag for renewing its exclusive rights to the NFL's Sunday Ticket that we mentioned in Chapter 3. The company has to decide whether they can do without the package or whether, as one analyst notes, many people only choose the satellite broadcaster because of the Sunday Ticket and "Lose the 'Ticket' and those customers will walk."[vi]

In this context, Ohio Art's status as a price taker is easier to understand. The Etch A Sketch is a unique and popular toy, but it is unlikely to motivate a special trip to the store, and it doesn't loom as large in the world of toys as, say, Apple products do in the world of technology. There are many other toys that consumers might consider buying instead, even if these other toys do not perform exactly the same functions.

5.3.2 Search Loyalty: Hard to Get, Harder to Measure in the Physical World

It is not easy to get the type of loyalty that makes consumers willing to search, especially if you are a CPG brand. Spam clearly had it, but in many cases, what looks like loyalty from a consumer's share of wallet or repeat purchases may, in fact, turn out to be habit. Make no mistake—habit *is* important to build; much of the low-involvement decision-making that characterizes grocery shopping is habitual. The consumer might try a product because she saw an advertisement, or it was prominently displayed in the store, or it was on promotion. If she decides she likes the product, the trial can start a sequence of repeat purchases or habit.[4] Habit is a marketer's friend, until something interrupts it, which is why A.G. Lafley, ex-CEO of P&G, cautions marketers to strengthen habits and not disrupt them.[vii]

Of course, a marketer wants not just habit, but also search loyalty. Although search loyalty is an intuitively appealing concept, for a few reasons it has been difficult for marketers to measure it. First, in addition to consumers, retailers are also in the audience for a suppliers' marketing pull activities. For example, an effective advertising

---

[4]Many marketing academics call this "state dependence." The term means that choosing a brand on one purchase occasion significantly increases the probability that it will be chosen the next time.

or promotional campaign can create genuine consumer loyalty that retailers observe in their stores, or it can simply cause retailers to *expect* the campaign to create that loyalty. That expectation, in turn, might cause retailers to stock the product, increase shelf space, ensure it doesn't go out of stock (OOS), and even advertise that they stock the brand. It can be difficult to separate true loyalty from expected loyalty.

Second, there are other behaviors that might be equivalent to search loyalty, such as stocking up on the product when it is on sale or mainly shopping in stores that the consumer knows will have the brand. Third, even when consumers search for OOS brands, their behavior will be difficult to observe. Consumers might just delay a purchase in that category until the next shopping occasion. Controlled experiments that intentionally disappoint consumers over a prolonged period are about the only reliable way to measure true willingness to search, but like conflict-induced "delistings," when a retailer might drop a manufacturer from its shelves, they can be expensive and also risky if consumers, when forced to interrupt their habit, decide the brand or store they switched to is actually pretty good.

One of us was involved in a unique experiment on consumer response to OOS products, which was conducted with the cooperation of a Dutch grocery chain.[viii] In the experiment, the complete product line (all SKUs) of the leading brand in five different product categories (cola, rice, margarine, detergent, and milk) was removed from selected stores of the leading grocery chain and OOS responses were measured by surveying consumers previously identified as loyal brand buyers. Brand switching ranged from a high of 65% for the cola brand to a low of 35% for the detergent brand. Those who did not switch brands were about equally likely to go to another store or delay purchase. Total purchases at the store did not appear to suffer beyond the specific product category.

But consumer response to a sustained delisting of a brand from the store shelf can be quite different from an OOS situation, which is generally temporary. There is a surprisingly large number of well-publicized spats in which retailers have delisted a manufacturer's products. The delisting of several Unilever products by Ahold's Albert Heijn chain in the Netherlands in 2002 and by Delhaize in Belgium in 2009, and Costco's decision in 2009 to drop Coca-Cola products, all arose from pricing disputes. The fact that the conflict escalated to the point of one party refusing to supply or carry products for the other suggests that both parties believed they enjoyed some consumer search loyalty and therefore some bargaining power. Otherwise, the weaker party would have caved to the other's pressure. But the resolution of these conflicts is more telling: they ended in quiet agreements, suggesting that both parties discovered they had something to lose and needed each other enough to settle. A manufacturer may have substantial power in one category but not in another, and a retailer who carries the manufacturer's products in multiple categories can use this to negotiate. Each is sometimes willing to put the other's power to the test by seeing whether consumers switch stores or brands when the manufacturer's brand is delisted.[ix]

5.3.3 Fake It Till You Make It?

Marketers can find ways to simulate (and maybe stimulate) search loyalty. For example, coupons, long a favorite tactic for introducing new products, can induce consumers to ask store managers for products they don't find on the shelf. If enough consumers ask about the products, there will be pressure on the retailer to stock them. Many advertising campaigns also encourage consumers to insist on the advertised brand and "accept no substitutes" or to search (when cigarettes were still advertised, one of the best-known slogans was "I'd walk a mile for a Camel"). Such tactics have a long history in marketing.

And what about fake loyalty? According to Linda Himelstein, writing in *The King of Vodka*, Pyotr Smirnov promoted his Smirnoff vodka in Moscow in the mid-1800s by paying a squad of otherwise unemployed imbibers to visit taverns and restaurants and ask for Smirnoff brand vodka. If it was unavailable, they were paid to refuse any other brand and then loudly announce their intention to leave in search of a tavern that did serve Smirnoff. Those tactics and others eventually made Smirnoff the world leader in vodka. Today, companies routinely implement seeding campaigns, especially on social media, that target certain numbers and types of consumers and give them incentives to spread word of mouth.[x]

5.3.4 Is Loyalty a Dinosaur in the Digital World?

With costless search online, have the very concepts of loyalty and willingness-to-search become obsolete? Costless search means that everyone can, and probably will, search online. Economic theory predicts that this should lead to more competition, lower prices, and lower dispersion of prices online. And, sure enough, for homogenous products like books and CDs, where the comparison is cleanest, prices were found to be 9% to 16% lower online, even after accounting for shipping-and-handling costs, and the lowest price was online rather than offline more than 80% of the time.[xi] Interestingly, though, prices vary just as much online as they do offline, and the highest-share e-tailers don't always have the lowest prices. Even consumers frequenting price-comparison sites, who presumably are price sensitive, often forego the lowest price on offer, choosing familiar and preferred e-tailers despite their higher prices.[xii] So, notwithstanding costless search, there is stickiness to e-tail sites just as there is stickiness to physical stores. Websites differentiate themselves with their product offerings, delivery and return services, and by learning about the consumer and making more relevant offers. And consumers are loath to incur the switching costs of setting up accounts with new websites. The upshot? Consumer loyalty to retailers continues to matter online.

What about loyalty to the brand? Search is now a preshopping activity not merely invoked when the assortment at the store does not match what the consumer wants. Increasingly, online and particularly mobile search means the consumer can check whether a product is in stock before she makes a trip to the store. We believe one way to think about brand loyalty is to examine whether the consumer searches for her preferred brand ("brand-primary"), simply searches for a product category ("generic") or goes to a preferred retailer's website and buys what is on offer there ("retailer primary"). And it isn't hard to measure this online. Figure 5.3 shows the most searched keywords in a few product categories, as reported by Google Trends. For some products, such as power tools and coffee makers, branded search significantly exceeds generic search. Brand name is more relevant in these categories,[xiii] so consumers go online seeking their preferred brands.

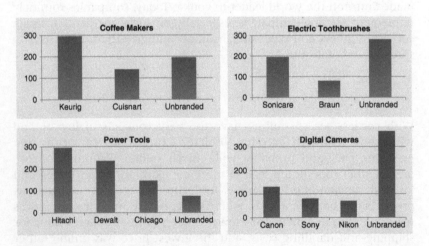

Figure 5.3 Branded versus generic search online.

In more feature-driven categories, such as electric toothbrushes and digital cameras, generic search is higher than branded search. But in either case, brands with strong equity are also the ones that show up high in the top searches—Keurig coffee makers, Hitachi power tools, Canon cameras. Brand equity offline begets branded search online.[xiv]

Our larger point is that the nature of a consumer's search has important implications for the channel power dynamic. Whether the consumer's search is generic, brand primary, or retailer primary determines the supplier's power relative to the retailer online.[xv] This is similar to the brick-and-mortar world, where a brand's power is related to whether the consumer will switch brands before she will switch stores. The more things change, the more they stay the same! No wonder marketers and analysts alike track metrics such as the percentage of product searches that originate on Amazon (over 50% by some estimates) instead of Google. The percentage of travel searches that begin on Google versus OTAs versus HotelBrand.com are similarly central to discussions of the travel industry.

5.4 ECONOMIC INDICATORS OF POWER

Many firms and academics assess outcomes of channel power, such as compliance with terms of trade, incidence of opportunistic behavior, and satisfaction with the partnership. As we will discuss in Chapter 7, these are extremely important to monitor for the health of the partnership and diagnosing problems before they are too far gone to be fixed. But, as we've said before, market power acquired in the horizontal market is generally exercised in the vertical market, and economists have their own tests of market power.

5.4.1 Monopoly Power: The Lerner Index and Price Elasticity

The Lerner index, or the percentage difference between a firm's profit-maximizing price and its marginal cost ($\frac{P-MC}{P}$), is widely cited in microeconomics textbooks as the classic indicator of monopoly power. True marginal cost is hard to measure, as economists have gone to great lengths to explain. But many suppliers are not hitting up against capacity constraints and operate on relatively flat portions of their cost curves, so average variable cost is often not that different from marginal cost. In practice, therefore, contribution margin, a concept that marketers know well and rely on for many decisions, bears a lot of similarity to the theoretical economic indicator of market power.[5] Brands (or retailers) that have little differentiation, consumer loyalty, and market power will earn low margins compared to those that have differentiated products (or services), loyal consumers, and strong market positions.

Still, neither marketers nor economists nor competition authorities rely solely (or even primarily) on the Lerner index as the gauge of market power. After all, high margins may reflect not a lack of competition but the fixed cost structure of the product category, or the innovation, superior quality, and efficiencies that result from effective competition.[xvi] Then there's the additional complexity introduced when a firm operates a multisided platform with customers on one side being subsidized by prices charged to those on the other side. But the Lerner index does tell us something about a firm's ability to control its own price, and changes in the index are often relevant for assessing potential anticompetitive effects of mergers and acquisitions.[xvii]

Perhaps more important for marketers to understand and appreciate is an "identity relationship": at a firm's profit-maximizing price, its Lerner index is equal to the negative inverse of the price elasticity of demand faced by the firm. In other words, the smaller a firm's price elasticity, the greater is its pricing discretion and market power, and the higher its margin. For many, it will be intuitive that firms can charge higher prices and earn higher margins if demand is less price elastic. Willingness to pay is, in fact, one of the many measures by which marketers assess how much their brands are valued by consumers. Still, other than an interesting bit of microeconomic trivia, why might this relationship be interesting?

Well, it implies that contribution margins (which, as we have argued, are often a reasonable approximation for the Lerner index) may provide insights into how marketers perceive the longer-term price elasticity of demand for their products,[xviii] at least to the extent that we believe they are pricing to maximize profits while taking into account competitor, reseller, and consumer responses. One might counter that marketers do a great job of estimating price elasticities directly, so why rely on assumptions about how firms are making their pricing decisions? The problem is that there are many different price elasticities and the lens through which we view them may be clouded.

---

[5]The cost of capital, which we will get to a bit later, is an important additional consideration.

The definition of price elasticity is simple enough—the ratio of percentage change in unit sales (demand) to the percent change in its price. But marketers estimate many variants of price elasticity, and they each capture rather different phenomena. For example, are price changes in the regular price of the product or week-to-week promotional discounts on a stable regular price? Are the sales changes being measured only in the short-term due to consumer response or do they also incorporate competitor and reseller response, which may show up over a longer time frame? Are the price and sales changes being measured for the brand in the overall market or in the store(s) of a particular retailer selling the brand? Most estimates of price elasticity that marketers measure reflect consumer response to short-term variations in price due mostly to promotional discounts. The price elasticity in the identity relationship with the Lerner index is the longer-term elasticity faced by the party whose power is being assessed. For a supplier, then, it is the change in its brands' demand in the overall market as a result of consumer, competitor, and reseller response to a change in its regular price. And that elasticity can be particularly hard to estimate.

5.4.2 Manufacturer versus Retailer Price Elasticity and How It Can Distort Power Assessment

We think it is especially important to caution the reader about the importance of *where* the price elasticity is measured. Economists are quite clear that the elasticity should be measured for the firm whose power you are trying to assess. But that point sometimes gets lost when marketers estimate their marketing-mix models. The most readily available assessments of price elasticity are taken from retail scanner data at the store or retailer level. But retailer-level price elasticity can distort the assessment of a brand's power. Consider Coke—a strong and widely distributed brand for which competition among retailers is probably high relative to competition in the soft-drink market. A researcher estimating price elasticity at the store level may find a high price elasticity for Coke: higher prices will reduce a retailer's Coke sales quite a bit because the store next door carries it too. But the high price elasticity faced by a retailer doesn't mean Coca-Cola doesn't have power—quite the opposite. The demand Coca-Cola faces from retailers is less elastic because retailers feel they have to carry Coke and price it attractively. The opposite is true when the brand is weak (i.e., inter-brand competition is high) and the retailer is strong (i.e., intra-brand competition with other retailers is low). This difference in price elasticities faced by the manufacturer and the retailer underlies the inverse relationship between manufacturer and retailer margins that we noted in Chapter 3.

While on the subject of retailer pricing, we remind the reader that retailers who advertise attractive prices for brands that have strong consumer pull are doing more than attempting to stimulate sales of the advertised brand. Recall from our discussion of loss-leaders in Chapter 3, for example, that the low prices on some products build traffic and sales in other categories and help the retailer achieve an overall low-price image. Retailers that offer broad assortments can focus on the profitability of consumers' entire shopping baskets over a period of time instead of insisting that each product earn a target return. We'll return to this topic when we discuss distribution performance metrics in Chapter 8 and channel pricing in Chapter 14.

5.4.3 Profitability as a Sign of Power

We expect that along with power will come the ability to earn what economists call supra-normal or supra-competitive economic profits *over the long term* if not in the short term. The opposite is also true—it is hard to argue that a firm is powerful if it is consistently on a downward spiral in profits and the ability to invest in its business. In a dated but telling 1992 interview with *Time* magazine, Robert Crandall, who was then CEO of American Airlines, had this to say when asked whether American had become too powerful: "It's a pretty sorry commentary on power when a company loses $40 million in 1990, when it loses $240 million in 1991, when it is compelled to cancel $8 billion worth of capital commitments such as new-airplane purchases, and when it formally gives up its long-term growth plan because of its inability to earn a return on its shareholders' investment. That's really not very much power, is it?"

Contribution margins and accounting rates of return are not great measures of economic profits, but over longer time periods, the trends in these measures are certainly informative about the increasing or decreasing power of a firm, be it a supplier or a reseller. Economic value added (EVA)—which, simply put, is a firm's net operating profit minus the cost of its capital—is widely believed to be a better measure of economic profit because it captures dollar profits (not just percentages) as well as capital intensity and risk. But businesses may be trading current margins for long-term market position. In such cases, revenues, growth rates, and market capitalization might be better indicators than even EVA.

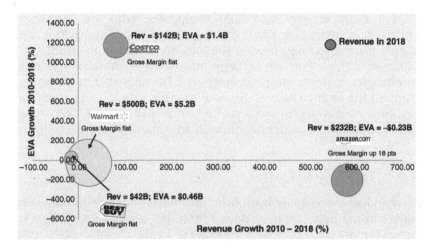

Figure 5.4 The performance of some retailers in this decade.

We have put Figure 5.4 together from Bloomberg financial data to show how some notable retailers have fared in this decade. The figure portrays five metrics for each retailer—revenue, EVA, revenue growth, gross margin growth, and EVA growth.[xix] The big takeaway is that none of these retailers is able to fire on all cylinders. Walmart is by far the largest in revenue and has kept fairly stable margins and EVA. Best Buy, a player that analysts watch closely as something of a bellwether for how e-commerce is affecting brick-and-mortar retail, has been running hard to stay in place. In contrast with both Walmart and Best Buy, Costco has been building very impressive EVA growth, while its gross margins are flat by choice. Recall Costco's policy of limiting its gross margins to less than 15%, which we cited in Chapter 3.[6] Finally, Amazon grew its revenues at a very high rate and also made gains in gross margin, but its EVA shrank and is negative because of the gigantic capital investments the company has made in its logistics infrastructure. These companies provide interesting examples of why revenues and growth, in addition to margins and EVA, are needed as financial-performance measures and potential indicators of power.

---

[6]Here is an interesting bit of trivia. In 2018, more cars were sold through Costco's Auto Program than by any retail automobile dealership in the U.S. And Costco does not make any money on those cars; it relies on membership fees from satisfied customers.

For example, we think CPG companies, who are sometimes criticized for their (excessive?) eagerness to partner with Amazon, are simply placing strategic bets on the long-term growth in online CPG purchases. Those bets are certainly not based on Amazon's historic profitability, nor on the percentage of CPG sales that currently go through the online channel. Instead, Amazon's dominance in online retailing, its logistics innovations, and its growth rate are likely what inspire CPG manufacturers' confidence in Amazon's future.

5.5 CONCLUSION

As marketers, we should learn from the efforts to define and measure power in the fields we have drawn from, but our marketing view of power is more concerned with the firm's ability to: (1) influence pricing and presentation of products to be consistent with its long-term strategy; (2) manage the breadth and depth of availability; (3) implement channel policies that ensure the provision of key channel services; and (4) sustain valuable channel alliances and create new ones that reflect strategic bets on where the future lies.

Conflict in the channel is inevitable, as is a constantly shifting power balance. But suppliers have to continue to work with independent channels; in fact, they have to work with more channels than they did before, and often while having less control than they had before. The challenge is for them to accumulate and preserve power, using it without using it up. That is our theme in the next chapter.

Summary

- Channel power is the ability of one channel "partner" to use the dependency of another to negotiate terms that it would otherwise not achieve.

- Channel power manifests in vertical interactions between firms at different levels of the distribution channel, such as suppliers and retailers, but derives from horizontal market power relative to competitors at the same level in the distribution system.

- Perspectives on power are diverse: social psychologists and organization theorists focus on dependence and investments in the relationship, and economists are concerned with market power and how it manifests in prices and margins.

- Consumer search loyalty is the ultimate source of channel power. It used to be easier to describe than to measure but access to consumer search behavior online has changed that. Patterns of generic and branded search online and where consumers conduct that search provide important insights into this loyalty.

- Willingness to pay is another loyalty metric, one closely related to the Lerner index and price elasticity, which are the classic economic measures of market power.

- There are many types of price elasticity, but long-term, strategic price elasticity is most relevant to power and it is hard to measure. Contribution margins may tell us more about managers' judgments of that elasticity than econometric estimates of consumer price sensitivity.

- Given management choices to trade off prices, and margins with volume and growth, growth in revenue and economic value added may be better indicators of power than margins.

- This is especially true because organizations accumulate channel power not simply to maximize current profits or as an end in itself, but to maintain the freedom to act and adapt to an uncertain and evolving future.

ENDNOTES

i. See, for example, these classic articles: Pfeffer, J. and Salancik, G. (2003). *The External Control of Organizations: A Resource Dependence Perspective*. Redwood City, CA: Stanford University Press. Casciaro, T. and Piskorski, J. (2005). Power Imbalance, Mutual Dependence, and Constraint Absorption: A Closer Look at Resource Dependence Theory. *Administrative Science Quarterly* 50: 167–199. Gaski, J. (1984). The Theory of Power and Conflict in Channels of Distribution. *Journal of Marketing* 48 (3): 9–29.

ii. Please see: http://data.parliament.uk/writtenevidence/committeeevidence.svc/evi dencedocument/eu-internal-market-subcommittee/online-platforms-and-the-eu-digital-single-market/written/26642.html%20-%20_ftn12#_ftn7.

iii. Ramachandran, S., and Sharma, A. (2014). Media Industry Grows Increasingly Worried About Comcast-TWC. *Wall Street Journal* (12 March), p. B1.

iv. Sharma, A. (2014). Riches and Risks for Fox in Time Warner Takeover. *Wall Street Journal* (18 July), p. B1.

v. Heide, J., and John, G. (1988). The Role of Dependence Balancing in Safeguarding Transaction-Specific Assets in Conventional Channels. *Journal of Marketing* 52 (1): 20–25. This article in the academic literature showed that this is just as true in business-to-business markets as in consumer markets.

vi. Flint, F. (2019). DirecTV's Zeal for Football Cools. *Wall Street Journal* (28–29 September), p. B3.

vii. Lafley, A.G., and Martin, R. (2017). Customer Loyalty Is Overrated. *Harvard Business Review* 95 (1): 46–54.

viii. Verbeke, W., Farris, P., and Thurik, R. (1998). Consumer Response to the Preferred Brand Out-of-stock Situation. *European Journal of Marketing* 32 (11–12): 1008–1028.

ix. An article published in the *Journal of Marketing* in 2017 studied the consequences of one such delisting and found that, though the retailer suffered more than the manufacturer overall, there was plenty of variation across product categories, depending on whether the manufacturer or the retailer had more leverage: Van der Maelen, S., Breugelmans, E., and Cleeren, K. (2017). The Clash of the Titans: On Retailer and Manufacturer Vulnerability in Conflict Delistings. *Journal of Marketing* 81 (1): 118–135.

x. The interested reader may find these articles useful: Haenlein, M. and Libai, B. (2017). Seeding, Referral, and Recommendation: Creating Profitable Word-of-Mouth Programs. *California Management Review* 59 (2): 68–91. Dost, F., Phieler, U., Haelein, M., and Libai, B. (2019). Seeding as Part of the Marketing Mix: Word-of-Mouth Program Interactions for Fast-Moving Consumer Goods. *Journal of Marketing* 83 (2): 62–81.

xi. Brynjolfsson, E., and Smith, M. (2000). Frictionless Commerce? A Comparison of Internet and Conventional Retailers. *Management Science* 46: 563–585.

xii. Smith, M., and Brynjolfsson, E. (2001). Consumer Decision-Making at an Internet Shopbot: Brand Still Matters. *Journal of Industrial Economics* XLIX (4): 541–558.

xiii. Fischer, M., Völckner, F., and Sattler, H. (2010), How Important Are Brands? A Cross-category, Cross-country Study, *Journal of Marketing Research*, 47 (5) 823–839.

xiv. While we know that high positions in search results get higher clicks, it is interesting that such position effects are less important for strong brands and for branded keywords. This is very consistent with our notion of search loyalty. See, for example: Narayanan, S. and Kalyanam, K. (2015). Position Effects in Search Advertising and Their Moderators: A Regression Discontinuity Approach. *Marketing Science* 34 (3): 388–407.

xv. Ruitong Wang, a PhD candidate from the Carlson School of Management at the University of Minnesota, proposes two interesting dimensions of search loyalty to a retailer: first, search prominence, which assesses how frequently the retailer is the first to be searched, and consideration prominence, which assesses how frequently the retailer is one of the retailers searched by consumers.

xvi. Elzinga, K., and Mills, D. (2011). The Lerner Index of Monopoly Power: Origins and Uses. *American Economic Review*, 101 (3): 558–564.

xvii. Werden G. (1998). Demand Elasticities in Antitrust Analysis. *Antitrust Law Journal* 66 (2): 363–414.

xviii. See, for example: Brynjolfsson, E., Hu, Y., and Smith, M. (2003). Consumer Surplus in the Digital Economy: Estimating the Value of Increased Product Variety at Online Booksellers. *Management Science* 49 (11): 1445–1615.

xix. Gross margins are different from contribution margins but they are a useful profit measure and easily available at least for publicly traded companies.

CHAPTER 6

Using Power Without Using It Up

6.1 INTRODUCTION

Consumer loyalty can create and communicate power, but it doesn't automatically translate into a sustainable channel strategy. Natural springs, rivers, and wells are good sources of water, but you need pumps and pipes to irrigate the fields. In the same way, power must be applied in designing channel strategies and instituting policies that will (1) encourage or require the desired behavior by channel partners; (2) result in higher sales, market share, profits, and growth rates; (3) reinforce horizontal power; and (4) enable more options in adapting to market developments.

Power is a resource to manage in the present and for the future. It should show up in a firm's performance in the longer term if not right away, but using power only to maximize one's current position or profits is not smart. Companies understandably want to be free from the constraints that powerful channel partners may want to impose on their ability to chart their own course. Properly accumulated and applied, power preserves an organization's freedom to act in evolving circumstances and an uncertain future. In fact, along the lines of speaking softly but carrying a big stick, just the knowledge of unexercised power may yield dividends, while, once used, power may be "used up," as Professor Ray Corey, was fond of saying.

6.2 APPLYING POWER IN CHANNEL RELATIONSHIPS

It is in the application of power that we believe the work of social psychologists can be most insightful. More than 50 years ago, social psychologists John French and Bertrand Raven proposed five "bases" of power: (1) *reward*, (2) *coercion*, (3) *legitimacy*, (4) *expertise*, and (5) *referent. Information* was soon added to bring the list to six. Over the decades, the six bases have been further sliced and diced to expand the total number—11 at last count![i] But the fine distinctions between ever-multiplying bases are, to our mind, not of great practical use. Instead, we believe it is more important to take stock of the various ways channel members can exercise power, and think about which ones are effective in influencing channel partners while still sustaining a productive relationship.

So how do these power bases relate to the everyday challenges of channel management? The first two are self-explanatory—*reward* and *coercion*, carrot and stick. Some of the most common examples are the ability of suppliers to reward good pricing and merchandising by resellers with trade allowances, and to withhold new products from those resellers that step out of line. Similarly, resellers can reward favored suppliers with the most desirable location on the shelf and special displays while cutting the visibility of a less favored supplier to a single facing.

The next basis of power, *legitimacy*, is seen in the ability to enforce investments and behavior specified in legal contracts, or to take recourse through regulatory restraints. While few would argue that specifying the terms of trade in a legal agreement is sufficient to ensure the channel operates smoothly, we seriously doubt anyone would disagree with our assertion that such an agreement is necessary. Much has been written about the long legal battles that the Coca-Cola Company fought with its bottlers in the 1920s and then again 60 years later because the original bottler contracts were deemed as being in perpetuity and tied the company's hands when it came to the price it could charge for concentrate sold to bottlers.[ii] Nowadays, the company's agreements with bottlers clearly spell out, among other things, its pricing authority. For example, here is an excerpt from an agreement with one of the company's largest bottlers, Coca-Cola Enterprises, archived at the SEC:*iii*

(a) The Company reserves the right, by giving written notice to the Bottler, to establish and to revise from time to time and at any time, in its sole discretion, the price of the Concentrate, the Authorized Supplier, the supply point and alternate supply points for the Concentrate, the conditions of shipment and payment, and the currency or currencies acceptable to the Company or the Authorized Suppliers.

(b) If the Bottler is unwilling to pay the revised price in respect of the Concentrate, then the Bottler shall so notify the Company in writing within thirty (30) days from receipt of the written notice from the Company revising the aforesaid price. In such event, this Agreement shall terminate automatically without liability by any party for damages three (3) calendar months after receipt of the Bottler's notification.

(c) Any failure on the part of the Bottler to notify the Company in respect of the revised price of the Concentrate pursuant to subclause (b) hereof shall be deemed to be acceptance by the Bottler of the revised price.

(d) The Company reserves the right, to the extent permitted by the law applicable in the Territory, to establish and to revise, by giving written notice to the Bottler, maximum prices at which the Beverage in Approved Containers may be sold by the Bottler to wholesalers and retailers and the maximum retail prices for the Beverage. It is recognized in this regard that the Bottler may sell the Beverage to wholesalers and retailers and authorize the retail sale of the Beverage at prices which are lower than the maximum prices. The Bottler shall not, however, increase the maximum prices established or revised by the Company at which the Beverage in Approved Containers may be sold to wholesalers and retailers nor authorize an increase in the maximum prices for the Beverage without the prior written consent of the Company.

Apart from whether they are contractual or not, behaviors may be perceived as "legitimate" relative to the norms accepted by the channel partners or regarded as "power plays." For example, when

Budweiser requires distributors to remove product from reseller inventories that has outlived its freshness requirements, this can be regarded as a legitimate policy to protect the brand franchise. On the other hand, if a powerful retailer decides to apply "deductions" from an invoice because they mistakenly ordered too much, that is unlikely to be accepted without protest. Indeed, such deductions by powerful retailers are sometimes perceived as strong-arm robbery, not the enforcement of practices that improve channel performance. So, another perspective on "legitimacy" is whether a policy or practice is perceived by the channel partner to reflect a genuine concern for the ability to deliver important, or at least valued, consumer services, or whether the practice is seen as merely lining the powerful party's own pockets.

The *information* or *expert* basis of power, meanwhile, is illustrated in the ability of one or the other channel partner to access, analyze, and use sales, logistics, and customer data. Amazon makes great use of this power to provide outstanding delivery service, decide which products are worth stocking and selling through its own retailer model versus the third party marketplace, and dynamically change their prices, and it guards these data zealously from suppliers.

Referent credibility as a power base is shown in a strong brand's ability to attract and influence distribution channel partners, and vice versa. Apple is known for innovative products, so it is no surprise that its products are rapidly adopted by retailers. But the same referent credibility can exist on the reseller side. Walmart and Amazon have such strong reputations for consumer traffic and logistics that suppliers find them hard to resist. Some resellers achieve particularly strong credibility within a product category, so they become a destination for consumers shopping for those items. We daresay Best Buy remains an example for electronics. The music streaming service Spotify now has almost 200 million listeners. It is arguably the most significant contributor of data used in the compilation of the Billboard weekly charts, a highly influential weekly tabulation of the popularity of songs and albums. This referent credibility means that even a top star like Taylor Swift, who had famously taken all her music off Spotify for a few years, found it hard to remain off the service and returned to it in 2017.

These power bases interact in important ways. Information and acknowledged industry expertise might provide the referent credibility for a supplier to qualify as category manager and therefore be able to suggest shelf layouts and merchandising and promotion strategies to the retailer. But they can also improve the design and amplify the effectiveness of a supplier's rewards. A supplier who has the data and analytics expertise to understand which promotional campaigns generate incremental sales and profitability—and which ones do not—has a big advantage when it comes to selecting the right carrots and sticks for channel members. And again, the same goes for the reseller side. The U.S. drug store chain CVS Caremark uses the insights from its Extra Care Loyalty Program to test and improve the effectiveness of its promotions to consumers. It also offers a subscription-based vendor portal to its suppliers, allowing them access to a limited set of reports from the database, and the option to pay for specific targeted promotions on their brands that are expected to be effective not just for the supplier but also for CVS.[1]

Another very stark example is the kind of contracts that Amazon is offering to sellers under its Amazon Accelerator program.[iv] The company is offering more prominent display and marketing support to sellers on its third-party platform but in exchange, it wants to be able to buy up the rights to the brand at short notice, and at a fixed price—around $10,000! Apparently, the designs, patents, and trade secrets will remain with the seller, but still, $10,000! The retailer is certainly using all its bases of power in what looks like a very lopsided program.

So, understanding power is not just about the balance of power and who has more, but also about the total stock of each party's power from these various bases. It also includes the investments and safeguards each partner puts into the relationship, which can motivate both partners to seek compromise and avoid losing the investments. We now turn our attention to such investments and safeguards.

6.3 INVESTMENTS AND SAFEGUARDS: EFFICIENT PARTNERSHIP OR POWER STRUGGLE?

6.3.1 Make Partner-Specific Investments with Open Eyes

A powerful channel partner is able to convince companies to implement policies that seem to further increase its power and enable it to negotiate ever-better prices and more attractive terms of trade. However, as Oliver Williamson, who received the Nobel Prize in economics for his work on transaction cost analysis (TCA) cautioned,

---

[1] We will have a lot more to say about the tension between promotion effectiveness for a supplier versus a retailer in Chapter 14.

investments in partner-specific assets don't necessarily imply a power shift.[2] Sophisticated suppliers and resellers go into these arrangements with open eyes. They deliberately make the investments, thus increasing their dependence, because it is beneficial and efficient to do so.[v]

Working with a demanding channel partner can spur a supplier into improving its logistics, for example. Although Levi's introduction of the low-priced Levi Strauss Signature sub-brand into Walmart in the early 2000s was far from successful when viewed through a sales revenue or brand equity lens, working with the retailer, who is known to be a supply chain pioneer, did force Levi's to spruce up its own supply chain. According to then Chief Information Officer David Bergen, "Our supply chain could not deliver the services Wal-Mart expected."[vi] Levi's could not track the location of product in the supply chain, nor did it know at any time how much inventory was in trucks or distribution centers and how many pairs of jeans were being manufactured in which factories. A new information system allowed the company to have better insight into how individual products in the company's lineup were selling in the stores of each channel partner and to speed up movement through the supply chain. On-time deliveries to retailers increased from 65% to 95%. We have heard executives from other companies tell similar stories about how working with Walmart forces them to improve their supply chain.

6.3.2 Safeguards Protect Each Party's Interests

Although the gains in supply chain efficiencies from cooperation can be significant, both suppliers and reseller customers need to be careful not to make partner-specific investments that further increase their channel partner's power without safeguarding their own interests. Carefully safeguarded investments have the potential for cementing a partnership and facilitating win-win cooperation between the two organizations.[vii]

P&G's early partnership with Walmart is often held up as an example of just such a partnership. In 1987, P&G opened an office

---

[2] Williamson and others who cite and build on his work use the term "transaction-specific assets" to designate investments made by a channel partner that don't have (as much) value outside the relationship. However, in the intervening 30-plus years, the term "transaction" became associated with short-term exchanges rather than longer-term relationships. Therefore, we favor the term "partner-specific" assets and beg forgiveness from those who are used to the TCA terminology.

near Walmart's headquarters in Bentonville, Arkansas, to make it easier to work with the retailer. The move was later followed by many other CPG manufacturers, but suppliers who recognize the new retail order before competitors can gain long-term advantages by being first to negotiate partnerships, and the Walmart-P&G relationship remained strong for two decades. Of course, picking the right partner(s), putting in safeguards, and monitoring the agreements is critical. Tracking retailer-specific P&L statements may be one basic safeguard. Another may be not leaving the same people in Bentonville too long, and locating teams in Seattle (for Amazon) and Minneapolis (for Target) as well.

Indeed, P&G also made an agreement with Amazon in 2014.[viii,ix] The agreement allowed Amazon to ship products to consumers directly from P&G's warehouses, and also made more P&G products eligible for Amazon's Prime Pantry and Subscribe & Save programs than any other CPG company's products, which cuts costs for both companies. The danger here may be less from P&G or Amazon engaging in "opportunism" than from their other channel partners' resentment of what might appear to be P&G favoring Amazon. Target determined, for example, that less reliance on P&G would make it easier to compete with Amazon. And Walmart has been pushing for lower prices from P&G to deal with competition not only from Amazon but from the German hard discount retailer Aldi, which has been making inroads in the U.S. market.

6.3.3 Safeguards Can Outlive Their Usefulness

On the flip side, safeguards can sometimes outlive their usefulness, at least for society. Depending on one's perspective, the automobile distribution system in the United States, in which new vehicles can only be sold through franchised dealers, is either a terrible or a wonderful example of safeguards implemented with the force of law. Strong state franchise laws protect dealers. While the details vary from state to state, here are some examples of the protections:[x] All states require dealers to be licensed, preventing cars from being sold through other means, such as the Internet. Direct sales from auto manufacturers to consumers are prohibited, as are manufacturer-owned dealerships. "Encroachment" regulations prevent manufacturers from establishing dealerships in another dealer's "relevant market area" without a demonstrated need. Manufacturers are prohibited from terminating a dealership without "good cause" as specified in the laws. Good cause usually includes factors like a dealer's conviction for a felony, fraud, insolvency, or failure to comply with a material term of the franchise agreement, not the manufacturer's desire to improve efficiency or profitability. If a dealership is terminated, most states also require the manufacturer to buy back unsold vehicles, parts, accessories, tools, and other equipment. Most states also prohibit manufacturers from price discriminating towards dealers. If a lower price is offered to one dealer, it also must be offered to all other dealers in the state or "relevant market area," making it difficult for manufacturers to reward more efficient dealers.

Clearly, therefore, the laws are designed to afford dealers a great deal of protection—too much, in the view of many observers. Some economists have concluded that these laws lead to higher costs, shorter hours of operation and therefore poorer service quality, and higher prices paid by consumers.[xi] Tom Keane, writing in the *Boston Globe*, cites a report by the Department of Justice that car prices are 6% to 9% higher than they need to be because car manufacturers are prohibited from selling their own products, and that 50% of consumers would buy from manufacturers "even if it didn't save any money."[xii]

Tesla Motors, the electric car company founded by Elon Musk and JP Straubel in 2003, is fighting to change the system. It has eschewed the traditional automobile dealer franchise system in favor of its own direct-sales model. The company has set up "galleries" in high-foot-traffic areas across the nation. Consumers can come into these showrooms and learn about Tesla electric cars from a "Product Specialist," who does not work for commission. Consumers can only test-drive the cars at special Tesla "Test Drive Events" or if they schedule an appointment at a Tesla Store. When a customer wants to buy a car, they place an order online with Tesla's production center in California. Tesla manufactures the car to the customer's specifications, and the customer receives it 6–12 months later. But Tesla has not had an easy time battling state franchise laws. It is encountering stiff resistance in almost every state.

6.3.4 How Automobile Dealer Safeguards Came to Be

But why do the state have such tough laws to protect dealers? To answer that, a short history lesson is in order. A franchise to sell steam automotives from General Motors, established in 1898, marked the beginning of the modern auto franchise system. Car manufacturers had realized the benefits of working with third-party sellers who had the sales expertise, capital, and geographic reach to sell their products. Early franchise agreements were relatively simple and short-term, and they could be terminated with a 30-day notice by either party. The franchise dealership structure gave auto manufacturers a controllable service and repair network without making capital investments of their own.

Demand for automobiles leveled in the 1920s, and as the market became more competitive, manufacturers demanded more from dealers. A dealership usually became affiliated with one auto manufacturer. The manufacturers defined the territory in which franchisees could market vehicles, while retaining the right to franchise other dealerships in the area. They set high sales targets, and in order to meet these targets, dealers had to increase investments in equipment, services, and inventory. Instances arose of dealers being exploited by manufacturers. One such incident occurred during the Great Depression, when GM and Ford forced dealers to buy inventories of new cars that were unlikely to sell. In the 1950s, the federal government investigated allegations of manufacturer antitrust violations that led to significant changes in the franchise system. For instance, GM extended the franchise agreement term to five years and agreed that franchise agreements would not be terminated without cause. The federal government passed the Automobile Dealer's Day in Court Act in 1956, which allows a dealer to recover damages if the manufacturer does not comply with the terms of the franchise agreement. But several states had their own auto franchise laws by the time the federal law was enacted and these state laws protect dealers more than the federal law does. One of the many examples of this is the law we mentioned previously that prohibits manufacturers from terminating a dealership without "good cause" and the desire to improve efficiency doesn't qualify as "good cause". We will return to the automobile industry, and its overdistribution problem in the U.S., in Chapter 10.

6.4 THE CHALLENGE OF PRESERVING POWER

It is a maxim that power corrupts. Research in social psychology finds that those who have power act more and act more variably; they are more selective information processors; more goal oriented; more oriented to rewards and opportunities and less to potential risks or disadvantages. As a result, they can be inattentive, "lazy" information processors, and make contradictory and risky judgments based on gut feelings. And much organizational research shows that organizations act like the individuals who work in them. Power leads organizations to "objectify," subordinating the needs and interests of those who have less power to those of the powerful.[xiii] Indeed, powerful firms can sometimes put in place practices that have the unintentional consequence of destroying their less powerful partners. The less powerful partner may be so abused that it no longer has anything to lose, and as the partnership disintegrates, the more powerful partner finds it has used up its power.

6.4.1 Using Up Power: The "Objectification" of Leather Italia USA

Recall LI, the upscale leather furniture producer we introduced in Chapter 3 who agreed to sell through Costco.com. The Costco deal required substantial changes in the way LI had done business with its other retailers, but also had the lure of substantial volume.

According to LI executives, the first step of the process of doing business with Costco was a review by Costco buyers of furniture items presented by LI and other vendors. Selected vendors who survived this review were then required to guarantee that a minimum of 100 items of the product selected for sale would be available at delivery-service warehouses before they were listed for sale on the Costco website. Costco had an approved list of six "white glove" delivery services from which a vendor could choose, all of which warehoused goods that were sold to Costco.com. If a product did not sell the full 100 items that were produced and shipped, Costco offered the vendor the opportunity to reduce the price and/or purchase other promotions such as an e-mail "blast" to the members.

The consumer purchase process went something like this. Consumers browsed the website, selected the desired item, and then typically paid by credit card. Costco communicated the order to the vendor, who sent the order to the delivery service. The item was unpacked in the delivery-service warehouse, supposedly checked for damages, and delivered to the consumer. As the product was shipped out of the warehouse and put on a truck to be delivered to the customer, the vendor billed Costco.com for the shipment and the customer's credit card would be immediately charged. Upon delivery, the consumer signed a receipt acknowledging that the item was indeed what they had ordered and in good condition.

When LI was selected as a vendor, it was required to sign Costco's standard vendor agreement, some portions of which are reproduced in the appendix to this chapter. LI chose a delivery service called HEP Direct from Costco's approved list. Other details were negotiated, such as product lines to be sold, pricing, and the start dates of any promotions in order to allow time for production and advance shipment to warehouses.

Costco offers consumers a generous no-questions-asked return policy. A consumer who wanted to return an LI item contacted Costco and initiated the returns process without having to provide a reason. But Costco's vendor agreement put the cost of the return squarely on LI's shoulders. For example, a consumer might decide after a few days or weeks that he or she simply did not like the way the furniture group looked. After a return request was initiated, Costco asked LI to commission HEP Direct to pick up the product from the consumer's home. As soon as HEP Direct had retrieved the product, the consumer was refunded in full. LI was required to pay an additional $450 to cover the expense of picking up the product. Costco deducted the manufacturer price from payables due to LI, effectively canceling the sale and reducing LI's margin from a typical $367 to a significant loss. In addition, the original furniture was, in many instances, now in less than saleable condition. Michael Campbell, founder and CEO of LI, noted that the "the vast majority of the product is returned due to buyer's remorse; e.g., the consumer didn't like color, product didn't fit in home, product wasn't as it seemed online, product was 'uncomfortable', consumer used it for a year and wanted to purchase another group to replace it." The return rate from Costco customers averaged around 20% and, as of late 2013, 3,913 furniture sets were returned. Of these returns, more than 60% were returned after more than a month, more than 10% were returned after more than three months, and nine sets were returned after an astounding three years had elapsed.

As a result of this delivery and return policy, the Costco.com account was hemorrhaging LI's cash flow and profitability within 18 months of starting business with Costco. Finding the association financially unsustainable, LI stopped doing business with Costco in September 2013 and took a long time to recover from the hit to its balance sheet.

This is clearly not a case of Costco wanting to destroy LI. But it does show how powerful firms can put policies in place that can seriously damage the interests of their less powerful and less sophisticated partners, perhaps without even realizing it. In this case, the difference in size and therefore power between the two parties was large enough that LI probably didn't have much leverage to change the rules imposed by Costco, so it would have been best for them to turn down the offer when it first came their way. Too much power imbalance in a mutually dependent relationship can reduce the frequency of exchange between the two parties and shrink the total pie to be shared, and the less powerful party finds ways to reduce its dependence or exit the relationship.[xiv] With LI at the brink of bankruptcy, Costco had nothing to show for its power.

6.4.2 Pushing Power Too Far or Giving It Up: Retailers and Their Private Labels

If a company fails to understand the limits of its power, it may make decisions that diminish that power. Consider the power that a strong private-label brand confers on a retailer. It is clear, both from academic research and from our discussions with CPG marketers, that having a viable private-label brand allows retailers to negotiate better prices and trade allowances from national manufacturers, and to build consumer loyalty.[xv] But it is also clear that this leverage is only effective to a point. If a retailer that sells both national and private-label brands pushes its private label too hard, it can hurt its position with both suppliers and consumers. Manufacturers of national brands may no longer see the value in negotiating with a retailer that mainly focuses on selling private labels. And the share of wallet that consumers spend at the retailer's stores will fall if they are unable to find their favorite brands on the shelves. From research that one of us has done, the turning point seems to be at a private-label share between 35% and 40%.[xvi] For many retailers, pushing the private-label share much beyond that risks using up power.

An interesting contrast is offered by retailers that sell only private-label goods. Consumers don't come into their stores expecting national brands, so these retailers don't need to balance national-brand and private-label products. Such retailers run the danger of losing the power of their private label in quite the opposite way. Consider Trader Joe's, a U.S.-based retail chain owned by Aldi of Germany that carried only private-label products with the exception of a few categories such as alcohol and chocolate. Given the competitive market in which private-label suppliers operate, the retailer enjoys a great deal of power over its suppliers while at the same time building considerable consumer equity for its Trader Joe's–branded products. The retailer's stores are still not densely located, but many consumers, including one of us, drive distances upwards of 30 miles to shop at Trader Joe's. However, the retailer is slowly adding more national-brand products to its assortment. Although the actions can be justified by the desire to differentiate from other private-label-only chains and to increase the share of wallet that it gets from consumers who shop their private-label brand in some categories but go elsewhere for national brands in others, we believe the benefit may not be worth the cost. On the supply side, Trader Joe's will not have nearly as much power over highly differentiated national brands as it does over private-label suppliers. And in the dynamics of the shopping aisle, placing national brands next to its private label on the shelf encourages consumers to compare the two in terms of prices, variety, and perceived quality, potentially putting its private label at risk.[xvii]

6.4.3 Should National Brand Manufacturers Produce Private Labels?

The above discussion begs the question: should manufacturers of national brands supply private labels? Certainly, many do so, even though the specifics of who supplies private label and to which retailers, are a well-kept secret.[xviii]

Over the years, many people have written about the virtues and pitfalls of national brands supplying private labels. John Quelch and David Harding, writing in the *Harvard Business Review*, advised manufacturers that do not produce private label not to start, suggesting it is better to close excess capacity than to go down the "slippery slope" of private-label production.[xix] They argued that any cost benefits from utilizing excess capacity and scale economies may be ephemeral because distribution and production complexities arising from the larger number of SKUs and labels can actually increase costs. Longer-term, they noted, manufacturers can come to depend on the private label volume to cover fixed costs, and the negotiation leverage can shift to retail customers. Other attractions of private label supply, such as more influence over the category assortments stocked by the retailers, can be similarly illusive, they maintained.

Dunne and Narasimhan, also writing in the same journal, made the opposite case, arguing that producing the premium tier of private label (think Alberstons' O Organics and Signature Reserve or Krogers' Private Selection brands in the U.S.) may boost rather than stifle innovation, while standard private label can be more effective for a market leader than introducing a "fighter brand" at a lower price point.[xx] They also argue that producing a private label for a retailer gives the manufacturer leverage in obtaining shelf space, and coordinating retail pricing and promotion for their whole brand portfolio.

We believe it is far too simplistic to make blanket statements about whether national brands should produce private labels.[xxi] It may make sense in some conditions and not in others. Pete and Gerry's Organic Eggs is a good example of when it makes sense. Pete and Gerry's is a New Hampshire–based company that sells free-range and organic eggs under the Pete and Gerry's and Nellie's brands to consumers through grocery, mass, club, and natural food stores in the U.S. The eggs come from over 120 family farms across the U.S. that work with the company. As the company is expanding distribution, it also needs to increase the number of egg farms to ensure adequate supply. It takes two to three years to convert a farm over to certified organic status. During that time, the company supplies the eggs as private label to selected retailers with whom it is building a relationship.

Like Pete and Gerry's, manufacturers need to be clear-eyed about why they are supplying private label and what they are getting in return for their efforts.[xxii] As Quelch and Harding advised, they should evaluate the full set of costs they incur in producing and selling private labels; negotiate favorable arrangements with retailers for the merchandising, pricing, and promotion of their national brands; and also educate those retailers on the actual profitability of national brands versus private labels, both for the private supplier and the retailer. Retailers do earn higher-percent margins on private labels than on national brands. But as one of us has documented, dollar margins can tell a very different story from percent margins, and private label purchasing is only associated with greater loyalty and profitability to the retailer to a point.[xxiii]

6.5 VERTICAL RESTRAINTS: WELFARE ENHANCING OR ANTICOMPETITIVE?

Finally, to ensure that power is preserved, it is crucial not to apply it in ways that would be viewed as anticompetitive by regulators. Channel partners apply their power in pricing and in a variety of other terms of trade. Retailers, for example, demand exclusive territories, special product lines and sizes (which often increase a manufacturer's costs), "swell allowances" (which are lump-sum payments for damaged goods), and a larger number of days for payables. As one executive told us, "Walmart will let you hear it if you don't perform. If they have excess inventory, they will make you do a spot media buy to help them sell that inventory." And on the other side, manufacturers' power may show up in their ability to move their trade promotion dollars from simple off-invoice discounts to pay-for-performance funding that is tied to specific retailer actions or performance targets.

In the language of economists and regulators, these and other terms of trade between firms at different levels of the distribution system that restrict the activities of a channel member, such as with respect to pricing, promotion, territories, and products sold, are called "vertical restraints." Vertical restraints on price might be the imposition by a supplier of a maximum or minimum resale price that resellers can charge (maximum or minimum resale price maintenance, or RPM), thus influencing distribution depth. Non-price restraints might be the granting of exclusive territories to resellers, or the requirement that they deal exclusively with the supplier, or that resellers be required to buy a presumably less desired product from the supplier if they want access to a more desired product (tying).

The stated purpose of U.S. antitrust policy is to prevent conduct that harms consumers and the competitive process. It would be fair to say that antitrust is much tougher on horizontal agreements and restraints between competing firms, whether they are suppliers or resellers, than on vertical agreements between suppliers and their downstream distribution channel partners.[3] In other words, threats to inter-brand competition come under scrutiny much more than practices that may reduce intra-brand competition between resellers of the same brand. The rationale is that there are possible pro-competitive reasons for vertical restraints, and limiting intra-brand competition may, in fact, increase inter-brand competition. A pro-competitive reason for vertical restraints is that it can discourage free-riding and provide resellers the incentive to increase distribution depth (i.e., invest in the services, infrastructure, marketing, and other efforts that the suppliers' products require). A new entrant can also use vertical restraints to gain a foothold in the market.

However, it is recognized that vertical restraints can be anticompetitive, especially when the firm(s) involved have dominant market share and therefore are likely to wield significant market power. As the Federal Trade Commission's guidelines are careful to point out, if there is evidence of anticompetitive effects, a restraint will not escape antitrust scrutiny just because it is labeled as a vertical arrangement.

One anticompetitive possibility is that restraints make collusion easier between suppliers. For example, if a group of manufacturers wants to collude on setting a higher manufacturer price for their products, minimum RPM reduces the likelihood that a "cheater" would gain by lowering price, since the RPM would prevent the price cut from being passed along to consumers and therefore prevent the cheater from gaining sales. Another is that restraints may be

---

[3]Note that "agent" relationships, which we defined in Chapter 4, are subject to more relaxed rules, generally not falling under regulations on vertical restraints.

exclusionary, preventing equally efficient competitors, either suppliers or resellers, from entering the market and/or achieving the minimum scale they need for efficiency. For example, if a dominant supplier takes the best distributors out of the market by requiring that those distributors deal exclusively with the supplier, a new entrant may not be able to find an effective route-to-market. Restraints may also be pushed upon suppliers by powerful retailers wanting to squelch their rivals. Or resellers may use RPM by suppliers to facilitate unlawful collusion in downstream prices.

The possibility of pro- and anticompetitive effects makes the navigation of vertical restraints tricky for marketers from a regulatory perspective. This is despite the fact that, overall, there has been a decline in U.S. regulation of vertical conduct in the last twenty years. Historically, there was a distinction between price and non-price restraints, the former being viewed with more suspicion. Non-price vertical restraints have been viewed under the less stringent "rule of reason" since 1977. Maximum RPM had been illegal per se since 1968 but became subject to the rule of reason in 1997. Minimum RPM had been illegal per se since 1911, but it too was brought under the rule of reason in 2007.

Through all of these changes, the *Colgate* doctrine has given manufacturers the option of a take-it-or-leave-it policy of selling only to downstream resellers whose retail price adheres to the manufacturer's suggested resale price (MSRP).[xxiv] So a manufacturer can always implement RPM unilaterally. However, this requires the manufacturer to terminate retailers who sell the firm's products at discount prices, a medicine that most manufacturers would view as too strong for the disease they may be trying to cure. Using the *Colgate* doctrine was also risky, especially in light of the per se illegal status of minimum RPM, because some aspects of the manufacturers' dealing with its channel members could be construed as an agreement among channel members rather than as unilateral action. As a result, manufacturers have been wary of using this route to prevent channel members from selling below a minimum price.

Historically, antitrust enforcement has been tougher on conduct by a group of collaborating firms than on the unilateral practices of a single firm.[xxv] It also is more concerned when a firm's vertical policies reference the sales of its rivals, not just its own sales. For example, in recent years, the FTC and Department of Justice have looked closely at a class of vertical restraints they call "conditional pricing practices," such as loyalty or share-of-wallet discounts.[xxvi] These are price discounts offered by the supplier that are contingent on a commitment by the reseller to purchase a specified share of its requirements in the category from the supplier, in effect putting a constraint on how much business the reseller can do with the supplier's competitors.

An aspect of vertical antitrust that has remained relatively unchanged despite some criticism[xxvii] is the *Robinson-Patman Act*. Subsections a and b of the Act make it illegal for suppliers to charge different prices for essentially the same physical product to different resellers *if* doing so is substantially injurious to competition in either party's horizontal market. Differences in costs, market conditions, and good faith efforts to meet competition are all acceptable defenses for price discrimination.[xxviii] In contrast, subsections d and e of the act make it illegal per se for a supplier to discriminate in providing allowances or services to competing resellers for promoting the resale of the supplier's products. Suppliers are required to offer such allowances and services on a "proportionally equivalent" basis to all competing resellers. Thus, from the perspective of suppliers, who should and do integrate their pricing strategies and promotional programs, the act creates a somewhat artificial divide between the two that has been criticized.[xxix]

A recent study examined cases involving Robinson-Patman from 1982 to 2010, concluding that it has become significantly less likely for courts to find defendants guilty of violating the act and the "no harm to competition" defense has become more effective.[xxx] The fact remains, however, that the Robinson-Patman Act is on the books and suppliers as well as resellers, especially those with dominant market shares, would ignore it at their peril.

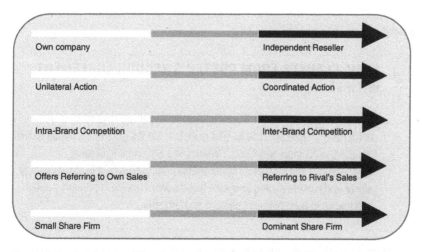

Figure 6.1 Regulatory red flags in exercising channel power: our lay view.

Our objective here is definitely not to provide legal guidance, but simply to offer a summary of the antitrust perspective on the types of activities and polices that firms may use in applying power on their channel partners and managing the channel. In that spirit, we summarize in Figure 6.1 our lay view of what is considered relatively benign (white shading at left side of the figure) versus a red flag (dark shading at right side of the figure), and refer the reader to the guidance provided by competition authorities and legal experts.[4]

6.6 CONCLUSION

Channel practices and policies can be evaluated with respect to whether they may be perceived by other members as self-centered exercises in power that will ultimately create resentment and their own reactions, or as sensible policies that improve the performance of the entire system. Of course, what one channel member regards as sensible and justified is not guaranteed to be accepted by other channel members. And while communications among channel members are part of the solution, data and metrics will make the case more compelling.

In Part II of the book, we offer specific metrics, tools, and an analytical approach for how companies should get to the right level and type of distribution coverage. Part III is about product line, pricing, promotion, and other policies for ongoing management of distribution once in the right ballpark.

APPENDIX

SOME CLAUSES FROM COSTCO'S VENDOR AGREEMENT WITH LI

■ Vendor shall comply with all packing (including pallets) requirements of the carrier and costco.com, and its cost is included in the price of the Merchandise. Vendor shall comply with Costco Wholesale's Structural Packaging Specifications and inspect all Merchandise prior to shipment to ensure quality, safety, and conformity and to ensure that the Merchandise is properly packed and loaded to prevent transit damage and tampering.

---

[4]For example, the Federal Trade Commission provides advice on its website at https://www.ftc.gov/tips-advice/competition-guidance/guide-antitrust-laws/antitrust-laws.

- Unless otherwise agreed in writing, Costco.com shall not be obligated to pay any invoice until thirty (30) days after delivery is completed under Section 6 above. Costco.com's payment to Vendor will reference Costco.com's Purchase Order number(s). Any claims submitted by Vendor to costco.com regarding unpaid invoices, partial payments, RTVs, rebate or audit deductions, etc. must be submitted on a Costco Wholesale Standard Vendor Claim Form. Vendor shall under no circumstances delay any shipment of Merchandise based on a delay in payment by costco.com.

- Costco.com may reject or revoke acceptance of any Merchandise returned by Customers for any reason stated in Section 13 above or for any other reason including buyer's remorse. Costco.com will ship to Vendor, at Vendor's expense, any Merchandise that is returned directly to a Costco Wholesale warehouse by a Customer.

- At Costco.com's option, Vendor shall grant a full refund to costco.com or, if Costco.com so elects, a credit or replacement with respect to any Merchandise shipment or portion thereof that costco.com rejects or for which costco.com revokes acceptance; and costco.com may offset any such amounts against amounts costco.com owes to Vendor. Costco.com may also offset costs associated with defective pallets, monies owed for regulatory fines or penalties (including associated attorney's fees), any rebates/incentive allowances and any other amounts owed by Vendor against amounts costco.com owes to Vendor. Costco.com may, at the end of a season, at the close of a business relationship, or otherwise, hold back a reasonable reserve for future claims against amounts owed. In the event there remains an outstanding balance owed Costco.com after such offset, Vendor shall immediately pay to costco.com said balance.

Summary

- Organizations accumulate channel power not simply to maximize current profits or as an end in itself, but to maintain the freedom to act and adapt to an uncertain and evolving future.

- Social psychologists have proposed several "bases" of power, including reward, coercion, legitimacy, expertise, information, and referent. This is a useful lens through which to view the application of power in channel policies and practices and assess how effective they are.

(Continued)

(Continued)

- Some practices may be perceived by channel partners as self-centered exercises in power that create resentment, and others as sensible policies that improve the performance of the entire system.

- Channel members make partner-specific investments in the relationship, and when these are made with eyes open and with suitable safeguards in place, they are efficient and beneficial for the system, not symptomatic of an undesirable power imbalance.

- However, the quest for short-term growth and profit can actually lead suppliers and resellers to use up their power needlessly or inadvertently give it up.

- The U.S. automobile distribution system, and how the state franchise laws that protect dealers came to be, offer a good lesson in the overuse of power, the development of safeguards, and how those safeguards can outlive their usefulness.

- Like Leather Italia, whose association with Costco.com was short lived, a party that suffers too much at the hands of a powerful partner's policies finds ways to reduce its dependence or exit the relationship.

- Retailers, their private label brands, and the manufacturers who supply those private labels are an interesting context in which there is the potential for one party to give up its power.

- Vertical price and non-price restrictions set by suppliers or their channel partners are viewed by competition authorities as having potential competitive and anticompetitive effects. One important aspect of not using up one's power is to make sure that it is not exercised in ways that would be deemed anticompetitive. This is especially, though not only, the case for a firm that has dominant market share.

ENDNOTES

i. Raven, B., Schwarzwald, J., and Koslowsky, M. (1998). Conceptualizing and Measuring a Power/Interaction Model of Interpersonal Influence. *Journal of Applied Psychology* 28 (4): 307–332.

ii. The book titled *Secret Formula*, written by Frederick Allen, describes the early battle with the company's parent bottlers, and details of the later case are available at https://www.leagle.com/decision/19911440769fsupp67111314.

iii. The agreement is available at https://www.sec.gov/Archives/edgar/data/1491675/000119312510223971/dex102.htm (accessed August 2018).

iv. Emont, J. (2019). Amazon Seeks More Brand Control. *Wall Street Journal* (19 July), p. B1.

v. Williamson, O. (1981). The Economics of Organization: The Transaction Cost Approach. *American Journal of Sociology* 87 (3): 548–577.

vi. Girard, K. (2003). Supply Chain Partnerships: How Levi's Got Its Jeans into Wal-Mart. CIO (15 July) at https://www.cio.com/article/2439956/supply-chain-management/supply-chain-partnerships--how-levi-s-got-its-jeans-into-wal-mart.html (accessed 15 August 2018).

vii. There is a rich academic literature on channel governance that builds on these and other elements of TCA. For the interested reader, we suggest two articles to get the lay of the land, one a nice review and another a recent piece that looks at the impact of initial partner selection, investments, and safeguards on ongoing costs that suppliers must incur to monitor the relationship: Rindfleisch, A. and Heide, J. (1997). Transaction Cost Analysis: Past, Present, and Future Applications. *Journal of Marketing* 61 (4): 30–54.

Wathne, K., Heide, J., Mooi, E. and Kumar, A. (2018). Relationship Governance Dynamics: The Roles of Partner Selection Efforts and Mutual Investments. *Journal of Marketing Research* 55 (5): 704–721.

viii. Ng, S., and Zibrio, P. (2014). P&G's Amazon Pact Prompts Retaliation. *Wall Street Journal* (3 March) p. B1.

ix. L2, Inc. (2014). The Digital IQ Index: Amazon 2014. L2 Intelligence Report (7 August) at https://www.l2inc.com/research/amazon-2014.

x. We have adapted much of this and the following discussion of U.S. automobile distribution from Lafontaine, F. and Morton, F. (2010). Markets: State franchise laws, dealer terminations, and the auto crisis. *Journal of Economic Perspectives,* 24(3): 233–250.

xi. See also: LaFontaine, F. and Slade, M. (2008). Empirical Assessment of Exclusive Contracts. In: *Handbook of Antitrust Economics* (ed. P. Buccirossi), Cambridge, MA: MIT Press.

xii. Keane, T. (2013). Is the auto franchise system a lemon? *Boston Globe* (26 May).

xiii. See the following book, for example, especially pages 154, 186, and 192: Guinote, A, and Vescio, T.K. (2010). *The Social Psychology of Power* (New York: Guilford Press).

xiv. See, for example: McAlister, L., Bazerman, M., and Fader, P. (1986). Power and Goal Setting in Channel Negotiations. *Journal of Marketing Research* 23 (3): 228–236. Piskorski, M., and Casciaro, T. (2006). When More Power Makes Actors Worse Off: Turning a Profit in the American Economy. *Social Forces* 85 (2): 1011–1036.

xv. Ailawadi, K., and Harlam, B. (2004). An Empirical Analysis of the Determinants of Retail Margins: The Role of Store-Brand Share. *Journal of Marketing* 68 (1): 147–165.

Meza, S., and Sudhir, K. (2010). Do Private Labels Increase Retailer Bargaining Power? *Quantitative Marketing and Economics* 8 (3): 333–363.

xvi. Ailawadi, K., Pauwels, K., and Steenkamp, K. (2008). Private-Label Use and Store Loyalty. *Journal of Marketing* 72 (6): 19–30.

xvii. Some readers may see a connection between the addition of higher priced products to a concept called "the wheel of retailing." The wheel describes a hypothesis that many retailers first enter a market as low-price and low-quality competitors, but then trade up to higher-quality and higher-price products to generate growth. The hypothesis was first formulated by Harvard Professor Malcolm McNair. For more of the history see: Hollander, S. (1960). The Wheel of Retailing. *Journal of Marketing* 25 (1): 37–42.

xviii. One of us is studying the patterns of who supplies private labels to major retailers in the Spanish grocery market, and early results reveal that "dual branding" (i.e., supply of both national brands and private label) by national brand manufacturers is very common. Across the six major retailers, on average almost 80% of the total number of private-label suppliers identified in the study are dual branders, and they are not just small fringe national brand manufacturers.

xix. Quelch, J., and Harding, D. (1996). Brands Versus Private Labels: Fighting to Win. *Harvard Business Review* (January–February).

xx. Dunne, D. and Narasimhan, C. (1999). The New Appeal of Private Labels. *Harvard Business Review* (May–June).

xxi. For a more detailed discussion of private label supply by national brands, we refer the interested reader to two books, *Private Label Uncovered* by Koen A.M. de Jong, and a recent one titled *Retail Disruptors: The Spectacular Rise and Impact of the Hard Discounters* by Jan-Benedict E.M. Steenkamp and Laurens Sloot.

xxii. One article finds evidence that top national brand manufacturers who supply private label to limited assortment retailers (Aldi in Germany and Mercadona in Spain) earn some goodwill in the form of shelf space for their national brands: ter Braak, A., Deleersnyder, B., Geyskens, I., and Dekimpe, M. (2013). Does Private-Label Production by National-Brand Manufacturers Create Discounter Goodwill? *International Journal of Research in Marketing* 30: 343–357.

xxiii. Ailawadi, K., and Harlam, B. (2004). An Empirical Analysis of the Determinants of Retail Margins: The Role of Store Brand Share. *Journal of Marketing* 68 (1): 147–166. Ailawadi, K., Pauwels, K., and Steenkamp, J.B. (2008). Private Label Use and Store Loyalty. *Journal of Marketing* 72 (6): 19–30.

xxiv. US. v. Colgate & Co., 250 U.S. 300 (1919).

xxv. Hovenkamp, H. (2005). *The Antitrust Enterprise*. Cambridge, MA: Harvard University Press.

xxvi. See details of a 2014 FTC/DOJ Workshop on Conditional Pricing Practices at http://www.ftc.gov/news-events/events-calendar/2014/06/conditional-pricing-practices-economic-analysis-legal-policy.

xxvii. Hovenkamp, H. (2005). *The Antitrust Enterprise*. Cambridge, MA: Harvard University Press.

xxviii. We refer the reader to the original law and to the FTC's guidance on it at http://www.ftc.gov/tips-advice/competition-guidance/guide-antitrust-laws/price-discrimination-robinson-patman.

xxix. See, for example: Steuer, R. (2012). Crossing the Streams of Price and Promotion Under the Robinson-Patman Act. *Antitrust Magazine* 27 (1).

xxx. Luchs, R., Geylani, T., Dukes, A., and Srinivasan, K. The End of the Robinson-Patman Act? Evidence from Legal Case Data. *Management Science* 56 (12): 2123–2133.

PART II

METRICS, TOOLS, AND FRAMEWORKS FOR GETTING THE RIGHT DISTRIBUTION

CHAPTER **7**

Metrics for Intensity and Depth of Distribution Coverage*

7.1 INTRODUCTION

Thus far, we have laid the groundwork for understanding the new channel ecosystem, from the nature of intermediaries to questions of conflict and power in channel relationships. With this fundamental knowledge in place, we can now turn to a crucial question for marketers anywhere, and especially in this multichannel

---

*Much of the material in this chapter was also published as part of an invited article in the 2017 special issue of the *Journal of Retailing* on "The Future of Retailing." The full citation is: Ailawadi, K., and Farris, P. (2017). "Managing Multi- and Omni-Channel Distribution: Metrics and Research Directions," *Journal of Retailing* 93 (1): 120–135.

environment: how much and what type of distribution coverage do we need? The first step in answering this question is to find the specific metrics that will facilitate reliable analysis of the relationship between distribution and marketing objectives. In this chapter, we set up a framework for doing this and discuss in detail metrics for distribution coverage and depth. In the next chapter, we focus on metrics for distribution performance.

Marketers have developed a number of measures to assess the state of their distribution. Many of these metrics have to do with the breadth or reach of their product availability, but just as important are those that reflect depth or quality of distribution, and the two are not independent of each other, as we noted in Chapters 2 and 3. Getting breadth right helps to get the depth right too. And together, breadth and depth of distribution drive performance in the market, both for the upstream supplier and its downstream resellers. Good breadth and depth metrics can guide the efforts of marketers to match distribution to market demand and "tune" the system to improve performance.

The basic metrics for measuring distribution breadth and depth in the brick-and-mortar world are well-known, but online and mobile commerce make some of these metrics less relevant and require some new ones. The metrics we present also address the need for marketers, both upstream and downstream, to change their mindset about the extent to which different channels compete with and complement one another. Suppliers are wise to consider whether channel partners are behaving in ways that will support the brand and customer experience for both sides and figure out how to measure, and reward, the contributions of different channel members along the path to purchase.

7.2 A FRAMEWORK FOR MEASURING DISTRIBUTION AND MATCHING IT TO DEMAND

Figure 7.1 is a useful way for marketers to think about measuring distribution breadth and depth, and managing them for sustainable channel performance. There are feedback loops between the four parts of the framework, as we noted in our organizing framework of Chapter 2. These loops need to be monitored and managed to keep the system in balance so that distribution doesn't get too far ahead of or behind demand, and so the performance of the supplier doesn't get too far ahead of or behind the performance of retail partners.

Recall from Chapter 2 that distribution breadth captures both the different types of distribution channels being used (e.g., omni-channel

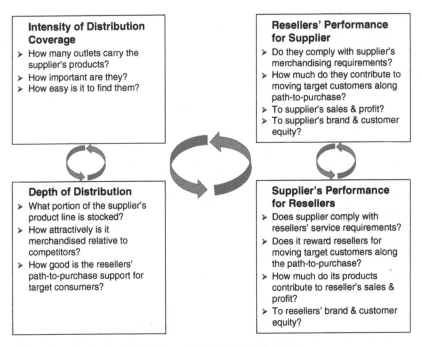

Intensity of Distribution Coverage
➤ How many outlets carry the supplier's products?
➤ How important are they?
➤ How easy is it to find them?

Resellers' Performance for Supplier
➤ Do they comply with supplier's merchandising requirements?
➤ How much do they contribute to moving target customers along path-to-purchase?
➤ To supplier's sales & profit?
➤ To supplier's brand & customer equity?

Depth of Distribution
➤ What portion of the supplier's product line is stocked?
➤ How attractively is it merchandised relative to competitors?
➤ How good is the resellers' path-to-purchase support for target consumers?

Supplier's Performance for Resellers
➤ Does supplier comply with resellers' service requirements?
➤ Does it reward resellers for moving target customers along the path-to-purchase?
➤ How much do its products contribute to reseller's sales & profit?
➤ To resellers' brand & customer equity?

Figure 7.1 Measuring distribution and distribution performance.

retailers, pure-play online retailers, marketplaces, direct-to-consumer stores/website/app) and the intensity of coverage, and distribution depth captures the quality of distribution. Since listing the types of distribution channels is fairly straightforward, we will focus here on metrics for the intensity and depth of distribution coverage.

Distribution coverage is about how easy it is for prospective buyers to find a stocking outlet—either because the brand appears in many outlets, or because it is stocked in the most important or prominently situated ones. Distribution depth, on the other hand, is about how findable and attractive the brand is relative to its competition within a stocking outlet. Depth is high when a large percentage of the brand's product line is stocked, it is conspicuously merchandised in the outlet, and/or the reseller is helps consumers navigate the path to purchase.

The feedback between coverage and depth in Figure 7.1 captures their interdependence. The breadth of a supplier's distribution impacts the motivation of the stocking resellers to invest in depth. Healthy competition among resellers can positively affect depth. Not enough breadth means too little competition, so complacent resellers don't put in enough effort. And an overabundance of breadth means resellers overcompete by cutting their prices. As their margins shrink, they attempt to lower costs by decreasing their stock and shelf space, and shirking important functions such as offering a full product line or having knowledgeable sales staff. We documented some examples of this in Chapter 3.[1]

But why the reverse effect from depth to breadth? Because suppliers regularly gauge whether they need to adjust coverage by examining the depth of distribution they enjoy. But there are also two other reasons that will become clearer as we get further into this chapter. One is that depth determines an important aspect of breadth in online channels—their findability, such as the position of websites stocking the brand on the Search Engine Results Page (SERP). Metrics like landing page experience, click-through rates, and bounce rates, among other things, determine how high up a website will be on the organic portion of the SERP. And its position on sponsored search is a function of how much it invests in search advertising for relevant keywords. All of these are aspects of distribution depth. The other reason is that improving the depth of distribution for brands that consumers care about increases a reseller's category sales and importance. This in turn increases distribution coverage metrics that are weighted by the importance of stocking outlets.

Moving along to the right side of Figure 7.1, the breadth and depth of distribution affect performance in the market for both the supplier and the resellers. Yet, each party has a distinct viewpoint. The supplier is concerned with its own brands and what the reseller does to support and sell them. The reseller pays attention to an entire category and store and is watching how the supplier and its brands affect that performance. This difference in perspectives is of a piece with the double marginalization that we introduced in Chapter 3. As we explained, there is inevitable conflict in how the total channel efforts and profit should be apportioned. The two-sided arrow between the supplier's and retailer's perspective on performance illustrates the

---

[1] For the interested reader, Randolph Bucklin and his colleagues provide another interesting example, this one from the auto industry. They found that the shorter the distance to the closest and the tenth-closest dealer, the higher the likelihood that a consumer will choose a particular brand. But the shorter the latter distance, which reflects the intensity of competition and therefore the ability of a consumer to comparison shop, the better the deal for the consumer (great distribution depth!) and the lower the margin earned by the dealer.

beneficial nature of a balance that can keep the channel partnership going. It's simply unsustainable for either party to focus on its own performance at the expense of the other, even if they have the power to do so in the short term.

Finally, the feedback loop in the center of Figure 7.1 highlights the need to calibrate distribution breadth and depth with the performance of both suppliers and retailers by aligning distribution to market demand. In most markets, there is an "equilibrium" between a brand's distribution coverage and market share. The brand must be available enough to support its goals for market share and resellers need enough sales and margin to justify the shelf space and inventories. It is a precarious balance, since competitors are always introducing new products that seek their own niche in the distribution ecosystem or making investments in pull and push to kick-start demand and grow distribution. Meanwhile, intermediaries with new revenue models disrupt the status quo. So, the system must be continually monitored and adjusted to create better performance.

7.3 MEASURING STOCKING OUTLET FINDABILITY: METRICS FOR INTENSITY OF DISTRIBUTION COVERAGE

Figure 7.2 lists the three standard metrics for assessing distribution coverage in the offline world: Numeric, %All Commodity Volume (%ACV), and %Product Category Volume (%PCV), as well as others we have compiled that are particularly relevant to online distribution. They follow from the three interconnected questions about distribution coverage in Figure 7.1: "how many," "how important," and "how findable."[2]

Numeric distribution is simply a count of the outlets that carry a supplier's brand(s), either the number of stores (or "doors") or the number of reseller accounts. The former is very important offline, but online, the latter is enough since a reseller will usually have only one or two websites even if there may be many affiliates through which the consumer can reach the website and many landing pages for the same website. All other measures of breadth consider how important or easy to find an outlet is.

---

[2]The more outlets a retailer has, the easier they are to find (at least offline). And the easier they are to find, the more consumers shop there and the more important the outlets become.

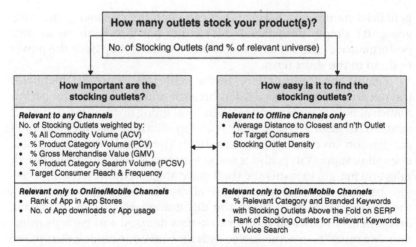

Figure 7.2 How to measure intensity of distribution coverage.

7.3.1 Importance of Outlets Can Be Measured by Their ACV, PCV, and GMV

Instead of just counting each stocking outlet equally, weighted measures reflect how important they are. %ACV weights outlets by their total sales of all commodities (All Commodity Volume). %PCV weights them by their total sales of the specific product category (Product Category Volume). For digital marketplaces, gross merchandise value (GMV)—the total dollar value of business done by third parties on their sites—is the appropriate analog to ACV. GMV, rather than the marketplace's revenue, reflects how important the marketplace is.[3]

We have constructed the graph in Figure 7.3 to highlight the difference between numeric and weighted (in this case by ACV) distribution. The graph uses 2018 data from Kantar on ACV and number of stores for those of the largest 100 retailers in the U.S. that sell at least some grocery products. We've sorted the retailers in order of their sales per store and plotted the cumulative percent of numeric stores versus the cumulative percent of total ACV. The retailers with the highest sales

---

[3]The revenue of the marketplace is made up only of its commissions (and advertising or other fees).

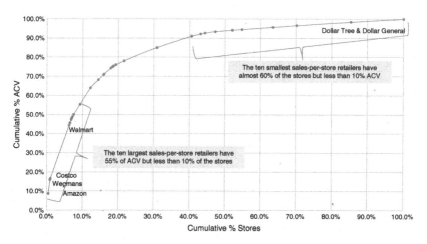

Figure 7.3 ACV versus number of stores of leading U.S. retailers selling groceries.

per store, at the lower left, account for 55% of ACV but make up less than 10% of total stores. In contrast, the flat part of the curve at the upper right shows that the long tail of small sales-per-store retailers account for about 60% of stores but less than 10% of ACV. So, ACV (and other weighted measures) collapse the long tail of outlets into equal percentage points of sales potential.

To illustrate the usefulness of weighted measures over numerical distribution, Figure 7.4 displays key data from 2013–2014 about the different channels in which running shoes are sold and the presence of the Brooks brand in each of these channels. It is the kind of distribution data that any good marketer should have at their fingertips, although we recognize that sometimes this advice is easier to offer than to implement. Especially when selling through wholesalers or distributors, it is easy for suppliers to lose sight of the reseller accounts that sell to end consumers.

Brooks is a leading performance running shoe brand that we will analyze in some depth in later chapters. But for now, let's look at this snapshot of its distribution breadth a few years ago and first go to the bottom row of the table. In total, the 4,376 stores that stock Brooks are just over 16% of the 26,781 stores in this retail "universe," but they account for almost half (48.6%) of running shoe sales.[4] So the brand's numeric distribution is 16% and its %PCV is 48.6%.

---

[4]In this computation, we have weighted each store within a channel equally. Ideally, one would weight individual doors, not just each channel, with their share of category

Channel Type	Channel's Share of Category	No. of Doors in Channel	No. of Doors Stocking Brooks	Contribution to Brooks PCV Distribution	Contribution to Brooks Numeric Distribution
Athletic/Gen. Sporting Goods (GSG)	48%	7800	1889	11.6%	7.1%
Chain Specialty	3%	557	235	1.2%	0.9%
Family Footwear	11%	2140	350	1.9%	1.3%
Specialty Running (SRA)	22%	1376	1376	21.9%	5.1%
Internet (pure play + omnichannel)	12%	66	66	11.9%	0.2%
Department Stores	2%	3366	100	0.1%	0.4%
Mass Merchants	0%	6076	0	0.0%	0.0%
Other	2%	5400	360	0.1%	1.3%
Total	100%	26781	4376	48.6%	16.3%

Figure 7.4   Numeric and PCV distribution for Brooks Running.

Looking at the types of retail formats that make up this universe, the department store and mass merchant channels have a lot of doors (as well as ACV), but they account for a miniscule share of running shoe sales. Brooks distributes most intensely in the specialty running accounts (SRA) channel—almost half of its %PCV (21.9% out of 48.6%) comes from SRA. As an aside, it is probably equally true that SRA stores, which target serious runners, are more open to proposals to stock Brooks shoes. Following SRA are the general sporting goods (GSG) and online channels, and the company has little to no presence in the long tail of department store and mass channels, which have a lot of stores but don't sell many running shoes.

So is one of these weighted measures more useful than the other? For mainstream products in mature CPG categories, %ACV and %PCV will likely provide a very similar picture of distribution coverage, especially if they are being tracked within a given retail format, such as the supermarket format or the drug store format. For new products in growing categories, %ACV is likely to be more useful because

---

sales. But Brooks does not have those data, despite its laser-sharp focus on distribution strategy, about which we will have much more to say in Chapter 12.

sales potential could be higher than the current size of the category. When the energy drink category was very new, it didn't make a lot of sense for Red Bull to use %PCV. In fact, in the very beginning, Red Bull selected "in" clubs with high visibility and the power to stimulate word of mouth, even if the actual sales and distribution coverage of these distribution outlets were not great. As the product market develops, ACV becomes more appropriate.[5] And even later, as the category matures and competition grows, suppliers need to become more focused on their share of the category, so %PCV becomes much more important.

In most other cases, especially for durable products in established categories, %PCV most closely expresses the share of the existing market reached through the stocking outlets. That's informative, but a shortcoming of %PCV is that it reflects where category sales are currently transacted, saying little about the possibility of increasing sales through other, growing channels. To that extent, it is a somewhat retrospective metric.

7.3.2 Traffic and Search Are Important, Perhaps Even More Than Sales Volume

An outlet without sufficient traffic can't garner many sales, and sales are increasingly not the entire picture. Even if many of the consumers who come through a high-traffic channel complete their purchases elsewhere, that channel can be valuable along the path-to-purchase. Furthermore, weighting distribution by traffic can be very useful for marketers of products that are purchased on impulse.

By the same token, outlets can be weighted by the volume of search that happens there, either overall or for a specific product category. In the shopper funnel, search is a little further down from visits, since consumers who search for something likely have some interest in buying it. It is also more future-oriented than %PCV.

For brick-and-mortar retailers, shopper reach and frequency are not reported as frequently as %ACV or %PCV, but can be meaningful indicators of sales potential and customer exposure. However, with mobile location data on large panels, market research companies can now offer such data. One example is Placed, a location

---

[5] Consider that much of 5-Hour Energy Shots' early distribution was in big-box stores (high ACV) and the marketing, unlike Red Bull, relied on heavy advertising to communicate product benefits.

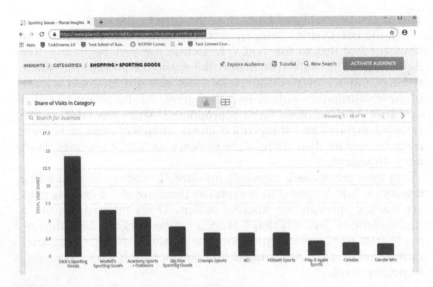

Figure 7.5 Visits to sporting goods retailers.

analytics firm now owned by Foursquare. Figure 7.5 is a screen shot of visit information to various sporting goods retailers from a free demonstration on the Placed website:[i]

Online, Alexa, Quantcast, ComScore, and other companies make it possible to monitor traffic and search metrics.

Traffic and search volume in the present are likely leading indicators of where sales are headed. Indeed, the increasing share of searches for more and more product categories that start on Amazon (versus, say, Google) give the e-tailer huge power over suppliers. Amazon probably nets the lion's share of purchases from those who search at the website, but many other retailers—both offline and online—don't. Weighting outlets by traffic and search, not just by sales, is necessary when consumers increasingly investigate products, check prices, make purchases, and pick items up (and maybe return them) all in different channels. Suppliers need to know where their target market searches and where it purchases—to measure and adjust distribution breadth, and to decide which channel partners need to be rewarded for what functions.

For a host of products (especially performance, prestige, and niche brands), what matters is not the total traffic (or search or sales) an outlet garners, but the traffic, category search, and category sales, it gets from the brand's *target consumers*. Daniel Lubetzky, founder and CEO of Kind LLC, writing about discipline in expanding distribution, says, "It's important to figure out which store sells to your true consumer—the most frequent, the most loyal buyer of your goods. You need to honor those accounts with a lot of TLC and support."[ii]

To see the distinction more clearly, review the Brooks distribution data in Figure 7.4. Judging by those numbers, a person might reasonably surmise that Brooks was under-distributed in some of the channels that sell many running shoes, especially in GSG. Nearly half the running shoes were sold through GSG, but this channel represented less than a quarter of Brooks' %PCV (11.6% out of 48.6%). Brooks, however, targets runners, not running shoe buyers. So it determines the importance of channels from where runners research and buy running shoes. Many people wear running shoes while, say, mowing the lawn or strolling in the neighborhood. These consumers focus on different shoe characteristics (style, color, and low price) than do Brooks' core target market of avid runners. SRAs have a larger share of what Brooks calls "running doors" than does GSG, and certainly a lot more than the family footwear channel.

7.3.3 Online or Offline, Stocking Outlets Have to Be Findable

For those convenience products consumers buy most frequently—and CPGs are a prime example—people are not interested in searching or traveling far. In the world of physical retail outlets, market coverage for these products is most strongly indicated by store density and the average distance that consumers must travel to the nearest store. Even for major purchases that consumers research heavily, such as automobiles, distance to the closest dealer is important. Yes, consumers trek farther for a car than for dish soap, but they also keep in mind the convenience factor of getting a car serviced near home. And because consumers also like comparison shopping, density and distance to, say, the tenth-closest dealer, are important as well.[iii]

Brands that either own or franchise their retail outlets (Starbucks), or use exclusive distributors (Stihl chainsaws) will find that ACV or PCV metrics are not particularly meaningful or relevant. Numeric distribution is useful for them but density and distance are even better, especially when these metrics are compared to competitors and calculated for relevant market segments. And, with the rich zip code and census tract level data on incomes, buying power indices, lifestyles, and preferences that companies like Claritas and LiveRamp (previously called Acxiom) offer, marketers have even more choices on how to weight outlets by their access to target consumers.

Distance and traffic volume are the bases for many models of retail site location. Franchise operators, such as hotels and fast-food restaurants, excel in developing models for locating new outlets based on traffic volume and flows, ease of access, and visibility. They have learned how to locate not only for visibility and traffic, but also to make it easier for consumers to find them as needed and relevant. Upstream marketers can employ similar models to estimate the probability of target consumers shopping at stocking outlets. In turn these probabilities can be used to weight the importance of retail outlets in assessing distribution coverage. Online, density may be irrelevant, but findability certainly is not. So we need measures of the ease with which a consumer searching for the product category or the brand can find a site that stocks it. The appearance of stocking outlets on the first SERP for a category or branded keyword is an effective gauge of findability. Placement at the top of the organic search section will probably correlate with PCV; after all, outlets with high sales of the searched-for category and/or the brand will logically be deemed more relevant by search engine algorithms. But even small outlets can appear "above the fold" (visible on the screen without scrolling down) on the SERP if they invest smartly in search advertising. And, as Google, Instagram, Pinterest, and others start offering "shoppable ads" with prices and the ability to buy embedded within the image of a product, that advertising becomes a distribution outlet![iv] This is why we said earlier that, in the online world, distribution and advertising are increasingly hard to separate.

On desktops, it may be less important to have the first position on the SERP. Click-through rates on ads go down faster than conversion rates with position.[v] Serious buyers, for instance, may examine lower positions more than mere window-shoppers and will also tend to buy more from outlets not at the top of the list. Also, prominent brands don't benefit as much from being in the top position as their less prominent competitors.[vi] But on small mobile screens and in voice searches, the top rank is very important.[vii] Furthermore, as mobile users switch from the mobile Internet to apps, the number of app downloads of stocking outlets, or the average rank of stocking outlets' apps in the app stores, become additional distribution breadth metrics to watch. While it's true that consumers never use many of the apps they download, app usage does increase sales.[viii] Moreover, if consumers don't download a stocking outlet's apps, the supplier's products may not make it into the consumer's purchase funnel at all.

The chart in Figure 7.6 compares online findability for the major running-shoe brands. Here is how we created the chart. We first

Brand	% Organic Sites Stocking the Brand	% Sponsored Sites Stocking the Brand	% PLAs Stocking the Brand
Nike	0.93	0.38	0.59
Asics	0.86	0.43	0.59
Brooks	0.86	0.24	0.48
Mizuno	0.86	0.23	0.47
Saucony	0.86	0.24	0.43
New Balance	0.86	0.36	0.79
Adidas	0.86	0.37	0.54
Reebok	0.57	0.46	0.46
Columbia	0.00	0.23	0.31
North Face	0.29	0.16	0.44
Puma	0.57	0.22	0.42

Read as: Across the ten highest volume category keywords, 93% of the sites on the first SERP in the organic search section stock Nike. The corresponding percentages for Nike in the sponsored search and PLA sections are 38% and 59% respectively.

Figure 7.6 Findability metrics for running-shoe brands online.

identified the ten highest-volume category keywords (e.g., "running shoes," "best running shoes," "trail running shoes," etc.). We then did a search with each keyword and checked whether each of the sites appearing on the first SERP (in organic, sponsored, and PLA sections) stocked each brand.[6] That allowed us to calculate the percentages shown in the chart. We have arranged the brands in decreasing order of market share (Nike has the highest share and Puma the lowest). There is low variation in these online breadth metrics across the larger share brands, which is reminiscent of the tendency of ACV and PCV for high-share CPG brands to cluster between 90% and 100%. The variation is even smaller for metrics based on branded keywords. This is due to the fact that—other than keyword poachers—the outlets appearing above the fold on the first SERP generally do carry the brand.[ix]

Finding the product is not particularly helpful unless the consumer can get it quickly, and the speed and cost (to the consumer) of delivery, especially in the online channel, is an increasingly important aspect of distribution breadth. As Amazon, Zappos, and other online retailers upped the ante on delivery, with two-day becoming standard and

---

[6]We did this analysis when organic search results were not pushed as far down on Google's SERP as they were later.

"same-day" becoming the objective, brick-and-mortar retailers have responded with click-and-collect and drive-by-windows or reserved parking for in-store pickup. But the cost to marketers of providing quick delivery is high, and not all online shoppers are looking for quick delivery all of the time. Some, like Walmart-owned online marketplace Jet.com, have experimented with offering lower prices to consumers in return for savings on delivery costs (e.g., when consumers accept slower deliveries or bundle their shopping from one seller, or choose a seller who is located closer by).

7.3.4 The Double-Edged Sword of Increasing Importance of a Channel Member

It is clear that the weighted metrics for distribution coverage can increase either because more channel partners are added or because existing channel partners become more important and therefore get higher weights. The better a specific channel or channel member is at performing the functions that consumers value (recall the functions we laid out in some detail in Chapter 4), the more important it becomes. Not all of these functions may be performed in service of the brand. In fact, most are performed to enhance the retailer's importance (as measured by traffic, ACV, and PCV in many product categories). Walmart's importance grew by leaps and bounds in the 1990s and the early part of the 2000s as it expanded its locational convenience with new stores and offered a vast assortment of categories under one roof, all at "always the low price." With this growth, the distribution coverage of suppliers whose products were stocked by Walmart grew even if they did not expand distribution with other retailers. And the distribution coverage of those who did not sell through Walmart shrank. The last decade has seen similar growth by Amazon, the "everything store" that delivers products to your doorstep, often in one day. The effective distribution coverage of products that are stocked by Amazon has been growing because the company has been performing some functions—product assortment and delivery—particularly well.

It is not hard to see how distribution that grows in this way can be a double-edged sword. On one hand, you want your distribution channel partners to perform channel functions well and you want the most important channels to stock your products, but on the other hand, you want consumers to build search loyalty to your brand, not to the channel partner. Netflix grew into the largest video streaming company through the large amount of programming that content providers licensed to it (in addition, of course, to its own investments in programming). Those content providers were happy to earn licensing revenue until the pressure that pay TV came under from cord-cutters spurred them to build their own direct-to-consumer streaming channels.[7] Now they face a formidable competitor in Netflix, the channel partner that their content helped make strong. They are taking back some of their most-watched content from Netflix—for example, reruns of *Friends* and *The Office* will only be available on Warner Media's and NBCUniversal's own streaming services, respectively.

Amazon's Accelerator program, which we mentioned in the previous chapter, is even more of a double-edged sword. Amazon is offering to increase distribution depth for sellers' brands but openly laying claim to those brands if or when they become successful—and that too at a low, low, fixed price.

7.3.5 Integrate Metrics Across Offline and Online Channels

To combine offline and online coverage into overall coverage, marketers can recompute each stocking outlet's ACV or PCV (or GMV for a marketplace) as a percentage of the total (offline plus online) in the geographical market. While not easy, it is well worth the effort to obtain the data on each outlet's online sales in the specific market. If a brand is looking to fill holes in offline coverage in widely dispersed, low-population areas, for example, the aggregation can be done at the brand level. On the other hand, if the goal is to improve availability of specific SKUs that are preferred only by small segments and therefore less likely to be stocked by offline stores, aggregation can be done at the SKU level.

Another way to aggregate offline and online breadth is by combining traffic. The challenge with traffic is that some consumers visit both stores and websites, and one needs that information so as not to double-count. It will comprise showroomers, webroomers, or multichannel shoppers, and the larger the overlap among channels, the greater the need for an integrated strategy.

Mobile is a great way for marketers to integrate digital shoppers with brick and mortar channels. It has expanded marketers' ability to help consumers locate and access brick-and-mortar outlets and is revitalizing the importance of numeric distribution, density, and distance. Location-based messages and maps can make it easier to find a store,

---

[7] We will discuss pay TV and media in more detail in Chapter 12.

as well as a shelf or product in the store. Furthermore, suppliers and retailers can use mobile to direct the consumer to a website or a product page online based on a scanned bar or QR code, a voice description, or an image.

7.4 METRICS FOR DISTRIBUTION DEPTH

The metrics for intensity of distribution coverage, whether are they weighted or unweighted, generally refer to "brand" distribution—if an outlet stocks at least one stock keeping unit (SKU) of the brand, it is considered a "stocking outlet." So, for brands that have a large product line and have garnered shelf space in most retail outlets, those

Any Channels	Offline Only	Online/Mobile Only
What portion of the product line is stocked?		
▪ Total SKU Distribution ▪ Share of Total Distribution in Category		
How attractively is it merchandised relative to competitors?		
▪ Share of SKUs in Store ▪ Store Within a Store ▪ % Time on Promotion ▪ % Promotional Discount	▪ Share of Shelf ▪ Share of Facings ▪ % Time on Special Display	▪ % of Reseller PLAs with Brand in Text ▪ Share of Thumbnails ▪ Brand on Landing Page ▪ Rank in Search Results ▪ Average Clicks to Find/Buy Brand ▪ % SKUs Above the Fold on Product Pages ▪ % Times with "Buy Box"
How well are buyers of supplier's products supported along the path-to-purchase?		
▪ Product Information Availability ▪ Inventory Information Across Resellers' Channels ▪ Ability to Buy Online and Pick-up/Return in Store	▪ No. and % of Staff Trained on Brand ▪ Ability to Order Online in store	▪ Availability of Chat Bots and Live Chat Staff Trained on Brand ▪ Inventory and Location Information in Nearest Store(s)

Figure 7.7 Distribution depth metrics.

Brand Distribution measures can be close to 100% and not vary much over time. These brands need more granular measures of distribution. Further, brand availability is just the first step. Astute marketers must also monitor how attractive the brand looks inside the store. Several years ago, P&G coined the term "First Moment of Truth" for what the shopper encounters in the store. Although there is now also a Z(ero)MOT, thanks to Google, the importance of the FMOT is far from diminished. In fact, many consumer goods manufacturers now have shopper marketing departments whose primary job is to partner with retailers to improve in-store attractiveness in ways that create win-wins for both parties. Figure 7.7 presents some important metrics for monitoring distribution depth, organized under the three questions about depth that we introduced in Figure 7.1: "how much," "how prominently merchandised," and "how well-supported along path-to-purchase."

7.4.1 Total Distribution Provides More Information Than Brand Distribution

Total Distribution measures the number of SKUs of a brand that are in distribution. Some companies also refer to it as Total Distribution Points. Specifically, it is the sum of ACV- or PCV-weighted distribution of individual SKUs of the brand. So it combines elements of distribution coverage with elements of the depth of that coverage. For the type of brands we mentioned earlier, whose Brand Distribution may be maxed out, Total Distribution is a more useful metric.[8] Figure 7.8 illustrates that with the two metrics for a major disposable diaper brand in one U.S. market. You can see substantial variation in total Distribution over time, while Brand %PCV Distribution is almost 100% for most of the four-year period.

But even growth in a brand's Total Distribution may not be worth much if the number of SKUs in the category is rising faster, or the SKUs being placed in distribution are not appealing to consumers. Marketers need to monitor competitive Total Distribution patterns closely to avoid falling behind, so a brand's share of Total Distribution in the category is a useful variant of Total Distribution that can assess the brand's presence relative to competitors.

---

[8]It is most useful when combined with the number of SKUs in distribution because Total Distribution of 1000% might mean 10 SKUs with 100% distribution each, 100 SKUs with an average of 10% distribution or any other combination of the number and average distribution of the SKUs in the product line.

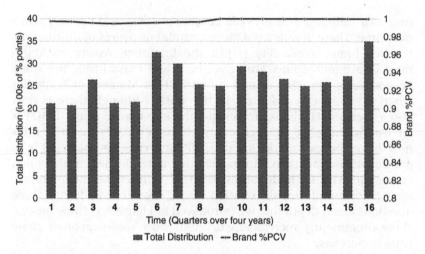

Figure 7.8 Total Distribution and Brand %PCV for a major brand.

7.4.2 Aggregate Other Depth Metrics Only Across Stocking Outlets

The remaining depth metrics all assess the prominence of a brand in stocking outlets.[9] Having a greater share of shelf and/or SKUs, or more frequent or more visible promotions in the store, will influence consumer choices at the point-of-purchase, whether online or in a physical store. The general location of the brand within the store, and the product categories it is next to, can also be an important aspect of distribution depth in some cases. Most of the time, a product will be placed along with others in its obvious category. But sometimes there is more than one place. Silk soymilk was originally distributed in the dry grocery section, because the product did not require refrigeration to maintain an extended shelf life. However, the company found that changing the package and relocating to the refrigerated section of grocery stores, next to cow's milk, was a turning point. Consumers don't expect to find "fresh milk" with dry grocery so they probably don't look there, and if they do see it there, they may think of it as processed and not fresh. But the refrigerated section of the store, being limited in

---

[9]Because the notion of distribution depth applies to each outlet that carries the brand, the depth within outlets is aggregated across outlets to get overall metrics for a brand in the market. This is important and confusing enough that some readers may find it worth their time to go through the example we have provided in the appendix.

space and more expensive to operate, comes with higher expectations for turnover rates and competent inventory management.

Unconstrained by physical shelf space, there is a huge variety of products available online. And that makes ensuring the prominence of a brand's SKUs on a website even more critical online (especially on mobile) than it is offline. Product thumbnails that are "below the fold" on the home page can easily lose sales to competitors that are easier to see. This is why apps offer (temporary) exclusivity to one or the other app store in exchange for premium placement on the home page or feature lists, and hotels fund Booking.com's discounts for members of its "Genius" loyalty program to get better placement on the online travel agent's listings. As consumers migrate online (especially on mobile) for convenience and ease of purchase, new metrics for distribution depth are becoming more and more important. These include a brand's presence on the stocking site's landing page, its rank in search results on the stocking site, the number of clicks it takes to get to it, whether it has the "Buy Box" on Amazon, or a voice assistant recommends it. Meanwhile, the location-based abilities of mobile are being leveraged to improve distribution depth offline. For example, consumers receive offers of assistance when they are in the store, and promotional offers when they are within a specified geographical radius of one's own outlet (called geo-fencing) or a competitor's outlet (called geo-conquesting).

7.4.3 Getting the Data to Monitor These Metrics

As we've seen, distribution metrics are easier to capture online than in the brick-and-mortar world. Figure 7.9 shows some of the online depth metrics for the same brands as in Figure 7.5. Most major brands are similar on metrics, such as the percentage of outlets in organic and sponsored search results where they appear on the landing page. But there is much more variation in others, such as the percentage of Product Listing Ads (PLAs) from outlets that have the brand on the landing page or mention the brand in the ad. PLAs by resellers are a type of "feature" on the SERP with limited space—just enough to show an image and a special price. The difference is notable between brands such as Nike, which is heavily promoted, and others like Brooks, which try to avoid heavy discounting.

For offline depth metrics, the workhorse is still store audits and salesperson visits. But marketers are beginning to use AI and machine learning tools to extract information from a variety of other sources of data. Some retailers deploy robots to go around the store every night taking pictures of the shelves and aisles that can then be processed to monitor in-store execution of planogram and displays, identify and

Brand	% Organic Sites with Brand on Landing Page	% Sponsored Sites with Brand on Landing Page	% PLAs with Brand on Landing Page	% PLAs with Brand Name in Text
Nike	0.71	0.26	0.34	0.31
Asics	0.79	0.32	0.14	0.08
Brooks	0.79	0.16	0.17	0.06
Mizuno	0.79	0.08	0.04	0.02
Saucony	0.57	0.08	0.01	0.01
New Balance	0.64	0.18	0.29	0.21
Adidas	0.64	0.21	0.02	0.00
Reebok	0.50	0.25	0.04	0.00
Columbia	0.00	0.06	0.00	0.00
North Face	0.14	0.04	0.04	0.02
Puma	0.50	0.03	0.00	0.00

Read as: Across the ten highest volume category keywords, 93% of the sites on the first SERP in the organic search section stock Nike. The corresponding percentages for Nike in the sponsored search and PLA sections are 38% and 59% respectively.

Figure 7.9 Online distribution depth for running-shoe brands.

predict out-of-stocks, and guide inventory management. There are also options for marketers who don't have the necessary expertise in-house to develop such tools. For example, Amazon Web Services has released DeepLens, a kit for developers that uses machine learning to identify people, objects, and so on, complete with programmable video camera, tutorials, code, and pretrained models and the company is exploring applications and demand in brick-and-mortar retail.

7.5 CONCLUSION

From the point of view of the upstream supplier, many of the "depth" measures are also indicators of how well the distribution channel is performing. But they are intervening measures and will not by themselves suffice to assess the health of the overall channel relationship. In the next chapter, we discuss the full set of performance metrics that marketers, both up- and downstream, should monitor to make sure distribution is being managed well and sustainably.

Summary

- As channel alternatives and data sources have multiplied, so have metrics for the breadth, depth, and performance of distribution.

▓ Many traditional metrics face challenges in transferring to online channels as the latter combine consumer search with availability and distribution with advertising.

▓ Distribution coverage is more about the importance and findability of stocking outlets than their number. Importance of stocking outlets in the brick-and-mortar space is measured by total sales, GMV, product category sales, traffic, and especially traffic from the target market. Findability of stocking outlets online is measured by position on the SERP and in voice search.

▓ Total Distribution is a more diagnostic metric than Brand Distribution, especially for brands with large product lines that already have at least one SKU on the shelf in most of the important outlets.

▓ Distribution depth was always, at least in part, a consequence of breadth, but the reverse is also true online, where depth affects findability.

▓ Depth is measured by share of SKUs and share of shelf space, but also by number of clicks to find the brand on a stocking outlet's landing page, the number of clicks to order it, and its appearance in response to voice search.

APPENDIX: AN EXAMPLE TO CALCULATE BASIC DISTRIBUTION METRICS

Figure A7.1 depicts the grocery market of a small but energetic U.S. town called Smallville. It has four stores. Each of these stores carries two of the largest brands of energy drinks, which the townspeople imbibe with great relish and frequency. The convenience store, supermarket, drug store, and mass merchant sell 20%, 30%, 15%, and 35% respectively of total product category volume in Smallville. Armed with a picture of how the energy drink aisle looks in each store, we can set about computing several measures of the distribution depth of Red Bull and Monster. We will take PCV weighted averages across the four stores (we could also have used ACV or any of the other measures of outlet importance discussed in the chapter).

Note, for starters, that all four stores stock at least one SKU of Red Bull but the drug store doesn't stock Monster at all. So Brand %PCV Distribution is 100% for Red Bull and 85% for Monster. But the number of SKUs stocked, the number of shelf facings, and promotions also vary across stores for the two brands. And depth metrics that are computed by averaging across all four stores will be different (and will look worse) for Monster than metrics that are computed by averaging only across stores that stock the brand. That is why we show two

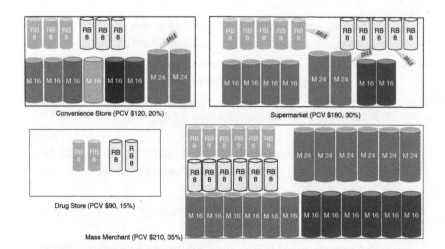

Convenience Store (PCV $120, 20%)

Supermarket (PCV $180, 30%)

Drug Store (PCV $90, 15%)

Mass Merchant (PCV $210, 35%)

Distribution Depth Metrics Across All Stores

Metric	Red Bull	Monster
PCV Weighted Total Distribution	200%	315%
PCV Weighted Avg. No. of SKUs in Store	2.00	3.15
PCV Weighted Avg. Share of SKUs in Store	46.0%	54.0%
PCV Weighted Avg. Share of Facings in Store	54.2%	45.8%
PCV Weighted Avg. Stores with Brand Promotion	30.0%	50.0%

Distribution Depth Metrics Across Stocking Stores

Metric	Red Bull	Monster
PCV Weighted Avg. No. of SKUs in Store	2.00	3.71
PCV Weighted Avg. Share of SKUs in Store	46.0%	63.5%
PCV Weighted Avg. Share of Facings in Store	54.2%	53.8%
PCV Weighted Avg. Stores with Brand Promotion	30.0%	58.8%

Figure A7.1 The Smallville energy drink market.

sets of metrics in the figure. Both are useful, but the first is affected by distribution breadth while the second is not. The first tells us how the brand presents on average across all stores. The second tells us how it presents in stocking stores.

Let's walk through the calculation of one metric—Total Distribution, which computes the PCV weighted distribution of each individual SKU and adds across all the SKUs of the brand that are in distribution. Red Bull has the same two SKUs in each of the four Smallville stores, so each of those two SKUs has 100% PCV Distribution, making Red Bull's Total Distribution equal to 200%. Monster, on the other hand, has a total of six SKUs, all of which are stocked in the convenience store. Three of them are also stocked in the supermarket and mass store, and of course, the drug store doesn't carry any of them. So, Monster's six SKUs have PCV Distribution of 85%, 20%, 20%, 20%, 85%, and 85% respectively, adding up to Total Distribution of 315%. In other words, we would expect that, on average, an energy drink buyer in Smallville would encounter 3.15 of Monster's SKUs and 2 of Red Bull's on a given store's shelf. Of course, we still need to monitor the 85% brand PCV distribution, which tells us that 15% of energy drink sales occur in a store that doesn't stock any of Monster's SKUs. If we only looked at Total Distribution of the two brands within stores that stocked them, Red Bull remains at 200%, while the number for Monster gets a little better at 371% because it is not pulled down by the absence of the brand in the drug store.

ENDNOTES

i. Placed.com (2019). Insights into shopping for sporting goods. https://www.placed.com/ui/insights/categories/shopping-sporting-goods (accessed 25 April).

ii. Lubtezky, D. (2015). *Do the KIND Thing.* (New York: Ballantine Books).

iii. See, for example, the article by Bucklin, Siddarth, and Silva-Risso that we referenced earlier: Bucklin, R., Siddarth, S., and Silva-Risso, J. (2008). Distribution Intensity and New Car Choice. *Journal of Marketing Research* 45 (5): 473–486.

iv. Forman, L. (2019). Instagram's Shopping Tabs Turn Clicks into Cash. *Wall Street Journal* (19 March) p. B1.

v. Agrawal, A., Hosanagar, M., and Smith, D. (2011). Location, Location, Location: An Analysis of Profitability of Position in Online Advertising Markets. *Journal of Marketing Research* 48: 1057–1073.

vi. Jeziorski, P., and Moorthy, S. (2018). Advertiser Prominence Effects in Search Advertising. *Management Science* 64 (3): 983–1476.

vii. Ghose, A., Goldfarb, A., and Han, S. (2013). How Is the Mobile Internet Different? Search Costs and Local Activities. *Information Systems Research* 24 (3): 499–882.

viii. Dinner, I., van Heerde, H., and Neslin, S. (2015). Creating Customer Engagement Via Mobile Apps: How App Usage Drives Purchase Behavior. Tuck School of Business Working Paper No. 2669817.

ix. Poaching in search advertising refers to a brand bidding on the branded keyword for one or more of its competitors. Here are some articles that study the phenomenon: Sayedi, A., Jerath, K., and Srinivasan, K. (2014). Competitive Poaching in Sponsored Search Advertising and Its Strategic Impact on Traditional Advertising. *Marketing Science* 33 (4): 463-620. Simonov, A., Nosko, C., and Rao, J. (2018). Competition and Crowd-Out for Brand Keywords in Sponsored Search. *Marketing Science* 37 (2): 177–331.

CHAPTER **8**

What Are You Managing Towards?*

Distribution Performance Metrics

8.1   INTRODUCTION

*"You cannot manage what you cannot measure" is one
of the oldest clichés in management, and it's either false
or meaningless. It's false in that companies have always
managed things—people, morale, strategy, etc.—that are
essentially unmeasured. It's meaningless in the sense that*

---

*Much of the material in this chapter was also published as part of an invited article in the
2017 special issue of the *Journal of Retailing* on "The Future of Retailing." The full citation
is: K. Ailawadi and P. Farris (2017), "Managing Multi- and Omni-Channel Distribution:
Metrics and Research Directions," *Journal of Retailing* 93 (1): 120–135.

everything in business—including people, morale, strategy, etc.—eventually shows up in someone's ledger of costs or revenues.

—Thomas A. Stewart[1]

In the spirit of Tom Stewart's comment that everything eventually shows up in the top and bottom lines, growth in revenue, margin, and Economic Value Added may be the ultimate indicators of successful distribution management just as they are of channel power. We believe, however, that there is an important role for intermediate as well as more granular indicators that diagnose whether distribution strategy is on the right path. Recall from the framework we introduced at the beginning of the previous chapter that metrics for distribution performance should measure both how well the supplier and its brand(s) perform for the retailer *and* how well the retailer performs for the supplier and its brand(s).

Before serving up a generous helping of the alphabet soup of performance metrics, let's summarize what is old but still worth reviewing, and what is new(er). Absolutely ancient is the difference between dollar and percentage metrics. Though "per centum" dates back to Roman emperors, it constantly surprises us how the tension between dollars and percentages reemerges again and again in newer, more sophisticated measures of profit and percentages. Some of this tension is a result of firms focusing on growth as well as efficiency. Dollars better reflect size and growth (e.g., sales revenue, total margin, EVA) and percentages better reflect efficiency (e.g., margin as a percentage of sales or inventory). Of course, the difference in perspective between manufacturers and resellers—the former focused on an individual brand's performance and the latter on the performance of an entire category and store—is not new either.

What is new is the metrics for how well consumers are supported along a path-to-purchase that spans multiple channels. What may also be new to some is the emphasis on evaluating the profitability of individual customers and vendors to augment category, brand, and SKU calculations, and on linking brand equity with customer equity. Towards this end, retailers are using "market basket analysis" and loyalty program data to dig deeper into their relationship

---

[1]Thomas A. Stewart is a journalist and management thinker perhaps best known for his writings on intellectual capital, including the 1997 book *Intellectual Capital: The New Wealth of Organizations.*

with individual consumers and shed light on how they can design effective promotions—some of which may look like money losers but are not—to keep customers loyal, or at least coming back. Finally, customers are being valued as assets with forward-looking metrics such as customer lifetime value (CLV) and its aggregate for the firm: customer equity. However important the short-term goals of building traffic and sales, neglecting the longer-term objectives of increasing brand and customer equity is at the peril of both upstream and downstream marketers.

8.2 A HIERARCHY OF PERFORMANCE METRICS

The quest for a single metric that will do it all has thus far been unsuccessful, and we don't expect that to change. But we want to be clear that more performance metrics are only part of the answer. Better metrics, and getting them organized into a useful hierarchy, are just as important. So rather than looking for the silver bullet of metrics, our advice is to buckle down and measure what you can and organize the metrics for insights.

We find it helpful to organize distribution performance metrics into the four groups in Figure 8.1: (a) metrics that track compliance with the requirements of the channel partner; (b) those that monitor support along the path-to-purchase across channels; (c) sales, profitability, and growth oriented metrics; and (d) metrics that speak to longer-term

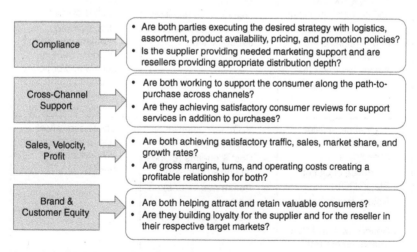

Figure 8.1 An organization for performance metrics.

brand and customer equity. In four separate figures, we offer a fairly comprehensive set of metrics in each group for easy reference. But instead of going through each one in detail, we highlight some major themes below.

8.2.1 Compliance Metrics Can Catch Problems Early

Intermediate compliance metrics such as those in Figure 8.2 are not ends in themselves. They can flag potential problems in the partnership before it is too late. Once suppliers decide to work with certain partners, they need to ensure that the partners provide the right distribution depth for their products and put to good use the money spent by the suppliers on allowances, marketing, or logistic support. So they monitor pass-through of trade promotional discounts to consumers, audit stores and websites for out-of-stocks (OOS), displays, and use their own staff or third-party companies to track abuses of minimum advertised price (MAP) or other resale price maintenance policies, and monitor whether too many visitors are walking out of a store without buying or abandoning their cart on a channel partner's website.

How Reseller Performs for Supplier	How Supplier Performs for Reseller	Comments
■ Trade Promotion Pass-through (in prices, markdowns, and/or merchandising) ■ Adherence to Resale Price Maintenance (RPM) or Minimum Advertised Price (MAP) policies	■ On-time payment of trade funds ■ Number of unauthorized resellers and % of supplier sales through them	■ Trade funding may be provided to maintain target retail prices or to offer discounts. ■ Unauthorized resellers may be due to poor inventory control and/or poorly designed promotional incentives that encourage diverting.
■ % On-time reseller deliveries to consumers ■ Incidence of Out of Stock (OOS) ■ Return rate by retailer's customers ■ Bounce rate and Cart abandonment rate	■ % On-time supplier shipments to reseller ■ Cost & on-time refunds on unsold inventory ■ Return rate by brand buyers ■ Cart abandonment rate	■ These can reflect poor performance of either supplier or retailer.

Figure 8.2 Compliance metrics.

Some elaboration is worthwhile here. Channel support in the form of trade promotions or other funding makes up a substantial portion of many suppliers' marketing budgets. In CPG, where more than half of the marketing budget is typically spent on trade promotions, suppliers are concerned about pass-through of those promotions in the form of temporary discounts. Pass-through rates can vary widely among suppliers and retailers. They tend to be low if the category is not very price sensitive, or if the retailer doesn't see an increase in its total category sales and profit when the supplier's brand is promoted, only a bump in the promoted brand's sales, if the retailer has more of the consumer's search loyalty than does the supplier and can negotiate a better deal for itself.[i] But trade funds may not always be intended to encourage discounts to consumers. Many suppliers, especially those who sell performance and prestige products (Apple, Nike, Brooks, and Samsung to name a few) may much rather have special displays, more effective in-store merchandising, than lower prices. In fact, they may want prices to be maintained rather than lowered. We will discuss these issues in detail in Chapters 14 and 15.

If a retailer is stocked out of the supplier's products, the fault may lie with either party. An out-of-stock (OOS) may have occurred because the supplier didn't ship complete orders on time, or because the retailer did not keep enough safety stock to supply consumer demand. Even the vaunted Walmart supply chain can face problems. The *Wall Street Journal* noted, "Grocery makes up 56% of the U.S. business and [Walmart] has been struggling to improve performance on its fresh products in the dairy, meat and produce aisles . . . trying to ensure items are in stock and on the shelves when customers want them."[ii] Some consider OOS to be a "good problem to have" if consumer demand surpasses the retailer's inventory or the supplier's production capacity. We don't agree—retailers don't have much patience for delayed shipments.[2] Even worse is the scenario in which a consumer is content to keep a given supplier's products OOS while switching consumers to other brands that it finds more profitable.

---

[2] According to one supplier, "If a product on their shelves sells well, and then you can't meet their inventory demands, they take your product out, and once you're out it's hard to get back in. It doesn't make sense for them to save shelf space for you if you can't give them inventory year-round." (*WSJ*, Nov 23, 2015, "Running the Show: Food Businesses Find Growth Hard to Digest.") Big brands are not immune from the ill effects of OOS either. In the summer of 2018, Michael Kors's sales per store dropped 2.1% from the same time last year and its share price dropped 15% in one day when the company ran out of stock, having cut inventory levels too much in anticipation of lower demand as they moved towards selling more products at full price.

The opposite scenario—excess inventory in the system—can also happen for many reasons. Authorized retailers may have ordered too much with the lure of volume discounts; product quality and/or consumer pull may be low; or the product portfolio may be bloated with a bad mix of items. The excess inventory brings its own problems. There are too many markdowns or product gets into the hands of unauthorized resellers. And that can happen faster online than ever before. As Mitch Ratcliffe, an entrepreneur and analyst in digital media, said, "A computer lets you make more mistakes faster than any other invention, with the possible exceptions of handguns and Tequila."

Other helpful intermediate metrics, such as high bounce rates and cart abandonment, have become particularly salient in online and mobile channels. These might indicate that the brand just isn't attractive enough, or retailers are not presenting it well, either because they don't want to make the effort, or because they don't know how and need guidance.

8.2.2 Cross- and Omni-Channel Metrics Are Increasing in Importance

The implementation of omnichannel strategies by retailers has increased pressure on suppliers to adopt and adapt by integrating across their many independent channels. Kurt Salmon consultants report on the evolving metrics needed to track these trends and we have included some important ones in Figure 8.3.[iii] A particularly sticky issue is frequent showrooming and webrooming by consumers. Suppliers and their channel partners have to decide whether they will minimize the opportunity and motivation for consumers to engage in these behaviors or embrace and them and try to manage them. Companies like LL Bean and Hallmark Retail that sell through multiple company-owned or licensed channels have made a lot of progress by rewarding their online and offline arms for total sales irrespective of where those sales are transacted. But, as we noted in earlier chapters, the job is much harder for a supplier who must deal with this practice across separate, independent retailers. Minimizing the opportunity and motivation may mean selling different products in different channels or reducing price differences across channels. Embracing it means some channel members must be rewarded for supporting a sale or the customer even if they don't make the sale.

It may not seem too difficult to motivate one retailer to deliver your product or accept returns on behalf of another. After all, Amazon is working with brick-and-mortar retailers like Kohl's to do just that, as you can see from the screenshot in Figure 8.4. But it is one thing for two

How Reseller Performs for Supplier	How Supplier Performs for Reseller	Comments
▣ Advocacy (Number or % of positive brand reviews by reseller's customers)	▣ Advocacy (Number or % of positive reviews by brand's buyers)	▣ Relevance of these metrics depends on number and type of channels and ease of tracking consumers across independent channels.
▣ Cross-Channel Conversions (Number of visitors served by reseller that subsequently buy the brand elsewhere)	▣ Own-Channel Support (Uniform price maintenance across channels, Exclusive products for retailer's channel)	▣ Whether own- or cross-channel support is relevant depends on whether goal is to discourage or embrace showrooming
▣ Cross-Channel Delivery or Returns (Number of purchases elsewhere delivered by, picked up at, and/or returned to reseller)	▣ Cross-Channel Support (Payments by supplier for cross-channel conversions, delivery and returns)	▣ Much easier to measure this behavior across a marketer's own online touch-points than across independent channels.

Figure 8.3 Omni- and cross-channel performance metrics.

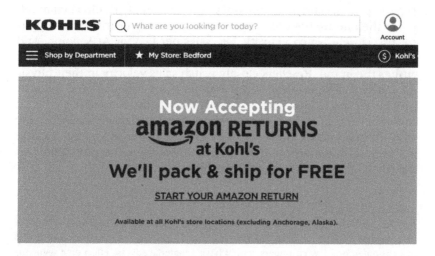

Figure 8.4 One retailer accepts another's returns.

retailers to work out a quid pro quo arrangement between themselves and quite another for a supplier to try to impose it on them.

As with compliance metrics, suppliers and resellers have their own perspectives on cross-channel metrics and agreement on who did what along the customer journey will be hard. Still, the metrics can flag a problem or an opportunity and begin the conversation—as long as both parties keep sight of the fact that these are only a means to an end. The end is the sales, profit, and longer-term performance metrics that we get to next.

8.2.3 Both Parties Care about Sales, Share, and Sales Velocity but in Slightly Different Forms

Sales and sales growth of their brands are the sine qua non for the health of the supplier, so these metrics, summarized in Figure 8.5, overshadow many others. Retailers care about sales and sales growth too, but, because they generally stock products from multiple suppliers and in several different categories, they care about total category and store sales in addition to the sales of particular brands. They can exchange low sales volume of a particular product for a high margin (recall double marginalization from Chapter 3).

Neither party wants to be too dependent on a single firm for a large portion of its revenue.[3] But resellers also don't want to put effort into brands if the giant share of sales goes to competing outlets, including or perhaps especially to online ones or to the supplier's direct channel.

In their desire not only to get but also to keep distribution, suppliers also closely watch velocity, i.e., sales per PCV or ACV point. And the Brand Development Index helps determine how much the retailer pushes the brand. Resellers closely watch sales velocity in their physical and virtual stores—per week and per square foot of shelf space or warehouse space. Low sales velocity is almost always a red flag when it comes to choosing which items to drop in order to make space for new ones. In many cases, however, they may be better served by tracking not only sales but also margin rates and watching the profitability of the customers drawn to their store by an item or brand.

---

[3]In fact, publicly traded companies are required to disclose their largest customers because that information is considered "material." The SEC requires disclosure if loss of a customer, or a few customers, would have a material adverse effect on a segment, while US GAAP (Generally Accepted Accounting Principles) requires disclosure of each customer that comprises 10 percent or more of total revenue.

How Reseller Performs for Supplier	How Supplier Performs for Reseller	Comments
▪ Brand sales (unit & $) per store and for total retail account ▪ Brand sales lift in market when on promotion at reseller ▪ Brand development index (brand's share of reseller's category sales, relative to brand's overall market share) ▪ Reseller's share of brand's total sales	▪ Brand sales (unit & $) per sq. ft. ▪ Category and store sales lift when brand is on promotion at reseller ▪ Retailer's share of total brand sales in market ▪ Share of total brand sales in the market that go to supplier's direct channel ▪ Brand's share of retailer's total sales	▪ Sq. ft. of warehouse space is relevant for online resellers. ▪ Portion of promotional lift that is incremental for supplier vs. reseller is quite different. ▪ Resellers are unhappy to lose sales to competitors or to supplier's direct channel. ▪ Neither party likes being too dependent on the other for its revenue.
▪ Brand velocity (sales per distribution point) ▪ Online sales per physical distribution point	▪ Brand velocity index (brand sales per sq. ft. ÷ category sales per sq. ft.) ▪ Brand's inventory turns (sales ÷ average inventory) ▪ Online sales per physical distribution point	▪ Sales and inventory may be measured in units or $. ▪ $ value of inventory is usually at average acquisition cost. ▪ Suppliers want to leverage physical availability to build online sales and resellers worry about cannibalization.
▪ Gross margin (GM) from retailer (unit and %, net of trade discounts) ▪ Total profit from retail account	▪ Gross and net margin from brand (unit & %) per sq. ft. ▪ Gross Margin Return on Inventory Investment from brand (GMROII = GM $s ÷ Average $ value of inventory) ▪ Direct Product Profitability (DPP)	▪ GMROII is increasingly important as retailers try to reduce inventory costs to compete in omnichannel environment. ▪ Turn & Earn, a relative of GMROII is % GM x Inventory Turns. ▪ DPP requires activity based costing.

Figure 8.5 Sales, velocity, and profit metrics.

8.2.4 Gross and Net Margins, Category, and Customer Profitability

Gross margin, as we explained in Chapter 5, serves as a foundation for marketers to evaluate pricing. On the face of it, gross margin is straightforward to calculate: the difference between selling price and cost of goods (a large part of which is manufacturer selling price from the retailer's perspective), expressed as a dollar value or a percentage of selling price. But in reality, it's more complicated. Promotions, uncertain pass-through rates, contingent rebates, markdowns, deductions, coupons and rebates with long expiration dates, and free goods are just a few of the reasons that figuring out gross margins for the thousands of SKUs in a typical retail operation is challenging. Suppliers deal with similar issues, with the additional complexity that accounting rules require them to deduct many promotional discounts from gross sales, while they may prefer to show them as marketing expenses further down in the financial statement because financial markets pay so much attention to top line growth.

A particularly relevant metric for resellers to manage their assortments is Gross Margin Return on Inventory Investment (GMROII). This metric, which combines inventory turns and gross margin, is crucial given that inventory can be one of a reseller's biggest costs, and one that traditional retailers are trying hard to control as they compete with online wizards of logistics like Amazon.

Because a retailer's other costs can vary widely, gross margins, even GMROII, don't paint the full picture. Direct Product Profit (DPP) subtracts from an item's net selling price all the costs associated with it—inventory carrying, stocking, shelf space, energy, checkout, delivery, returns, and so on. Activity-based costing (ABC) is used to ensure that the costs attributed to individual categories and items are not arbitrarily spreading overhead. DPP can discern between items with the same gross margin but very different net profitability for the retailer. Because it is a dollar metric (it also can be expressed as a ratio to sales), DPP can also separate items that have low and high sales rates—for instance, in comparisons of DPP per week. A word of caution: don't ignore delivery and return costs here, which classically didn't figure in DPP calculations but can ruin profitability. These costs are substantial overall but also vary widely across categories and across items in a category. Even Amazon, the master of logistics and delivery, is focusing on what are called CRaP ("Can't Realize a Profit") items within the company and either eliminating them or selling them in larger multi-unit packs at higher prices, demanding that suppliers change the packaging and also having them ship directly from their own warehouses.[iv]

We said earlier that retailers are concerned not just with individual items and brands but with the performance of the whole category and the whole store. Isn't the whole just the sum of the parts, you might ask? Well, yes, but . . . no. Attractive merchandising or temporary deals on one brand take sales from other brands in the store, so resellers (should) monitor the impact of one brand's marketing on sales and profit of the entire category—a topic we will return to in some depth in later chapters. Categories may also play specific roles for retailers and may be associated more with some types of retailers than others. For example, some build traffic or burnish the retailer's image; others attract frequent shopping trips and longer-term store loyalty. Depending the category's job for the retailer, item, brand, and even category profitability may be more or less significant. This is especially true of loss leaders, which we discussed in Chapter 3. Some deeply discounted items are temporary "door busters" to get immediate increases in sales and traffic, whereas others, like baby products, are routinely sold at small or even negative margins to get loyalty and share of wallet from growing families with children. These are not only excellent customers to attract in terms of their current shopping baskets, but they may offer even greater prospects for future sales and profits as children and appetites grow.

Which brings us to customer profitability and Figure 8.6. Marketers have always cared about and focused on satisfying their customers (at a profit, of course). CPG manufacturers often don't (can't?) measure the profitability of their millions of individual customers, but retailers regularly collect customer-transaction data from the members of their loyalty program. Increasingly, the more technologically savvy retailers are using loyalty programs not just to deliver discounts but to have a better understanding of the economic value of their customers. As a result, the retailers can gauge not only the sales and margins of various brands, but also the value of the consumers who buy those brands.[4] This effectively brings together the notions of "brand equity" with "customer equity."[v]

---

[4]Professor Yuxin Chen and his colleagues coined the term "marketing profits" in a 1999 article in the journal *Marketing Science* to assess how profitable a category is to a retailer based the profitability of the consumers who are drawn to the retailer because of the category. The term seems not to have caught on, but the concept remains important.

How Reseller Performs for Supplier	How Supplier Performs for Reseller	Comments
▪ Total brand sales to reseller's customers ▪ Lifetime value of channel's and reseller's customers for supplier	▪ Total sales and profit from brand customers (those who visit the reseller seeking the brand) ▪ Lifetime value of brand buyers for reseller	▪ Determining whether customer visited seeking the brand is difficult offline, but worthwhile. ▪ Online, those who arrive at a site after searching for a supplier's branded keyword can be identified.

Figure 8.6 Equity metrics.

As an example, one of us studied the profitability of private label products and product label buyers for retailers.[vi] It turns out that, while retailers earn higher percent gross margins on private label than on national brands, the dollar margins, especially net of all costs, are not necessarily higher. Furthermore, heavy users of private label are less loyal to, and less profitable for, retailers overall than medium users.[5] This is important for retailers to recognize, but also for their national brand suppliers to understand so that they can effectively negotiate with retailers. As another example, when Netflix negotiates with content producers on the licensing fee it pays for shows, and determines how to offset the loss of *The Office* and *Friends* (which, as we noted in Chapter 7 are being held back by content companies for their own streaming channels), Netflix needs to understand not just what percentage of their subscribers watch those shows and how much, but the extent to which those shows help them attract and/or retain subscribers to their service.

Taking this concept a step further, the value of customers can be assessed based on the "lifetime" profit they generate. Customer Lifetime Value (CLV) is usually defined as the net present value of the expected cash flows from a customer relationship. It is calculated from estimated sales and customer-retention rates, margins, marketing spending directed at retaining customers, and a discount rate. Among other applications, the CLV values are used to evaluate customer-

---

[5]This is for retailers who carry a mix of national brand and private-label products, not those like Aldi and Trader Joe's who sell primarily private label.

acquisition costs, to fine-tune marketing spending for acquisition versus retention, to make long-term sales forecasts, and to establish "customer equity" (the aggregate value of a firm's customers). The textbook formulas for CLV use retention rates with no fixed time horizon, but many retailers consider a fixed (say, five-year) time horizon more practical.

Is it worth the trouble to compute the profitability of individual customers? We are wary of citing the infamous 80-20 rule, which is overused in our opinion, but it is true that there are wide variations in the profitability of individual customers for resellers. The "whale" curve, a hypothetical version of which we show in Figure 8.7, is produced by calculating the profits from individual customers, ranking them from most to least profitable, and then plotting the cumulative profit in a graph. The graph is named after the appearance of a whale rising from water. The "water line" is at 100% profit, so the curve shows that the most profitable SKUs (or customers) add up to the majority of total profits, often even more than the total profit, whereas those in the tail (where the graph curves down) are unprofitable. The higher the whale rises above the water, the more worthwhile it is to distinguish between the best and worst customers.

For a supplier, there will probably be much more variation in costs and profitability across different retailers and channels than across individual items of a brand. That is why they don't often measure DPP, but they have account-specific Profit & Loss statements for each retailer. These can be an effective tool in negotiating assortments,

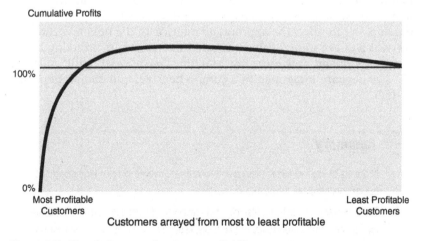

Figure 8.7 The whale curve of customer profitability.

pricing, plan-o-grams, marketing support, and promotion plans. Lastly, the types of consumers who visit different retailers can vary in how well they mesh with a supplier's brands, which therefore affects their value to the supplier. For that reason, suppliers should try to monitor the average lifetime value of consumers who patronize different channels and even different retail accounts.

8.3 CONCLUSION

> *"I would not give a fig for the simplicity this side of complexity, but I would give my life for the simplicity on the other side of complexity."*
>
> —Oliver Wendell Holmes

Our perspective on distribution metrics is in the spirit of Holmes's advice. Marketers should understand the entire compendium of what they *might* measure even if they then decide to focus on a few key metrics. We have presented that compendium through the organizing framework of the opening figure in the previous chapter, and our discussion of channel metrics in the sequence of breadth, depth, and then performance. The system of metrics that companies choose to monitor reflects what they believe to be the key marketing priorities, strategies, and competitive challenges at a particular time.

A friend who specializes in sales management dashboards has observed that "when strategy is right, marketing is easy, and when marketing is right, sales are easy." We would add that when the marketing strategy is clear, channel strategy will also be clear and it is much easier to select the appropriate metrics. In the next few chapters we will address some of the strategic frameworks for thinking about channel strategy and ensuring that the "push" and "pull" sides of the business are integrated in a comprehensive, and comprehensible, system.

Summary

- In the era of omni-channel, metrics and rewards are needed not just for closing sales but for support along the path-to-purchase.
- The partnerships must be profitable for both reseller and upstream marketer. But defining and measuring profitability can be tricky, especially when retailers have their own strategic goals for different product categories and brands.

- Profits from SKUs, brands, categories, consumers, and channel partners are all being measured with increasing frequency and increasing granularity.

- A host of intermediate distribution performance metrics (out-of-stocks, markdowns, bounce rates, cart abandonment rates) are useful for diagnosing causes of profit problems.

- But we also cannot lose sight of the ultimate metrics that capture the lifetime value of a brand and its customers for a retailer, and vice versa, the value of a retailer's customers for the brand.

- Rarely will a single metric be sufficient to indicate whether the organization is learning, growing, and becoming more efficient in distribution.

ENDNOTES

i. Ailawadi, K., and Harlam, B. (2009). Retailer Promotion Pass-Through: A Measure, Its Magnitude, and Its Determinants. *Marketing Science* 28 (4): 782–791.

ii. Banjo, S. (2014). Corporate News: Wal-Mart's Merchandising Chief Resigns – With Departure of Duncan Mac Naughton, U.S. Chief Greg Foran Restructures Store Operations with More Direct Reports. *Wall Street Journal* (26 November), p. B3.

iii. Sambar, A., Goldman, D., and Scrimale, J. (2015). Bring Store Performance into Focus. http://www.kurtsalmon.com/en-us/Retail/vertical-insight/1380/Bringing-Store-Performanceinto-Focus.

iv. Stevens, L., Terlep, S., and Gasparro, A. (2018). Amazon Targets Unprofitable Items, with a Sharper Focus on the Bottom Line. *Wall Street Journal* (17 December), p. A1.

v. Leone, R., Rao, V., Keller, K., Luo, A., McAlister, L., and Srivastava, R. (2006). Linking Brand Equity to Customer Equity. *Journal of Service Research* 9 (2): 125–138.

vi. Details are available in: Ailawadi, K. and Harlam, B. (2004). An Empirical Analysis of the Determinants of Retail Margins: The Role of Store Brand Share. *Journal of Marketing* 68 (1): 147-166. Ailawadi, K., Pauwels, K., and Steenkamp, J. (2008). Private Label Use and Store Loyalty. *Journal of Marketing* 72 (6): 19–30.

CHAPTER 9

The Challenge of Optimizing Distribution Breadth

9.1 INTRODUCTION

In the previous two chapters we described many of the most useful metrics for monitoring distribution breadth, depth, and performance. Measurement is necessary, but it's only the first step in matching distribution coverage and depth to demand. Recall from Chapter 3 that many of the conflicts that occur between suppliers and their resellers can be traced to under- or over-distribution, or to the division of work and pay as new layers of intermediaries slide between suppliers and end consumers. Matching distribution and demand, so that neither gets too far ahead of the other, is a constant challenge in the ever-changing marketplace. One side of the equation is to tailor the type and intensity of distribution coverage to demand, which we take on here and in the next couple of chapters. The other side of the equation is to use products and channel incentives to "adjust" demand and effort across channels and over time to match distribution, and we will discuss those activities in subsequent chapters.

Online and mobile channels are making the classic categorization of products into specialty, shopping, and convenience goods somewhat obsolete. Further, beyond the general recommendation that these three types of products correspond to exclusive, selective, and intensive distribution coverage respectively, there is relatively little to be found in the marketing textbooks on how to determine a sustainable level of distribution breadth. Managers need guidelines, because it is often more difficult to determine the best level of distribution than it is to optimize pricing, advertising, and promotion. The approaches we recommend are more about getting into the right "ballpark" than making precise recommendations about the optimal breadth of distribution. This chapter and the next discuss considerations and signals that can indicate when strategic stances toward distribution coverage need to be revisited. Once in the right ballpark, sales response models and distribution elasticities coupled with a deeper understanding of consumer search behavior can help managers get closer to their brand's just right or "Goldilocks" level of distribution coverage.

We introduced the dangers of under- and over-distribution in Chapter 3 and reprise them in Figure 9.1. Executives we speak to tell us they track metrics such as average price points, volume sold on

The Perils of	
Under-Distribution	**Over-Distribution**
Not available: Sales are lost because the product is not available where consumers search or buy. Consumers forego buying or switch to competing products. Competitive entry is encouraged.	**Service Problems:** Excessive reseller competition leads to low retail prices and margins, making them less enthusiastic about investing in effort needed to sustain the brand. In the extreme, "bait and switch" leverages the brand to attract shoppers and then switches them to higher-margin products.
High Prices: Sales don't reach their potential at stocking resellers because resellers price too high or put in too little merchandising and sales effort (double-marginalization).	**Upstream Pricing Pressure:** The pricing pressure faced by retailers can travel upstream to suppliers, who lower their prices, possibly compromising product quality to preserve margins.
Inefficient Marketing: Suppliers' spending on marketing pull (e.g. advertising, coupons, samples, and even direct selling) becomes less effective because consumers can't find the promoted products, which leads to cuts in pull spending and further decrease in sales.	**Resellers Dump the Line:** Adding distribution that is not supported by sales velocity will irritate stocking resellers and take up valuable salesforce time. When the products are inevitably dropped, normal sales are disrupted with "close-out" promotions or product that is past the shelf-life.

Figure 9.1 The signs and perils of under- and over-distribution

discount, and store sales growth, to determine whether distribution is too intense or too light, which makes sense. The challenge, of course, is to get strategy and distribution coverage approximately right *before* suffering the negative effects or engaging in "fine-tuning" to get to a precisely wrong level of coverage.[1]

9.2 CLASSIC CATEGORIZATIONS OF PRODUCTS AND DISTRIBUTION COVERAGE

Distribution coverage both reflects and constrains suppliers' ambitions for sales growth. But the appropriate level of distribution coverage required to reach sales and market share goals depends on consumer search and shopping behavior. The conceptual frameworks and advice found in the "classics" of marketing theory on distribution strategy generally advise marketing managers to first think through expected consumer shopping patterns for the goods and services they are selling, and then to match the "intensity" of distribution coverage to those consumer shopping patterns. Marketing textbooks have distinguished between convenience, shopping, and specialty goods since 1932.[i]

> *Convenience* goods are those for which consumers have little or no intention to search, at least in the short-term. These are typically frequent purchases for immediate needs, often on a shopping list and replenished with "one-stop" shopping trips. Consumers expect to find these products on their regular shopping trips to groceries, drugstores, and mass merchandisers. Even if they are *willing* to search for a favorite brand (consumer search loyalty for Heinz Ketchup, say), that doesn't mean they *want* to search. Still, consumer search loyalty might lead to long-term changes in store preferences if stores do not stock favorite products.
>
> *Shopping* goods tend to be purchased infrequently (think big-ticket items such as home furnishings, automobiles, or consumer electronics). There is usually a lack of consumer expertise in these categories, and therefore the desire to compare products before buying and minimize "post-purchase dissonance."[2]

---

[1] The quote "It is better to be approximately right than precisely wrong" is often attributed to the famed economist John Maynard Keynes.

[2] Post-purchase dissonance is the regret that consumers have subsequent to a major (or risky) purchase about having made the purchase and/or the specific product chosen. Generous retailer return policies can ease the fear of this dissonance, but as we saw with Leather Italia, at what may be a high cost.

Specialty goods are those wherein consumers know what they want, but don't expect to find them everywhere and are willing to make a "special" trip to locate them. They are not purchased as frequently as are convenience goods. Examples are high-end cosmetics, designer apparel, and other luxury products.

Almost, but not exactly, corresponding to the above classification of goods is the three-part division of distribution strategies into *intensive, selective, and exclusive* distribution strategies. As the names imply, the terms represent a spectrum of availability.

Intensive distribution means the products are, like Santa Claus, everywhere. Few restrictions exist, at least within a specific channel (e.g. supermarkets)—most resellers are encouraged to stock convenience goods because consumers are generally not willing to search for them. If they are not stocked and easily available for purchase, consumers will switch brands or forego a purchase and both retailer and manufacturer will likely lose some sales. And who knows, if consumers are forced to switch once, they might decide they like what they were "forced" to try even better than the previous favorite. So it is rare that even leading brands of convenience goods turn down distribution opportunities though they may offer different SKUs in different outlets.

Exclusive distribution policies are at the other extreme. These can restrict resellers to a single outlet for a defined geographic area. For niche specialty goods, it is more important to let consumers know where to find them, and to have them presented according to the exclusive image the supplier wants to portray, than to be broadly distributed.

Selective distribution is somewhere between exclusive and intensive, with some limits on both the type and number of resellers in a given market. Highly differentiated products can motivate consumers to shop more consciously and energetically, seeking out stocking retailers. Such products are therefore the *least* in need of wide market distribution for a given sales objective.

Very simply put, the more consumers are willing to search—for your product category and your brand—the less distribution coverage you need. Certainly, this is a simple and intuitive classification that provides some strategic guidance regarding distribution coverage. But its utility was limited historically and is even more so today. Why? First, even if a brand were to fall neatly into one of the three product types when it is first introduced, goods often migrate from one type to another after the initial purchase or as consumers gain experience with the product category. For serious runners, for example, running shoes may first be a shopping good as they explore options to find the right fit and feel, and then a specialty good as they search for the specific brand and model for their replacement pair. Conversely, many foods begin as specialty goods and then migrate to become convenience products (think Greek yogurt, sushi, or Sriracha seasoning).

Second, the web and mobile are further blurring distinctions between the three types of products. Almost everything (from specialty products to frequently bought packaged goods) is in danger of becoming a shopping good. Shopping activity today need not involve visits to multiple brick-and-mortar stores, or, indeed, to any seller. A mobile app can do that with a single touch. So exclusive distribution based on geographical territories may be a thing of the past, and even purveyors of the most exclusive luxury products are finding themselves being "shopped." On the other side, even if consumers are willing to make a special trip to find a particular product, if it is available on the web and can be delivered tomorrow (or later today), why should they bother to travel? Programs like Subscribe and Save and Amazon's Alexa help marketers circumvent the shopping list with a form of "hyper-convenience."

And, third, even if you could clearly classify a product/brand as one of the three classic types, it still raises an important question: just how exclusive, selective, or intensive should distribution be? Even convenience packaged goods can fall prey to over-distribution. CPG suppliers cannot reasonably expect to sustain a distribution strategy that literally has their entire product line "everywhere." Conversely, brands with exclusive distribution need to figure out how much protected territory each outlet should have. Most suppliers have to find the right level of selective distribution coverage in the space between those extremes, and also choose the right partners. What kind of brand image do I want? How much price competition between resellers is healthy? What kind of selling investments do I need resellers to make? How much power do I have to obtain those investments? A supplier needs answers to these questions, and others like them, to get into the ballpark of the right level of distribution coverage and to choose the specific channel partners.

9.3 CONSUMER SEARCH LOYALTY AND DISTRIBUTION ELASTICITY

We have used two terms in the title of this section, "consumer search loyalty" and "elasticity," in earlier chapters but they are important enough to deserve some elaboration here. "Consumer search" in general refers to the practice of visiting multiple resellers to gather information, examine individual brands and products, and compare prices before buying something in the product category. In the online retail world, "visiting" multiple outlets is much easier than in the brick and mortar world, just as it is easier to visit multiple outlets in urban versus rural areas. So, consumer search and comparison-shopping across brands in a category can indicate a lack of loyalty to a particular brand or product. "Consumer search loyalty" on the other hand refers to the willingness of consumers to search at multiple resellers until they find the specific product or brand they are seeking, perhaps at a price they like. Recall that we discussed this in some detail in Chapter 5. We keep returning to this concept because it is so very central to the management of distribution breadth. In any case, understanding and measuring consumer search behaviors is a requirement for understanding the effects of adding distribution coverage to generate incremental sales, as we will explain in this section.

The second term, "elasticity," as we noted in Chapter 5, is a term of art among economists and data analysts to measure how responsive markets are to specific marketing decisions. It reflects the percentage change in one metric that corresponds to or results from the percentage change in another. Elasticity is a popular term, because in the language of data analysts it is "unitless" and can therefore be used to compare sales response to different marketing variables. The elasticity of sales revenue to distribution indicates the percentage change in sales that is expected to be associated with a 1% change in distribution measured, say, as the number of retail "doors" or %ACV.[3] A .5 elasticity means that we would expect an increase of distribution from 50% ACV to 52% (4% change) to be associated with a 2% increase in sales revenue.[ii] Similarly, an advertising elasticity of .5 would mean that a 1% increase in advertising spending would result in a .5% increase in sales revenue. But we note that clarity on the specific metric used for the marketing variable is essential to evaluating the economic significance of the response. For example, a percentage change in the number of "doors" of distribution (i.e., numeric distribution), is quite different from a percentage change in %ACV distribution. We'll document some of these differences in just a couple of pages.

---

[3]Recall from Chapter 7 that %ACV is ACV-weighted distribution breadth of a brand; it refers to the percentage of all commodity sales in the relevant market that outlets stocking the brand account for.

9.3.1 How Consumer Search Loyalty Reduces Distribution Elasticity

With the tedious business of defining terms out of the way, let's look at how propensity of consumers to search for the brand they prefer can reduce the incremental sales response to increases in distribution breadth. Consumers generally shop in multiple stores. If they don't find a favored brand in one store, some will find another store that stocks it, so when additional stores start to stock the brand, they will cannibalize sales from existing ones to some extent. Strong search loyalty is a great thing for brands, as we've said before: the kind of attachment that motivates search also allows marketers to charge premiums for their products and gives marketers a better power position in negotiations with resellers. However, the same search loyalty means that some of the volume in newly acquired stores will likely come from existing distribution. Some consumers, who are loyal searchers, were already searching for and buying the product even when it was not available in the stores they typically frequented. All else being equal, increasing distribution coverage does increase sales—a lot, as will document in the next section—but it causes average sales *velocity* across all stores to decline. So expect diminishing returns to additional distribution, or, in the language of economists, distribution elasticities that are less than one. The boxed insert provides an example, complete with arithmetic.

HOW SEARCH LOYALTY CAN CREATE DIMINISHING RETURNS TO DISTRIBUTION BREADTH

KA Iced Tea is sold in a regional market and has achieved 50% PCV distribution. With monthly sales of 600 cases, KA's sales velocity is 12 cases per month per point of PCV distribution (600 ÷ 50).

Market research has shown that 200 cases are bought by fanatically loyal KA drinkers. They find and buy KA Tea wherever it is stocked. The remaining 400 cases are purchased by non-loyals who like KA Tea and buy it because it happens to be available where they shop; otherwise, another brand of iced tea would be fine with them.

KA's sales manager convinces PF Kaching, a local chain of convenience stores, to add KA to their shelves. As a result, KA's distribution breadth increases to 60% PCV from 50% PCV. Monthly sales increase, but only among the non-loyal buyers because the loyal searchers were already finding and buying KA Tea elsewhere. The 400 cases sold to non-loyals increases to 480 cases and the 200 cases sold to loyal buyers remains stable. The net result is that monthly sales increase from 600 to 680 cases.

So distribution has increased by 20% (60% PCV versus 50%), while sales have only increased by 13.3% (680 cases versus 600), implying a distribution elasticity of 0.665 (13.3 % increase in sales ÷ 20% increase in PCV distribution). Velocity has declined from 12 cases per PCV point to 11.3 cases (680 ÷ 60).

Strong search loyalty is a wonderful marketing asset, but, somewhat perversely, it can lead to lower distribution elasticities.

9.3.2 Empirical Evidence of Distribution

Elasticities Less Than One

Unlike price and advertising elasticities, of which there are tens, if not hundreds, of estimates to be found in the academic literature, estimates of distribution elasticity are a bit of a rarity. Professor Berk Ataman and his colleagues have estimated them for several CPG categories. They measure distribution breadth as Brand ACV% and document elasticities of about 0.74. Diminishing returns, but we do note that the magnitude is six times larger than the advertising elasticity they estimate, and ten times larger than other estimates of advertising elasticity. That certainly reinforces the importance of distribution in driving sales![4]

One of us, along with colleagues, also estimated market response models for a number of CPG categories, using Share of Total Distribution as our measure of distribution, and found lower distribution elasticities—around 0.45.[iii] Consumer search loyalty also explains why Brand %ACV or %PCV elasticity may be higher than Total Distribution elasticity. An increase in a brand's total distribution often adds SKUs to an existing assortment in stores, while an increase in %PCV adds stores that previously did not stock any SKUs of the brand. And consumer search loyalty is likely higher for the brand than for a particular SKU of the brand. Consider Pete and Gerry's, the company we introduced in Chapter 6, which is expanding nationally %ACV distribution around 55% in 2019. A loyal Pete and Gerry's consumer might prefer to buy the dozen carton of Pete and Gerry's eggs. She will likely buy the six-pack of their eggs if the store she's shopping in doesn't stock the

---

[4] As an aside, those researchers also include a brand's product line length in their model and document a substantial elasticity for it. The product line is measured as the number of SKUs of the brand in distribution, a metric that, the reader will recall from Chapter 7, is closely related to total distribution and distribution depth.

dozen-carton she really wants, though she'll be darned if she switches to another brand. So, when the store adds the dozen-carton SKU, that loyal consumer won't end up contributing to a Pete and Gerry's sales increase, only to an SKU switch.

Professor Randolph (Randy) Bucklin and his colleagues report on new car distribution elasticities in the article we referenced in Chapter 7.[iv] They examine several metrics of distribution coverage, and look at the impact of distribution not only on car purchases by consumers but also on the profit made by dealers. They measure the distribution intensity of each car make (e.g., Honda, Toyota) from the perspective of individual consumers using the exact geographic locations of consumers and new car dealers. Their two main distribution metrics—dealer accessibility (the buyer's distance to the nearest outlet for each make) and multiple dealer choices (the buyer's distance to the tenth closest dealer)—are correlated but each is useful in its own right, as we noted in Chapter 7.[5] In a nice illustration of how higher distribution coverage increases manufacturers' sales but lowers retail prices and retail margins, these authors document a positive effect of both metrics on sales but a negative effect of the multiple dealer choices on dealer profit margins. Further, they find fairly large variations in distribution elasticities of the different car makes in their analysis, underscoring the importance of marketers measuring the elasticity of their own brand. But the average distribution elasticity they report is 0.6—again, large in magnitude but still diminishing returns.

These examples are set in physical stores, but the phenomenon is likely to be even stronger online. As a supplier with strong search loyalty expands its online distribution beyond the first several points of %PCV and %PCSV (recall from Chapter 7 that %Product Category Search Volume is a particularly relevant metric for distribution breadth online), sales returns to online distribution are likely to diminish even faster because search online is so much easier than search in physical stores.

The upshot of all this is that the more search loyalty the brand enjoys, the more likely it is that returns to distribution coverage will be diminishing, at least after some critical mass of coverage has been achieved, and especially as online distribution coverage increases.

---

[5]They also measure dealer dispersion (i.e., how unequally the dealers are spread away from the buyer), but we think the first two measures are the most intuitive and the most insightful.

9.3.3 Feedback Effects and Longer-Term Distribution Elasticity

Search loyalty is not the entire story, however. Another important question to ask is how distribution depth is expected to change with distribution points gained or lost. In some cases, the gain in distribution breadth might be accompanied by increased depth compared to competing brands. Convenience stores, warehouse clubs, and airport shops typically have more limited assortments. So if a brand manages to be on their shelf at all, the result may be a more prominent position. In fact, if these structural differences between the first few and the last few points of distribution coverage are big enough, they may even offset search loyalty and reflect themselves in increasing rather than decreasing returns to distribution breadth.[v]

In other cases, adding more points of distribution may intensify the competition between retailers and reduce their margins so much that they reduce their selling effort and distribution depth suffers. Correctly estimating the longer-term distribution elasticity means that these effects have to be accounted for. There are also other feedback loops in the system of Consumer Pull, Distribution Push, and Performance that we introduced in Chapter 2. For example, higher distribution can make advertising more effective because consumers are reminded of the advertising when they see the brand stocked in the stores they shop at. And broader distribution begets higher sales, which encourages more retailers to stock the brand. The work by Berk Ataman and colleagues that we cited above captures this last performance feedback, but it is difficult to specify a system that can fully capture all the feedback effects and provide good estimates of longer-term distribution elasticity. And that longer-term elasticity is a key input to any kind of "optimization," which we discuss next.

9.4 THE DIFFICULTIES OF OPTIMIZING DISTRIBUTION COVERAGE

For data-savvy managers, thinking about the right level of distribution will bring the notion of optimization to the fore. Although the term may suggest that the absolute best solution can be found, it is more accurate to think of optimization in the context of a dynamic marketing environment, where companies constantly strive to improve the efficiency of their marketing mix decisions. The increased granularity of market response data, and the ability to analyze those data in real time, have certainly enabled marketers to make better decisions on prices, promotions, and advertising, which lead to improved profits.[vi]

The typical approach to optimization involves: (1) estimating how sales could be affected by different degrees of the marketing decision being optimized (i.e., elasticity), and (2) combining that elasticity with data on the corresponding marketing costs to project the effect on profits net of marketing. More and more, such optimization is being done dynamically, and not just for the overall market but for segments, individual consumers, and shopping occasions. Estimating sales response is usually the more difficult part, requiring reliable data from experiments, sales histories, surveys, or a combination of all three, generously seasoned with management judgment. Then costs, margins, and hurdle rates can be applied to find the price or promotion or advertising levels that maximize profits over the desired time horizon. Predicting how competitors and channel partners will react further complicates the process, though there are helpful tools available from game theory that specify or estimate who leads and who follows, and structural models that can be used to simulate the impact of policy changes.

So shouldn't managers try to optimize distribution coverage using the same data-based techniques that include collecting and analyzing historical data and executing carefully designed market experiments? Of course, but, as we've said, distribution elasticities are a tough nut to crack and there are additional wrinkles when it comes to distribution that are not easy to iron out.

9.4.1 The Complexity of Distribution Costs

First, distribution costs are more complex and come in several categories, as Figure 9.2 illustrates. So the cost of distribution is much more difficult to know with any degree of certainty, or to model, compared to the costs of advertising and promotion. Large wholesale and retail customers can stretch out payables, impose arbitrary deductions, and represent major financial risk, and the servicing costs to reach small, dispersed retailers can be fairly high relative to the revenue stream they provide.[6]

---

[6]When financial problems beset channel partners, the risk travels up very fast. As sales of newsstand magazines fall, distributors try to survive by offering deals to retailers that they cannot afford. Source Interlink, who used to be the second largest magazine wholesaler in the U.S. had to shut down after Time Inc. stopped supplying through them because of unpaid fees. Time, in turn, said it would have to write off over $25 million in receivables and revenue.

Slotting allowances and free goods for initial inventories are typical up-front costs for expanding distribution. Even within existing reseller accounts the addition of stores or SKUs can involve significant expenses. For new accounts, the supplier may also be expected to purchase and dispose of inventories of the product line being replaced. Some suppliers and some retailers claim that they have moved away from "slots" to plans that support the retail customer with advertising, promotion, and the right products. But trade funds to support additional slots on the shelf, by any name, are still trade funds.

Allowances and sales support, including cooperative advertising, can crop up in unexpected ways. Some new customers (e.g., Walmart) may insist on dealing directly with manufacturers, while others will prefer to purchase through their own supply chain of wholesalers and distributors. One major U.S. retail chain we have worked with has at least twenty-five different accounts into which various types of supplier funding flows.

Receivables and risk of bad debts - opening new accounts can mean extending credit to new retail customers, increasing working capital, and incurring the risk that not all will pay. Large department stores typically pay their vendors in 30–60 days but each day added to or reduced from days payable can have a major impact. Sears, for example, under pressure from vendors who were wary of supplying to the retailer in its financially weakened position, started paying some of them faster than it used to. Each day shaved from its payment cycle was estimated to tie up about $48 million in working capital.[vii]

Inventories and warehousing to support new distribution will affect working capital and sometimes capital expenditures requirements. How to trade these off against the risk of higher receivables and need for timely order fulfillment can be a real challenge, especially for products with limited shelf life and/or specific storage requirements.

Ordering, invoicing, and shipping costs can also be different for new distribution, in particular for geographical expansion and/or customers that order in smaller or larger quantities than usual. Walmart's Retail Link and SPARC software systems are especially well-known examples of suppliers needing to get trained on their retail customers' systems. With the demise of Toys R Us, Hasbro and others have to ship smaller quantities at short notice to thousands more small retail outlets.

Returns and deductions for new distribution can be quite different from what upstream suppliers experienced with existing customers. Recall Leather Italia's problems with Costco. Some packaged goods retailers expect "swell allowances," which are a percent of sales, instead of processing and charging for goods that are actually damaged.

Producing additional SKUs to support new distribution (e.g. all-natural options for health stores, smaller packages and case packs for dollar stores and larger ones for club stores, and easy-to-ship, not easy-to-display, packages for Amazon) can add costs to production and/or packaging.

Figure 9.2 The complexity of distribution costs.

9.4.2 Discontinuities Arising from Retail Structure

Second, changing distribution coverage in today's retail environment can be uneven because it means beginning to sell through a different type of reseller or to a different retail format. Snapple and Red Bull launched their products through smaller, independent resellers, but quickly expanded to chain supermarkets and, eventually, to club stores, mass merchandisers and beyond. For these products, expanding to different store formats was mainly a question of managing the logistics and the costs in Figure 9.2, and that is challenging enough. But adding Amazon.com, Walmart, or even one of the dollar store chains is by no means a "small" adjustment. It will potentially be perceived as signaling a shift in strategy and a lessening of "commitment" to existing channels, creating a series of reactions that are hard, if not impossible, to codify in game theoretic or econometric models. Of course, we don't mean to suggest that dealing with larger retailers is inevitably an "all or nothing" arrangement. For example, Ukrop's specialty foods has arrangements with only some regional Kroger stores and a subset of Food Lion outlets. However, it will be difficult to resist further expansion should those retail customers request (require?) it.

9.4.3 Distribution Is Not under the Complete Control of the Supplier

A third issue is that even the best brand marketers who sell through independent resellers, including those with the most restrictive and exclusive distribution strategies, are never in complete control of where and how their product is sold. They can't *require* independent resellers to stock their products, and even when they "buy" distribution with slotting allowances or other arrangements, the deals are often loose arrangements that survive only as long as the economics works for everyone in the supply chain. So even if a well-calibrated market response model were to point to a specific profit-maximizing level of distribution coverage, there is no assurance that marketing and salespeople can actually achieve or maintain that new level of distribution. Much more so than other marketing decisions, working through independent resellers requires collaboration and commitment to long-term goals that are acceptable to the channel as a whole. So, unless there is good reason to believe that the new level of distribution can be sustained, it probably isn't worth the marketing and organizational effort to try.

9.5 CONCLUSION

In this chapter we argued that the standard marketing classifications of goods and distribution strategies have become somewhat outmoded. The web has not only increased the ability to shop (compare features and prices), it has moved consumers toward higher expectations for convenience and transparency. Nevertheless, distribution coverage and depth remain things to be actively managed and coordinated with demand. Consumers' search loyalty is the ultimate indicator of a brand's power, but it also means that sales returns to additional distribution coverage may be decreasing. In other words, distribution elasticities may be less than one, although they are much higher than other marketing mix elements, notably advertising. Feedback effects, the lumpiness of distribution decisions, the difficulty of estimating total distribution costs, and the lack of direct control over whether and how products are adopted by independent retailers are all challenges in using a traditional "optimization" approach to finding the "Goldilocks" level of distribution. In the next chapter, we introduce velocity graphs that show distribution coverage and share positions versus competition. They can inform the balancing act between too much and too little coverage. Once in the right ballpark, suppliers can use distribution elasticities and even optimization to fine-tune coverage.

Summary

- Matching distribution to demand is largely about understanding and responding to buyer search and shopping patterns.
- Marketers often categorize products as convenience, shopping, or specialty goods and these correspond (roughly) to recommendations for intensive, selective, and exclusive distribution.
- But neither is the distinction between the types of goods clear as online search accelerates the migration from specialty towards shopping and even convenience goods, nor are the recommendations precise enough to be actionable.
- Elasticities are a common metric for estimating consumer response to marketing changes. Distribution elasticities are much higher than those of other marketing mix variables like advertising, but they are usually less than one, implying diminishing returns to additional distribution breadth.

▨ Strong consumer search loyalty is a wonderful marketing asset but, somewhat perversely, it can lead to lower distribution elasticities.

▨ The relationship between breadth and depth of distribution, as well as other feedback effects mean that short-term elasticities, that are easier to estimate, can be quite different from long-term elasticities that more difficult to measure or project.

▨ Optimization to find the Goldilocks' (just right) extent of distribution coverage is made more challenging by the difficulty of estimating all relevant costs, the potential "lumpiness" of distribution coverage decisions, and the inability to directly control independent resellers.

▨ Once in the ballpark, however, elasticities and traditional optimization can be used to fine-tune coverage.

ENDNOTES

i. Copeland, M. (1932). Relation of Consumers' Buying Habits to Marketing Methods. *Harvard Business Review* (April): 282–289.

ii. Here a brief discussion of the difference between arc elasticities and point elasticities.

iii. Datta, H., Ailawadi, K., and van Heerde, J. (2017). How Well Does Consumer-Based Brand Equity Align with Sales-Based Brand Equity and Marketing-Mix Response? *Journal of Marketing* 81 (3): 1–20.

iv. Bucklin, R., Siddarth, S., and Silva-Risso, J. (2008). Distribution Intensity and New Car Choice. *Journal of Marketing Research* 45 (5): 473–486.

v. See, for example: Reibstein, D., and Farris, P. (1995). Market Share and Distribution: A Generalization, a Speculation and Some Implications. *Marketing Science* 14 (3 supplement): G190–G202. Friberg, R. and Sanctuary, M. (2017). The Effect of Retail Distribution on Sales of Alcoholic Beverages. *Marketing Science* 36 (4): 471–643.

vi. Here are a couple of examples of optimized prices and promotions that have been demonstrated to improve firm profits in simulated or field tests: Natter, M., Mild, A., Reutterer, T., and Taudes, A. (2007). An Assortment-Wide Decision-Support System for Dynamic Pricing and Promotion Planning in DIY Retailing. *Marketing Science* 26 (4): 576–583. Zhang, J. and Wedel, M. (2009). The Effectiveness of Customized Promotions in Online and Offline Stores. *Journal of Marketing Research* 46 (2): 190–206.

vii. Kapner, S. (2015). Jittery Suppliers Press Sears to Pay Up Faster. *Wall Street Journal* (19 March), p. B1.

CHAPTER **10**

Using Velocity Graphs to Guide Sustainable Distribution Coverage

10.1 INTRODUCTION

Specifying a model that provides valid estimates of longer-term distribution and other marketing mix elasticities, complete with all or at least most feedback effects, is not easy. But it would be essential if one were to rely on that route to optimizing distribution coverage. In this chapter, we provide a simpler way for a supplier to get to the approximately right level of distribution coverage that is sustainable—by placing itself on a graph showing the cross-sectional pattern of distribution and market shares of competitors in the marketplace.

10.2   THE CONCEPT OF A VELOCITY GRAPH

Figure 10.1 depicts a graph for a hypothetical product category, where each brand is located in the two-dimensional space of Brand PCV% on the x-axis and market share on the y-axis. Such a graph is easy to generate since companies usually have data on share and distribution coverage for their own products and their key competitors. If you don't have these data, the value of velocity graphs should be a reason to collect them. They are often more accessible than the longitudinal data on sales and all its major drivers needed to properly estimate market response models.

We refer to graphs of this type as "velocity graphs" because the slope reflects share velocity (i.e., market share per distribution point for brands that compete in the market). In this particular example, the graph happens to be increasing in velocity with distribution coverage (i.e., convex). This convex shape is representative of Brand PCV and ACV graphs for packaged goods, as explained by the boxed insert.[i] But the shape will be different for velocity graphs based on other distribution metrics, and there are lots of choices, as we will soon illustrate.

WHY IS THE SLOPE OF THE %ACV OR %PCV BRAND VELOCITY GRAPH "INCREASING"?

1. Consumers buy what is available and only a few are willing to delay or forego buying if a favorite brand is not stocked.

2. Brands that have wide consumer preference and/or search loyalty will be stocked by more retailers because they don't want to lose the consumer to another store.

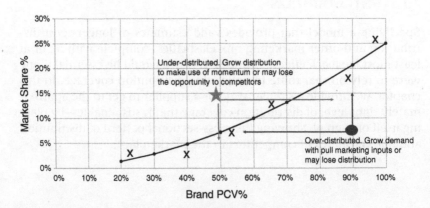

Figure 10.1   Velocity graph for brands in a hypothetical category.

3. Such brands penetrate limited-assortment outlets where they encounter fewer direct competitors and tend to get a larger share of the retailer's category sales. Usually, you can only find one brand of ketchup in convenience stores: Heinz.

4. Such brands are also able to get marginal SKUs (sizes, flavors, etc.) in large-assortment stores that the small brands can't.

5. Other "rich-get-richer" effects for such brands are lower reseller margins and more frequent promotions/displays.

Note: Recall, also that ACV% and PCV% metrics collapse the long tail of small and limited assortment outlets into their collective share of total or category sales. Other distribution metrics can yield different patterns.

It is important to underscore that velocity graphs do not represent any direct "causal" effect of distribution on share. They combine the effect of distribution on sales, the effect of sales velocity on distribution, and the effects of other factors on both sales and distribution. So they are not useful for predicting the share gains from additional distribution coverage; those, as we explained in the previous chapter, are likely to show diminishing rather than increasing returns. But these cross-sectional graphs show what has happened in the market and, as we will explain, they yield important insights into what combinations of distribution and share are likely to be sustainable over time without extraordinary support or some other structural advantage. Comparing velocity graph positions between time periods is even better for providing a window into distribution trends in the market.

10.2.1 Sustainable Positions Likely Lie Close to the Velocity Graph

Whatever the shape of the velocity graph, at any given time most brands will be located close to the curve, but there may be some brands that sit well above or well below it. In our hypothetical example, the Xs represent brands whose %PCV and market shares are about in line with the equilibrium in the market. The circle represents a brand with much lower sales velocity than the market equilibrium. In order to sustain its relatively high distribution coverage, it will need to increase its pull activities and bring share up, or it will lose distribution over time. Either way, over time, the tug of economic gravity will likely move it closer to the equilibrium curve. In contrast, the brand represented by a star is garnering substantially higher market share than its distribution coverage would lead one to expect. It is likely investing much more in pull and has a highly differentiated product that consumers are willing to search for. Unless it continues to sustain this heavy investment, over time either its share will fall back more in line with its distribution coverage or it will get broader coverage.

10.2.2 Special Logistics Can Allow a Brand to Persist "Off" the Graph

Velocity graphs are very useful, particularly in identifying "out-of-sync" situations, but we caution that marketers should be careful about choosing the brands when assembling the cross-sectional relationship. As in everything else in marketing, the definition of the market and category is key, but even in a well-defined market, some outliers may be where they are for good reason.

Different brands in the same category may use very different logistics and inventory management systems, and a special system can allow a product to remain alive and well off the graph. For instance, fast-selling products such as soft drinks, beer, and snack foods can justify their own, dedicated, direct-to-store delivery systems. Consider Frito-Lay: distributing directly from its own trucks to the retail outlet, the company may be able to put only a single bag of an exotically flavored potato chip on a store's shelves. That could achieve variety, supply demand, and not endanger product freshness. Another snack product, being delivered through chain distribution center, might be subject to the "whole case pack-out" rule—either demand justifies an entire case being placed on the shelf, or the store drops it from the chain-supplied assortment.

At the other end of the sales velocity spectrum, small-share, low-turnover, niche brands often use distributors and wholesalers to supply even their large retail customers. These distributors can break bulk, place less-than-case quantities on the shelf, and tailor retail inventories to fit sales velocity, thereby maintaining acceptable turnover for resellers. Other niche brands may be able to persist off the graph because they have a very loyal, albeit small, customer base that will switch stores before they switch brands, and retailers are loathe to lose their shopping baskets. Think Spam, the brand whose consumer search loyalty we noted in Chapter 4.

10.2.3 Three Main Variants of Velocity Graphs

Velocity graphs will always have either sales or market share on the vertical axis and the choice is largely a function of market maturity and strategic focus. The choice of distribution metric for the horizontal axis generates several variants, each with its own particular strengths, which we will illustrate next.

The Brand Distribution graph plots Brand %ACV or %PCV on the x-axis. It provides a simple picture of the strategic position of the brand, and is particularly useful for new or growing brands. But it tends to be relatively insensitive to trends and changes at the margin because brand distribution does not reflect the more volatile changes or differences in the number of SKUs carried by resellers. The outliers on the graph are informative, however. They may be more or less permanently "off the graph" because they represent different strategies or logistics systems, or they may foretell important dynamics (e.g., a brand is likely to lose/gain share or distribution).

The Total Distribution graph plots a brand's total distribution. Recall from Chapter 5 that this is usually the most sensitive metric for revealing changes in a brand's distribution. One could also plot a brand's Total Distribution as a percentage of the category's Total Distribution. Together, the two Total Distribution velocity graphs help detect gains and losses in strategic positions vis-à-vis competitors as well as the breadth and depth of distribution required to keep pace with competitive trends.

The SKU Distribution graph plots %PCV for individual SKUs of a brand. The management of a portfolio of SKUs in distribution is a major challenge for brands. Velocity graphs constructed at this level are most relevant to that task by pointing out SKUs that are off the curve. We'll save a discussion of this particular variant till we get to Chapter 13 on distribution and product line strategy.

10.3 INSIGHTS FROM VELOCITY GRAPHS: AN ILLUSTRATION WITH LAUNDRY DETERGENTS

It is worth illustrating the types of insights about distribution that can be gleaned from these three varieties of velocity graphs with a real product category and set of brands. We use an example from the consumer packaged goods industry, using store-level supermarket scanner sales data from Symphony IRI.[ii] These and other similar "syndicated" data from providers like Nielsen and GfK are readily available to CPG manufacturers and retailers, though they don't come free.

10.3.1 Brand Distribution Velocity Graphs

Figure 10.2 shows the Brand %PCV velocity graph for laundry detergents in two time periods, ten years apart. Tide's market share is so high

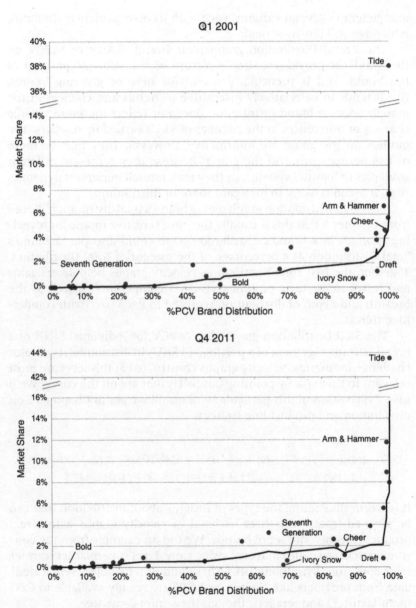

Figure 10.2 Laundry detergent Brand Distribution velocity graph.

that we have broken the axes to more clearly illustrate the positions of the remaining brands.

Let's first look at three brands that were located in the lower right area "below the curve" in 2001: Bold, Dreft, and Ivory Snow.[iii] All three had substantially lower market share for their distribution coverage than was the norm for the category. Ivory Snow is positioned in somewhat of a niche as a gentle care detergent, which might give it some leeway. Dreft has an even clearer niche position as a product for babies. Bold has no such niche. And these brands don't have any special logistics or other structural distinction that would enable them to sustain high distribution despite underperforming on market share. These positions below the curve might suggest to their marketers that if the brands did not make significant market share gains, they would be unable to sustain the broad distribution coverage they had built up. Indeed, by 2011, Bold and Ivory Snow had lost distribution and share and migrated left. Although the Brand %PCV velocity graph is not sensitive to small movements, the shifts are visible over the ten-year period. Dreft's niche allowed it to sustain distribution and persist below the curve but it too should worry about how long this can continue.

In contrast, Seventh Generation, a relatively new brand, gained share and distribution and progressed towards the right. It, too, was starting to fall below the curve by 2011 and should invest in the consumer pull needed to gain some market share points and move up. Of course, the heavyweight, Tide, was putting pressure on all brands. Its %PCV was maxed out so no gains were possible, but it managed to increase share by five percentage points. Among the other brands whose %PCV was maxed out in 2001, there was still a lot of variation in share, with some like Arm & Hammer much higher than others like Cheer. By 2011, Arm & Hammer had accumulated more share to sustain its high Brand Distribution, while Cheer slid downwards and to the left.

The point here is that, as a brand expands its market coverage and sales, it can keep track of whether it is moving along the Brand PCV velocity graph or straying from it, and take necessary action. It can also use the graph to monitor the positions and velocities of its competitors and get some foresight into their prospects. Also, forecasting sales of new products always requires an assumption about the distribution the product is expected to achieve. A velocity graph can validate the reasonableness of assumptions regarding the distribution a new product is expected to achieve. The combination of market share and distribution breadth being presented can be put to a reality check by seeing where the product falls on the graph. Too far below and it is likely the new product will not sustain the distribution that the salesforce sought (bought?) for it. This means the retailers who initially put the product on the shelf in return for hefty slotting allowances will soon drop it, making the new product launch one more statistic among the thousands of failed ones each year. Too far above, and management should question whether the forecasted market share is feasible at the level of distribution they expect to achieve.

10.3.2   Total Distribution Velocity Graphs

For mature brands, total distribution provides more granular information about distribution coverage. This metric is more relevant than ever, since most product categories have been growing the total number of SKUs in distribution. Total Distribution graphs can quantify those category trends and indicate which brands have been managing their distribution with more success in matching SKUs with consumer preferences. Figure 10.3 depicts the Total Distribution velocity graph for our laundry detergent brands.

One interesting point to note is that the spread of brands above and below the curve on the Total Distribution velocity graph is quite a bit lower than on the Brand Distribution graph. One product category, which is all we have shown here, doesn't make a generalization, but this is also the case for other CPG categories we have examined. One reason is that retailers find it a lot easier to drop SKUs (and shelf facings) of a brand that is not generating enough volume than to delist the brand entirely and risk antagonizing its small but potentially loyal customer base. So brands have a harder time staying off the Total Distribution curve than off the Brand Distribution curve. The insights to be had from this graph may therefore be more about tracking where a brand is relative to its competitors and whether and how fast it is moving up or down the curve.

This velocity graph reveals the difference between brands like Tide and Arm & Hammer that were clustered at 100% PCV in the previous graph. Tide was far and away the strongest in distribution and share in 2001, and yet it showed the biggest growth in total distribution over the next ten years—from 2,700% in 2001 to 4,500% in 2011. Even the leading brand has to be sure it can sustain such a large increase, and its market share did go up five points over this period.[1] Arm & Hammer, in the number two place, also added to both total distribution points and

---

[1] In a sign that the brand may have overshot its mark, Tide's total distribution actually went up to almost 5,500% in 2008 before dialing back.

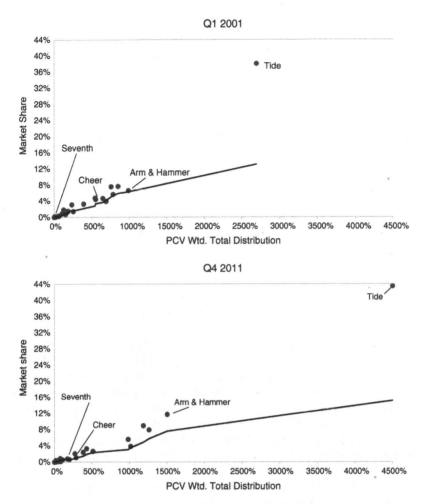

Figure 10.3 Laundry detergent total distribution velocity graph.

share, moving up more steeply than Tide. Although it is hard to see on the graph's scale, Seventh Generation made slow gains, reaching total distribution of 201% by 2011. The fact that it increased Brand %PCV from about 10% to about 70% reflects that it was focused on expanding to new outlets rather than increasing the number of SKU in existing ones—not a bad strategy for an upcoming brand.

But growth in a brand's own total distribution may not be worth much if the number of SKUs in the category is rising faster. In this case, total distribution in the category went from 10,447% in 2001

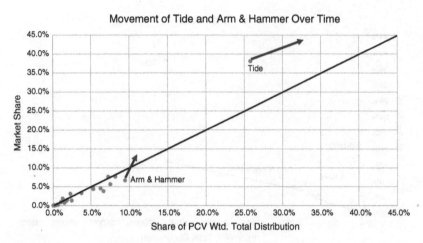

Figure 10.4 Brands line up near 45° line on the share of total distribution velocity curve.

to 13,477% in 2011, an increase of almost 30%. The velocity graph in Figure 10.4, plotted with Share of Total Distribution can assess the brand's position relative to competitors.

This graph shows the position of various brands in 2001 and the arrows depict the gains that the two biggest players, Tide and Arm & Hammer, made at the expense of most of the other brands in the ensuing ten years. This particular type of velocity graph is usually quite stable unless there have been major shifts in competitive positions. It also has most brands aligning close to a 45-degree line. Tide was well above the 45-degree line in 2001, with market share greater than total distribution share; it increased both over time but migrated a bit closer to the line. Arm & Hammer moved upwards to just above the 45-degree line by 2011, while most other brands are behind it, either on or somewhat below the line. Why a little below? Because retailers are prone to give their own private label a greater presence on the shelf than its market share might justify and because a small number of leading brands—in this case Tide—can command even greater shelf presence than their already high share justifies.

10.4 VELOCITY GRAPHS, STATE FRANCHISE LAWS, AND OVERDISTRIBUTION OF U.S. AUTO MAKERS

Our focus in this book is on managing distribution through multiple independent channels. In line with that, this chapter has taken the perspective of upstream suppliers managing distribution coverage among independent resellers who sell multiple brands and product categories. Of course, suppliers in many categories distribute through own-branded stores that are company- or franchisee-owned. Some of the best-known examples are quick-serve restaurants (think McDonald's and Subway), automobile part and service shops (think Jiffy Lube and Goodyear tire centers), and, of course, car dealerships. As we pointed out in Chapter 7, the relevant distribution metrics for such cases are not ACV, PCV, and Total Distribution, but rather numeric distribution, density, or average distance to an outlet.

Numeric distribution does not collapse the long tail of smaller outlets. Further, when distribution outlets are dedicated to one brand, the differences in assortment size that tend to favor large-share brands in multi-brand outlets and contribute to the convex shape of the %ACV/%PCV brand distribution velocity graph are no longer applicable. So numeric distribution can produce different patterns when charted against sales or market share for brands in such cases. But even for this type of distribution structure, velocity graphs can be helpful, as we now illustrate with the automobile industry.

We constructed the velocity graph in Figure 10.5 for Asian and U.S. car brands using 2017 dealer census data published by *Auto News*. It is immediately evident that the U.S. makes are over-distributed—most of them have more dealers and lower sales than the Asian makes. In fact, when we fit one velocity curve for both sets, most of the Asian makes appear to be under-distributed. But they hug their own velocity curve (which we also show in the figure) quite tightly.[iv] This state of affairs is no accident. In Chapter 6, we provided a brief history lesson on how

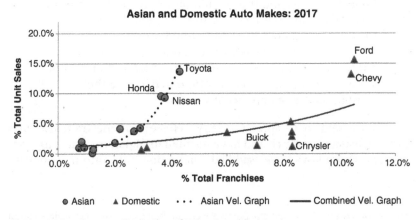

Figure 10.5 The over-distribution of U.S. automobile brands.

the state franchise laws that protect automobile dealers came to be. We pick up from there.

During the 1970s, domestic car makers started facing strong competition from Asian imports. However, the domestics had expanded their dealer networks before many of the state franchise laws came into being.[2] In contrast, imports planned their distribution taking the laws into account. Although the domestics tried, over the decades, to reduce the number of dealerships in line with their shrinking market share, the laws made it difficult and expensive to terminate dealers—they could only do so through normal attrition and consolidation in smaller markets. Hence the over-distribution of U.S. car makes that continues through today, despite a significant pruning after the 2008 financial crisis. The financial crisis hit U.S. auto manufacturers hard. With bankruptcy imminent for both Chrysler and GM, the government authorized emergency financial help through the Troubled Asset Relief Program (TARP). This help was contingent on Chrysler and GM restructuring their operations to achieve long-term viability, and as part of restructuring, the companies were allowed to prune their dealer network without legal repercussions from state franchise laws. Here is an excerpt from the report of the Special Inspector General for TARP, explaining the rationale:

> The Auto Team's view about the need for GM and Chrysler to reduce their dealership networks and do so rapidly was based on a theory that, with fewer dealerships (and thus less internecine competition), like their foreign competitors, the remaining dealerships would be more profitable (through more sales volume and less floor plan financing costs) and thus would permit the dealerships to invest more in their facilities and staff. For GM and Chrysler, the theory goes, this would mean better brand equity (*i.e.*, better consumer perception through more attractive facilities and better customer service) and would allow the manufacturers over time to decrease their substantial dealership incentives.

As we said in Chapter 6, many believe that the franchise laws protect dealers too much and have resulted in higher car prices for consumers. Those laws have "saddled" many domestic auto makers with

---

[2]Indeed, as we noted in Chapter 6, the laws were put into place to protect dealers against exploitation by the domestic car makers.

too many dealers, many of them located in sparsely populated areas of the U.S. that have been losing population and buying power. The velocity graph shows the over-distribution of U.S. car makes. The history of how the industry and the laws got to where they are explains why.

Should regulations be revised and/or technology change, the economics of automobile distribution could change radically. Tesla continues to experiment with more reliance on online sales, even as their attempt to reduce physical locations was somewhat frustrated by lease obligations. Also, we have observed that many of Tesla's service centers are not located in high-traffic "auto miles" and are supplemented with a growing number of mobile service vans. Increased emphasis on electric vehicles, separation of sales from service, and accompanying changes in economics might produce entirely different patterns in velocity graphs.

Summary

- Velocity graphs simply plot the market share of various brands in the market against their distribution coverage. These cross-sectional plots represent the equilibrium relationship between distribution breadth and market share and are useful to get to an approximately right level of distribution. From there, market response models can help fine-tune.

- A brand that is situated below the velocity graph for its market is over-distributed in that its market share is well below the level needed for its current level of distribution breadth to be sustained. Conversely, a brand that is situated above the velocity graph has the market share momentum to justify and retain more distribution breadth than it currently has.

- The shape of, and the insights from, a velocity graph differ depending on the specific metric used to measure distribution breadth. %ACV or %PCV Brand distribution graphs are generally convex, with the most widely distributed brands having more market share per point of distribution than those with lower distribution levels.

- Some brands may be able to thrive off the Brand Distribution graph, because they have logistics systems like direct-to-store delivery or because they have a small but very loyal group of customers whose shopping baskets retailers are loath to lose.

- Brands will generally have a harder time thriving off the Total Distribution graph because retailers can easily delist some of a brand's SKUs from their stores even if they hesitate to delist the brand entirely.

(Continued)

(Continued)

■ Velocity graphs can also provide some insight on sustainable distribution coverage for single brand outlets like automobile dealerships, although it is important to take into consideration the different strategies, economics, and constraints of various competitors.

ENDNOTES

i. For documentation of a similar convex shape for the SKU-level %ACV/%PCV velocity graph, see: Reibstein, D., and Farris, P. (1995). Market Share and Distribution: A Generalization, a Speculation, and Some Implications. *Marketing Science* 14 (3 supplement): G190–G202. Wilbur, K., and Farris, P. (2014). Distribution and Market Share. *Journal of Retailing* 90 (2): 154–167.

ii. The initial dataset, which was subsequently expanded to cover more years, is described in: Bronnenberg, Bart, Michael Kruger, and Carl Mela (2008), The IRI Marketing Data Set. *Marketing Science* 27 (4): 745–748.

iii. We sorted the brands in increasing order of %PCV and then drew a smoothed "trendline" using the moving average of five observations. Other options for drawing the trendline include using the exponential or power functions available in Excel. Reibstein and Farris (1995) and Wilbur and Farris (2014) have used more flexible nonlinear functions.

iv. We used exponential trendlines in Excel to draw the curves in this figure.

CHAPTER **11**

Augmenting the Distribution Mix: Digital Channels and Own Bricks and Clicks

11.1 INTRODUCTION

In the previous chapter, we illustrated how velocity graphs can help to match the intensity of distribution coverage to the volume of demand. But matching distribution to demand is not only about how much coverage is needed; it is also about choosing the types of distribution channels in such a way that product availability and selling effort pair well with where consumers are searching and buying. In this chapter, we offer a systematic approach for expanding the type of distribution with additional routes-to-market to match where demand is headed. In particular, we'll look at two important phenomena: (a) many suppliers now "make *and* buy," by building their own physical and/or web stores to augment distribution by independent resellers; and (b) the challenges and opportunities of digital channels.[1]

11.2 A VARIETY OF OWN-STORES TO AUGMENT DISTRIBUTION BY INDEPENDENT RESELLERS

Suppliers selling through independent resellers should think long and hard about *why* they are adding their own stores to the distribution mix. This will help ensure they do so in the right locations, with the right intensity, and the right (portion of their) product line, and so that they can evaluate the performance of the stores with the right metrics. As Figure 11.1 shows, own-stores come in many varieties and associated costs. Furthermore, they differ in their purpose, coverage, and sales and therefore in the conflict generated with their independent channel partners. We have sorted them in increasing order of the potential for conflict. Stores-in-stores, flagship, and outlet stores are at the lower end of the conflict spectrum. But beyond them lies a danger zone in which suppliers, going direct, compete with their own customers and can risk losing depth of coverage by independent resellers.

We've placed the showrooms of digital native vertical brands in their own unique category at the bottom of the figure and shaded it. Their only or primary route to market is a direct-to-consumer digital channel and they have no channel conflict to worry about, at least not yet. The purpose of the showrooms is not to stock large inventories and make sales but to provide an opportunity for consumers who might otherwise hesitate to buy online to see, feel, and try on products before ordering them and having them delivered to their home.

11.2.1 Store-Within-a-Store to Improve Distribution Depth

For some suppliers, setting up a "counter" or a "store-within-a-store" in partnership with their resellers is an effective way to control distribution depth—at a cost that is usually far less than opening a dedicated retail outlet. Across the many examples of store-in-store, the product

---

[1] Much been written about the factors that influence a supplier's decision to "make" rather than "buy" distribution (i.e., only to sell directly to end consumers). We refer the interested reader to channels textbooks like those by Robert Palmatier, Adel el Ansary, and Lou Stern for a review.

Type of Store	Examples	Purpose and Channel Implications
Stores-in-Stores	MAC, Clinique in Department Stores, Samsung, Apple in Best Buy	Relatively low cost and low conflict way to control distribution depth among independent retailers. Retailers may need some convincing to relinquish control of retail space but may also welcome the support to compete against online players.
Flagship Store(s)	Burberry, Niketown	Showcase the brand in high visibility, high traffic locations frequented by consumers from far and wide. Can establish benchmarks for brand price and presentation but low conflict because not a significant portion of total sales. High cost per store but limited number.
Outlet Stores	Coach, Brooks Brothers "outlet stores"	Dispose off excess, obsolete, damaged, and returned merchandise to prevent uncontrolled markdowns and unauthorized distribution. Potential for conflict not high. Some suppliers have even developed special lower-priced brands or brand extensions for their outlet stores.
Regular Physical Stores	Coach, Apple	Additional distribution points intended to turn a profit, plus set price and merchandising benchmarks for independent resellers. "Competing with your customers" means high potential for conflict. High cost per store, need several to make a dent in coverage, and require large product assortment to generate sufficient traffic, sales, and profit per store.
Web Store	Most suppliers	To sell to consumers searching and buying online. Again, high potential for conflict. Costs of managing the technology and especially the logistics are significant and often under-estimated.
Showrooms	Warby Parker, Bonobos, Zalando	Opened by digital native vertical brands (who use solely or primarily direct-to-consumer online distribution) to provide opportunity for consumers to see, touch, and try on products before ordering. No/few independent resellers so no conflict concerns, at least not yet. Need locations like flagship stores but probably greater numbers.

Figure 11.1 The many varieties of own-stores.

ownership and payment model (and therefore costs) can vary significantly, but all of them afford the supplier more control than they typically have over independent resellers. In the case of counters such as those set up by cosmetic brands like Clinique or Lancôme at department stores, the retailer often takes ownership of the product and earns a margin, but the brand rents the space and the "beauty advisors" work for and are paid by the brand. In the case of a store-within-a-store, like Sephora inside JCPenney, it is like having a mini-Sephora in the department store—Sephora owns the product, makes pricing and promotion decisions, employs the staff, and pays JCP rent and a commission on sales.[2]

Resellers may need some convincing to relinquish control of their retail space. For instance, it wasn't easy for luxury brands like Gucci and Prada, who wanted more control over the presentation of their products in U.S. department stores, to convince retailers to allow them to operate a store-within-a-store. But with luxury spending on the rise again after the 2008 recession, retailers like Saks agreed to try such arrangements, sometimes in return for exclusive rights to carry a particular brand in a particular market. In other cases, and we believe these are increasingly likely, resellers welcome the support in their battle against online competitors like Amazon. Electronics suppliers like Apple, Samsung, and Sony have invested heavily in mini-stores to merchandise their products within Best Buy stores. Although Best Buy still takes ownership of the product inventory, the suppliers get to showcase their products the way they want and the retailer gets to differentiate itself without adding to its expenses.

The third-party marketplaces of retailers like Amazon and Walmart, which allow them to be the "everything store" and offer "endless aisles," are somewhat analogous to the notion of offering suppliers a store-within-a-store. In the second half of this chapter, we will explore the advantages of doing business with Amazon in this way.

11.2.2 Flagship Stores and Outlets Stores Are at Two Extremes of the Branding Spectrum

The main purpose of flagship stores is to showcase the brand in an environment that is more differentiated and that displays a larger inventory than any single reseller is likely or able to carry. These stores are not intended to directly transact a substantial percentage of the brand's

---

[2] We thank James Black for his insights on these models.

total sales. They are more about generating consumer pull than about distribution push, and are best located in high-visibility, high-traffic areas, frequented not only by the local population but also by travelers from far and wide. Niketown stores on Regent Street in London or Fifth Avenue in New York City are a good example. Burberry's global flagship store, also on Regent Street, is, in the words of McKinsey & Company, a walk-in website that is part store, part event space, and part digital channel.[i] Other objectives for flagship stores are to establish benchmarks for recommended retail prices and to gather consumer data that can guide a range of marketing activities, from pricing and promotion to new product development. Keurig's flagship store in Burlington, Massachusetts, for example, serves as a testing and launching ground for new products. Their prime real estate and high cost of operation make flagships an expensive proposition but a brand usually has only a small number of such stores. Their performance is best measured not by store revenue or profit, but by the traffic they attract and ultimately by their impact on total system sales and prices.[3]

At the other branding extreme, carefully located discount outlets can safely dispose of obsolete products, products with minor defects, and returned merchandise, thus preventing them from flooding the market with markdowns or finding their way to unauthorized sellers. These "factory" or "outlet" stores, common to many fashion, electronics, and household product brands, are typically in remote "outlet mall" locations and have avoided incurring the wrath of the company's valued retail customers because of the limited assortment they carry. But conflicts may increase even in this space, as more retailers who previously unloaded their unsold inventory to off-price retailers (think TJ Maxx) open their own off-price or outlet stores, often right next to their regular stores. Outlet stores do need to pay for themselves, so revenue and profit per store is relevant, but their performance should also be measured by their ability to reduce unauthorized distribution and undesirable markdowns by authorized resellers. Some brands have even created lower-priced, outlet-only

---

[3] A 2018 article on how omni-channel retailers can use geospatial analytics to quantify the economic value of each of their stores, beyond the actual sales transacted within those stores, is relevant here. Although it is set in the context of a retailer, the same analyses can be applied by suppliers who open flagship stores. Article accessed July 2019 at https://www.mckinsey.com/industries/retail/our-insights/whos-shopping-where-the-power-of-geospatial-analytics-in-omnichannel-retail?cid=other-eml-alt-mip-mck-oth-1808&hlkid=78bc477367f0421cafbf7ea3561c3305&hctky=1384445&hdpid=e257e96e-8ca5-401d-b75a-d4616e647b73.

brand extensions, such as Brooks Brothers 346, and must deal with potential challenges of brand dilution and confusion, about which we will have more to say in Chapter 13.

11.2.3 Look Before You Leap with Regular Physical and Web Stores

Regular own-stores are opened with the intention of selling products and turning a profit, in addition to setting pricing, promotion, and merchandising standards for independent resellers. Naturally, therefore, they exist in larger numbers and in mainstream locations where consumers shop. Competing with one's channel customers in this way can generate even more resentment than just over-distributing, because the supplier's own stores or website are perceived to get priority over independent resellers (for example, priority access to the newest styles and models or to products in short supply).

These conflicts may be alleviated to some extent if own-stores are used to selectively fill "holes" in distribution that other channel members can't or won't take on, or to cater to consumers who don't need or value channel functions or who want services that channel members are unwilling or unable to provide. That was Apple's stated rationale when the company opened its first retail stores. The company responded to unhappy retailers by asserting that it was opening stores in airports and other locations to reach new consumers and expand Apple's reach and market share, not to shift sales away from retailers. Still, the company had legal battles with channel members. Some filed suit for what they deemed unfair business practices, claiming, among other things, that Apple sold products at a net loss in its own stores and eliminated the level playing field it had promised. Apple reportedly settled these suits in the next couple of years.

No wonder many other manufacturers, even of shopping or specialty products, still refrain from doing more than showcasing their products and providing dealer locators on the company websites (think Baker furniture or Stihl chainsaws).[ii] In other instances they don't offer their entire product line on their websites, presenting the newest styles plus special services like customization, and a small selection of sale items (think many apparel brands who depend on department stores and other retailers for a large portion of their revenue).

In addition to conflict with channel partners, suppliers wanting to add a direct-to-consumer channel must think about fixed costs. Whether for stores or websites, there are upfront fixed costs to be incurred in order to gain the benefit of broader reach and higher margins on direct sales. Web stores and the resources needed to build and run them—including collecting and maintaining customer databases, and the logistical challenges of managing inventories, delivery, and returns—are far from trivial, as we pointed out in Chapter 4. Even retailers, who are in the business of selling directly to consumers, have a difficult time managing their web business. For over a decade, Target outsourced nearly all of its online operations to Amazon, which provided software, hosted Target sales through Amazon.com, ran the call center, managed warehouse operations, shipped products to customers, and even handled customer service.[iii] Even operations-savvy Walmart struggled to get Walmart.com up to speed, making significant annual investments in e-commerce since 2011, spending over $1B in 2015, and buying Jet.com for $3B in 2016 to gain an edge in its e-commerce competition with Amazon.

You would be right if you argued that suppliers do not face the same complexity because they deal with a much smaller assortment of products. But that's a mixed blessing. As we noted in Chapter 4, one of the most important functions of a reseller is to aggregate assortment across many different categories and many different suppliers to provide a one-stop and comparison shop to the consumer. Suppliers selling directly can't offer that. So, unless you have a wide assortment of product categories, or you sell a specialty good or a high-ticket shopping good, your own stores will struggle to garner much in the way of traffic and sales. Even for specialty goods manufacturers who try to increase reliance on own stores, the pressure to expand their product line and therefore improve store performance, is high. Coach, for example, bought women's luxury footwear maker Stuart Weitzman and then accessory and apparel brand Kate Spade to expand its assortment. Then it changed its name to Tapestry to try to bring all these brands and products under a large umbrella. We'll return to this in more depth in Chapter 13.

Even the higher margins on sales in own-stores can be ephemeral when suppliers find themselves having either to learn to perform several channel functions themselves or to pay new intermediaries, like bulk-breaking warehousing services, payment processors, delivery companies, and reverse logistics providers.

Apple is a wonderful example of a supplier that managed a successful forward integration into retailing. In spite of that spectacular success, few other manufacturers will be able to pull off the same trick. So what made Apple exceptional? The list is long: deep pockets; consumer loyalty that borders on fanaticism; a flair not just for product but also for store design; a product line that benefits from display, hands-on consumer trial, and advice from a knowledgeable sales force; and great timing to boot. When people start waiting in line a week before your new products are even formally announced, let alone made available for purchase, you can get away with a lot of choices that other companies cannot.

Even so, early performance was not stellar. Apple needed sales of $10 million per store just to cover the cost of space it was leasing in high-rent districts for its first stores.[iv] The first 25 stores opened during 2001–2002 had sales of $19 million that year, compared with total company sales of $5.4 billion, and they didn't break even for another two years. But the company quickly followed up the retail store openings with innovative digital products at the convergence of computers and consumer electronics that consumers visited stores to see, experience, and purchase. By the first quarter of 2004, Apple stores were a hit, with $273 million in sales and $9 million in operating profit from its approximately 100 retail stores. By late 2014, Apple stores accounted for 12% of the company's total sales and attracted 1 million visitors a day.[v] The average store generated $6,000 per square foot.

All of this may make you wonder: what is the purpose and future of Google and Microsoft stores? Far from compelling, to our minds. If management cannot articulate a clear and compelling reason for adding their own stores, it will not be possible to generate metrics to assess their success or strategies to manage conflict with their channel partners.

11.2.4 Showrooms Are a Little Like Flagship Stores

Digital natives like Warby Parker and Bonobos have attracted much attention, first with their online success and then with their decision to open physical stores to function as showrooms. These showrooms generate brand awareness so they are somewhat like flagship stores, and to that extent, their locations, numbers, and success metrics may be similarly determined. But there is an important difference—these digital natives do not have an extensive network of independent brick-and-mortar retail partners where consumers can see, touch, and experience the products. The showrooms, or so-called "guide shops," provide that function so that consumers become comfortable with the "high-touch" products before turning into regular online customers. The original concept was that these stores would display the full array of products but not carry large inventories for sale in the store. Instead, consumers would check out the products on display and order for later delivery to their homes. That means success should be determined not only by store traffic and sales, but also by higher conversion rates, lower return rates, and higher repeat purchase rates of first time "triers" acquired through the showrooms.[vi][4]

Bonobos seems to be sticking with the idea of a limited number of guide shops, although it is also expanding its physical availability by distributing its products through an independent retailer (Nordstrom), presumably to expand opportunities for touch and feel. Warby Parker appears to be expanding its physical footprint more like regular stores. By the end of 2018, there were around 100 stores across the country, with locations chosen according to where latent demand was forecast to be the highest. Continuing at that rate can chip away at the cost advantages that came with being primarily digital, but the company has also been experimenting with temporary pop-up stores and stores-on-wheels to contain costs.

11.3 THE INEVITABILITY AND CHALLENGE OF ONLINE DISTRIBUTION

11.3.1 Whether to Be Online Is No Longer Debatable

For more than a few reasons, the question that most suppliers face today with respect to their online presence is not whether they should make their products available for sale online, but why and how. "Why" and "how" are our focus, but we begin with the main reasons why the "whether" question is no longer debatable for all but the most narrowly targeted, niche- or experiential of brands.

First, and perhaps foremost, today's consumers switch between channels all the time. As they use both physical and digital channels "constantly, interchangeably, and simultaneously" retailers scramble to become omni-channel.[vii] This is particularly true as Wall Street puts pressure on brick-and-mortar retailers to strengthen their online arms and reduce reliance on expensive real estate and other capital. And if retailers are omni-channel, then their suppliers must embrace and manage online distribution.

Second, suppliers may face significant holes in their brick-and-mortar coverage despite much analysis and planning to locate their products in stores that line up with consumer demand. The expanded reach of online distribution can fill in these holes. The holes may be

---

[4]David Bell and his co-authors document just such an effect in their analysis of the impact of Warby Parker showrooms. Their 2014 Sloan Management Review article on winning in an omni-channel world is an interesting read.

in markets where there is latent demand for the brand but which have been left underpenetrated due to the patterns of adoption by large multi-market retail accounts.[viii] Or the holes may be in small, isolated, and rural areas, where brick-and-mortar availability is thin.[ix]

Third, even in markets with an abundance of offline distribution coverage, online distribution can complement, not just compete. Most categories have a long tail of products that exist because there are small segments of consumers who have a strong preference for them. The product assortment stocked in brick-and-mortar stores is (or at least should be) tailored to local preferences. Because shelf space is limited, these stores are more likely to stock products that appeal to the majority of local consumers. Demand in the market is insufficient to motivate these stores to stock the specialized, niche items that appeal to a small segment of consumers called the "preference minority." Professors Choi and Bell describe the example of young parents who live in areas where the majority of the population is elderly.[x] Stores in such areas are unlikely to carry very large assortments of disposable kids' diapers, especially given their bulk and stocking cost. So the young parents who are a minority in the area have limited choice. Those young parents who have a preference for specialty diapers, such as the Seventh Generation or Honest Company brand, being an even smaller preference minority, are even more out of luck! The web can enable companies to augment brick-and-mortar distribution of the long tail of products for preference minorities.

11.3.2 Coverage Versus Control Is a Steeper Trade-off Online

As we said in Chapter 9, even the most differentiated products can migrate over their life cycle from being specialty goods to shopping goods, sometimes even becoming convenience products that the consumer is not willing to search for at all. If it is not carefully managed, online distribution can accelerate that migration, leading to an erosion of prices, brand image, and ultimately quality. The lack of geographical boundaries and the ease of search and price comparisons online and on mobile phones puts greater pressure on prices.[5] This is despite the fact that people shop online not just for low prices but also for

---

[5] Mobile provides the opportunity to tailor not only prices and promotional offers but also web pages and assortment to a shopper's location. It can help marketers bring prices back

other reasons, such as convenience and a broad product selection. Listed prices are usually lower online as pure play e-tailers first offer lower prices and omni-channel retailers then try to match them. So suppliers who want to control the price and presentation of their brands have to be even more careful about how they are distributed online.

Barriers to entry are relatively low online. Anyone can set up shop with a website and a small inventory of what industry lingo calls "broken sizes" (i.e., missing the most popular sizes), and advertise it on Google Shopping. Such sites may not garner much in the way of sales, but they can do a lot of damage to price points. So controlling unauthorized distribution is especially important online. Bait and switch is also easier online—retailers can bid on your branded keywords, give the false impression that they carry your brand, and then try to switch consumers to other brands once they get them on their sites.[6] Brands used as "bait" are rightfully concerned. Monitoring is expensive, and demanding that the practice be discontinued may not be effective, so they have to try to work with search engines to control this practice.

One vivid example of this, from Golfnow.com, a website that offers tee times online, hits especially close to home. One of us was a part owner of a golf course called Magnolia Greens in Wilmington, North Carolina. At the time, Magnolia Greens had never permitted Golfnow .com to act as its reseller or agent. Yet when we entered "Magnolia Greens Golf Course Wilmington North Carolina" into a Google search engine box, the SERP listed Golfnow.com at the top of the paid search results, with text offering "Tee Times @ Magnolia Greens." Clicking through, we found Magnolia Greens on the pull-down menu for Coastal North Carolina. So we tried to book a tee time. That did not work so well. Instead of being offered a choice of tee times, we got this message: "How About a Mulligan? We're sorry, but there are currently no available tee times for one of the following reasons." The website listed three reasons for a potential customer being unable to book at time through Golfnow.com website: (1) the course is closed, (2) tee times for sale are already sold, or (3) the tee time requested is too far in advance. Not only were none of the reasons valid, but all would have encouraged prospective golfers to look for other courses.

---

up from the lowest common denominator that integrating online and physical channels often leads to. We'll discuss this topic at some length in Chapter 14.

[6] "Poaching" a competitor's keywords to try to switch consumers away is not uncommon but it is the "bait" part of bait and switch that we are referring to here.

Yet another link invited browsers to "View the next available tee times at Magnolia Greens." Those who clicked on this link were then invited to call Golfnow.com customer service.

Management requested that Golfnow.com remove the course from those listed for potential tee times, but even two months later, a search for "Magnolia Greens Golf Course Wilmington North Carolina" still produced a SERP with a Golfnow.com ad that offered "Tee Times @ Magnolia Greens." While the deeper links that suggested the course was closed, sold out, or not taking tee times for specific dates had been removed, Golfnow.com was still advertising services that they did not and could not supply: tee times at Magnolia Greens.

Clearly, the most control you can have is by using only a direct-to-consumer channel online. But even with a great deal of pull and consumer search loyalty for their *brands*, suppliers of most products will find that the pull for their *direct channel* simply isn't enough and they need intermediaries to ensure that their brand meets users where and when they are searching online. Most consumers want a one-stop shop for most categories, even online. Further, the small assortment of products a typical supplier offers also means lower relevance in organic search algorithms. It also means that bidding on many category keywords will be expensive. The upshot (or, rather, downshot) is a low rank on the SERP for many category keywords, and therefore low findability online. Suppliers also have to watch the bottom line—delivery and returns can really cut into margins especially as consumers in hard-to-reach places with fewer brick-and-mortar options increasingly shop online for bulky but low-ticket items.

Subscription services are one way that suppliers can try to alleviate some of these disadvantages. Those can work for suppliers of mid- to higher-ticket products that are repurchased fairly frequently, and that have significant consumer pull. Nike's Adventure Club for kids is a good example of a subscription service from a supplier.[xi] For a monthly price from $20 to $50, Nike will ship sneakers for kids every ninety days to every month, with free exchanges (at least for the wrong size) within a week of delivery. There is also a recycling program: twice a year, parents can send back the worn shoes in a prepaid bag, to be donated or recycled, depending on their condition. Success in such programs depends on the ability to match sustainable pricing with consumers' willingness to pay, the quality and consumer pull of the product, and efficient logistics.

11.3.3 How Viable Is the Online Channel's Revenue and Profit Model?

Each intermediary takes a slice of the total channel profit and close monitoring is needed to ensure that they bring new sales revenue, build the brand, and/or perform other valuable functions to earn their slice. If there isn't enough revenue and total profit to be had in the new channel, the division of work and pay is a moot point. In the media and entertainment industry, for example, traditional two-sided markets, where advertisers subsidize content for consumers, have become difficult to sustain. This is because ad revenues are becoming harder to come by, while the number of online businesses looking to advertising as the sole or primary source of revenue is mushrooming. The online channel needs subscriptions to survive and it is not easy to get consumers to pay, especially for content that they were used to getting free or almost free. If there are several links in the chain from supplier to end consumer, the problem is exacerbated as costs, revenues, and revenue models at every link are affected. In the pay-TV business, for example, content created by artists goes through production companies, distributors, and aggregators, to delivery platforms like cable providers and online streaming companies, which reach the end consumer. How and how much the downstream channel gets paid determines how much is available to share with upstream intermediaries and the original suppliers of content (i.e., the artists).

11.4 BE CLEAR ABOUT "WHY" TO DECIDE "HOW" TO DISTRIBUTE ONLINE

These considerations of control over price and brand, consumer search loyalty, work versus pay, and financial viability of the online channel make the decision of how to go online a very challenging one. It requires careful analysis of why you need to be online. "Why" is, at the most basic level, obvious—at least some consumers shop and/or buy online, and being unavailable online means you might lose customers to competitors. But that observation is not enough to guide online distribution strategy. "Why" has to do with a deeper understanding of which consumer segments you want to reach online and why they migrate there? That understanding will guide how to go online, as we depict in Figure 11.2. We depict the likely connections between the different answers to "why" and "how" by using three different outline

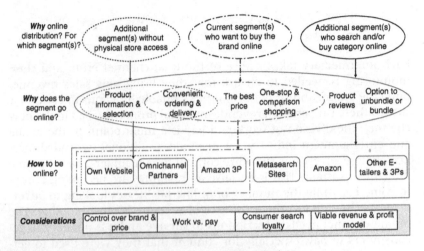

Figure 11.2 "Why" should guide "how" in online distribution.

patterns (small dots, longer dashes, and a solid line). The connections are not perfect, but you can see that the broader the segment you want to reach online, the more varied their reasons for going online, and the more ways you will need to reach them.

11.4.1 Which Segments Are You Trying to Reach and Why Do They Go Online?

Is online distribution intended to help you plug holes in physical distribution and reach consumers who want your brand but don't have access to it? Or do you want to go online because consumers in your core segment prefer to make at least some of their purchases online and you need to be where they want to buy? Is it to expand your reach to a broader segment of potential customers who shop your product category online but may not (yet) have knowledge or preference for your brand?

Filling holes in physical distribution for a long tail of products sought by widely dispersed but niche segments, and by preference minorities, is an easy proposition. These segments are likely to have high search loyalty and you could use your own website, perhaps along with a few omni-channel partners. It is also least likely to generate conflict with existing channel partners and most likely to expand total revenue in the system.

But our experience is that online sales are often higher in the vicinity of brick-and-mortar outlets. As an example, we show in Figure 11.3

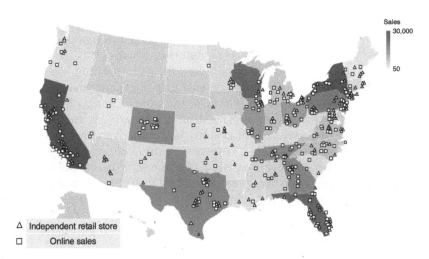

Figure 11.3 The location of independent retailers and online sales for a consumer brand.

the locations of one supplier's brick-and-mortar retail outlets (marked by triangles) and its direct-to-consumer sales (marked by squares) in the U.S. Areas with higher total sales are shown in darker shades. As you can see, online sales come largely from the same areas where the supplier has brick-and-mortar distribution. Is this because both are high where demand is high, in which case perhaps there aren't really any "holes" to fill? Or is there latent demand in the holes without physical distribution but online availability alone is not enough to generate awareness and activate that demand? Does physical store distribution create brand awareness and/or allow consumers to see, touch, and feel products, serving as billboards and showrooms that the online channel can leverage while growing total demand? Or is this simply a case of cannibalization? Suppliers would do well to research shopper behavior for answers to these questions. Their brick-and-mortar channel partners are likely to suspect the worst.

Regular surveys of where consumers search, which channels they consider, and where they prefer to buy are needed to keep distribution strategy moving with (and maybe just ahead of) the market. But such insights needn't rely on surveys alone. Fortunately, as we illustrated in Chapter 3, consumers' search loyalty to the product and to the store is easier to understand online than it used to be in the physical world, by examining the keywords they are searching for. A plethora of tools, some of them free, allow marketers to do this—for example, Google Trends and Keyword Planner, SEOBook.com, and Wordtracker.com.

And companies like ComScore provide data on the websites where consumers are visiting, browsing, and purchasing different products.

Once you understand which segments of consumers shop online and for which portion of their purchases, the next question is another "why"—why do they shop online? Is it just to get the lowest price? Because ordering is easy, saving a trip to the store or the mall? Because the selection is wider, with special sizes, colors, and styles? Because they want to research several options or comparison shop without going to several stores (or even websites) before deciding what to buy? Because they don't believe they need all of the services and advice that traditional channel partners provide or they want to pick and choose what they want instead of having to buy a prepackaged bundle, say of songs or cable channels? Depending upon the answers to these questions, suppliers may find it necessary to use additional intermediaries online.

11.4.2   Own Website Is Usually Not Enough and Omni-Channel Retailers Will Expect to Sell Online

If anyone can set up shop with a website, then suppliers themselves certainly can, and many do. Setting up one's own storefront on the web offers control, and may be easier and achieve greater coverage than several physical storefronts. But, as we noted earlier, the costs are often higher than is appreciated, and a limited product assortment and associated lower traffic and search loyalty to the direct channel means that relying only on one's own website to generate and meet demand online is likely not to be enough for most suppliers.

Should upstream brands rely on their brick-and-mortar resellers to sell their products online? Most retailers will want that option as they beef up their online arms. But the brick-and-mortar legacy business may hold these retailers back from serving online shoppers and becoming true omni-channel marketers as quickly or effectively as upstream suppliers would like. Many of them are spending large amounts of money but struggling to get their operations up to speed so as to deliver on the promise of omni-channel.[xii] In which case, should you also sell through pure play online resellers? They provide broad geographic coverage and may be more efficient because they are focused on an online business. But they are also likely to scrimp on some services and be prone to compete on price, driving prices and brand equity down.

11.4.3 Think Hard About the Functions That Pure Play Web Intermediaries Perform

Of all the web-based intermediaries that are sprouting up every day, how many and which ones does a supplier really need? Asking "why" helps determine which new intermediaries should be welcomed and how they should be paid, monitored, and managed. The one unique function many web intermediaries provide, that a single supplier simply can't on their own, is aggregation—consumers can comparison shop at one convenient site, usually with access to peer reviews. And the one reason why at least some of them may be hard to bypass is that they have become the sites of choice for consumers to (re)search and comparison shop. Think Booking.com, Expedia, and increasingly Google for travel, and Amazon for pretty much everything else. What are the commissions paid to these intermediaries worth? A lot to small suppliers who don't have much in the way of assortment options and/or the consumer's search loyalty, and a little less to larger multi-product suppliers who have the loyalty and the resources to spend on broad-based search advertising. But even for the latter, breaking bulk for small orders, shipping them, and handling complaints and returns, is an expensive proposition, in contrast with Amazon's logistics infrastructure. By 2017, half of the U.S. population had an Amazon warehouse within 20 miles, and with the acquisition of Whole Foods locations that infrastructure got even better.

11.4.4 Whether and How to Do Business with Tech Behemoths Is a Strategic Question All Its Own

Should a supplier of consumer products sell through Amazon? It is the largest online retailer by far and gets a large share of online traffic and search. So in many categories, having sufficient distribution coverage online, as measured by % PCV or %Product Category Search Volume, necessitates being available on Amazon. The "everything store" makes everything easy—for the consumer. But Amazon's size also gives it power over suppliers and other retailers and as its assortment of categories and brands and its customer base increase, its power to price and present brands in ways that benefit Amazon most will only increase too. Not to mention that Amazon does not share any customer data with its vendors, making very clear its view that any

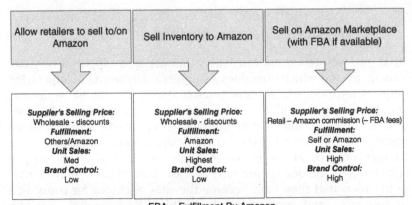

FBA = Fulfillment By Amazon
Amazon does not share customer data under any option

Figure 11.4 Doing business with Amazon.com.

sale made on its website is to an *Amazon* customer, not to the vendor's customer.[7]

If a brand does decide to make itself available on Amazon, there is still the question of "how"? Should they sell inventory to Amazon or be a seller on the third-party (3P) marketplace? Should they let their other retailers do so? Figure 11.4 shows these options and the trade-offs they entail between coverage and control, and between margin and volume. At one end, an open policy allowing retailers to sell your brand to or on Amazon as they please affords little control. Suppliers can disallow this, although the costs of monitoring and enforcement will not be trivial. At the other end, being a 3P seller and paying Amazon a commission on sales affords control of the brand and its pricing. Amazon's commissions range between 6% and 50% of sales, but most sellers supposedly pay between 8% and 15%.[xiii] And if the option of Fulfilment by Amazon (paying to use Amazon's warehouse and logistics network) is available, so much the better. In between is the option of selling inventory to Amazon at wholesale price so the e-tailer decides how to present, price, and promote the brand.

Why would a supplier not choose the 3P option, especially if it is able to use FBA and even be eligible for Amazon Prime delivery? Well, for one, it is easy, especially for small suppliers, to get lost among

---

[7] Amazon 3P and other marketplaces are basically online malls. But no physical mall we know had either the ability or the power to gather data on what consumers were buying in the stores of their tenants. So it is an interesting contrast that Amazon and Alibaba are building large advertising revenue streams from their customer traffic and data.

the millions of items on offer by over two million third-party sellers. But for another, the supplier may not have the choice. Amazon is happy to let the long tail of products be sold by 3P sellers but prefers to control high-demand products itself. The company is known to keep close track of 3P products, demand for which is initially uncertain, identify high-potential "mid-tail" products, and then try to procure and sell them directly.[xiv] Many vendors were already nervous that once they built large enough volume on 3P, Amazon would find a source of supply and take over direct sales and pricing control, becoming a formidable competitor.[xv] And that nervousness got a whole lot worse with the Amazon Accelerator program we noted in Chapter 6!

Sellers should be similarly cautious about how to engage with Google and Facebook when those tech giants become distribution partners. Whether Google shopping takes the consumer to the seller's website or completes the transaction on Google may seem like a small detail, but the ramifications for whether the consumer has the opportunity to browse the seller's other product offerings, and for who builds the customer relationship, are far from small. Whether newspapers should insist on being paid for the newsfeed they provide to Google and Facebook, and whose websites any subscriptions stimulated by those feeds should be completed on, are similarly important questions.

We illustrate these challenges in the next chapter with an in-depth discussion of three case studies from three very different industries: athletic footwear, hotels, and media.

SUMMARY

- Matching the type of distribution to demand is largely about understanding consumers' search behavior and responding to their needs for one-stop and comparison shopping while making the right trade-off between coverage and control.

- Many suppliers are jumping in with own physical and online stores in addition to distributing through independent resellers. But the functions and associated costs of bulk-breaking, aggregation, and logistics have not gone away.

- Clarity on the purpose of own physical stores, from flagships to discount outlets to showrooms, is necessary to choose the right number, locations, and success metrics.

- With respect to online, the question is not so much "whether" to have web sales options, but "why." The answer will inform decisions on "how, how many, and who."

(Continued)

(Continued)

- One-stop and comparison shopping are just as important in the online world as in the physical world. They are an important reason that simply setting up one's own web store is unlikely to be enough for a supplier.

- Web-based intermediaries can fill gaps in coverage where consumers search, but they accelerate the loss of control over how the brand is presented. So choose the right partners.

- The online channel will inevitably cannibalize sales from traditional channels. The question is how much and how fast. Before committing, be sure that the new web channel offers a viable revenue model and a fair division of work and pay.

ENDNOTES

i. Desai, P., Potia, A., and Salsberg, B. (2017). *Retail 4.0: The Future of Grocery Retail in the Digital World*. McKinsey & Company.

ii. For a formal analytical model that assesses this and other strategies, see: Tsay, A. and Agrawal, N. (2004). Channel conflict and coordination in the E-Commerce Age. *Production and Operations Management* 13 (1): 93–110.

iii. Zimmerman, A., and Talley, K. (2011). Target to Launch Revamped Website. *Wall Street Journal* (18 August).

iv. Edwards, C. (2001). Commentary: Sorry, Steve: Here's Why Apple Stores Won't Work. *Bloomberg Businessweek*, http://www.businessweek.com/stories/2001-05-20/commentary-sorry-steve-heres-why-apple-stores-wont-work.

v. Kapner, S. (2015). Apple Stores Upend the Mall Business. *Wall Street Journal* (10 March), p. B1.

vi. David Bell and his co-authors document just such an effect in their analysis of the impact of Warby Parker showrooms. Their 2014 *Sloan Management Review* article on winning in an omni-channel world is also an interesting read: Bell, D., Gallino, S., and Moreno, A. (2018). Offline Showrooms in Omnichannel Retail: Demand and Operational Benefits. *Management Science* 64 (4): 1477–1973. Bell, D., Gallino, S., and Moreno, A. (2014). How to Win in an Omnichannel World. *Sloan Management Review* 56 (1): 45–53.

vii. Verhoef, P. et al (2015). From Multi-Channel Retailing to Omni-Channel Retailing. Introduction to the Special Issue on Multi-Channel Retailing. *Journal of Retailing* 91 (2): 174–181.

viii. Bronnenberg, B., and Mela, C. (2004). Market Roll-Out and Retailer Adoption of New Brands. *Marketing Science* 23 (4): 500–518.

ix. For a good review of this and other issues related to online and offline sales, see: Lieber, E., and Syverson, C. (2011). Online vs. Offline Competition. In: *Oxford*

Handbook of the Digital Economy (ed. M. Peitz and J. Waldfogel). (Oxford, UK: Oxford University Press).

x. Choi, J., and Bell, D. (2011). Preference Minorities and the Internet. *Journal of Marketing Research* 48 (4): 670–682.

xi. Perez, S. (2019). Nike Launches a subscription service for kids' shoes, Nike Adventure Club. *TechCrunch* (12 August) at https://techcrunch.com/2019/08/12/nike-launches-a-subscription-service-for-kids-shoes-nike-adventure-club/ (accessed August 2019).

xii. As one example, see: Chao, L. and Norton, S. (2016). Race for Web Sales Leaves Some in the Dust: Athletic Retailer Finish Line Shows the High Stakes of Retooling for E-Commerce. *Wall Street Journal* (29 January), p. B1.

xiii. Loten, Angus, and Adam Janofsky (2015), Sellers Need Amazon, but at What Cost? *Wall Street Journal* (16 January) p. B4.

xiv. Jiang, B., Jerath, K., and Srinivasan, K. (2011). Firm Strategies in the "Mid-Tail" of Platform-Based Retailing. *Marketing Science* 30 (5): 757–944. See also: Zhu, F., and Liu, Q. (2018). Competing with Complementors: An Empirical Look at Amazon.com. *Strategic Management Journal* 39 (10): 2618–2642.

xv. See: Loten, Angus, and Adam Janofsky (2015), Sellers Need Amazon, but at What Cost? *Wall Street Journal* (16 January) p. B4. See also: Jiang, B., Jerath, K., and Srinivasan, K. (2011). Firm Strategies in the "Mid-Tail" of Platform-Based Retailing. *Marketing Science* 30 (5): 757–944.

CHAPTER **12**

Three Cases on Online Distribution

12.1 INTRODUCTION

The previous chapter provided a framework to analyze which segments of consumers are being targeted online, why those consumers go online, and therefore how the supplier should go online to meet those consumers where they want to search and buy, while preserving as much control as possible over brand, price, and profitability. In this chapter, we use three very different cases—running shoes, travel services, and media and entertainment—to illustrate how our framework can help suppliers navigate the online channel.

12.2 THE SAGA OF BROOKS RUNNING AND AMAZON.COM

Let's first revisit Brooks Running, the company we introduced in Chapter 7. It is 2013. While Brooks is the number one performance running shoe brand in specialty retail, it is number three overall, with market share in the low teens, so there is plenty of room for growth. The company must manage its distribution to stay apace with its share growth goals. Reckoning with online distribution is the most challenging part of this balancing act.

The frequent runner buys 2.6 pairs of shoes per year. Brick-and-mortar stores are still important for gait analysis, fit, and advice for the first shoe, but the second and third shoe is increasingly a price or convenience buy online. So Brooks cannot afford to fall behind in the growing online channel. But its goals are to effectively service convenience-seeking runners on the web without devaluing the brand and continue to be the vendor of choice and a profitable brand for running's best retailers. So what type of online distribution coverage does the company need to accomplish its goal?

12.2.1 What Do Segments of Runners Search for Online and Where?

For the runner in the lower part of what is referred to as the purchase or conversion "funnel" who knows that she wants to buy and Googles "Brooks shoes" or "Brooks Ghost Size 11" online, it is probably enough if a few trusted options with good distribution depth show up above the fold on the SERP. This consumer will easily find what she is looking for as long as a handful of stocking sites—say Brooks' own website and a few of its strongest omni-channel partners—have good search engine optimization and one or more of them bid on Brooks-branded keywords. Brooks certainly has the most complete product line, and potentially so do its best partners. So if they invest in efficient online marketing and logistics, together they can balance findability with distribution depth for the convenience-seeking runner who knows what she wants.

What about the runner in the upper part of the purchase funnel who is looking for a good pair of running shoes and hasn't yet settled on the Brooks brand? He might Google "best running shoes." In order to get into this runner's consideration set, some strong sites that stock Brooks had better show up above the fold on the SERP. As in the previous example, this requires good SEO. But for top-of-page sponsored search positions, it also means bidding on category (or what academics call "generic") keywords, which tend to be more expensive. But even in this scenario, Brooks can probably limit its online distribution to its own website and its omni-channel retailers, as these are likely considered "relevant" enough to running shoe searches by Google's algorithm.

But what about the runner who searches not on Google but on the website of a particular seller such as Amazon? This is increasingly likely to happen as Amazon grows its share of product searches online. If the runner searching on Amazon doesn't find Brooks, will she leave the Amazon site and search elsewhere? If she is a Brooks loyalist, maybe yes, otherwise, no, especially if she has Amazon Prime. If Brooks wants to target this runner whose search loyalty lies more with Amazon than with Brooks, it had better be available on Amazon.

Here is how Brooks analyzed the situation at the time. It wanted to be available where most runners shop. As we pointed out in Chapter 4, this is not be the same as being available where most running shoes are sold. The company's market research showed that over a third of runners shop for running shoes online and a significant percentage of them buy their shoes on Amazon. However, a deeper examination showed that their core segment of frequent and regular runners was half as likely to buy on Amazon as occasional runners or "dabblers." Further, this core segment was much more likely to search for a specific brand or model than for running shoes in general. This is consistent with the pattern of search for keywords associated with "running shoes" on Google. As Figure 12.1 illustrates, branded search is more frequent in running shoes than generic search.[1] The upshot of Brooks' analysis was that online distribution does not need to be broad in terms of number of outlets as long as the outlets that carry the brand are "findable" by runners looking for Brooks in particular or for running shoes in

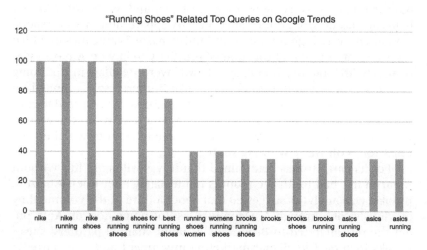

Figure 12.1 Branded search more frequent than generic search for running shoes.

---

[1] As an aside, there is valuable insight to be had from comparing the search volume for one's own branded keywords, competitors' branded keywords, and generic keywords over time.

general. Selling on Amazon was desirable but only if the brand was presented and priced the way Brooks wanted.

12.2.2 Coverage without Sacrificing Control

Among the options we laid out in Figure 11.4 of the previous chapter, Brooks saw no benefit in allowing its retailers to sell on Amazon; it therefore prohibited the first option. Amazon preferred the second option of being sold inventory, which is what Brooks did for quite a while. But Brooks was unhappy with how its brand was presented and priced by Amazon and decided to become a 3P marketplace supplier instead. The company would have loved to have Fulfilment by Amazon (FBA), which Amazon uses to attract sellers to its marketplace.[i] But Amazon, unhappy with Brooks's decision to stop selling inventory to Amazon, did not allow that. So Brooks took on its own logistics.

It was unclear how long this arrangement would continue, however. Brooks stood its ground and insisted on doing business only as a third-party supplier while Amazon made clear its preference to take over inventory. Ultimately, Amazon did not renew Brooks's 3P contract in 2015 in what (multiplied by many other brands in Brooks's situation) could well become an example of using up one's power. For Amazon, Brooks may be a relatively small vendor in terms of revenue, but the e-tailer was trying to bring prestige brands on board, whether in luxury, fashion, or performance. Luxury apparel and specialty sports equipment were high on the list of "anti-Amazon" categories in which service is important and consumers' proclivity to buy on Amazon was relatively low. Luxury brands like LVMH were steadfast in not doing business with Amazon, though some, like Burberry, sold a limited set of SKUs through the e-tailer. In return, though, Amazon agreed to control unauthorized Burberry resellers.[ii] So, at a time when the e-tailer wanted to woo high-equity brands, we have to wonder whether cutting Brooks off was a winning strategy.

For its part, Brooks determined that it was willing to live without Amazon if it had to. In the months immediately after it left Amazon, Brooks' web analytics suggested that about a third of the volume they previously sold through Amazon was lost to competitors on Amazon, but the rest migrated to Brooks' or its omni-channel partners' sites.[2] Brooks increased its digital marketing investment and also started a consumer catalog to offset the Amazon revenue loss.

---

[2]This is an illustration of how consumers' willingness to search leads to lower returns for incremental coverage, a phenomenon that we described in Chapter 9.

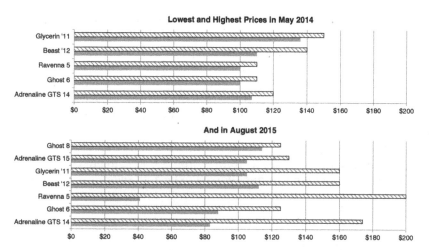

Figure 12.2 Brooks shoes on Amazon before and after leaving third-party marketplace.

Unauthorized resellers of Brooks shoes cropped up on Amazon and the company couldn't expect any help from Amazon. We tracked the dispersion in prices of Brooks shoes on Amazon's marketplace in mid-2014 when Brooks was a third-party seller and again in mid-2015, a few months after it left. The results, in Figure 12.2, speak for themselves. There were many more small sellers selling odd sizes of Brooks shoes at widely varying price points. And many of them were actively supported by Amazon—they got to use FBA even though Brooks had not been allowed that option.

This situation is not unique to Brooks. Amazon offers preferential treatment to firms like Burberry and Levi's who partner with it, and is known to permit, or at least turn a blind eye to, unauthorized third-party resellers of brands who don't.[iii] The decision not to sell to Amazon is therefore not one that can be taken lightly, even if one is willing to take a sales hit. Selling to Amazon entails a loss of control because your brand may not be presented and priced the way you would like. Not selling to Amazon may entail a different loss of control, as unauthorized resellers show up on the third-party marketplace unless you are willing and able to do what it takes to track and get rid of them.[3]

---

[3] You have to do that even if you do sell to Amazon. Nike made a Burberry-like deal in 2017 to sell a small number of items to Amazon but terminated it in 2019, apparently disappointed that unauthorized distribution on Amazon continued.

But the market continues to evolve and so must Brooks's distribution strategy. More runners have migrated online and, at the same time, many brick-and-mortar running stores have gone of business, leaving holes in physical distribution. Brooks is investing more heavily in search advertising as well as other targeted digital advertising to get into the consideration set of runners in the top or middle portion of the purchase funnel. It has also permitted some of its best omni-channel retailers to sell on Amazon 3P, which, somewhat ironically, Amazon has allowed. Equally ironically, as Amazon builds up its advertising business to fully monetize its traffic, Brooks is able to advertise on the website even though it is not allowed to be a 3P seller.

12.3 AGGREGATION: WORK WORTH THE PAY IN THE ONLINE TRAVEL CHANNEL?

If Amazon is increasingly becoming the place where consumers begin and/or end their search for products online, Google and travel sites like Expedia, TripAdvisor, and Booking are the ones that consumers visit to search for hotel rooms and reviews. Expedia and other online travel agents (OTAs) offer rooms to comparison-shopping travelers. Until recently, their prices were no higher than the ones available directly from the hotel chains, and they charged hotels commissions of 15% to 30%. Small independent hotels with a handful of properties and little brand awareness, let alone any search loyalty, are much more dependent on OTAs and can pay commissions as high as 50%.

Individual travelers can visit a hotel's own "brand.com" website (e.g., Hilton.com), or call its central reservation number or an individual property to make a direct booking. Alternatively, travelers may go through an online intermediary (or two, or three...). They might visit a meta-search site like TripAdvisor or Google's new Google Travel to explore options, see what other travelers think of them, search for the best deal, and make a booking at an OTA or with the hotel. Or they might go to an OTA like Expedia or Booking. They may either make a booking there directly or use these sites as billboards, to comparison shop and then make a booking directly at the hotel (something that the hotel loves but the OTA hates!). Of course, they may start at Google Search and either go from there to any of the sites that show up in sponsored or organic search or click on a hotel in Google's own Hotel Ads.

Meta-search sites provide information to travelers in one convenient-to-search place but transfer them to the OTA or brand .com to complete the actual booking, earning a listing fee, and a fee per click or per conversion. OTAs make actual bookings and the industry historically distinguished between so-called "merchant" and "agent" models. The terminology is a misnomer because the OTA doesn't act any more or less like an agent in the two models—it does not take ownership of room inventory and usually does not set the price. It sells room bookings to consumers and takes a prenegotiated commission. The difference turns on who gets paid when, and who has the relationship with the traveler. In the merchant model, originally used by Expedia, the consumer pays the OTA at the time of booking, who keeps the commission and passes the rest along to the hotel after the stay. In the agent model, with which Booking.com was extremely successful, the consumer pays the hotel directly at the time of stay. The hotel then pays the OTA its commission and gets the customer data. For obvious reasons—not having to wait months to be paid, being able to build relationships with travelers and more easily monitor rates—hotels prefer the agent model. Coming under competitive pressure from Booking, Expedia started giving consumers the choice of paying the hotel at the time of their stay or paying Expedia while booking.[4]

12.3.1 Why Online Travel Intermediaries Thrive

OTAs and metasearch intermediaries survive, and thrive, because travelers value the aggregation function they perform. While the road warrior with high status in one or more hotel loyalty programs may go straight to brand.com, many other travelers search at intermediaries. Hotel rooms are not like running shoes. For one, hotel brands are likely more substitutable for the traveler than running shoes are for the serious runner. People do have travel preferences, especially business travelers, and loyalty programs attempt to make those preferences sticky. But people don't travel only to places where their preferred hotel brand has a property, and the average traveler is a member of multiple loyalty programs. Furthermore, even price-insensitive travelers may want to compare options at their destination, for convenient locations and high

---

[4]There is also a "wholesale" distribution channel to which hotels sell a block of rooms at a discounted price. The wholesalers commit to paying the price whether or not they are able to sell the rooms. They sell the rooms on to other OTAs and outlets. Generally, the rooms that are sold through wholesalers are supposed to be part of bundled packages or in otherwise "opaque" offers in which the discounted room rate is not visible. Unsurprisingly, though, that does not always happen.

ratings if not for the best price. Few travelers would want to check dozens of different hotel websites, one at a time, each time they travel.

The chart in Figure 12.3 shows monthly traffic from Alexa .com (measured as number of visitors per million people in Alexa's

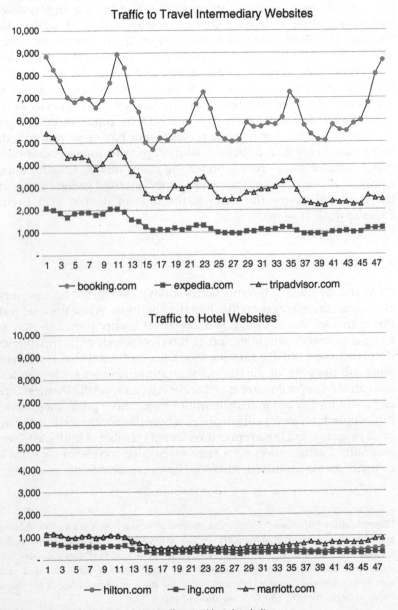

Figure 12.3 Traffic at travel intermediary and hotel websites.

global panel) to some intermediary and brand.com websites. The time period is from September 2015 to August 2019. The relative magnitudes across the different websites are more reliable than the absolute numbers (since absolute numbers can vary depending upon the measurement method of the data collection company) and they serve our purpose just fine. Traffic, as we said in our discussion of metrics in Chapter 7, is a prerequisite for sales. The large intermediaries have much more traffic than even the largest brand.com sites, and this is after the hotel companies have consolidated to build up scale.[5] As an equity analyst for the hospitality industry, Dan Wasiolek, said, "Hotel scale matters, but Expedia's reach of 750 million monthly visitors to its platform versus only 35 million that visit Marriott.com each month also matters. Both have leverage in negotiations."[iv]

12.3.2   Power from Consolidation and Pull Marketing

The OTAs have had strong leverage partly because of the traffic their sites get and partly because, after a spate of acquisitions, the two big OTAs, Priceline Group and Expedia Inc., became behemoths. In contrast, the hotel industry is highly fragmented, even after the Marriott-Starwood merger and even more so in Europe, for example, than in the U.S.

OTAs spent vast sums of money on advertising. Booking Holdings (then called the Priceline Group) was the number two advertising spender on Google in 2014 (with spending of $82.3 million), second only behind Amazon. And Expedia was number four with $71.6 million.[v] By 2016, Expedia's U.S. advertising spending was $1.6 billion and Booking Holdings' was $415.3 million.[vi] Even the largest hotel chains had a hard time matching this type of spending. Given their vast offering of hotel rooms, OTAs' advertising can pay off in potential bookings in many more locations, even if their revenue per booking is only a fraction of the hotel's. Even if hotels tried to spend more on advertising widely, those dollars would be wasted, given their limited number of properties. They felt that OTAs earned hefty commissions for not a lot of work, so they could invest in search advertising, thus

---

[5]The traffic to Expedia.com is relatively low, but the Expedia Group also owns many other sites, including Hotels.com, Travelocity.com, and Trivago.com, and together they garner much more traffic than any hotel brand.com. Also, Marriott and Hilton.com traffic compares much more favorably with the OTAs in the U.S. As of mid-2019, Marriott .com had about half the traffic of Booking.com in the U.S.

increasing traffic to OTA sites even more and making the hotels even more dependent on them.

The result of all this was that hotel companies needed the two big OTAs more than the big OTAs needed any one hotel company.[6] Large, well-known hotel chains and those in the upscale or luxury market were in a somewhat stronger negotiating position than middle- and lower-market chains and independent hotels. But even the largest hotel companies didn't have the consumer search loyalty that the OTAs do. Their contracts with OTAs, until 2016, included "rate parity" and "last room available" clauses. These clauses meant that hotels could not offer lower prices on their own brand.com websites or elsewhere, nor could they hold back from the OTA any rooms that were available for booking on brand.com or elsewhere.

Recognizing the importance of aggregation and the value of one-stop search to travelers, a group of large hotel companies banded together some years ago to form Roomkey, the website we mentioned in Chapter 4, where travelers could book a room on any of the thousands of properties belonging to these hotel companies. To try to keep its marketing costs low, Roomkey relied on "pop-under" ads. When a visitor to the brand.com website of a participating hotel chain was leaving the site without making a booking, a Roomkey ad popped up under the site. However, this meant that Roomkey depended only on traffic that came to the hotel websites to begin with. And to make matters worse, the pop-under ad strategy ran into trouble as Google, Apple, and others offered software to block such ads. In the absence of enough marketing pull, Roomkey accomplished very little.

12.3.3 Limits to Power from Regulation and Competition

Big as they are, and despite the traffic they get, the power of OTAs is increasingly contained. For one, the large hotel companies are consolidating too—witness the creation of the largest hotel company with the merger of Marriott and Starwood. For another, OTAs got in the crosshairs with competition authorities, at least in Europe, where price

---

[6] Another reason why hotels became dependent on OTAs, which we have heard from a senior hotel executive, is how they responded in the wake of the September 11 World Trade Center attacks. As travel dropped precipitously, hotels "rushed into the arms of OTAs" to fill up their rooms while airlines focused on improving their yield management systems.

parity clauses came under scrutiny because they can protect OTAs from having to lower their commissions and increase the prices paid by consumers. First Booking.com and then Expedia loosened price parity restrictions, paving the way for hotels to offer lower prices elsewhere.[vii] That was the harbinger of a similar trend in the U.S., where Hilton's renegotiated contract with Expedia in 2016 was hailed as a major milestone in the so-called direct booking wars. [viii] The company then began not only offering lower rates to its Hhonors reward program members, but marketing them in a very public and concerted way with its "Stop Clicking Around" campaign. Other hotel companies followed suit with mass advertising campaigns to attract customers to their sites and special "gated offers" to loyalty program members, as well as substantial investments in their loyalty programs to retain those customers.

Other players in the travel ecosystem also experimented with getting into the booking game. TripAdvisor, which has been very successful in meta-search with the draw of its consumer reviews, tried a foray into booking. Its revenue traditionally came from listing fees and commissions per click or per acquisition, but many travelers don't go straight from TripAdvisor to the OTA or brand.com to complete a booking. Presumably in an effort to get full credit (or "attribution" in the lingo of digital marketing) for the bookings it generates, the company introduced its own Instant Booking. A person searching on TripAdvisor could make a booking right there instead of having to click through to the hotel or OTA's website. What happens on the back end was in flux for a while. In 2014, before launch, TripAdvisor talked about how the benefit to partners would be higher conversion rates, though they would not own the customer data. By 2016, the company's website said that partners own the traveler profile and collect deposit payments; they pay TripAdvisor a commission of 12–15% only on bookings that turn into stays.[ix] And, by 2018, TripAdvisor appeared to have deemphasized instant booking. The company is increasingly building its consumer pull around being an "experience" provider with tours and activities, and it is also getting into the meta-search business for cruises.

"Book With Google" was another example. Here is how it was supposed to work: Travelers book hotels in Google search, Google handles the payment on its own system, charging a commission to the hotel or OTA partner, who then handles the confirmations and customer service. But, given how much advertising revenue Google generated from OTAs, directly competing with them is risky business, and we believe that neither an OTA nor a hotel company with any leverage should be willing to give up control of its customer relationship. It appears that

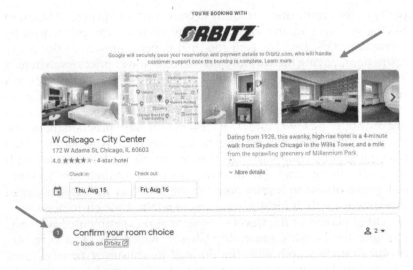

Figure 12.4 Screenshot of Book With Google.

Google is not actively promoting it to consumers. Figure 12.4 shows what one of us encountered when we searched for a hotel in Chicago on Google on August 9, 2019, and clicked on an offer by Orbitz in Google Hotel Ads.

The screenshot in Figure 12.5 shows the explanation we got of how booking on Google works when we clicked on "Learn More." Also notice the option, albeit in small print, to book on Orbitz. When we clicked on that to take a quick peek and were about to leave the Orbitz site, Orbitz gave us a "Wait, don't go" message with a coupon code for 10% off the booking if we booked on Orbitz.

Even if Google has been treading warily with Book With Google, it is charging ahead in the travel business overall. In 2019, it launched "Google Travel"—a website that aims to be a one-stop shop for travel, with flights, hotels, vacation packages, trip-planning tools, and recommendations, all in one place. These features are also available in Google Search and Google Maps. Bookings are done at its travel advertising partners' websites, but the search loyalty that such an offering can draw means travel companies—suppliers and OTAs alike—become even more dependent on advertising with Google.[x]

The devil, they say, is in the details. To us, this flux is evidence of the tightrope that TripAdvisor, and also Google, walk between the advertising and meta-search business on one hand, where the OTAs are customers, and the booking business on the other hand, where it

---

Book hotels on Google

In some cases, when you search for hotels on Google and select a hotel to book, you'll stay on Google to complete the booking process. You can complete the reservation quickly using contact and payment info stored in your Google Account.

1. Search for hotels on Google.
2. If you select a hotel that can be booked on Google, follow these steps:
3. Check your dates and number of guests.
4. Select a room.
5. Provide guest details:
   - Contact information stored in your Google Account will automatically load if you're signed in.
   - If you're not signed in, click **Sign in** at the top of the page.
   - Or you can manually enter your contact info.
6. Click **Continue**.
7. If you're signed in to your Google Account, you can use Google Pay:
   - Select a stored payment method from the drop-down menu and click **Continue**. If you're not signed in, enter your card details and click **Continue**.
8. Review your booking details and click **Reserve**.

Google will securely pass your reservation and payment details to the hotel or online travel agency that processes the booking and charges your card. Once your booking has been processed, you'll receive a confirmation email from the booking partner. You may also receive a summary email from Google.

Figure 12.5 More on Book With Google.

competes with those same OTAs.[7] Google has an additional balancing act to perform as it, along with other tech giants, comes under scrutiny by regulators and legislators for its monopoly power and accusations that it unfairly prioritizes its own business over organic search. The company was accused of talking out of both sides of its mouth when it argued during U.S. Congressional hearings that it is not a monopoly and that when people search for travel they start at "dedicated travel specialists," yet their advertising business sells advertisers on the importance of Google Maps and Google search.[xi]

---

[7]No discussion of new competition would be complete without recognizing Airbnb's meteoric rise. The home-sharing company began in 2008, and by early 2016, it had hosted 70 million guests. In the first quarter of 2019, it reportedly booked 91 million room nights to Expedia's 80.8 million, although its gross bookings of $9.4 billion were less than a third that of Expedia's (Skift Report by Dennis Schaal, August 22, 2019, Airbnb Beat Expedia in Booked Room Nights). As Airbnb takes a big bite out of leisure travel bookings, gears up to do the same with business travelers, and even dabbles in hotel bookings with its acquisition of HotelTonight, hotel companies and OTAs alike are trying to protect their hotel business, while also solidifying their foothold in the vacation rental space.

12.3.4 What Is Sustainable?

The issue for all parties is the sustainability of the distribution channels. One aspect of sustainability relates to the division of work and pay. What functions do the OTAs perform—for consumers and for the hotels? What is a reasonable payment for those functions? The most important function, we've said more than once, is the aggregation of supply for travelers in one easy-to-search place. Some also provide after-sales service, dealing with cancellations, refunds, and complaints. Others simply hand the traveler over to the hotel for these services. The OTAs should think about what functions they provide and what slice of the profit pie is sustainable. Of course, they would like to keep their functions narrow and therefore their costs down. But that becomes difficult as travelers want more or better services, competitors grow, and hotels work harder to cut out the middleman. The OTAs clearly recognize this: they have relaxed contract restrictions, reduced commissions, and invested in more services for the traveler.

Hotels, for their part, would do well to figure out which aspects of their OTA contracts are most worth changing in negotiations. A lower commission is not the be-all and end-all of negotiations. On the other hand, while rate parity seems to have become a bad word and hotel companies are happy to be freed from its restrictions, it is worth remembering that it was the hotels that originally demanded rate parity because they did not want OTAs to compete prices down. While hotels may now want the flexibility to offer special rates for direct booking, OTAs will not sit still either, and it could become a race to the bottom if such discounts are not managed well. In contrast, if hotels can extricate themselves from the "last room available" clause, they can more effectively use their yield management systems, only releasing rooms to OTAs that are in danger of going unsold. Our understanding is that some protection of search advertising is also in the works, whereby an OTA may not bid on a hotel company's branded keywords and vice versa. It does appear that the closely watched contract renewal negotiations between Marriott and Expedia, completed in 2019, were not just about commissions but also about other clauses.[xii]

Hotels should also carefully analyze the true costs of their direct and OTA channels. There are commissions on one side and mass marketing, search advertising, and loyalty program costs to drive traffic, findability, and consumer search loyalty on the other. They also should get an accurate estimate of how much they benefit from the billboarding effect. There is controversy about how big (or small!) the effect is, and the answer depends, not surprisingly, on who you ask. One online marketing firm serving the hotel industry claimed, based on surveys of several thousand hotel guests each year, that approximately 20% of direct bookings occur after the consumer finds the hotel on an OTA site.[xiii] Another study, sponsored by Expedia, reported an even higher magnitude.[xiv] A third, done on behalf of the hotel industry, suggested that the OTA billboard effect, if any, is on the decline.[xv]

Hotels should also correctly compute the lifetime value (LTV) of the customers acquired through each channel. Conventional wisdom would suggest that OTA channel users are not engaged with the hotel brand and are less likely to be loyal than those who are loyalty program members and book direct. True, but a frequent traveler acquired through an OTA can subsequently be converted into a direct channel repeater through good service and data captured at the hotel property, followed by targeted communications and loyalty program benefits. The LTV of that traveler may be very attractive, and she may not have found and tried the hotel if it weren't for the OTA. Other consumers who use OTAs may be occasional travelers whose trips may well take them to places where the hotel may not even have a suitable property, and who would take a long time to build up enough points to earn a reward with one hotel company. Such travelers may not be worth trying to switch over to direct booking but are well worth getting through OTAs.

Perhaps most of all, it is important for all parties in the ecosystem to remember that a partner today may become a competitor tomorrow and that the balance of power shifts over time. So all parties should work hard to earn the consumer's search loyalty and accumulate power. They should also try to use that power without using it up, as we said in Chapter 6. Barry Diller, under whose watch Expedia became the largest seller of travel, said: "I understand that leverage ebbs and flows in some cycles. The leverage is on one side and then in other cycles, it is on the other side. I learned very long ago that when the leverage is on your side, don't push it through the wall because when it switches, you're going to be the recipient of revenge." [xvi]

12.4 BUILDING A VIABLE REVENUE MODEL ONLINE: NEWS, MUSIC, AND TV

As we have seen, entering a new channel, especially online, not only exacerbates conflict with existing channel partners but raises the issues of maintaining control over how the brand is priced and presented, and agreeing on the pay and other support the new and existing channels deserve for the work they do. As if that is not challenging enough, in many cases the new channel not only can erode prices and cannibalize existing channel members, but it also may not have a clear revenue and profit model to sustain itself.

12.4.1 Online Erosion of a Two-Sided Platform's Business Model

Ironically, at the same time suppliers find themselves having to work with online intermediaries, many of whom, like Amazon and TripAdvisor, operate two-sided platforms, other classic two-sided platforms are becoming untenable. The digitization of the media and entertainment industry is probably the starkest example of this. As consumer demand migrates online, the pressure to meet them there is high but the viability of a revenue model for the online channel is far from certain. Almost every day during the few years preceding this writing, there was a new story in the press about the pressures being felt in the media world from such migration online, and conflicts between content providers and their distribution channels—news publishers versus Google and Facebook, networks versus cable and video streaming companies, artists and record labels versus music streaming companies.

In a quintessential example of two-sided platforms, newspapers and magazines had long relied on advertising revenue to subsidize subscriptions, providing their content at rock-bottom prices to subscribers. The typical newspaper got 75% of its revenue from advertising and only 25% from subscriptions and newsstand sales.[xvii] But with the digitization of news, consumers shifted their reading online, and the newspapers gave their content away free, fearing that consumers would go elsewhere if they tried to charge for content. As eyeballs moved away from print, advertisers cut their print advertising spending and digital advertising didn't pick up the slack, leaving the old revenue model in shambles. Over a period of just five years, from 2005 to 2010, total advertising revenues for newspapers fell by almost 50%.[xviii] In the ensuing shakeout, many stalwarts of the publishing business went out of business or have struggled to survive. The industry is still trying to carve out a viable revenue model online by erecting paywalls, albeit porous ones, so that readers get some, but not the majority, of their content free. We'll say more about this in Chapter 15 on pricing.

Digital advertising has grown exponentially, especially with the potential of targeting and the rise of mobile and now accounts for more than half of total U.S. advertising spending. But as digital businesses of all colors and stripes rely on advertising to monetize their content and services, we believe there is a limit to how much advertising the consumer will endure, let alone pay attention to. By mid-2016, P&G—considered by many as the bellwether for consumer goods companies—was backing off on highly targeted Facebook ads.[xix] And companies are increasingly skeptical about the returns they get on their digital advertising spend.[xx] Dependence on advertising has become even trickier as more consumers use ad-blocking software, and as problems increasingly surface with the context in which ads appear on YouTube and other digital venues.

Just as hotels rushed to OTAs when their occupancy rates were down, publishers rushed to Google and Facebook when their traditional advertising revenues were spiraling downwards. The lure of younger and much bigger audiences than they could attract on their own led them to give content away for free. They hoped to make enough in advertising revenue and possibly higher subscriptions, but gave up control over their advertising, customer data, and content in the process.[xxi] This only helped the tech giants get stronger—Alphabet and Facebook together took in more than 60% of digital advertising revenue in 2017, though Amazon has been eating into their share since then. And it is unclear how much benefit in the form of increased traffic and subscriptions publishers have received from these partnerships. Google's "one click free" policy, which is discontinued as of this writing, required them to offer free access to up to three articles per day that showed up in a user's search results. And Facebook's changes to its news feed algorithm in the wake of "fake news" during 2017 left publishers uncertain and with little control over how they would be affected. No wonder publishers like the *New York Times* and *Washington Post* have thought twice, and thrice, about whether to enter into agreements with Apple for its Apple News+ subscription service. At launch in 2019, the service allowed users unlimited access to recent content (e.g., the last three days) from participating publishers for a monthly subscription of around $10, half of which Apple kept for itself, with the remainder distributed among participating publishers in proportion to user engagement with their content.[xxii]

12.4.2 Music and Pay-TV Tread More Carefully

Just as newspapers and magazines have to make enough revenue to pay for the content their journalists create, music and TV/video streaming companies have to make enough to pay for the content they stream. They appear to have learned some lessons from news and are treading more carefully. Content providers have been more forward-thinking in the deals they make with digital third parties. For example, artists with strong consumer search loyalty and their music labels required that their music be made available only on paid subscription channels (recall Taylor Swift's disagreement first with Spotify and then with Apple Music).

There are also some differences between the industries that have a bearing on the viability of the online channel.[8] For one, the print channel for newspapers and magazines is two-sided, where consumers were used to getting content for very little fee. Music, on the other hand always had to be paid for in the recorded music channel (except for digital piracy in the age of Napster, which streaming services claim to have reduced, especially with their free, ad-supported options). For another, the segment that reads the news only or primarily online tends to be a light, occasional, or seasonal user, whereas the segment that listens to streaming music tends to be a heavy user. Spotify or Apple Music subscribers listen to music an average of 27 hours a week, more than twice as much as non-streamers, according to market research firm MusicWatch.[xxiii] Further, streaming subscribers listen to a lot of old songs, so it is a way for labels to make money from catalogs that would otherwise bring very little in new sales. News organizations also archive old articles but those are not read anywhere near as much as old music is streamed. Third, artists generally make more money from touring concerts than from music sales, and streaming grows the fan base, letting them sell more concert tickets at higher prices. Revenue from getting their music into shows, films, commercials, and the like, while small as a percentage of the total, is also growing at a fast rate. There is little in the way of such positive externalities for news and magazines.

Still, profitability in these digital channels remains elusive. In the music industry, there is a long chain from songwriters to artists to publishers to record labels, each of whom need to be paid from the

---

[8]The availability of news also has important policy implications that don't apply to music. News is information and policy makers want to see the population at large continuing to benefit from that information. The European Commission, in particular, is concerned about the ability of cash-strapped newspapers to continue investing in news content. It has stepped in with new copyright laws that make online news aggregators and search engines like Google pay for any snippets of news articles they display from newspapers other than headlines.

revenues generated by a streaming service like Spotify. It is clear that ad-based free service will not suffice.*xxiv* These various upstream content providers divvy up the lion's share of streaming revenue between them. Spotify, for example, pays out about 70% of its revenue in royalties.[9] Despite being the industry leader with 232 million monthly users and 108 million premium subscribers in 2019, Spotify is yet to turn a consistent profit. Its expansion into podcasts can help boost margins because the payout rate there is substantially lower than 70%. And of course, the bigger the streaming channel grows and the higher its share, the more leverage it will have in future negotiations. As of 2019, streaming accounted for 80% of all music consumption in the U.S.

In the pay-TV world too, the major players have treaded more carefully with the online streaming channel, though they were initially quick to license their old shows to Netflix for easy revenue when that company evolved from being a distributor of DVDs to a streamer around 2007.[10] Networks asked Netflix to clearly display their logos on the shows they license to the streaming company, in an attempt to preserve their own brand equity in the minds of consumers. NFL, Disney, NBCUniversal, and others hesitated to make deals with Facebook for its "Suggested Videos" and "Facebook Live" products, not wanting to cede control.*xxv* Around 2016, Apple, in negotiations for the streaming TV service it was trying to launch, asked for terms such as a freeze in the rate paid to networks, and on-demand access to full seasons of hit shows with the ability to skip advertising. TV companies resisted and, three years later, Apple was still figuring out its TV business, investing heavily in creating its own content. Various players are entering the online streaming channel with limited, specially designed bundles of programming for specific segments, and none of them are free. In a *New York Times* Op-ed, Michael Wolff said that TV "is mastering the model of the future: Make 'em pay. And the corollary: Make a product that they'll pay for."*xxvi*

All the major players in the industry, up and down the value chain, are jostling for position to get access to that "product," which in this

---

[9]The early payment structure in which it paid a per-stream rate was clearly not sustainable since consumers only pay Spotify and other streaming companies a flat monthly subscription fee, irrespective of the number of streams.

[10]Yes, we know it is confusing, but note the distinction between pay-TV *distribution channels*, which include traditional cable and satellite distributors and online streaming services, and *television channels* like CNN, ESPN, and Nickelodeon.

industry is content, as well as control over distribution. AT&T's acquisition of Time Warner gave it access to premium cable channel HBO, other cable networks like TNT and CNN, as well as the Warner Bros. film and television studio. Disney's acquisition of 21st Century Fox assets was motivated by the desire to expand content for direct streaming channels to compete with Netflix. And the merger of CBS Corp. and Viacom is also all about more content for streaming companies and potentially for their own streaming service, as well as better negotiating leverage with pay-TV distributors over carriage fees. Nor are companies in the streaming business standing still. From Netflix to Amazon to Apple, they have been investing heavily in content to reduce their dependence on content providers.

Online channels spell the demise of traditional bundles—bundles of content and advertising, as well as large bundles of content much of which the average subscriber has little interest in. But that doesn't mean the demise of all bundling. Content providers must decide which portions of their older and new content will be made available for streaming, through whom, when, in which parts of the world, in what packages, and at what price. This is the digital version of what many suppliers of physical products do—aligning different product lines with different channels based on the preferences and needs of customer segments who frequent those channels, and pricing accordingly. Sling TV CEO Roger Lynch's assertion that "consumers are putting their own content puzzle together" notwithstanding, the consumer doesn't want to go to ten different places to put together the content she is interested in, nor will she save very much money if she has to pay ten monthly subscriptions of $7.99 or $9.99 each.

New, skinnier, and sustainably priced bundles have to be created for different segments, and they have to be better curated. Differentiating the content is hard enough. Pricing it is an even bigger challenge. On one hand, there is enormous pressure to price low to compete with Netflix and because the primary motivation of "cord-cutters" and "cord-nevers" is their unwillingness to pay high prices for bundles of stuff, a lot of which they don't care about. But on the other hand, content is extremely expensive and prices need to be raised to turn a profit. It appears that the price difference between cable and custom bundles of multiple streaming subscriptions is steadily narrowing.[xxvii]

And these new bundles have to be made easy to navigate. David Pierce, writing in the *Wall Street Journal*, said it better than we could, so we'll just quote him:[xxviii]

Talking about how great cable is in 2019 sounds like bragging about my horse-drawn buggy in the age of the Model T. The future of TV looks mostly like Netflix, Hulu, Disney+ and other streaming services. But what we're discovering is, in this cable-cut, streaming-dominated world, every set of shows we want to watch comes with its own app, password and ever-increasing monthly fee. Gee, it'd be great if someone could bundle all that content together in one place! And maybe consolidate all my bills down to one, and hand me a nice box to run it all. We could call it—and I'm just spitballing here—"cable."

Streaming video distributors like Roku, Amazon's Fire TV, Apple TV, and Android TV, whose set-top boxes or plug-in sticks make it easy for consumers to bring all their streaming subscriptions together, may well become the cable companies of streaming and they are flexing their muscles in negotiations with content providers over their share of subscription revenue and advertising time.[xxix]

12.5 CONCLUSION

With these three cases, our goal was to illustrate the importance of being selective about which channels and channel partners to pursue online, guided by (a) a deep understanding of where different segments of consumers are searching for your product or category, and why; (b) an equally clear understanding of the functions provided by each channel to each segment, its revenue model and costs, and its impact on the entire channel ecosystem; and (c) the lifetime value of consumers acquired in each channel, taking into account that they may be retained in other channels. The cases also underscore the need to sweat the details (see Figure 12.6) in everything from the revenue model, costs, and profit in the channel, to who owns the customer data and relationship, to which products are authorized in which channel, to who has what influence over price.

The right selection of type and intensity of coverage is critical, but ongoing decisions about product line, pricing, trade promotions, and other channel incentives are required to keep the multichannel machinery well-oiled and running smoothly. That is what we will tackle in the third and final part of this book.

Issue	The Details	Examples
Revenue & profit model of channel	▪ How attractive are the consumer segments?	Brooks; OTAs; Music and TV Streamers
	▪ Is a two-sided market model being eroded?	News and Magazines
	▪ What is the total revenue and profit available?	Music Streaming and Spotify
	▪ Is there over-dependence on advertising revenue?	News and Magazines;
Work & pay	▪ What is the value of customers who visit a channel but buy elsewhere?	OTAs; Showrooming and Billboarding
	▪ Who is responsible for delivery and returns?	Fulfilment by Amazon
	▪ Who gets paid when?	OTA "Agent" vs "Merchant" vs "Wholesale"
	▪ What % of revenue/profit goes to channel?	Amazon, OTAs, Music Streaming
Customer data & relationship	▪ Who does the customer transact with?	Amazon inventory and 3P marketplace
	▪ Whose site/store does customer see?	TripAdvisor Instant Booking; Book with Google
	▪ Who sees and owns the customer data?	Amazon; OTAs, Facebook News
Control of the product line	▪ What part of product line is offered in the channel?	Burberry on Amazon; Music Streaming; LRA to OTAs
	▪ What about in each bundle and each segment?	Pay TV & Slim Bundles
	▪ Who takes inventory risk?	Brooks, Hotel Wholesale Channel
	▪ Who controls unauthorized resellers?	Burberry, Nike on Amazon
Pricing	▪ Who sets the price? And promotions?	Amazon 3P Marketplace
	▪ One price across channels or different?	OTA Rate Parity, TV Streaming
	▪ Can prices and other offers be targeted? On what basis?	Hotel Closed Group Rates

Figure 12.6 Sweat the details.

ENDNOTES

i. Bensinger, G. (2014). Amazon Tempts the Anti-Amazons: Talks With Abercrombie, Nieman Marcus, Others Come Amid Plans to Boost Price of Prime Program. *Wall Street Journal* (24 February).

ii. Roberts, A. (2014). Burberry Goes Solo in Perfume Challenge With Amazon Deal. Bloomberg (20 May).

iii. Bloomberg (2014). Amazon Favors Brands Like Burberry, Levi's With "Pay to Play" Strategy. Business of Fashion.com (August 7). https://www.businessof fashion.com/articles/news-analysis/amazon-favours-brands-like-burberry-levis-pay-play-strategy (accessed September 2019).

iv. Quoted in Ting, D. (2019). Marriott's New Contract With Expedia Signals a Shift in the Direct Booking Wars. https://skift.com/2019/04/11/marriotts-new-contract-with-expedia-signals-a-shift-in-the-direct-booking-wars/ (accessed July 2019).

v. Peterson, T. (2014). Amazon Tops List of Google's 25 Biggest Search Advertisers. *AdAge* (15 September). http://adage.com/article/digital/amazon-tops-list-googles-25-biggest-search-advertisers/294922/ (accessed September 2018).

vi. Pasquarelli, A. (2018). Overbooked: Expedia and Priceline Battle the Digital Duopoly. *AdAge* (19 March). https://adage.com/article/cmo-strategy/expedia-priceline-battle-digital-duopoly-airbnb/312769 (accessed January 2019).

vii. Fitzgerald, D. (2015). Expedia Yields on European Hotel Rate Listings. *Wall Street Journal* (1 July).

viii. Schaal, D. (2016). First Look at the Exclusive Rates Hilton Wrested From Expedia. https://skift.com/2016/01/20/first-look-at-exclusive-rates-hilton-wrested-from-expedia/ (accessed 2 August 2016).

ix. FAQ: Instant Booking on TripAdvisor (2019). https://www.tripadvisor.com/TripAdvisorInsights/n2513/faqs-instant-booking-tripadvisor.

x. Schaal, D. (2019). Google Travel Is Now One Step Closer to One-Stop Shopping. https://skift.com/2019/05/14/google-travel-looks-more-like-an-online-travel-agency-by-putting-all-the-pieces-together/.

xi. Schaal, D. (2019). Google to Congress: We're Not a Travel Monopoly. https://skift.com/2019/07/16/google-to-congress-were-not-a-travel-monopoly/.

xii. Ting, D. (2019). Marriott's New Contract With Expedia Signals a Shift in the Direct Booking Wars. https://skift.com/2019/04/11/marriotts-new-contract-with-expedia-signals-a-shift-in-the-direct-booking-wars/ (accessed July 2019).

xiii. Soler, M. (2014) Where Do Direct Bookings Come From 2014, originally at http://blog.wihphotels.com/publication/where-do-direct-bookings-come-from-2014/ (accessed July 2016). Later at https://web.archive.org/web/20170227082636/http:/blog.wihphotels.com/publication/where-do-direct-bookings-come-from-2014/ (accessed Sep 2019).

xiv. Anderson, C. (2011). Search, OTAs, and Online Booking: An Expanded Analysis of the Billboard Effect. https://pdfs.semanticscholar.org/aafa/633b053cc05a0fb4c bdcd3fae004731be76b.pdf.

xv. O'Neil, S. (2015). The Billboard Effect is dead, says a study of hotels listed on OTAs. (30 July). https://www.tnooz.com/article/the-billboard-effect-is-dead-says-a-study-of-hotels-listed-on-otas (accessed 10 August 2016).

xvi. McCartney, S. (2016). The Middle Seat: Behind Your Online Travel Booking With Barry Diller. *Wall Street Journal* (14 July), p. D1.

xvii. Vogel, H. (2010). *Entertainment Industry Economics*. (Cambridge, UK: Cambridge University Press).

xviii. Kumar, V., Anand, B., Gupta, S., and Oberholzer-Gee, F. (2013). The *New York Times* Paywall. Harvard Business School Case 512-077.

xix. Terlep, S., Seetharaman, D. (2016). Biggest Ad Buyer Rethinks Facebook. *Wall Street Journal* (10 August), p. A1.

xx. Vranica, S., and Shields, M. (2016). Doubts Rise on Digital Ads. *Wall Street Journal* (24 September) p. A1.

xxi. Alpert, L., and Trachtenberg, J. (2015). News App is Latest Shift in Distribution. *Wall Street Journal* (9 June), p. B4.

xxii. Mullin, B., Alpert, L., and Mickle, T. (2019). Publishers Balk at Fine Print of Apple's 'Netflix for News' Plan. *Wall Street Journal* (13 February), p. B1. See also: Alpert, L. (2019). Journal Joins Apple in News App. *Wall Street Journal* (26 March), p. B3.

xxiii. Shah, N. (2016). The Summer When Streaming Conquered the Music Business. *Wall Street Journal* (26 August) p. D1.

xxiv. An empirical analysis of streaming consumers by Professors Wloemert and Papies finds little evidence of people moving from free to fee, establishes that streaming cannibalizes sales from other channels like downloads; and shows that the net revenue impact for music labels is negative for free advertising-based streaming but positive and substantial for subscription-based streaming: Wlomert, N., and Papies D. (2016). On-demand streaming services and music industry revenues—Insights from Spotify's market entry. *International Journal of Research in Marketing* 33 (2): 314–327.

xxv. Ramachandran, S., and Perlberg, S. (2016). Ad Sales Concerns Lead TV to Balk at Facebook Video. *Wall Street Journal* (11 August), p. B1.

xxvi. Wolff, M. (2015). How Television Won the Internet. *New York Times* (29 June).

xxvii. FitzGerald, D. (2019). Online TV Lifts fees, Closing in on Cable. *Wall Street Journal* (12 April), p. A1.

xxviii. Pierce, D. (2019). Streaming Revolution Gives Cable a Boost. *Wall Street Journal* (22 April), p. B1.

xxix. Mattioli, D., Patel, S., and Haggin, P. (2019). Amazon, Disney Clash Over TV. *Wall Street Journal* (4 October), p. B1.

PART III

ALIGNING THE MARKETING MIX TO MANAGE DISTRIBUTION

CHAPTER 13

Using the Product Line to Manage Multiple Channels

13.1 INTRODUCTION

None of us likes having too few choices, but research documents that too much choice is not a good thing either. An overload of options can cause fatigue and unhappiness, and induce us to make poorer and less confident decisions—or forego a decision altogether. These findings, as you might guess, are highly relevant to consumer purchase behavior. *The Paradox of Choice*, by psychology professor Barry Schwartz, is a particularly well-known book on the topic. It argues that decreasing the number of consumer choices can relieve shopper anxiety. The book has had its share of critics, but there is plenty of research to support the idea that reducing the number of options on the shelf, if done right, can increase the odds that someone will actually make a purchase. Other costs of too many choices include the wasted development and marketing costs to suppliers, and the high opportunity cost to channel members of investing scarce shelf space and sales effort on products that turn out to be duds. Yet product proliferation continues unabated on retail shelves. The number of individual items carried by the typical U.S. grocery store, for example, has grown from about 9,000 in 1974 to 45,000, with larger grocery stores approaching 60,000 SKUs on the shelf.[i] So what gives? Are suppliers, channel members, and consumers all just wasting time and money, and would everyone be better off with drastic reductions in the length of the product line?

At any given point in time, a supplier or reseller could improve sales and profit by reallocating production capacity, inventory, shelf space, and marketing effort from certain slow-moving items to those in higher demand. However, over time, product lines almost inexorably move toward greater variety and complexity. Strong brands, as well as presence in distribution channels, are intangible marketing assets generally built with years or decades of investment in selling, warehousing, and delivery systems, and spending on push and pull marketing programs. It is only natural that suppliers are eager to expand their product line to leverage both assets for sales growth. Variety works because "sometimes you feel like a nut, and sometimes you don't," because different consumers have different price sensitivities and tastes, and those tastes evolve and change over time. Suppliers fear losing precious shelf space to competitors; they also want to be present in more channels and more outlets, but without the counterproductive conflict that can result from over-distribution. Some of their new products can eventually become like Diet Coke or Bud Light, keeping the brand and category energized and relevant.

WhiteWave Foods (now owned by Danone) built the company's Silk brand with the slogan "Silk is Soy," as soy came to be considered a healthy alternative to cow's milk. Although Silk had 80% of soy milk sales in the U.S., the outlook dimmed as soy milk lost ground to other "plant-based beverages." One of these, almond milk, grew so fast that in early 2014 the CEO of WhiteWave, Gregg Engles, said that the company was "shifting shelf space away from soy to almond milk."[ii] By late 2014, the company's sales of almond milk exceeded that of soy-based products. It is doubtful that the Silk brand would have enjoyed near the same success without the reallocation of effort to the trending category, almond milk.

Of course, not all new products have this kind of success, and channel members complain about an explosion of SKUs, most of which fail. But product line expansion is as much a result of channel members' needs and demands as it is of suppliers' desire to innovate and grow. Channel members want products that fit the differentiated image they want to portray, and they also want to stock something "special" that their competitors don't have. Both parties struggle with trying to predict which products will do well, and both struggle with decisions about which of the suppliers' SKUs and brands should be stocked in which channels. Product line expansion to meet channel needs is just as prevalent in digital products as in physical ones, as we illustrated with the media industry in Chapter 12.

How suppliers can and should use their product line to balance the needs of their channel members with their own need to grow and manage the channel, especially in times of change, is the topic of this chapter. There are many aspects of innovation, positioning, and brand strategy that are relevant to managing the product line. We do not attempt a treatment of all of these topics. Our focus is on those aspects that we consider most relevant to channel management.

13.2 CHANNEL-MOTIVATED EXPANSION OF SKUs, BRANDS, AND CATEGORIES

Figure 13.1 serves as a starting point, by showing how three levels of product line expansion by suppliers—more SKUs, more brands, and more categories—interplay with the needs and preferences of channel members and their target consumers, and with the supplier's channel management goals. The figure also shows some of the costs of such expansion, which, though known, are often underestimated.

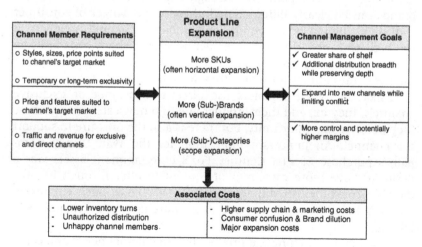

Figure 13.1 Product line expansion and channel management.

In the grocery industry, for example, warehouse club stores like Costco sell in bulk to both upscale and middle-market customers, and the brands and SKUs they seek to stock must reflect both aspects. Dollar stores are at the polar opposite, catering to less affluent customers who generally buy smaller quantities. Amazon is also interested in large sizes and multi-packs, but it wants packaging that reduces shipping costs and waste and is less interested in how the package looks on a physical shelf. So CPG manufacturers offer portfolios of SKUs for these formats that differ in size and packaging. It is not that some SKUs are better than others, which is why this is an example of "horizontal expansion." Still, the separation reduces what would otherwise be head-to-head price competition between the various grocery formats. Of course, the SKU proliferation also means more complexity and costs in the supply chain, as well as bigger marketing budgets to support distribution.

Suppliers often create separate brands or sub-brands for different channels to fit their price positioning and the affordability of their target consumers. Apparel and accessory designers are an example. MICHAEL Kors, Marc by Marc Jacobs, RED Valentino, and Miu (a Prada brand) were all created to expand into lower-priced channels for different consumer segments than the ones these designers' eponymous brands targeted. This is generally referred to as vertical (higher- and lower-price) expansion and the purpose of the new (sub-)brands is to protect both the equity of the original high-end brand and the price points of the high-end channels. But unless the brands can be clearly differentiated, there is the danger of consumer confusion, diluted brand equity, and unhappy channel members at the high end, not to mention escalating supply chain costs and the increased likelihood of unauthorized distribution, as products find their way into outlets for which they were not intended.

Especially when suppliers use direct-to-consumer or exclusive channels, they expand their product line into new categories because they perceive an opportunity, but there is also the pressure to support the channel. An important motivation for the Walt Disney Company's purchase of 21st Century Fox's entertainment assets was a desire to have more categories of content to offer through its own direct-to-consumer streaming channels. Of course, such expansion requires large investments—the final purchase price topped $70 billion.

In general, matching the product line to channel needs and capabilities and, of course, to the preferences of shoppers in those channels, is one way of tailoring coverage to minimize conflict and maximizing relevant availability. And it continues to be a strategy that many manufacturers employ. When it works, separate product lines can help keep the peace between channels. But it is often difficult and sometimes impossible to truly differentiate between the product lines, and the cost and complexity of managing a large product line and/or multiple brands and maintaining fences between channels should not be underestimated. Suppliers, resellers, and consumers learn to handle the complexity. But just because they learn to handle it doesn't mean they like unnecessary complexity or the costs that accompany it. The complexity must be managed well. We don't have a magic bullet for doing that, but we offer some guidance in the remainder of this chapter, devoting a section each to SKU expansion, (sub-)brand expansion, and (sub-)category expansion.

13.3 PORTFOLIOS OF SKUs FOR A PORTFOLIO OF CHANNELS

13.3.1 Product Line Length Is Tied to Marketing and Distribution Structure

Different brands, even in the same category, have very different product line strategies. Generally, the broader the segments of the market the brand serves, and the more varied the channels that carry it, the longer will be the product line, and the larger the investments needed in both pull and push marketing programs. Consider Nike versus Brooks in athletic footwear. Nike's product line spans shoes for sports from running and soccer to golf and cycling, as well as shoes that are intended mainly to make a fashion statement. A search for shoes on its website reveals over 800 options under "Lifestyle," and 147 under "Running." In contrast, Brooks, as we described previously, targets the performance running segment with a product line that is orders of magnitude smaller. Its website shows a total of only 100 options, divided evenly between men and women.

Nike spends heavily on advertising, and its wide availability means a consumer shopping for an athletic shoe is unlikely to be in a situation where some sort of Nike shoe is not on offer. But Nike assigns different parts of its product line to different channels. On the other hand, Brooks CEO Jim Weber jokes, "Nike spends more on advertising in one day than we do in a year." The Brooks brand, as we said in the previous chapter, wants to be in channels "where runners shop" and it encourages all of its channel partners to carry the full line. Its relatively small product line allows the company to excel on inventory management, shipment and returns, and on improving GMROII (Gross Margin Return on Inventory Investment) for its channel members.

Variety is a fundamental part of the positioning in some categories and especially for some brands. Such brands need to have especially strong control over their supply chain so that they can control costs and flexibly change production lines according to demand. And they need a distribution structure and delivery system that allows for a large variety of SKUs to be economically delivered and displayed in a given amount of shelf space. In many CPG categories such as beverages, greeting cards, salty snacks, beer, or bread and baked goods, representatives of suppliers deliver products directly to the store and merchandise them in what is called a Direct to Store Delivery (DSD) system. Because these representatives are in the store many times each week replenishing the shelves, it becomes easier to manage a much larger number of SKUs. Out-of-stocks on fast-moving SKUs can be minimized, and slower-moving SKUs that the supplier believes have potential can have some space and time to grow.

13.3.2 Product Line Guidance from Total Distribution and SKU Distribution Velocity Graphs

A brand supplier should have a good sense for how many SKUs they are likely to sustain, and which of them are promising and therefore deserve investments in push and pull. As the number and variety of SKUs proliferate and "mega-brands" tuck them all under a single umbrella, even the strongest brands need to police whether individual SKUs deserve the extent of distribution that the sales force has obtained for them. Often, the distribution is "bought" with slotting allowances, which, as the term suggests, are allowances that are paid to retailers in return for obtaining a "slot." If they don't have enough sales velocity, those SKUs may simply become part of the ever-shifting group that never quite earns permanent slots despite the allowances paid up front.

On the other hand, suppliers can't afford to be too slow to expand. Red Bull founded the energy drink category in the U.S., but Monster became the volume share leader. From its beginning, Monster has offered more beverage for less money, but it was also quick to launch new flavors, different sizes, and different package designs (e.g., resealable tops), while Red Bull for many years had one size and two varieties, regular and sugar-free. Then the new flavors and sizes came in what looked like a relative rush.[iii] Red Bull might be accused of being a little late to expand their product line.

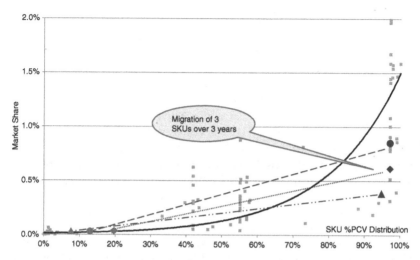

Figure 13.2 Tide SKU distribution velocity graph in one market.

In Chapter 10, we introduced the reader to velocity graphs. Velocity graphs of Total Distribution and Share of Total Distribution can provide very useful insights on whether a brand is matching the size of its SKU portfolio with demand.[1] SKU Distribution velocity graphs provide insight about individual SKUs at a more granular level. Because the distribution and share of SKUs can vary a lot across markets, and because different channel types often carry different sets of SKUs, these graphs should be drawn for individual markets and retail formats.

Returning to the detergent category we examined in Chapter 10, Figure 13.2 shows the graph for Tide SKUs in the supermarket channel in one U.S. market in one year. It uses %PCV as the measure of SKU distribution. Many SKUs cluster near zero on both share and %PCV and there is a highly dispersed scattering of SKUs at the top right of the convex graph.[iv] There are several SKUs with close to 100% distribution but with much lower shares than the highest-performing ones. As an illustration, we have selected three of these (depicted by a triangle, a circle, and a diamond) and we show with dotted lines where they ended up three years later. They were unable to sustain their prior distribution levels and migrated left and down, ultimately being discontinued.

---

[1] Total Distribution, you will recall from Chapter 10, adds up %ACV or %PCV distribution for each of a brand's SKUs.

Like any other tool, this one too should not be used without careful thought. Some SKUs that seem to be in unsustainable positions can survive. One reason is that preferences vary across markets. An SKU that is well below the curve in one market may do quite well in another, and because large retail chains often make centralized stocking decisions, such a SKU may be able to keep distribution in multiple markets—at least for a while. The brand marketer can easily distinguish between such SKUs and consistent duds by examining the velocity graphs for multiple markets. Suppliers may have good reasons to support some other SKUs that sit below the curve. It is possible that an SKU appeals to a small but highly loyal consumer segment that the retailer does not want to risk losing, even more so if that segment is a very profitable one.[2] Or one SKU may be needed to ensure sales of others. For example, a candy or snack bar manufacturer needs the smaller-sized SKUs to be "tastemakers"—for consumers to try at a lower price point before they would be willing to buy the big bags. If the small size is dropped because it appears to not carry its distribution weight in market share, the consequences will likely be felt in other sizes. It is important to consider such connections between individual SKUs, but there are also other connections, which we note next.

13.3.3 Use the Opportunity to Be a "Category Captain" Judiciously

Retailers' data are trump cards that are shared sparingly with supplier partners, but the retailers acknowledge that suppliers often hold specific category expertise. A lead supplier can be influential in shaping the plan-o-grams that specify which brands and SKUs belong where on the shelf and in what quantities. A common term for that lead role is "category captain." Captains typically gain access to retail data and can improve their position versus competitors as long as the retailer trusts them to recommend an assortment and shelf layout that places the retailer's interest first and their own second.

One of the first steps in category management is to specify the role of the category for the specific retailer. The way these roles are conceptualized varies greatly. Some researchers have proposed classifications such as "staple, niche, variety enhancers, and fill-in" categories for grocery products.[v] Other role descriptions are "destination, convenience,

---

[2]However, we think such instances are more likely at the brand rather than the individual SKU level.

routine, and seasonal." Still other role descriptions focus on whether the category is intended to enhance store traffic, market share, profits, or store image.[vi]

Within the strategic role of the category, a good category manager or captain will not only evaluate the relative performance of individual SKUs and brands, but also understand and help evaluate the effectiveness of the assortment as a whole, something that often relies on assortment optimization models. These models share the basic elements to evaluate individual SKUs. They sort the SKUs on a few major metrics (usually unit sales and margin), making sure that the margin accounts not just for manufacturing costs but also activity-based costs of storage, transportation, and so on—and recommend the low end of the tail for elimination. Some add consumer penetration (the percentage of consumers in the category who buy the SKU) and, when the information is available, the value to the company of consumers who buy the SKU, as additional metrics.

But the more sophisticated ones also account for connections between the SKUs. For example, how do the SKUs combine into a portfolio that offers true variety to consumers? If we think of SKUs as bundles of attributes that consumers care about, a large portfolio of SKUs can be described in terms of a handful of attributes. For example, the attributes of Colgate Palmolive's toothpaste product line include sub-brand (Colgate Total, MaxFresh, Kids, etc.), flavor (mint, fruit, etc.), type (gel or paste), added ingredient (baking soda, fluoride, etc.), size (trial size, 3.2 oz., etc.), pack (single, twin-pack, etc.), package type (tube, pump, etc.), and special benefit (whitening, cavity protection, sensitivity relief etc.).[3] Understanding the preferences of a channel's consumers for these attributes, and quantifying the "distance" between pairs of its own as well as competitors' SKUs on the attributes, can help Colgate design a portfolio that is diverse enough to cover the needs of the consumers and effectively compete with other products on the shelf, while limiting redundancy and cannibalization.[vii]

"Context effects" are another way in which SKUs are connected to one another. What consumers choose is influenced by the context at

---

[3]There may be many more attributes and levels underlying these physical attributes that are not visible or meaningful to the consumer but add variation and cost to the manufacturing and logistics. Examples might be different recipes, ingredients, or packaging materials. Consulting firm Bain and Co., writing about reducing assortment complexity, calls this "below-the-skin" variation, as distinguished from "above-the-skin" variation noticed by consumers.

the shelf or on the web page. As one example, you might not choose the higher-priced, more heavily featured version of a brand (call it product A) if the alternative (product B) has a lower price with fewer features, but add an even higher-priced, slightly better-featured third option (product C) and the odds that you will choose product A go up significantly because it now looks like a good compromise. Incorporating these and other context effects can, at least in some product categories, significantly improve the profit potential of the product assortment.[viii]

In a nutshell, category management is a field where retail strategy meets stocking heuristics and practical guidelines (such as case pack-outs,[ix] heavy items on the bottom shelf, kids' products at shopping cart level) and both integrate with, and sometimes face off against, sophisticated assortment optimization models. The models are useful even if they are sometimes challenging to apply in a dynamic environment where the universe of products is constantly changing and expanding, and the available shelf space is changing too as the category growth rates and retailer strategy change.

We should add that regulators and academics have pointed out that the role of category captain can be abused to restrict shelf presence for new and smaller competitors. The consensus seems to be that though there are potential dangers of competitive exclusion (a category captain can keep competing brands out or raise those competitors' costs), and the possibility of facilitating collusion between rival manufacturers or rival retailers, there are also benefits for retailers and consumers, and opportunism and anti-competitive conduct are, for the most part, in check.[x] Still, suppliers would be well advised to keep the potential for accusations of anti-competitive behavior in mind when acting as category captains.

13.3.4 Be Clear About Why and How SKUs Are Aligned with Channels

Should certain SKUs simply be emphasized for certain channels because they fit better with the positioning and target market of those channels, while also making them available to any other channels that want to stock them? Or should fences be erected between channels so that some SKUs are only available in some channels? It is important to be clear on the answer and then consistently execute on it.

For example, warehouse clubs, as we mentioned earlier, primarily stock large sizes or multi-packs of CPG products, so suppliers create those SKUs for the club channel but may either allow or not allow other channels to stock them. Of course, in effect, those SKUS will become aligned with the club channel because they are less popular in supermarkets, drug stores, and dollar stores. Organic items are more important for some grocery retailers, like Whole Foods, than for others. A supplier who doesn't have them in its portfolio will have a hard time getting on the shelf there. In fact, Silk lost shelf-space in many Whole Foods stores when they expanded to nonorganic soy milk. But that doesn't mean other channels won't also want to stock the organic SKUs, so this is more a question of ensuring that channels have the SKUs they value the most, rather than raising fences that prevent them from stocking other SKUs.

In contrast, appliance manufacturers often sell different models of the same brands at different types of retailers (e.g., Lowes and Home Depot versus Best Buy versus higher-priced specialty retailers) to meet the price points desired by target markets of each type. In fact, sometimes the same products would be sold under different model numbers at different retailers, presumably to reduce price competition. In the era of technology, the tactics of selling the same electronic appliance in Circuit City versus Best Buy under different model names and numbers no longer work (and not only because Circuit City no longer exists). Mobile apps make it easy to find the same product elsewhere with just a bar code or even a photo. Distributing different SKUs with different features through different channels, and fencing them off to reduce channel conflict, is something that has to be done thoughtfully, with clear differentiation between the SKUs. The fences also have to be monitored and enforced, which requires leverage over channel members, and the will and resources to exert that leverage.

The freedom to build such fences by holding back certain SKUs from certain channels should be written into contracts with channel members. Otherwise, suppliers are liable either to find their hands tied or to create unhappy partners. It is far easier to expand the product line made available to a channel than to take it away. Recall, for example, that the contracts that the large OTAs like Booking and Expedia have negotiated with hotel companies include "Last Room Available" clauses. This means hotels cannot fully exploit their yield management systems by only releasing room inventory to these channels at times of low demand (we are thinking here of rooms in different locations, in different types of properties, and at different times, as the equivalent of SKUs). It is only recently that the largest hotel companies like Marriott seem to be having some success in relaxing those clauses.

The agreements that brands like Burberry made with Amazon, in contrast, limit the product line sold through Amazon to a small number of selected SKUs, and in return Amazon is supposed to help control unauthorized sales of their products. As we saw in Chapter 12, not selling to Amazon may make the brand more vulnerable to discounting by unauthorized third-party resellers. An L2 report noted that there are many more SKUs of brands like Gucci and Dolce and Gabbana—brands that don't do business directly with Amazon, but that are available on the third-party marketplace—than SKUs of the brands who do business directly with Amazon, but limit the items they sell there.[xi] One e-commerce consulting company, CPC Strategy, goes further and pronounces that "selling only a limited assortment of products on Amazon is your #1 tool to combat [intellectual property] infringement."[xii]

In some cases, one channel may be given exclusive access to a product on a temporary basis. A toy company executive one of us worked with spoke about how Target would ask for temporary exclusives before the big holiday season, while Walmart was focused on the lowest prices and supply chain efficiency. Apple and Google compete intensely to woo game developers so that new, top-tier games are first available on their respective operating systems.[xiii] Game developers offer the two companies short periods of exclusivity for new titles in return for which they receive top placement on the App Store home pages and feature lists. And, up until her latest album, *Lover*, Taylor Swift's new albums were available only for download and in retail stores for a few weeks before also appearing in streaming channels like Spotify.

13.4 PORTFOLIOS OF BRANDS TO PROTECT EQUITY AND MITIGATE CHANNEL CONFLICT

All of the issues we have discussed so far in the context of SKU expansion and alignment with different channels apply just as much to the expansion of brands. Multiple brands or sub-brands sold through different channels can be a core part of achieving coverage while minimizing conflicts. But there are some additional opportunities and challenges when it comes to aligning brands with channels, which we highlight next.

13.4.1 Get Clarity on Your Brand Portfolio Strategy and Brand Architecture

The inevitable drive to reach new consumers who differ in the product features they seek, or the prices they are willing to pay, or the channels in which they like to shop, means that suppliers will often find it necessary to add new sub-brands or even entirely new brands.

Just as a single brand can only be stretched so far, especially across very different price points, it may only be able to be distributed across so many different channels without creating needlessly intense price competition and unhappy resellers. One solution is for suppliers to create additional brands and sub-brands to target segments of consumers with different preferences for price and feature combinations who shop at different channels. Of course, channels blur over time and consumers channel-hop, so the brand-channel-consumer alignment may not remain water-tight. But clarity on the brand portfolio strategy and the architecture that connects the different brands and sub-brands in that portfolio will go a long way in guiding and sustaining the match-up.[xiv]

One of the more complex arrangements of channels and brands has been developed over many years by L'Oréal. L'Oréal's portfolio

L'Oréal Division	Main Brands	Main Channels	Consumers
Consumer Products	L'Oréal Paris Soft Sheen Maybelline New York Garnier Essie	▪ Mass ▪ Drug ▪ Food	▪ Want to spend less money ▪ Look for promotions, earn loyalty card points ▪ Like convenience of buying while grocery shopping or picking up prescriptions
Luxe	Lancôme Paris Kiehl's Giorgio Armani Yves Saint Lauren Ralph Lauren Fragrances	▪ Department stores ▪ Specialty retailers (e.g., Sephora, Ulta)	▪ Enjoy the shopping experience ▪ May use advice of beauty consultants
Professional	L'Oréal Professionnel Redken Kérastase Paris	▪ Salons	▪ Value advice of stylist who understands individual needs
Active (skin products)	La Roche-Posay Vichy Skin Ceuticals	▪ Dermatologists ▪ Doctors' offices ▪ Drug/specialty outlets	▪ Look for solutions to skin care problems ▪ Recommended/ endorsed by health professionals

Figure 13.3   The brand and channel architecture of L'Oréal USA.

of cosmetics brands is distributed internationally through a varied set of retail types and formats. Consumers shopping these different channels often differ by what they expect the product and retailer to offer. Figure 13.3 shows how the brands, channels, and consumer segments are aligned in the U.S. market. The company is a "house of brands," owning many different brands in each of the different channels. In the mass consumer product channel, for example, L'Oréal Paris spans the full spectrum of cosmetics, Maybelline is primarily in the makeup category, Garnier is primarily in the hair care category, Soft Sheen is an ethnic beauty brand for people of color, and Essie is in nail care. The L'Oréal parent brand name is used only in two of the channels—the mass channel and the salon channel. The completely different brand names in the different channels alleviate channel conflict and consumer confusion, and so do the different portfolios of SKUs and price points for the same product categories.

13.4.2   Real Differentiation Is Harder than It Looks

Differentiation in product features, positioning, and pricing of the (sub-)brands aligned with different channels, and a sufficient marketing budget for pull and push are essential ingredients to make the recipe appealing. Even these may not be sufficient differentiators if consumers and retailers do not appreciate (i.e., understand and value) the differences. That seemingly obvious fact is sometimes lost on marketers in their eagerness to reduce cutthroat competition among resellers. And to be fair, it is often difficult to know in advance which differences consumers and retailers will fully appreciate.

In Chapter 3, we related the story of DuPont's highly successful launch of Stainmaster branded nylon carpeting, and how they then lost control of the brand because of over-distribution. The company tried to rectify the situation with what it called "MasterPlan." Masterplan introduced three new Stainmaster sub-brands—Stainmaster Plus, Grand Luxura, and Masterlife—and made Masterlife available only to a subset of retailers who were designated as "Master Stores." But consumers and retailers may have been unclear on the points of differences among the three sub-brands, and the marketing budget was not sufficient to support them all, so the many brand extensions became unmanageable and took the company's focus off its key asset—the core Stainmaster brand.

John Deere arguably had more success in introducing a new line of "D-class" lawn tractors to be sold at big-box home stores. That new line not only had a lighter-weight frame, but substituted a Briggs and Stratton engine for the Kawasaki engine in tractors sold by dealers.

These features are easy to distinguish, as is the price. Consumer Reports gave the new line positive reviews. But it also pointed out that dealers now offer an in-between "compromise" choice—models with Kawasaki engines combined with the lighter "D" frame, priced only a little more than the big-box models, which begins to blurs the distinction between the lines.[xv]

The creation of slim bundles for the streaming channel in the TV industry is similar to creating new brands. Traditional players from the pay-TV system got their feet wet gradually—NBC Universal with a comedy-focused subscription web video service, Viacom with Noggin for preschoolers, and HBO with its HBO Now app. But now they are forging ahead. Disney must differentiate its much ballyhooed Disney+ streaming service from Hulu, which it now controls, whether it offers them separately or in a bundle. AT&T planned to offer three versions of a streaming service with content that came with its contentious acquisition of Time Warner but is realizing that the tiers are hard to differentiate effectively. They need to carefully design the right bundles at the right price to target segments of consumers who will stream but are not willing to pay for large bundles of traditional pay-TV. And they need to be able to retain these consumers. After all, "If you're the fourth or fifth subscription service people pay for every month, you're as easy to leave as to try," says Forrester Research media analyst James McQuivey.[xvi] At the same time, networks need to shore up the attractiveness of their offerings in the traditional pay-TV channel so that those consumers don't feel cheated and accelerate their migration online.

13.5 EXPANDING TO SUPPORT AN EXCLUSIVE OR DIRECT CHANNEL

In Chapters 4 and 6, we discussed the value to consumers of one-stop shopping. Consumers may not deem it worth the effort to visit a store or website that carries neither multiple brands nor multiple categories. That is why, when suppliers use either exclusive or direct channels, which do not carry competing brands, they feel the need to offer a wider array of categories.

13.5.1 Enticing Consumers to the Direct Channel Requires Greater Scale and Scope

As you may recall from Chapter 6, one reason why online travel agents (OTAs) were able to build up such strong positions in the hotel industry is variety. They can offer the traveler a variety of rooms at many price points in any given location. After the failure of RoomKey from lack of marketing support, among other things, the large hotel chains have been trying to boost traffic to their direct-to-consumer channel, through advertising and improved loyalty programs. By some accounts, the drive towards consolidation among hotel chains, such as the merger of Marriott International and Starwood Hotels & Resorts, is motivated by building the scale necessary to make both the loyalty programs and direct booking more attractive to consumers. The more likely it is that a traveler will find a room to suit their needs at a brand.com website, and the easier it is both to earn and to redeem loyalty points, the more likely she is to book a room in one of the hotel company's properties and do so using the direct channel. The Marriott-Starwood merger created the world's largest hotel company, with 1.1 million rooms in more than 5,500 hotels spanning as many as 30 brands. As industry watchers noted at the time, the merger offered "millions in cost savings, and more market share to fend off competition from online travel agencies and emerging threats from short-term rental companies like Airbnb."[xvii]

In a similar vein, media companies, both content providers and distributors, are investing heavily in content so as to have a larger variety of offerings for direct-to-consumer streaming and other platforms. We previously mentioned the Walt Disney Company's motivation to buy Fox media assets. Disney also acquired a 60% stake in Hulu, the direct-to-consumer video streaming service, as part of that deal. AT&T's hard-fought $81 billion acquisition of Time Warner is towards the same purpose—the company needs content to offer in skinny bundles for cord-cutting consumers, such as the WatchTV bundle it unveiled in 2018, and acquiring Time Warner ensures it will have willing programmers to make that content accessible. Needless to say, such expansion of scale and scope comes at a high price, the benefits of which should be evaluated carefully before jumping in. AT&T is already being criticized by some investors for having lost focus and taken on a lot of debt in its acquisitions without yet having a clear strategy for its direct streaming channel.

Also, as suppliers go direct, they may stop distributing their products through independent channels in order to promote their direct channel, but they need to think hard about whether the direct channel has built enough awareness and interest among consumers. Twenty years after Progressive Insurance opened up a direct channel, over half of its revenues were still coming from independent agents. Less than 10% of Apple's iPhone sales come through its direct channel. So we would advise AT&T, Disney, and others to tread slowly and softly as they decide to stop licensing their content to Netflix and other streaming services, and make it exclusively available on the new streaming channels they themselves launch.[xviii] In this case, there is the added complication that the creators of the content, who get a cut of the revenue, would understandably not be happy to see their earnings constrained by the companies' decision to air the shows only on their own channels. This is not unexpected; in the past, content providers have not been pleased when their channels were excluded from slim bundles. ESPN sued Verizon for unbundling its channels out of the FiOS "Custom TV" plan and offering them as add-ons, saying the practice violated their contractual agreements. It took a year for the companies to settle, with Verizon offering a second "Custom TV" bundle that includes ESPN and ESPN2. This is an important reason why Disney, AT&T's Warner Media, and others are increasingly paying high upfront fees to content producers instead of a share of profits from future reruns on various platforms.

13.5.2 Sometimes It Makes Sense to Sacrifice Profits to Support the Channel

The Porsche Boxster debuted on January 26, 1997, during Super Bowl XXXI, and marked the introduction of Porsche's first major new model in many years. In fact, the company had recently pared back the product line drastically, eliminating both lower- and higher-priced two-door models compared to the mainstay, the 911, because they had not succeeded in the market.

To woo a larger audience, the Boxster was initially priced at $39,980, a far cry from the $63,750 commanded by the base model 911. It was backed by a $20 million first-year marketing budget. Executives claimed that one of the Boxster's primary goals was also to attract a younger audience and to increase the number of female Porsche buyers.

In one sense, the Boxster was very successful. For the first five years Boxster sales in the U.S. exceeded 911 sales and total Porsche sales more than doubled. But by another measure, profits, the picture was quite different. According to a 2003 Lehman Brothers report, Porsche made more money on the 700 GT2 models it sold in that year than on *all* of the Boxster sales. Another model, the 911 Turbo, sold slightly more than 4,000 units and generated over four times as much profit as the 18,000 or so Boxsters sold. So why would the company risk cannibalizing its highly profitable high-end sales with this new sub-brand?

Industry observers have commented that while one goal of the Boxster was to pump up sales to other demographics, another aim, even more critical, was to shore up the declining dealer network. Porsche's position as the performance sports car that can be driven every day relies on dealers to provide service. Unlike (even) more exotic sports cars (e.g., Ferrari and Lamborghini), this "everyday" positioning relies on having convenient access to dealer service. In the decades prior to the Boxster's introduction, the Porsche dealer footprint had declined sharply. Several states had only one dealer and at least five had none by 2003. We believe the profit data support the view that the Boxster introduction did far more for their dealers than for Porsche company profits. To some extent this was a rather unique case of a strong brand franchise with opportunities to grow beyond a narrow definition of "performance' sports cars. Later models, especially the SUVs, have generated profits for both the company and their dealers, but the Boxster showed the way and buttressed dealers at a critical time in the brand's history. Sales have grown mainly through stronger dealers, not more dealers. It is also noteworthy that even with an expanded product line that now includes three four-door models, two of which are SUVs, demand for Porsche is still concentrated in economically prosperous areas. The company has had success in introducing new, well-differentiated models that leverage the brand and existing dealers in urban areas, as opposed to expanding coverage in thinly populated regions.

13.5.3 But Make Sure the Long Tail Is Not Wagging the Strategy Dog

As you expand distribution into more and more channels, and you expand your product line to satisfy the needs of those channels, the danger of the tail wagging the dog is a very real one.

In earlier chapters, we documented the discipline with which Brooks Running approaches its distribution strategy. But that was not always the case. The company was founded in 1914, and its early products included ice skates and fashion bathing footwear, but it quickly moved into cleated footwear in the 1920s and 1930s. By the 1970s, Brooks designed and manufactured numerous product lines for a variety of different sports. The company benefited from a nationwide jogging craze at the time and reached its pinnacle when its running shoes ranked as one of the top brands in the U.S. In 1979, the world champion Pittsburgh Pirates wore Brooks cleats, and the company had the endorsements of quarterback Dan Marino and marathoner Zola Budd. But the company had overextended itself, having expanded into all kinds of footwear (basketball, aerobics, baseball, and more) and into all kinds of channels (specialty retailers, national chains, promotional retailers, and discount chains). Brooks shoes were being sold at prices as low as $20. And manufacturing quality took a nosedive. Nearly 30 percent of the shoes were returned, compared with an industry average return rate of 1 percent.

The company declared bankruptcy in 1981 and accumulated $60 million in losses during the eighties, suffering eight consecutive years of unprofitability. Beset by financial problems, Brooks tried to lower costs by using less expensive materials. By 1993, when the company was sold to Rokke Group, U.S. sales had plateaued at $25 million and Brooks had fallen from the number three brand in the late 1970s to number twenty-five, with only 0.4% of the market. In the words of Jim Weber, president and CEO since 2001, "Brooks had lost its way. We tried to be everything to everybody. We had become barbecue and lawnmower shoes. We were present but unimportant. Nobody would have missed us if we disappeared." Many analysts believed that the Brooks brand had suffered from the pursuit of "growth for growth's sake." Weber focused Brooks on performance running with a strategy to have a premium product and premium brand in a premium chan- nel. In a series of bold moves over two years, Brooks pulled out of the discount channels, walking away from $20 million in revenue. The company eliminated 55% of its product assortment, and it rechanneled distribution through the specialty stores and focused on competencies that were important to that channel. The challenge for Brooks was to rapidly expand distribution in this specialty channel and grow sales of high-end, technically superior running shoes, something that it did successfully within a few years and has maintained ever since. Today, prestige brands like Burberry and Coach are following similar strategies to recover from over-expansion.

13.6 CAUTIONS AT ALL THREE LEVELS OF PRODUCT LINE EXPANSION

13.6.1 Preempt, Monitor, and Control Unauthorized Distribution

More products in the lineup, and more restrictions on who is allowed to sell what in which channel, means more opportunities for unautho- rized distribution. The proportion of sales that goes through unautho- rized dealers is generally much lower than their numeric counts would suggest, but they can wreak considerable havoc on price points. For as long as we can remember, diverting has been a problematic issue, especially for high-value, easy-to-ship products. But the difficulty of tracking where the diverted product came from and where it is sold is magnified when retailers that historically had their reach effectively confined to a local geographic market can sell through their own websites and aggressively seek business with a national, or in some cases global, source. Amazon.com and eBay have enabled many small retailers to sell well outside the boundaries of what upstream marketers originally imagined. (Though, recall from Chapter 2 that, in principle, the same issue was present with the 1-800 sales of wallpaper).

Suppliers can (and do) try to monitor and pursue these unauthorized resellers after the fact, but perhaps the most effective way to deal with the problem is to plug the sources from which they get their hands on the product. The sources may be closeouts of part of the product line, inventory liquidations from previously legitimate and/or bankrupt dealers, or diverted merchandise from unintentional or intentional overstocks by authorized resellers. Technologies like RFID, QR codes, and blockchain can help track unauthorized products to their source.

But it is better to prevent a problem from occurring than to try to solve it later. Preventing excess inventory from finding its way into the marketplace means first running a tight ship with respect to sales forecasting and shipments, and then buying back unsold inventory if necessary. But it also means making sure that pricing and promotion policies are not exacerbating this problem. As we will discuss in the next chapter, the far too common practice of offering volume discounts to resellers not only can encourage the largest resellers to divert product but can also make it extra profitable for them to do so.

Upstream marketers may tolerate gray markets in order to generate some sales from markets that they are not otherwise planning to enter, or to generate volume and price discriminate (charge higher or lower prices according to local market demand conditions), but they often find that the longer-term channel conflict and price erosion are not worth it.[xix] The wholesale distribution channel in the hotel industry that we briefly mentioned in Chapter 12 is a good example. Hotels use it to sell excess inventory and reach markets they may otherwise not have access to, but many believe that this leads to undercutting prices because the rooms find their way into markets they are not intended for.[xx]

13.6.2 Curation Is More Important than Ever

As choices explode and search costs decrease, consumers are expanding their horizons and trying more new products, from packaged foods to services to music and television shows. They also are less tolerant of being forced into buying bundles of things that include items they don't want. But the cost of search is lower, not zero, and the importance of curating large assortments to individual preferences is growing, not decreasing. According to David Pierce, a technology writer for the *Wall Street Journal*, the race among music services "won't be decided by the largest library or the most exclusive content—or even the best app. It's the battle of intelligence: curation and personalization, voice recognition and search. It's a battle to be the one who responds when you turn to your speakers and shout, 'Play me some music!'"[xxi]

Case in point: Nike, the world's leading marketer of athletic footwear, apparel, equipment, and accessories for a wide variety of sports and fitness activities, is making a major push to sell directly to consumers through what it calls its "Consumer Direct Offense" strategy. The company purchased Zodiac Inc., a consumer data analytics company, to help power 1-to-1 curation, selling, and relationship building with consumers. Nike's Adventure Club for kids, the subscription service we mentioned in Chapter 11, offers a curated set of products for a specific target market, with the added advantage of a somewhat assured subscription revenue stream, even though the subscription can be cancelled at any time.

Catalina Marketing is a company, now in a joint venture with A.C. Nielsen, that works with CPG clients and uses shoppers' purchase behavior to implement targeted promotions and advertising. It conducted a large-scale analysis of more than 30 million shoppers across almost 10,000 grocery stores and found that on average, shoppers bought just 0.7% of available SKUs over the course of a year.[xxii] The percentage was not much bigger even for top shoppers, who accounted for 80% of retailers' sales—they bought only 1% of SKUs. That may sound like evidence for excessive product proliferation. But Catalina also noted that no two of the millions of shoppers they analyzed bought the same set of SKUs over the course of the year, underscoring the importance of targeting curated products and offers that meet the individual preferences of consumers.

13.7 CONCLUSION

This chapter has dealt with modifying the product line supply not just to match demand but also to manage multiple distribution channels. But suppliers need to adjust other aspects of supply to manage their channels: that can mean changing pricing schedules, ramping trade promotion up or down, designing incentives that reward certain channels for performing certain functions, and managing the pull side of marketing. We will discuss channel pricing and promotion strategies, and channel incentives, in depth in the next two chapters, and then bring the push and pull sides together in the final chapter.

Summary

- Channel relationships and distribution presence, like brands, are important intangible marketing assets. Suppliers attempt to both leverage and reinforce those assets by expanding their product line.

- At any point in time, reducing the product line to focus on the strongest items can improve sales and profits. Over longer time horizons, however, product lines of successful companies tend to grow, and with good reason. The goal should be to manage the resulting complexity, not necessarily eliminate it.

- Suppliers expand their product lines along three dimensions: adding more SKUs of a brand within a category, introducing additional brands or sub-brands in a category, and expanding into more categories or sub-categories.

- Portfolios of SKUs and brands are tailored for different channels to reflect differences in consumer preferences, the demands of channel members, and efforts to reduce channel conflict.

- Distribution velocity curves, an attribute-based view of SKU diversity, and a good understanding of context effects and other connections between individual SKUs, are useful tools to manage the SKU portfolio.

- A clear brand architecture that aligns differentiated brands with channels and consumer segments is similarly important to manage the brand portfolio. But meaningful product differentiation (beyond attempts to merely make direct comparisons difficult) is harder than you might think, and technology is making it ever harder to maintain fences between channels. So, product line expansion can easily result in confused consumers and unhappy channel members, while increasing supply chain and marketing costs.

- Expanding product lines and trying to align them with different channels also means more unauthorized distribution, and the web has exacerbated that problem. Suppliers must control inventory if they want to contain unauthorized distribution.

- Growth often requires that suppliers expand into new categories but they feel especially pressured to do so when they use exclusive or direct channels because a wider assortment is needed to bring consumers into the store and generate sufficient revenues for the channel.

- But such expansion of scale and scope is costly, so it needs to be done with a clear understanding of the right profit metrics and the right time horizon to assess them in.

- The online channel is a great un-bundler, but consumers still value curation, so designing more relevant bundles for different segments (channels, consumers, and occasions) is key.

- In all of this channel driven expansion of the product line, it is easy to lose sight of one's brand and channel strategy. So don't let the tail wag the dog!

ENDNOTES

i. Ellickson, P. (2016). The Evolution of the Supermarket Industry From A&P to Wal-Mart. In: *Handbook on the Economics of Retail and Distribution.* (Cheltenham: Edward Elgar Publishing), pp. 368–391.

ii. https://www.investors.com/research/the-new-america/whitewave-foods-growing-on-plantbased-alternative-milk/.

iii. Although Red Bull did market a water under a different brand name and a cola product under the Red Bull brand, there was no early visible response to Monster's product variety.

iv. This pattern is very common. One of us, along with a colleague, Kenneth Wilbur, conducted a large-scale analysis of the national distribution-share patterns for 37 CPG categories covering over 79,000 SKUs and 9,000 brands. We found wide dispersion of market shares and distribution across SKUs, with even brands that are category leaders offering large numbers of low-performing SKUs. In the average category, the maximum SKU market share was about 32 times larger than the average and the maximum distribution was about 15 times larger than the average. See for details: Wilbur, K. and Farris, P. (2014). Distribution and Market Share. *Journal of Retailing* 90 (2): 154–167.

v. Dhar, S., Hoch, S., and Kumar, N. (2001). Effective Category Management Depends on the Role of the Category. *Journal of Retailing* 77 (2): 165–184.

vi. The latter are from an undated presentation by Gordios Consulting, "Efficient Consumer Response."

vii. Professors Pete Fader and Bruce Hardie first proposed a model in which preferences for, and choices among, large numbers of SKUs are recast as preferences for levels of a much smaller number of attributes. As you might imagine, this can make the modeling a lot easier, and Professor Robert Rooderkerk and his colleagues have recently applied this attribute-based modeling to the otherwise very complicated task of optimizing a retail store's SKU portfolio in a category: Fader, P., and Hardie, B. (1996). Modeling Consumer Choice among SKUs. *Journal of Marketing Research* 33 (4): 442–452. Rooderkerk, R., van Heerde, H., and Bijmolt, T. (2013). Optimizing Retail Assortments. *Marketing Science* 32 (5): 679–826.

viii. See, for example: Rooderkerk, R.P., van Heerde, H.J., and Bijmolt, T.H.A. (2011). Incorporating Context Effects into a Choice Model. *Journal of Marketing Research* 48 (4): 767–780. However, not all types of products and not all types of purchase environments may lend themselves to context effects. These effects are more likely to show up in practice when product features are concrete and easy to compare so that the consumer can tell, for example, whether one product dominates another, when most consumers value the same features (camera or screen resolution, processor speed, diamond clarity), and when their preferences are not very strong. These articles offer a good discussion: Frederick, S., Lee, L., and Baskin, E. (2014). The Limits of Attraction. *Journal of Marketing Research* 51 (4): 487–507. Huber, J., Payne, J., and Puto, C. (2014). Let's Be Honest About the Attraction Effect. *Journal of Marketing Research* 51 (4): 520–525.

ix. If stores receive shipments of individual SKUs in case quantities, this means that the designated shelf space will have to be sufficient to hold the case quantities, plus the safety stock. Or, in some cases, back room inventory held for periodic restocking. These logistical constraints can affect the viability of proposed shelf layouts.

x. See, for example: Klein, B. and Wright, J. (2006). Antitrust Analysis of Category Management: Conwood v. United States Tobacco Co. https://www.justice.gov/atr/antitrust-analysis-category-management-conwood-v-united-states-tobacco. https://www.antitrustlawblog.com/2012/05/articles/articles/planogram-and-category-captain-marketing-programs-held-non-exclusionary/. Desrochers, D., et al. (2003). Analysis of Antitrust Challenges to Category Captain Arrangements. *Journal of Public Policy & Marketing* 22 (2): 201–215. FTC (2005). Category Management: An Interview with FTC Commissioner Thomas B. Leary, https://www.ftc.gov/sites/default/files/documents/public_statements/category-management-interview-ftc-commissioner-thomas-b.leary/050328abainterview.pdf (accessed August 2019). Gooner, R., Morgan, N., and Perreault, W. (2011). Is Retail Category Management Worth the Effort (and Does a Category Captain Help or Hinder)? *Journal of Marketing* 75 (5): 18–33.

xi. Zaryouni, Homa (2014), "Why Hasn't Amazon Cracked Fashion?" *L2 Daily* (November 26).

xii. CPC Strategy (2018). Proactively Protect Your Brand From Unauthorized Sellers on Amazon. Webinar recording. https://www.slideshare.net/CPCStrategy-ConvertRetailIntent/proactively-protect-your-brand-from-unauthorized-sellers-on-amazon (accessed 20 August 2018).

xiii. Sherr, I. and Wakabayashi, D. (2014). Apple, Google: Game of Apps. *Wall Street Journal* (22 April), p. B1.

xiv. David Aaker and his co-author write extensively about brand architecture in this book: Aaker, D., and Joachimsthaler, E. (2000). *Brand Leadership*. (New York: Free Press).

xv. Perratore, E. (2015). Nothing Runs Like a Deere You Buy at the Dealer. *Consumer Reports*, https://www.consumerreports.org/cro/news/2015/05/nothing-runs-like-a-deere-you-buy-at-the-dealer/index.htm (accessed August 2019).

xvi. Jurgensen, J. (2019). Short Cuts: Hollywood's Next Big Test. *Wall Street Journal* (31 August), p. B1.

xvii. Ting, D. (2016). Starwood Rival Takeover Bid: What It Means for Brands, Executives, and Shareholders. https://skift.com/2016/03/15/what-the-starwood-rival-takeover-bid-means-for-brands-executives-and-shareholders/.

xviii. FitzGerald, D. (2018). AT&T Plans 3-Tier Streaming. *Wall Street Journal* (30 November), p. B3. Al-Muslim, A. (2018). Verizon Warns of Disney Blackout in Spat. *Wall Street Journal* (27 December), p. B3. Flint, J. (2018). Netflix Nabs Ex-Disney Talent. *Wall Street Journal* (18 December), p. B1. Schwartzel, E., and Armental, M. (2019). Disney Spends Big on Its Streaming Bet. *Wall Street Journal* (8 May).

xix. For a good review, see: Antia, K., Bergen, M., and Dutta, S. (2004). Competing with Gray Markets. *MIT Sloan Management Review* (Fall).

xx. See, for example: Trivago Business Blog (2019). How Can Hoteliers Deal With Wholesale Distribution Dilemma. https://businessblog.trivago.com/wholesale-distribution-dilemma/ (accessed October 5 2019).
Hospitality Net (2019). Wholesalers Are the Biggest Issue in Hotel Distribution. https://www.hospitalitynet.org/news/4091868.html (accessed October 5, 2019).

xxi. Pierce, D. (2018). A Search for Music Streamers' High Notes. *Wall Street Journal* (25 June), p. B1.

xxii. Catalina (2013). Engaging the Selective Shopper. https://www.catalina.com/news/press-releases/new-study-shoppers-purchase-less-than-one-percent-of-available-products-at-their-grocers/ (accessed June 2018).

CHAPTER 14

Harnessing the Power of Price and Price Promotions

14.1 INTRODUCTION

With a few exceptions, suppliers distributing through independent middlemen don't set the retail price to be paid by the end consumer. However, suppliers do influence middlemen's selling prices with their own actions, such as the prices and incentives they offer to channel partners (and there are many others). The influence process is often messy, and dissatisfaction with pricing is central to all four root causes of conflict we laid out in Chapter 3: (1) The myopic tendency of each party to maximize only its own profit can result in retail prices that are too high for the good of the whole channel; (2) over-distribution puts pressure on retailers to price too low, and this tendency is exacerbated for brands with strongest consumer search loyalty;[1] (3) the division of

---

[1] As we explained in Chapter 3, the more a consumer is willing to search for a brand, the more pressure a retailer feels to price competitively so as not to lose the consumer, and their entire shopping basket, to a competing retailer.

pay between suppliers and channel members depends in large part on the price and promotion levels each party sets; and (4) at least some of the angst about the future is about the ability to charge a price that sustains the functions needed in the face of new, especially online, distribution channels.

Channel incentives don't substitute for making the right decisions with respect to the breadth and type of distribution, or even for offering a competitive product line, which is why we discussed those issues before getting to this topic. But once those decisions are made, smart pricing, promotions, and other incentive programs can oil the channel machinery to ensure that it operates more smoothly. Pricing, of course, is a big topic, with several books devoted entirely to it; the same is true of promotions. As we did with product line management, we focus our discussion, in this chapter and the next one, on those aspects of supplier pricing and incentives that we consider most relevant to managing distribution. We'll lay the groundwork in this chapter with a discussion of why a single supplier price is generally not a good idea; the role of price promotions offered to channel members; and the challenges in assessing their costs and profit impact. In Chapter 15, we'll build on this foundation by offering guidance for building pricing and incentive programs that work for suppliers and their multiple channel partners.

14.2 WHY ONE "EVERYDAY" PRICE TO RESELLERS IS USUALLY NOT A SMART IDEA

14.2.1 Variable Supplier Prices Can Alleviate Double Marginalization

As we showed with a simple example in Chapter 3, when a supplier charges a fixed price to the channel member, the channel member will in turn set its selling price to maximize its own profit. And, especially when the channel member doesn't face competitive pressures, that price will be too high to maximize the total profit pie. The example in Chapter 3 was adapted from an article we wrote to illustrate the double marginalization problem and how a supplier can mitigate it by making its own selling price conditional on the selling price charged by the channel member.

We return to that example here. Figure 14.1 reiterates the point we made in Chapter 3: when the manufacturer charges a single, fixed price (in this case $4) for a bottle of table wine, the channel profit is maximized ($333) at a retail price of $6, but the retailer is tempted to charge $9 to maximize its own profit ($220.50).

Figure 14.2 shows that the manufacturer can set up a variable pricing schedule to encourage the retailer to choose the channel-profit-

Retail Selling Price (RSP)	$5	$6	$7	$8	$9	$10	$11
Bottles Sold (Q)	160	111	81	62	49	40	33
Manuf. Selling Price (MSP)	$4	$4	$4	$4	$4	$4	$4
Retailer Profit	$80.0	$166.5	$202.5	$217.0	$220.5	$220.0	$214.5
Manufacturer Profit	$240.0	$166.5	$121.5	$73.5	$60.0	$49.5	$40.5
Channel Profit	$320	$333	$324	$310	$294	$280	$264

Retailer Profit = Q * (RSP - MSP -$0.50)
Manufacturer Profit = Q * (MSP-$2.50)

Figure 14.1 A single manufacturer price is susceptible to double marginalization.

Retail Selling Price (RSP)	$5	$6	$7	$8	$9	$10	$11
Bottles Sold (Q)	$160	$111	$81	$62	$49	$40	$33
Manuf. Selling Price (MSP)	$4.0	$4.0	$5.5	$5.5	$5.5	$5.5	$5.5
Retailer Profit	$80.0	$166.5	$81.0	$124.0	$147.0	$160.0	$165.0
Manufacturer Profit	$240.0	$166.5	$243.0	$186.0	$147.0	$120.0	$99.0
Channel Profit	$320	$333	$324	$310	$294	$280	$264

Retailer Profit = Q * (RSP - MSP -$0.50)
Manufacturer Profit = Q * (MSP-$2.50)

Figure 14.2 A variable manufacturer pricing schedule can alleviate double marginalization.

maximizing retail price (i.e., to "coordinate" the channel). By offering a list price of $5.50, for example, and lowering it to $4.00 if the retailer charges a retail price of $6 or less, the supplier can accomplish the objective of maximizing channel profit and sharing that profit equitably (in this case, equally) with the retailers. Of course, the specific pricing schedule and the specific profit split will depend on the work each side does, the risks they take, and the negotiating power they have, but the point is that variable supplier pricing linked to reseller pricing can accomplish what a single price cannot. Note that in this case and others we will discuss, the upstream marketer has "increased" list price and offered discounts from that increased list price. By "increased" we simply mean that list price is higher than the profit-maximizing single price of $4.00 that would have been charged with full channel coordination. Some marketers refer to this practice as "pricing up and dealing back."[2]

---

[2]Volume discounts can alleviate the double-marginalization problem, but, as we will discuss later in this chapter, they can lead to other problems such as resellers buying more than they intend to sell to their own customers and diverting the excess to other markets or holding higher inventories for sale at a higher price in later periods.

The Coca-Cola Company uses a linked pricing model for selling concentrate to its bottlers, who manufacture the company's branded beverages and are responsible for obtaining and managing retail distribution for those beverages. Exclusive distribution arrangements, such as those granted by the company to its bottlers, are particularly vulnerable to double marginalization. So Coca-Cola directly links the bottler's selling price to their retail customers to the bottler's purchase price of concentrate from Coca-Cola. Concentrate is the main cost in the production of the beverage. This linked pricing is called "incidence pricing" within the Coca-Cola system (which consists of the company and its bottlers). In essence, if the bottler raises its beverage selling price, the concentrate selling price charged to the bottler by the company goes up too.[i] By linking its own concentrate selling price directly to the bottler's selling price, the company is able to align the incentives of both parties and move the bottler selling price closer to what is good for the health of the combined system: the total channel profit to be shared between Coca-Cola and the bottler.

In a different example of Pricing Up and Dealing Back, an HVAC equipment manufacturer that one of us worked with believed that only with exclusive distribution could they motivate distributors to stock sufficient inventory, service the equipment when repairs were needed, and otherwise put in the efforts to develop the market to its full potential. The manufacturer also faced a situation in which prevailing market prices of equipment sold to residential buyers were much higher than prices of similar equipment sold to large commercial buyers. The company's solution was to set its list price high with the knowledge that distributors could profitably mark up this price and still be competitive in the residential market. For commercial sales, especially those subject to competitive bidding, the distributor could request discounts from the manufacturer that would enable the distributor to place competitive bids and still earn sufficient margin should they win the contract. Periodically, the manufacturer audited invoices issued by the distributor to large customers to ensure that the agreed upon prices were indeed invoiced to the customers. Although the system imposed an administrative burden on both parties, it enabled the partnership to remain competitive, even in the face of large fluctuations in market demand and prevailing prices as well as systematic price differences for commercial versus residential segments.

14.2.2 Trade Promotions Fund Retail Promotions to Consumers

Cooperative advertising and market development funds, discounts, and many other incentives that resellers demand from suppliers, and suppliers provide to resellers, are often referred to as "trade promotions" in the CPG world. In return for these trade promotions, suppliers expect resellers to stock their product line, price and merchandise it attractively, and offer special deals or "retail price promotions" to consumers. For example, manufacturers often feel retailers don't do enough to promote their brands. They can use trade promotions to reward retailers for offering a temporary price promotion to consumers, featuring their brand in the retailer's weekly flier at the special promotional price, or setting up a special display. Similarly, retailers often feel manufacturer prices are too high. One of the ways they can reduce the effective wholesale price they pay is to ask for an allowance to support their merchandising efforts and retail promotions.

Retail promotions to consumers have so many well-known reasons for being that we simply remind the reader of two that are particularly important, one economic and the other psychological. Promotions are an effective means for price discrimination, allowing marketers to charge a higher price to those who have more money than time, while providing discounts to those who need them the most and are willing to work for their savings by, for example, waiting for a special price, visiting multiple stores to cherry-pick deals, searching for coupons, or redeeming rebates. And they offer psychological satisfaction to consumers—making them feel like smart shoppers and even providing some entertainment value. Even Walmart, long considered one of the most EDLP (which stands for "everyday low price") retailers, regularly uses month-long promotions it calls "price roll-backs."

While retailers do fund some retail promotions to consumers on some products some of the time, for the most part, if suppliers cut their trade promotions, retailers will be less willing and able to offer retail promotions to consumers. Trade promotion is often the largest dollar item in the marketing budget, and with good reason. In two major and well-publicized endeavors to cut back promotions that marketers have attempted in recent years, the result was not pretty. P&G initiated its "value pricing" move in the 1990s, implementing it not just in the U.S. but also abroad. Some company executives were convinced that the large amount of money being spent on trade and consumer promotions could be put to better use in other parts of the marketing program like advertising. The company overhauled its pricing strategy to one of consistent list prices to retailers with little, if any, promotional spending. Trade promotions (and therefore retail promotions to consumers) were cut, wholesale prices to retailers were decreased from the original list prices, and advertising was increased.

One of us, working with colleagues, examined how competitors, resellers, and consumers reacted to this move.[ii] We found that P&G incurred significant market share losses in many of the product categories in which it played, averaging a five-percentage-point loss per category. Despite the reduction in P&G's wholesale prices, net prices paid by consumers rose significantly because of the promotion cuts. Retailers were unhappy with the move and major competitors did not follow P&G down the path of promotion cuts. Consumer penetration of its brands fell significantly, without the offsetting improvement in repeat rates and loyalty that was hoped for in shifting spending from promotions to advertising. The company's "cost-cutting czar," Durk Jager, who spearheaded the value pricing move, rose quickly from executive vice president to president during this time, and then to CEO, but lasted in the CEO position for less than two years, quitting in 2000 as P&G's stalled growth and earnings sent the company's stock price tumbling. The company, which is known to innovate, experiment, and learn from its experiments, backed off on "value pricing" within a few years.

If even P&G, with their house of powerful brands, could not thrive without promotions, it is no surprise that JC Penney, a retailer in a much less differentiated position, could not do so either. Ron Johnson, the CEO under whom JCP tried to scrap promotions, had to leave in 2014 as the company scrambled to return to its original marketing strategy. More recently, Kraft Heinz, which had to cut the value of its Kraft and Oscar brands by over $15 billion in early 2019, alienated retailers when they reduced promotions on Kraft cheese, Capri Sun, and other products. As we wrote in an article for the *Wall Street Journal* and in a commentary on *Forbes'* CMO Forum, promotions remain a durable feature of consumer marketing because manufacturers, resellers, and especially consumers all love a deal![iii] The challenge is to design promotional programs that achieve their goals effectively and profitably.

14.3 THE MANY VARIETIES OF TRADE PROMOTIONS

One of us worked with a major U.S. consumer goods retailer who had thirteen different accounting buckets for the various types of trade promotion funding it received from suppliers—in fact, it took quite a bit of effort even to bring those thirteen buckets together to assess the total funding situation, because different individuals and even different departments in the retailer's organization negotiated and managed the various buckets. Figure 14.3 depicts some of the wide variety of trade funding that we have seen used by marketers. Some are straight discounts per case purchased by the retailer, while others are discounts linked to retailer actions—giving a product shelf space, selling it to

Type of Trade Promotion	Description	Timing and payment
Slotting fees	Payments to obtain shelf and warehouse space, may also include failure fees or cost of inventory to be replaced, and pay-to-stay fees	One time payments, in free goods or cash or discounts on future orders
Off-invoice & seasonal discounts	Discount per unit ordered during a specific time period, sometimes on specific items	Temporary reduction from invoice
Payment terms	Typically, discounts or reimbursements based on early payment	Regular invoice adjustments often contractually determined
Bill-backs, Scan-backs, Hold-backs	Unit payments/discount paid on evidence of retail sales typically at reduced price for specific time period	Periodic invoice reductions
Quantity and bundled discounts	Discounts for meeting individual order quantity and/or breadth of product line purchases	May be ongoing reductions or end of period
Rebates & market development credits	Rebates and credits conditional on retailer meeting sales, growth, share, or other targets	Usually end of period, sometime spread over forecast units
Advertising, display, and sales support allowances	Payments to fund specific retailer advertising, features in weekly flyers, displays, or personnel devoted to product.	May be lump sum or unit discounts for specific periods
Deductions and damage allowances	Discount from invoice by retailer for wrong, damaged, or late shipments; sometimes simply an exercise of power	Usually one time, but often unexpected
SEO fees	Payments to cover retailer's costs for search engine optimization	One-time or periodic payments
Listing fees	Fees to obtain good search rank on retail site	Periodic or ongoing dollar amounts

Figure 14.3 Different types of trade promotions.

consumers at a special price, achieving a certain volume of sales or sales growth, and so on. Some are lump sum payments to support advertising, features in the retailer's flyers, and the like, while others are per-unit discounts. Most are relevant to both online and offline channels, while some, like SEO (search engine optimization) and listing fees, are only relevant for online channels. Some are paid ahead of time, while others are rebated later, after proof of sales, sales growth, or customer satisfaction is available.

Why such a large variety? One reason is that they can each be used to accomplish somewhat different goals, often at different stages of the product's life cycle.

14.3.1 Trade Promotion Goals Evolve Over the Product Life Cycle

Some trade promotion goals are ongoing—the quest for growth means suppliers are invariably looking to improve consumer penetration and beat out competition to increase their own the share of consumers' category requirements. Others are tactical—there may be excess or obsolete inventory that needs to be cleared before new models and fresh stock can be brought out into distribution, or a supplier might want to load up retailers and consumers in advance of a competitor's new product launch. But there is also a systematic evolution of sales and distribution goals as a product progresses through its life cycle, as we show in Figure 14.4.

Early in the life cycle, the primary goal is to get distribution and encourage resellers to merchandise and promote the product so as to generate product trial and then encourage pantry-stocking by consumers. Increases in shelf space may come next. Often the shelf space is needed for increases in store inventories to accommodate at-shelf promotions such as coupons and other trial-focused tactics. Then come additional SKUs.

Let's take some likely examples for Coca-Cola's Fairlife product (high-protein, low-sugar, lactose-free milk), even though it is still far from the mature stage of the product life cycle. First, it needed shelf space for a basic offering on a crowded, expensive refrigerated shelf. Then it expanded the product line to various combinations of fat content, chocolate flavoring, and enhanced DHA (mainly for children). With each new SKU, a very constrained area in the store (the cool cabinet) needs to be rearranged. Trade allowances encourage retailers to do the required work. Periodic temporary price reductions on some or all SKUs encourage trial and allow more price-sensitive consumers to stock up, keeping them out of the market for promotions

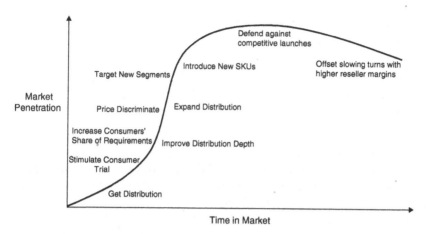

Figure 14.4 Strategic goals of channel incentives over product life cycle.

by competitors. (Fairlife has a relatively long shelf life). It is easy to sell out of some popular SKUs during temporary price reductions and if in-store personnel don't or can't restock, much of the potential to increase sales and trial customers is lost. So they need incentives to execute the promotions. As some SKUs fail to hit required minimums, new ones are introduced to take their place. And, of course, competitors whose shelf space allocations are being most directly affected don't take this lying down. The best ones anticipate and prepare counter moves and trade promotions of their own.

14.3.2 Pay-for-Performance Trade Promotions Tie Funding to Reseller Actions

Some trade promotions, notably off-invoice discounts, which are offered for a limited period of time, are not explicitly tied to reseller actions or targets, although suppliers hope that resellers will pass the discount through to consumers or invest in other merchandising to boost sales, like special displays or additional shelf space or additional salesperson effort. Others are conditioned on performance. Some discounts, for example, require evidence of retail price discounts in the form of scan-backs or bill-backs (i.e., the reseller receives a rebate on its invoice on the basis of scanner data evidence of sales to consumers on a discounted retail price), or other visible and verifiable efforts by the reseller on merchandising, displays, and so on. In our experience with a variety of consumer goods companies, we often see end-of-quarter or end-of-year discounts or rebates linked to mutually agreed-upon sales and sales growth targets.

Some pay-for-performance trade promotion discounts may reference what the reseller does with respect to competing products. Anytime discounts depend on some sort of share—be it share of shelf space or category sales, competitors are implicitly being referenced. One reason companies condition allowances on "share" measures may be because total sales (either of the category or of the individual brand) are dependent, at least in part, on factors outside the reseller's control and such conditions are aimed at ensuring that the brand gets its fair share of the reseller's effort. Another reason may be that the Robinson Patman Act, which we discussed in Chapter 5, requires suppliers to offer proportionally equivalent deals to different resellers. Instead of trying to agree on the right sales target for each individual reseller according to its size, the market conditions it faces, and so on, they may find it convenient to base allowances on share of category sales, thus putting smaller retailers on a competitive footing with large ones.

However, such "loyalty discounts" that reference competition are likely to attract antitrust scrutiny, especially if the supplier who uses them is a dominant player. The reasoning is that a high market-share supplier who offers significant discounts to resellers for buying a high share of their total requirements from that supplier can effectively bar distribution access to competitors and prevent them from reaching the scale they need to be efficient. One of us was a panelist in a workshop on conditional discounts held jointly by the Federal Trade Commission and the Department of Justice.[iv] An important takeaway for marketers is that it is wise to design trade promotions that focus on generating reseller push for one's own products rather than to link the discounts, directly or indirectly, to what the reseller does with competitors' products. Also, both suppliers and resellers should be clear about their rationale and goals for promotional programs, keeping track of why those programs are tweaked and modified over time, both so as not to lose sight of the forest for the trees, and for regulatory purposes.

14.4 THE CHALLENGE OF ASSESSING THE COSTS AND PROFITABILITY OF TRADE PROMOTIONS

Trade promotions are often seen by upstream marketing managers as headaches, even symptoms of greedy retailers or other problems like weakening brand equity. A survey that one of us conducted several years ago asked marketing managers which marketing task they most disliked. The clear loser was planning, implementing, and evaluating promotions, especially trade promotions, which are regarded as an administrative pain—even though they are essential to managing distribution. Making matters worse, it can be challenging to assess their costs and effects on profits. This is true even in the simplest scenario where the trade promotion is in the form of a temporary discount offered to resellers and the resellers pass it through to consumers in the form of a temporary price promotion.

14.4.1 What Is the Cost of a Trade Promotion?

Let's start with a basic question that is often asked: "How much does a company/brand/product spend on trade promotions?" Lump-sum payments can simply be added up. But what about the various kinds of discounts—off-invoice, scan-backs, bill-backs, hold-backs, rebates, and so on? Simple arithmetic would estimate the average amount of the discounts offered and multiply this by the number of units sold "on deal." If list price was $10/case and the average amount of the discount was $2/case, and if 100 cases were sold on discount, then $200 was spent on that trade promotion. What's the problem? Most price promotions are reductions from list price and list price is generally higher in the presence of promotions. Pricing up and dealing back is one of the standard practices for designing profitable price promotions, where pricing up is often on the time frame of strategic long-term decisions, while dealing back is a program of tactical, month-to-month, quarter-to-quarter, channel-customer-to-channel-customer moves. In one five-year period, cigarette sales in the U.S. declined more than 5% while marketing spending (mainly promotions) increased 50%. You might think that profits dropped, but in the same period operating profits almost doubled. The reason is that list selling prices also almost doubled. Merck & Co's percentage of gross revenue for discounts and rebates increased from 27.1% in 2010 to 45% in 2017. Such increases are almost never sustainable without increasing prices. Of course, we are not implying that more discounts always mean higher net prices and profits. Between 2016 and 2017, Merck's net prices fell by 1.9% even though list prices grew by 6.6%.[v]

Our main point here is that merely counting discount dollars or expressing them as a percentage of gross revenues doesn't make much economic sense unless all else is equal, which it almost never is. By themselves, those numbers leave the main question unanswered: "What would list prices and net revenues be if there were no promotions?" Most likely, prices would be somewhere between the current list price and the current discounted price. If that hypothetical number, the price that would be charged without any promotions, were available (and only rarely have we seen companies actually estimate it), it would be a better benchmark against which to compute the "cost" of the trade promotion.[3] So leaving aside hypothetical numbers and the question of what the true "cost" of a trade promotion is, can we decide whether a given trade promotion discount generated more profits than not offering the promotion at all? At least when the reseller passed the discount through to consumers in the form of a retail price promotion? Well, maybe. [4]

To evaluate the sales and profit impact of such a trade promotion, managers must first answer two questions about the retail price promotion that it led to: (1) What "baseline" level of sales would have been expected without the promotion, all else being equal? (2) What are the margins (price – variable costs) before the price promotion?

Baseline sales measurement requires econometric controls for what the brand is doing with its marketing, what its competitors are doing with theirs, and what seasonality and other external factors are in play.[vi] Once you have the baseline, calculating the promotional bump in sales seems easy—just subtract the baseline from actual sales. As we said in Chapter 5, variable costs are as close as the typical manager gets to the economic concept of marginal costs (the incremental costs of providing a single additional unit for sale). But even variable cost can be difficult to nail down. Some of the reasons include the fact that suppliers' own material costs will change with volume, that both sales revenue and invoice amounts depend on payment terms, and accounting systems have limited ability to attribute costs to specific SKUs.

14.4.2 How Much of the Sales (and Profit) Bump Is Incremental for Whom?

Baseline sales and variable costs are just the beginning, even if the reseller passes along the trade promotion discount to consumers in the form of a temporary retail price promotion. For packaged goods, the lift

---

[3]For a further explanation with a numerical example, see the appendix at the end of this chapter.

[4]For trade promotions that are not fully passed through to consumers in the form of retail price promotions or where retailers buy more on promotion than they intend to sell on promotion to consumers, things will be more complicated.

in retail sales during a promotional week can be anywhere from 150% to 500% of a product's regular weekly sales. But not all of that lift is "incremental," which is why it is called the "gross lift." Some parts of the gross lift are incremental only for the supplier, some only for the retailer, and some are incremental for both, as we depict in Figure 14.5.

When the promotion attracts "new" consumers, who buy and consume something on deal that they would not have bought otherwise, both the supplier and the retailer benefit—that sale is incremental for both. Both also benefit when consumers buy more on promotion or sooner than they otherwise would, and then consume the product at a faster rate than they otherwise would.[5] But promotions also encourage consumers to simply shift their purchases in time (buy more or sooner than they would have otherwise or lie in wait for a deal) and/or in space (buy a different brand or from a different store than they would have otherwise), without increasing their usage rate. When such a shift involves switching from one brand to another but not the store where it is bought, the sale is incremental for the supplier but not for the retailer. And, of course, the converse holds, too—a store switch is incremental for the retailer but not for the supplier.

It is important to have a good understanding of the incrementality of retail price promotions for both the supplier and the retailer—it has to work for both parties. Resellers may not pass through a large fraction of trade promotion discounts to consumers for some brands and categories because promoting those products to consumers does not generate enough incremental sales for the reseller. Academic research, which has been conducted almost entirely on CPG products, suggests that on average about a third of the promotional sales bump in a given store is taken from sales of other brands in the store (and therefore is incremental only for the supplier, not the retailer). Further, 30 to 50% of the bump can be increased consumption (and therefore incremental for both parties), but that varies widely across products. Obviously, if you are a supplier of yogurt or snacks or even soup and canned tuna, there is plenty of room for incrementality because consumption rates are flexible—consumers buy more and use it up faster. You may find you can get by with smaller trade deals and that encouraging

---

[5]Such stockpiling has some benefits even if there is no increase in consumption. As our friend Erv Shames notes, "a loaded customer is a loyal customer" and one of us has estimated the benefits of promotion-induced stockpiling for suppliers. See Kusum Ailawadi, Karen Gedenk, Christian Lutzky, and Scott Neslin (2007), "Decomposition of the Sales Impact of Promotion-Induced Stockpiling," *Journal of Marketing Research* 44 (3): 450–467.

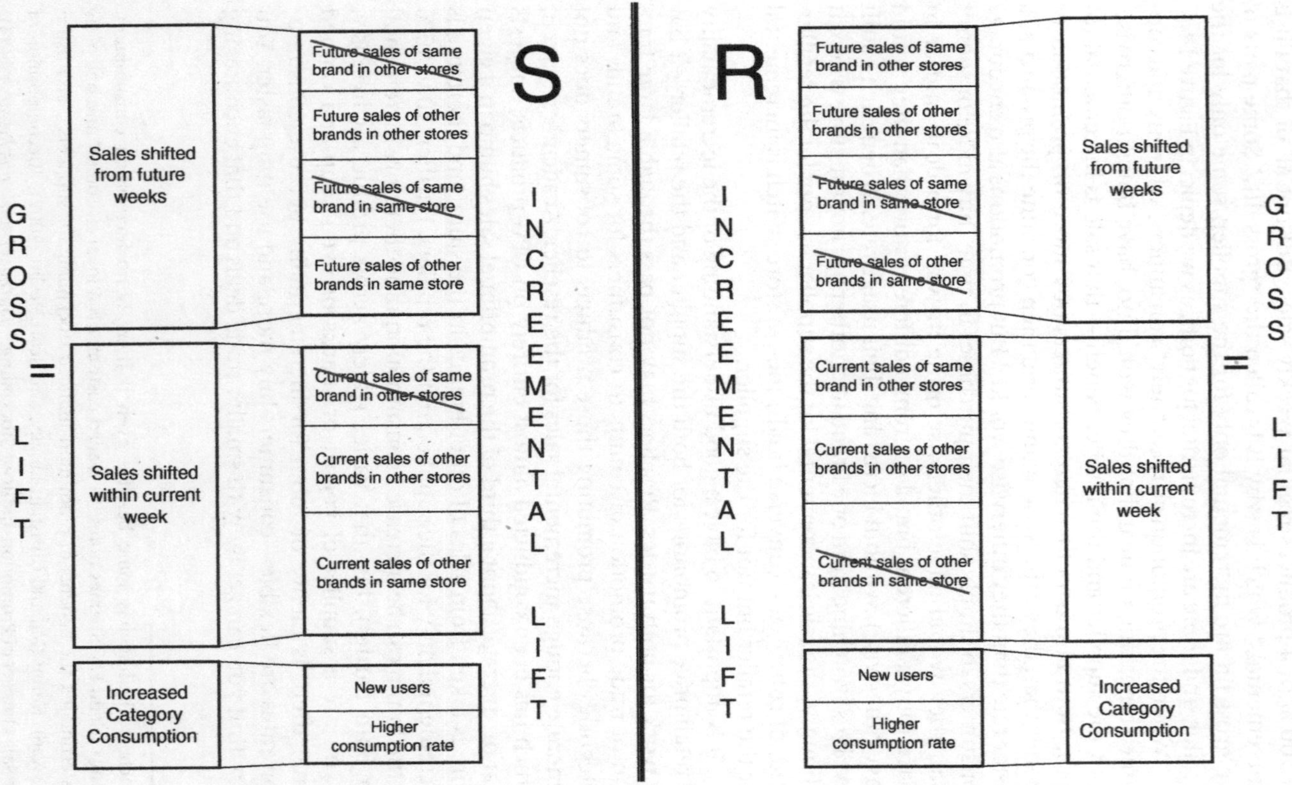

Figure 14.5 Incremental promotional lift for suppliers versus retailers.

resellers to offer multiple-unit-promotions like Buy-One-Get-One-X% off (BOGOs) is particularly effective.

Although a major source of incrementality for a reseller is when a promotion persuades the consumer to switch from another reseller, there isn't much evidence of promotion-induced store switching in CPG. Perhaps this is because, for the most part, a promotion in one grocery category is unlikely to make any but the most deal-sensitive cherry-picking consumers visit a different store. But it is important to keep in mind that consumers typically shop at more than one store in a given week. If they happen upon a promotion in one store on a product that they would usually buy in another, they are quite likely to make use of the deal in what researchers have called an "indirect store switch."[vii] Still, the point remains that it may be harder for a CPG retailer to get incremental sales from a promotion than it is for a supplier. One of us conducted a large-scale promotion impact study with U.S. drug store retailer CVS, and found that, on average, about 45% of the promotional sales bump was incremental for CVS but the fraction varied widely across individual promotions.[viii] Another study of a CPG retailer found that retail price promotions increased revenues for suppliers but the effect on retailer revenues was mixed.[ix]

All of this refers, of course, to frequently purchased (and consumed) packaged goods. Marketers of durable products ranging from apparel, accessories, and footwear to electronics, cars, and home furnishings also have frequent promotions, but it is harder to collect the data needed to assess how well they work. Because consumers are much more likely to search for durable products, and searching is so much easier online, retailer switching has to be a substantial portion of any promotional sales bump—otherwise showrooming wouldn't be such a big issue. And, though durable products aren't literally "consumed up," promotions do grow the category because consumers buy products on deal that they otherwise would not have bought, or replace/upgrade them earlier than they would have otherwise.

Our point is that retail promotion response varies widely across product categories and the better a supplier is able to assess incrementality not just for itself but for the reseller, the higher the odds that its trade promotions will be effective.

14.4.3 Additional Metrics for Key Value Items and Loss-Leaders

So far, we've talked about promotional lifts and incrementality in the product and category promoted. But a consumer attracted to a particular store by a good deal in one category may also make an incremental purchase in a different category. Marketers clearly believe in the ability of attractive promotions on certain categories, brands, and even specific items to grow traffic and therefore store sales, to the point that retailers are willing to take losses on such products, as we discussed in Chapter 3—hence the term "loss-leader." Many retailers have a list of "key value items" or KVIs, guarded quite zealously, that they believe it is critical for them to have attractive price points on. Recently, some researchers have attempted to identify what they call "lighthouse" categories—categories whose prices play a large role in forming consumers' perception of how expensive the store is but which do not account for a large portion of sales (so that it is not too expensive for the marketer to promote these categories heavily).[x] Suppliers of products that are in lighthouse categories or otherwise prone to be used as loss-leaders may find that their trade promotion dollars are better spent on getting more shelf space or higher positions on website listings. They should also make sure that the metrics they highlight to retailers are not item margins or even category incrementality, but the bump in total store sales and the total profitability of their brand's buyers for the retailer. In situations where the retailer is incurring the loss in item margin but not getting the hoped-for gain in customer and store sales, the supplier's trade promotions are better conditioned on maintaining prices than on consumer discounts—basically to protect the retailer from itself.

14.4.4 Baseline Sales Evolve Over Time

Promotions are also known to influence baseline sales over time, which adds another important issue for marketers to get a handle on. Management may make good use of promotions to achieve in-store visibility and competitive prices at key times, increasing the share of requirements among existing users and stimulating trial by new users. Strategically timed and targeted promotions defend shelf and users against competitive entries and introduce new SKUs that expand the category as well as market share. In that case, baseline sales are likely to increase over time, as shown in Scenario 1 of Figure 14.6.

On the other hand, excessive price promotions stimulate stock-piling by both consumers and resellers, and they learn to lie in wait for deals. Competitors respond with their own promotions, deepening and extending post-promotion dips. Management becomes increasingly dependent on promotions to make their numbers at the end of the quarter. Marketing and production are so busy managing the complexities of inventory booms and busts that long-term product and brand development suffer. Baseline sales decline over time, as shown in Scenario 2 of the figure.[xi] It is easier to see this pattern over

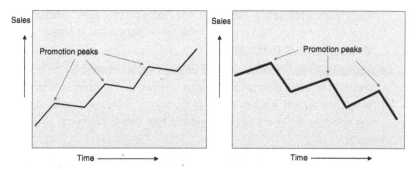

Figure 14.6 The evolution of baseline sales.

longer periods, but if you are in the thick of battle, it may not be so obvious.

We conclude this chapter with what we believe is an important message. Trade promotions are an important tool in the arsenal of a marketer looking to influence the prices and non-price selling efforts of its channel members. Yes, their effects are complicated to assess. Yes, if poorly designed and executed, they can hurt baseline sales and erode the equity of a supplier's brands. But the solution is not to cut them out. The solution is to design better trade promotions, tie them to desired reseller actions, and work with resellers to create targeted retail promotions that are beneficial for both parties. We are now ready to move on to a broader discussion of different kinds of channel incentives, their goals, and how they can be used to manage pricing across multiple channels of distribution.

Summary

- Charging a fixed manufacturer price is rarely a good idea. That is true despite the challenges of implementing and evaluating effective trade promotional programs. For good reasons, suppliers, resellers, and consumers all love a deal!

- Effective trade promotions are not just about maximizing the percentage of trade promotion dollars passed through to the consumer. They are about ensuring the reseller improves distribution depth and increases sales of the supplier's products in a way that sustains and strengthens the brand's health.

- The accounting cost of trade promotion discounts will appear larger if one compares the promotional price to the prevailing list price, but that would be an overestimate because

(*Continued*)

(Continued)

of pricing up and dealing back. The list price would be lower if there were no discounts. It is much better to keep track of average net prices and margins than to worry about the accounting cost of the trade promotion.

- Accurate estimates of baseline sales and variable costs are essential but are only a first step to assess the profitability of a trade promotion. The promotional sales "bump" over baseline is almost always an overestimate of incremental sales. And what is incremental for the supplier is different from what is incremental for the reseller.

- Promotions also influence baseline sales over time. Managers need to keep track of whether promotion programs are improving the baseline with better distribution breadth and depth, and higher consumer penetration and repeat rates, or depressing it by encouraging retailers and consumers to lie in wait for deals and then stockpile goods.

- Coke's incidence pricing, P&G's value pricing experiment, and CPG promotional bumps provide interesting illustrations of our main points in this chapter.

APPENDIX: TRADE PROMOTION, RETAIL PRICE DISCRIMINATION, AND PROMOTION "COST": A NUMERICAL EXAMPLE

In this stylized example, life is fairly simple for the manufacturer and the retailer. There are two consumer segments in the market, one more price sensitive than the other. We know what demand will be at different retail prices in each segment. The retailer sets retail price to the consumer by simply adding $0.20 to the manufacturer's selling price. The table shows the two segments; demand at various retail prices; and the manufacturer's price, variable cost and margin per unit, and total profit.

In this carefully constructed example, the best manufacturer price for the less price sensitive segment is $2.00, while the best manufacturer price for the more price sensitive segment is $1.40. If one price is to be charged for both segments, that is $1.60. If two different prices can be charged, say using well-targeted promotions, then perfect price discrimination would increase the average selling price as well as total sales and profits.

	Units Sold	Retail Price	Manu-facturer Price	Manu-facturer Variable Cost	Manu-facturer Margin	Manu-facturer Profit
Less Price	70	$2.20	$2.00	$0.75	$1.25	$88
Sensitive	75	$2.00	$1.80	$0.75	$1.05	$79
Segment	80	$1.80	$1.60	$0.75	$0.85	$68
	85	$1.60	$1.40	$0.75	$0.65	$55
More Price	0	$2.20	$2.00	$0.75	$1.25	$0
Sensitive	30	$2.00	$1.80	$0.75	$1.05	$32
Segment	60	$1.80	$1.60	$0.75	$0.85	$51
	90	**$1.60**	**$1.40**	**$0.75**	**$0.65**	**$59**
Best Single	70	$2.20	$2.00	$0.75	$1.25	$88
Price	105	$2.00	$1.80	$0.75	$1.05	$111
Across	**140**	**$1.80**	**$1.60**	**$0.75**	**$0.85**	**$119**
Both	175	$1.60	$1.40	$0.75	$0.65	$109
Segments						

Sales and Profits with Perfect Price Discrimination through Promotion

Sales at List	**70**	**$2.20**	**$2.00**	**$0.75**	**$1.20**	**$88**
Sales on Deal	**90**	**$2.60**	**$1.40**	**$0.75**	**$0.60**	**$59**
Total Sales	**160**	**$1.86**	**$1.66**	**$0.75**	**$0.85**	**$147**

Cost of Trade Promotion?

Units Sold at Discount	Average Discount	Cost of Promotion
90	**$2.00 – $1.40 = $0.60**	**$54**

Although we might compliment management on their pricing and promotion acumen, what if someone asks, "How much was spent for price promotions?" The "standard" answer is to calculate the "deal price" discount ($0.60) and multiply by the number of units sold "on deal" (160 units), yielding a "cost" of promotions of $54—over one-third of gross profits. While it makes sense to track this number over time and be aware of trends, this $54 is not a "cost" in the same sense that we use the word for other expenditures, such as advertising media, cost of goods, or even the cost of holding inventory. We believe it is far more important for management to track the average net prices and margins that result from a well-designed and targeted program of trade promotions.

ENDNOTES

i. See, for example, Incidence Pricing Agreement (2016). https://www.sec.gov/Archives/edgar/data/317540/000119312516535534/d157746dex101.htm (accessed 25 December 2018).

ii. See: Ailawadi, K., Lehmann, D.R., and Neslin, S.A. (2001). Market Response to a Major Policy Change in the Marketing Mix: Learning from P&G's Value Pricing Strategy. *Journal of Marketing*, 65 (1): 44–61.

Ailawadi, K., Kopalle, P., and Neslin, S. (2005). Predicting Competitive Response to a Major Policy Change: Combining Game-Theoretic and Empirical Analyses. *Marketing Science* 24 (1): 1–184.

iii. Ailawadi, K., and Farris, P. (2013). How Companies Can Get Smart About Raising Prices. *Wall Street Journal* (22 July), p. R1.

iv. Conditional Pricing Practices: Economic Analysis and Legal Policy Implications. FTC-DOJ Workshop in Washington, D.C. (23 June 2014).

v. Grant, Charley (2018). New Pain in Drug Supply Chain. *Wall Street Journal* (12 July), p. B1.

vi. We refer the interested reader to these articles that estimate baseline sales to get at short-term promotion effects: Abraham, M., and Lodish, L. (1993). An Implemented System for Improving Promotion Productivity Using Store Scanner Data. *Marketing Science* 12 (3): 213–338. Bucklin, R., and Gupta, S. (1999). Commercial Use of UPC Scanner Data: Industry and Academic Perspectives. *Marketing Science* 18 (3): 195–462. Ailawadi, K., Harlam, B., Cesar, J., and Trounce, D. (2006). Promotion Profitability for a Retailer: The Role of Promotion, Brand, Category, and Store Characteristics. *Journal of Marketing Research* 43 (4): 518–535.

vii. Bucklin, R., and Lattin, J. (1992). A Model of Product Category Competition Among Grocery Retailers. *Journal of Retailing* 68 (3): 271–293.

viii. Ailawadi, K., Harlam, B., Cesar, J., and Trounce, D. (2006). Promotion Profitability for a Retailer: The Role of Promotion, Brand, Category, and Store Characteristics. *Journal of Marketing Research* 43 (4): 518–535.

ix. Srinivasan, S., Pauwels, K., Hanssens, D. and Dekimpe, M. (2004). Do Promotions Benefit Manufacturers, Retailers, or Both? *Management Science* 50 (5): 617–629.

x. Lourenco, C., Gijsbrechts, E., and Paap, R. (2015). The Impact of Category Prices on Store Price Image Formation: An Empirical Analysis. *Journal of Marketing Research* 52 (2): 200–216.

xi. Academic work in CPG has provided evidence that excessive retail price promotions to consumers depress baseline sales over time but distribution breadth and depth as well as feature and display activity, which well-designed trade promotions engender, have the opposite effect. See, for example: Kopalle, P., Mela, C., and Marsh, L. (1999). The Dynamic Effect of Discounting on Sales: Empirical Analysis and Normative Pricing Implications. *Marketing Science* 18 (3): 195–462.

Ataman, M., Mela, C., and van Heerde, H. (2008). Building Brands. *Marketing Science* 27 (6): 949–1136.

CHAPTER **15**

Managing Prices and Incentives Across Channels

15.1 INTRODUCTION

In the previous chapter, we made the point that offering variable price schedules and trade promotions, rather than charging a fixed supplier price, allows suppliers to influence the prices that resellers charge to consumers and coordinate the channel. We also laid out the challenges of designing and assessing the effectiveness of trade promotions, especially those whose goal is to encourage price promotions by resellers to consumers. However, many trade promotions and incentives offered by suppliers to their channel partners are not aimed at reducing prices to consumers. Channel incentives, more broadly, try to motivate resellers to stock, price, merchandise, and support products to consumers in the way the supplier would like, while generating profitable sales in the market. For example, their goal may be to *not* let prices go down, to reward non-price selling effort, to support specific channels that perform other valued functions and/or are vulnerable to being showroomed.

Control over reseller pricing can be one of the most important aspects of keeping the peace in distribution channels. When new types of distribution channels emerge and are adopted, pricing challenges can and often do increase. Certainly, that has happened with the growing prevalence of online channels. In this chapter, we first offer a way to organize the many types of channel incentives that exist in the market according to their goals and implementation challenges. Then, we provide some guidance on how suppliers can use those incentives to manage prices across multiple channels, containing conflict and realizing potential synergies.

15.2 THE GOALS AND CHALLENGES OF CHANNEL INCENTIVES

15.2.1 Sales and Channel Management Goals

We have tried to organize the most important goals and the most significant challenges in designing and implementing channel incentives in Figure 15.1. The goals are separated into suppliers' sales objectives in the marketplace and their channel management objectives, but keep in mind that sales goals will not be profitably and sustainably met unless channel management goals are met too. Sales goals may be for specific new or existing products, or at specific times to preempt a competitive launch or defend against competitor actions. They may be broader such as to expand penetration among consumers, build market share and loyalty, or ensure that consumer needs along the path to purchase are satisfied. Channel management goals span a wide spectrum. They can focus on one channel, through expanding distribution coverage and influencing reseller prices and other selling efforts. And they can focus on keeping the peace across multiple channels, especially when one channel (usually physical) is being showroomed (recall that this is the practice of visiting a store or stores in order to examine a product before buying it online at a lower price) and needs to be shored up while another (usually digital) channel is able to free-ride on the investments made by the showroomed channel.

15.2.2 Challenges in Implementing Incentives

But implementing channel incentives is far from easy. The previous chapter took a deep dive into the complexities of determining the sales and profit impact of trade promotions that are intended to encourage retail price promotions to consumers. But there are many

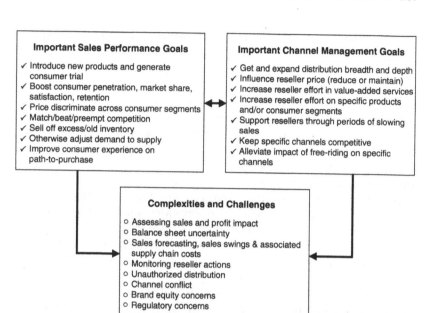

Important Sales Performance Goals

✓ Introduce new products and generate consumer trial
✓ Boost consumer penetration, market share, satisfaction, retention
✓ Price discriminate across consumer segments
✓ Match/beat/preempt competition
✓ Sell off excess/old inventory
✓ Otherwise adjust demand to supply
✓ Improve consumer experience on path-to-purchase

Important Channel Management Goals

✓ Get and expand distribution breadth and depth
✓ Influence reseller price (reduce or maintain)
✓ Increase reseller effort in value-added services
✓ Increase reseller effort on specific products and/or consumer segments
✓ Support resellers through periods of slowing sales
✓ Keep specific channels competitive
✓ Alleviate impact of free-riding on specific channels

Complexities and Challenges

○ Assessing sales and profit impact
○ Balance sheet uncertainty
○ Sales forecasting, sales swings & associated supply chain costs
○ Monitoring reseller actions
○ Unauthorized distribution
○ Channel conflict
○ Brand equity concerns
○ Regulatory concerns

Figure 15.1 Goals and challenges of implementing channel incentives.

other challenges too, certainly for other types of channel incentives but also for trade promotional discounts. For example, it's not always easy to monitor whether the reseller is actually taking the actions that the incentives are tied to. If you have a store audit system in place or can routinely access data on your resellers' prices and promotions to consumers, such behavioral monitoring can work well and it may be more feasible in online channels than in physical ones. Of course, with the ability for things to change by the hour and minute, not just by the day, the monitoring has to be continuous. New technologies and third-party services are rapidly becoming available to monitor online prices, availability, and compliance with brand policies (e.g., ChannelIQ and PriceSpider), with some specializing in business with Amazon (e.g., Amazzia) and others promising similar information for brick-and-mortar stores as well (e.g., Minderest and Rocket Wagon).

Added to this are other organizational complexities such as the need for good sales forecasting systems to anticipate the inevitable swings in sales on and off promotion and manage the impact on supply chain costs. Supply chain managers have labeled the swings in inventory the "bullwhip effect," because the differences between the low and high points of demand and inventory tend to get more extreme at the upstream positions of suppliers versus downstream resellers. Delays in ordering and shipping and more levels in the distribution systems, e.g., from supplier to wholesaler to distributor to retailer, create even more problems with forecasting.

As an example, consider the simplest type of financial incentives that suppliers offer to their retailers—the off-invoice discounts we mentioned in the previous chapter. Strong brands generally don't have to worry about discounts not being passed through to consumers, so off-invoice discounts can eliminate a lot of administrative hassles for them. But, for other suppliers, they are ripe for opportunism by retailers, who buy extra quantities of product either to divert to other (unauthorized) resellers or to sell later at full price. Apart from the problems of high prices and products showing up in unauthorized channels, this forward-buying also amplifies spikes and troughs in demand, increasing supply chain costs even more.

It is not only resellers who can abuse channel incentives. Instances abound of suppliers using trade promotion incentives to encourage their distribution partners to load up on inventory in order to make the supplier's revenue numbers. This kind of behavior occurs most frequently at the end of a quarter or year, or in advance of a merger or acquisition deal, even though they (the suppliers) know full well that the excess stock will be difficult to sell through to consumers.[i] In some other cases, the largest channel partners who get the biggest discounts can also be very expensive to serve. Consider UPS. In the days before e-commerce took off, the company gave large quantity discounts to its business-to-business customers. The same quantity discounts were then offered to Amazon and other e-commerce companies, but their cost per package was going up with all the small packages that these companies were shipping to widely dispersed locations. In 2016, for example, Amazon got discounts of up to 70% and was a $1B UPS account, but, at least in part due to that account, the average cost to handle a parcel at UPS went from about $6.50 to $8.00. Add to that the extra costs of dealing with the swings in delivery orders from Amazon during the Christmas season. In 2014, for example, UPS had hundreds of trailers of last-minute Christmas orders from Amazon and was later forced to help underwrite millions in customer refunds.[ii]

There are also balance sheet reporting requirements to be met. Many discounts are reported as reductions from gross sales. But other financial incentives may have to be allocated to different portions of the product line and/or listed as contingent liabilities. The latter, which include funds that are rebated back at the end of a quarter or year if the retailer meets sales performance goals, come with uncertainty about whether or not they will be paid out, and when. One of us was on the board of a retail chain that was forced to defer finalizing a quarterly income statement pending the arrival of a large check from an important supplier. The reliance of both upstream marketers and downstream resellers on these payments is a fact of marketing life.

If different types and amounts of incentives are offered to different channels to encourage them to provide different types of services to consumers, there is a danger that channel conflict may be exacerbated rather than alleviated, and there is constant need to ensure that the incentives don't run afoul of regulations. And a final caution on the kind of incentives that are aimed at encouraging retail promotions to consumers: in implementing these, suppliers must make sure that their programs strengthen the equity of their brands and don't erode it.

15.2.3 Conditioning Incentives on Reseller Efforts or Performance

So, on one hand, suppliers would do well to remember that channel incentives do not need to be only in the form of per-unit discounts. There is a large variety to choose from. In fact, they don't even have to be only financial incentives—some, as we will discuss below, can be in the form of special support services or privileges. On the other hand, suppliers also have to consider the challenges involved in administering the incentives and balance their goals against those challenges. As we said in the previous chapter, trade promotion discounts are often set up to "pay for performance." The same is, or should be, true for other incentives. Some incentives are conditioned on specific reseller efforts (inputs) and others on reseller performance (outputs). We provide some examples in Figure 15.2.

Conditions that tie incentives to reseller performance (e.g., sales and sales growth of suppliers' products) give the reseller flexibility in how to achieve the required performance. In our experience with a variety of consumer goods companies, we often see end-of-quarter or end-of-year discounts or rebates linked to mutually agreed-upon sales and sales growth targets. In some cases, manufacturers cede complete control of promotional decisions to their reseller partners, as long as the target sales or growth rate is met. This might be efficient, and there is something to be said for the reseller (who is closest to the end consumer) knowing best how to achieve that target. But the other side of reseller flexibility is lack of supplier control over how the products are presented and sold. Also, sales and sales growth are a function of several factors, not all of which can be controlled or even anticipated (e.g., macro-economic conditions or competitor activity).

That is why some suppliers tie at least some incentives to consumer satisfaction metrics. In the automobile industry, for example,

Examples of Channel Incentives	Tied to
	Reseller Efforts (Inputs)
▪ Slotting Allowances	▪ Shelf space, location, and facings for supplier's products
▪ Scan-back & bill-back discounts	▪ Retail price promotion timing, depth, frequency
▪ Cooperative advertising allowances & materials	▪ Feature placement, size, location, Special displays
▪ Market development funds	▪ Minimum (Advertised) Retail Price
▪ SEO funds	▪ Search engine optimization
▪ Listing fees	▪ Rank and visibility of supplier listings
▪ Employee training, cost-sharing	▪ Store-in-Store
▪ Special privileges (e.g., priority for shipments, new products)	▪ Consumer support along path-to-purchase
	Reseller Performance (Outputs)
▪ End-of-period rebates	▪ Sales and sales growth of supplier's products
▪ Bundled discounts	▪ Sales and sales growth of a bundle of supplier's less and more desirable products
▪ Hold-backs	
▪ Special privileges (e.g., permission to sell on 3P marketplaces)	▪ Consumer satisfaction with reseller

Figure 15.2 Channel incentives can be tied to reseller effort or reseller performance.

some manufacturers base their end-of-year bonus payments, as well as preferential treatment in supplying high-demand vehicles to dealerships, on the dealers' customer satisfaction scores. But there is inflation in these scores, just as in school grades and online reviews, and dealers openly beg for (even demand) perfect scores. Buyers have grown used to receiving calls from dealers after buying a car and before receiving the satisfaction survey, asking if there is "any reason you will be unable to give us a perfect 10." The ability of resellers to manipulate the metric instead of truly satisfying customers argues for basing incentives on visible and verifiable efforts by the reseller on pricing, merchandising, displays, store-in-store space, etc.

Lest the reader think that these are issues only for physical products, consider this. Volume discounts and other creative promotional arrangements are very prevalent in the world of digital entertainment. In something that is reminiscent of manufacturers using slotting allowances and free cases and volume discounts to get their new products on retailers' shelves, content producers traditionally offered shows to networks at deep discounts per episode if they committed to buying an entire season. They also waived large amounts of upfront money in exchange for a sizeable portion of the profits if the show succeeded.[1][iii] In another example, as pricing pressures increase in the pay-TV world, distributors are resisting paying high carriage fees for programming. Traditionally, TV channels are paid based on the number of subscribers to the channel, irrespective of whether they watch it. That may change in the future. When AT&T introduced its WatchTV skinny bundle app in 2018, the company said it wanted to pay based on the number of subscribers who spend significant time using the app.[iv]

15.3 HOW TO MAINTAIN RESELLER PRICES

15.3.1 Incentives to Keep Reseller Prices from Being Too Low

Recall our illustration in the previous chapter of how a variable supplier pricing schedule or trade promotion can help solve the problem of double marginalization, i.e., too-high retail prices. Well-designed channel incentives can be just as effective to solve or at least mitigate the problems of retail prices being too low. Many prestige brands keep manufacturer prices very close to suggested retail prices, thereby reducing the ability of resellers to offer steep discounts. They make this work by offering authorized resellers "market development" and "cooperative advertising" funds as incentives; in return, retailers agree to maintain retail prices at acceptably high levels while stocking the full line and investing in selling and merchandising effort.

For many years, Apple has successfully maintained the retail price for its devices by making its marketing development funds contingent on retailers' pricing. Even the largest retailers such as Best Buy and Walmart did not discount the advertised prices of Apple products. They did, however, come up (ingeniously) with promotional offers that accompany Apple purchases, such as $50 gift cards and $100 trade-in allowances that effectively constitute lower prices. Figure 15.3, for

---

[1]As we noted in Chapter 13, that is changing as all parties in the pay-TV system figure out how to play in the streaming channel. Distributors, wanting to control content while retaining flexibility in streaming channels, are offering content producers larger amounts of money up front instead of the rights to later profits if the shows succeed and go into syndication.

Figure 15.3 Best Buy gift card offer.

example, is an offer that one of us received. One might argue that this suits Apple just fine since the retail price of its devices is being preserved. In our opinion, though, that would be short-sighted. Whether a retailer cuts into its margin by lowering the price of an Apple product or by giving away gift certificates, the fact remains that its margin is being cut and ultimately that makes for an unhappy retailer. Unless, of course, Apple is funding those gift certificates!

15.3.2 Control Inventory to Control Price

Too little inventory causes stock-outs, which reduce sales, frustrate consumers and resellers, and open the door to competitors. So many incentives are designed to help resellers finance inventories and ensure that they order early and in sufficient quantities to meet demand. Invoice dating and extended payment terms are some examples. Another common tactic is to offer off-invoice and quantity discounts that are valid for orders placed in a specified period. These discounts are relatively easy to implement for both buyer and seller. For suppliers and products with very little or a lot of market power, off-invoice discounts can be practical. Weaker brands, for instance, are less able to negotiate pay-for-performance requirements. Strong brands, meanwhile, may not worry about requiring resellers to pass along the discounts; a bigger concern for them is restricting orders to quantities that the resellers can realistically sell to consumers.

But, as we said earlier, such discounts that load up resellers can backfire if the resellers don't intend to sell all that they bought. Even if they intend to, they may not be able to. And unsold inventories sitting on the shelves and in the warehouses of independent retailers too often results in fire-sale prices and diverting said items to unauthorized resellers. To control inventories residing at independent retailers, you need to be sure that your own incentive programs are not contributing to the problem. One supplier we know offered substantial quantity discounts to its authorized channel, with logic that made sense on the face of it: reward your largest customers. The largest channel partners bought a lot of product to achieve the fattest discount, and then, finding they could not sell it, diverted it to an unauthorized discount channel. The rest of the authorized channel found itself having to compete with the significantly lower prices in the discount channel and was understandably unhappy. The supplier was caught in a bind because it hadn't put in place an account-level forecasting and shipment analytics system that could have helped it pinpoint specific sources of the diversion. To make matters worse, it didn't really have the will to stop the practice, having become accustomed to the additional revenue generated in the discount channel! Even people closest to the action (e.g., the sales force) may be tempted to turn a blind eye to such practices if the result is sales growth.

Forecasts have to be made, and inventory levels planned, for all promotions and channel incentives that encourage resellers to build inventories. And, recognizing that a world of perfect forecasts is not the one that most marketers live in, contingency plans on what to do with excess inventory need to be made. Many brands—Brooks, Tory Burch, and many luxury watch makers among them—take back unsold inventory from retailers to avoid having it steeply marked down and/or to make room for new items.[v] Some, like Burberry, have received unwanted press coverage for destroying (in Burberry's case burning) millions of dollars of excess inventory. These practices can become very expensive in the absence of reasonable forecasts. Our advice to suppliers and their authorized resellers is this: cooperating by sharing the data and analytics needed to forecast demand, track shipments, monitor inventories, and actual sales (especially during promotional periods) is an important activity that keeps the brand healthy, price points at desirable levels, and unauthorized distribution to a minimum.

A good example of a cooperative arrangement is the 2019 agreement between Marriott and one of its largest OTA partners, Expedia, according to which Expedia became the exclusive distributor for the hotel company's wholesale business.[vi] As we noted in Chapters 12 and 13, the rooms that go through the wholesale distribution channel often cause problems for hotels because of unauthorized price undercutting. Expedia will now have an additional revenue source by being the exclusive channel from which redistributors who don't have a direct connection with Marriott can access rooms. And Marriott's burden of policing unauthorized resellers and discounted rates will be considerably reduced.

15.4 DECIDE WHETHER TO DIFFERENTIATE OR HARMONIZE ACROSS MULTIPLE CHANNELS

As if it isn't hard enough to influence pricing and other efforts of independent channel partners when there is just one type of channel, things only get more complicated when you are managing an array of channels that may provide different types and levels of services to consumers and compete with one another, often quite fiercely. Although upstream suppliers will almost always be concerned about the level and variation in downstream reseller prices, it does not always follow that suppliers should strive to equalize retail prices to consumers across channels.

15.4.1 Different Products, Retail Prices, and Retail Services Across Channels

It may be that different consumer segments shop at different channels, look for different product features and services, perhaps buy in different quantities, and differ in their willingness to pay. If so, an upstream supplier wanting to satisfy those segments might expand its product line and distribute different portions of it through different channels, much like Nike, as we discussed in Chapter 13. In that case, whether retail prices are different in different channels is not an issue; different products have different prices! The challenges of managing a broad product line and the potential conflict with channel members who don't get to stock their preferred products will remain, of course, and they are far from trivial.

Sometimes, the purchase contexts are so different that neither consumers nor channel members expect the same prices and service, even for the same physical product. We expect to pay more for the same wine in a white-tablecloth restaurant than a wine warehouse, and the same goes for buying a toothbrush in the hotel gift shop compared to walking down the street to a drug store. In other cases, the costs of serving consumers are so different that suppliers may accommodate and even encourage different retail prices. But they will need to work with their channel partners to educate consumers about the costs so that the price differentials consumers see across channels are not perceived as being unfair.

Progressive Insurance explains on its website why consumers should expect their auto insurance prices to vary, depending on whether they use the agent or direct channel.[vii] Even retailers who embrace omni-channel are finding that setting the same prices in their physical and digital channels is not viable, at least for products that are either expensive to ship, or whose penny profits (i.e., unit margins) are so thin that even a small shipping cost can wipe them out, or when the costs of high return rates have to be recouped. Walmart, for example, began showing different online and in-store prices for some items and encouraging consumers to buy them online and pick up in store to get the lower price. And a survey reported in a 2018 *Sloan Management Review* article suggest that the majority of consumers are tolerant of reasonable price differences across channels.[viii]

15.4.2 Harmonized Retail Prices Across Channels Can Reduce Showrooming

Historically, the thorniest channel pricing challenge for a supplier is managing a system in which the target consumer shops for the same product(s) in multiple independent channels and those channels don't all perform the same functions or provide the same level of services. One channel, often a brick-and-mortar channel, might be an effective showroom where consumers can see, feel, and try your products before making purchases in a different, often online, channel that is not saddled with the overhead of a physical outlet. If unchecked, there is the danger of price and brand equity erosion we pointed out in Chapters 2, 11, and 12, exacerbation of conflict between the showroomed physical and free-riding digital channels, and even the potential demise of the showroomed channel.

New technologies encourage free riders, at least from the perspective of existing channels, but showrooming is not a new phenomenon, as we illustrated with the story of the wallpaper industry in Chapter 3. The mail-order system combined with 1-800 numbers allowed consumers to browse wallpaper patterns in their local store and then order at substantial discounts for direct delivery. Many in the wallpaper industry believed that the free riding by 1-800 dealers contributed to the decline of local shops and, ultimately, overall wallpaper sales. Wallpaper suppliers recognized the value that local brick-and-mortar stores provided by stocking "pattern books" with hundreds, maybe thousands, of patterns, and enabling consumers to find something that matched their own tastes and budgets and would be unlikely to be identical to what their neighbor had selected. Could they have put in place policies and incentives to slow or minimize the decline? Maybe.

Not having large differences between channels can reduce some of the motivation for showrooming. Like Apple, therefore, you don't want retail prices to consumers to be different across channels, at least for your best-selling and new models. Lower prices in one channel are likely to quickly set off a downward spiral as other channels cut their prices to compete. As we said in Chapter 6, the *Colgate* doctrine does give suppliers the ability to prescribe a specific retail selling price, and setting a minimum retail price was also declared no longer to be per se illegal by the U.S. Supreme Court in 2007. However, suppliers are understandably wary of using these options to prevent price erosion, because the *Colgate* doctrine requires the manufacturer to unilaterally terminate a noncompliant reseller contract, no questions asked, and the several states have their own laws prohibiting minimum resale price maintenance. Instead, suppliers can make use of a minimum advertised price (MAP) policy.

15.4.3 Minimum Advertised Price (MAP) Policies Can Help

MAP policies set a lower bound on the price that a reseller can *advertise*. Offline, MAPs generally refer to prices advertised outside the physical store (e.g., on radio, TV, and in print). Online, in many cases they serve like minimum RPM because they apply to all prices. In other cases, they apply to searchable prices—prices that are displayed only when a product is clicked on or when it is placed in the shopping cart, are not considered to be "advertised." Many suppliers combine the carrot of channel incentives with the stick of withholding some or all of their product line to enforce adherence to MAP.

MAPs must be credible to be effective, which means that suppliers must specify clearly the consequences of a violation, monitor advertised prices, and notify violators as well as enforce the terms of the policy when they find a violation. Professor Ayelet Israeli has documented a 40%–80% reduction in MAP violations among authorized retailers of a manufacturer who modified its MAP policy: a "three strikes" enforcement protocol with detailed explanations of the consequences of each violation and intermediate email notifications to retailers each time they violated the policy.[ix] Brooks Running runs a tight distribution ship and, in addition, put in place a unilateral MAP policy that is specific, monitored, and strictly enforced. Other athletic footwear manufacturers also have such policies. As an example, the appendix to this chapter presents excerpts from Mizuno's policy, as listed on the company's website.

Of course, MAPs can only be applied to authorized resellers—unauthorized resellers don't officially source product from suppliers by definition, so a policy that threatens to discontinue supply is meaningless for them. This again underscores the importance of controlling inventory in the marketplace and thereby limiting gray markets and unauthorized distribution points. Suppliers also walk a fine line between unilateral MAPs, which are legal, and "agreements" or negotiations when there are violations, which come under scrutiny. In addition, monitoring the marketplace for violations can be a time-consuming and expensive process even though there are companies such as the ones we listed earlier to whom the task can be outsourced. Hence our caution that, while these are one more tool in managing distribution, it would be dangerous to open up wide distribution coverage and rely solely or even primarily on such policies for enforcing channel discipline.

15.4.4 Differential Incentives for Valuable Channels that Serve as Showrooms

Consumers don't engage in showrooming only because prices vary across channels and they are looking for a lower price. They may feel they can find a higher-quality product online after having checked out fit and feel in a physical store, or they may be dissatisfied with the level of service they received in a store.[x] Irrespective of the reasons for showrooming, morale in the showroomed channel is likely to decline (along with its service quality) if channel partners feel the fruits of their investments and efforts are being enjoyed by others. But the showrooms perform important functions. So, while suppliers may work to keep retail prices consistent across channels, they also need to find ways to reward the channel that provides more functions (at higher costs). Wanting to equalize *retail* prices across channels does not mean that *supplier* prices and especially channel incentives need to be equalized as well. Quite the opposite, in fact!

Although it might be desirable to reward one channel for behaviors that contribute to sales in another channel, this is easier to conceptualize than actualize. The analysis of billboarding in the hotel industry that we discussed in Chapter 12 is a good example. Recall the divergent views on how much a hotel's direct channel benefits from online travel agents (OTAs) serving as a "billboard." In that case, one can get objective data on traveler visits to and bookings on the different websites. Getting agreement is even harder when each channel simply presents its own view on the role it has played in helping another channel close a sale in the much more typical case where a consumer's path-to-purchase spans physical and digital channels. What about when Best Buy is showroomed, say, and the purchase is made on Amazon? Or when Amazon is webroomed to compare prices and features, and the purchase is made at Best Buy? Resellers will be happy to take credit for being showroomed but not happy to give credit to other resellers for enabling the transactions they themselves close. Also, despite all the different types of data we described in Chapter 1 that marketers now have access to, it is still very difficult to connect all the dots and touchpoints across the individual consumer's physical and virtual paths-to-purchase.

But even if that type of granular "attribution" for purchases is not (yet) practical across independent channels, suppliers generally do (or at least should) have a good understanding of which channels add value and incur higher costs and which ones free ride on investments by different channels. Bigger trade promotion discounts may be provided to the former, but those discounts may be competed away. Other forms of support that are less likely to be competed away and are directly aimed at shoring up a high-value channel can be more effective. One example is the funding and assistance that Apple and Samsung provide to build up and man their stores-in-stores for retailers like Best Buy. We have also seen suppliers support specific channels in other ways. Progressive Insurance provided advertising support and built a for-agents-only website to make it easier for independent agents to get quotes, renew policies, and process claims even as they recognized and acted on the need to have more competitive prices in their direct-to-consumer channel. Natura did something similar for its independent sales consultants—a digital consultant received a personalized Rede Natura URL to their own web page on the company's website that the consultant could promote to their own network.

Brooks Running supports its omni-channel retailers in many ways. If a runner shopping at a Fleet Feet store finds that the particular model, size, and color of the pair of shoes she wants is out of stock, the salesperson in the store can place an order directly with Brooks, which ships the shoes to the consumer while crediting Fleet Feet for the sale.[2] In a few major U.S. cities, the company has experimented with same day delivery from local stores on orders placed at BrooksRunning .com. According to the company "In addition to delivering gear to runners within 24 hours, same-day delivery will create new sales for our specialty running accounts by introducing new customers to their local stores."[xi] Recall from Chapter 12 that Brooks is no longer allowed by Amazon to be a third-party supplier on Amazon's marketplace. However, Brooks rewards some of its best, MAP-abiding omni-channel retailers by allowing them to sell Brooks on the marketplace, and it also helps to support the Amazon marketing and operations of those omni-channel retailers. The retailers are happy with the additional source of revenue and the support they receive for their Amazon business. Brooks is happy because it reaches Amazon shoppers and can continue to exert influence over how its brand is priced and presented to them.

15.4.5 Use Targeting to Reduce Channel Conflict

When, as in the examples we discussed above, different regular prices in different channels are not desirable, targeted promotions offer flexibility in aligning net prices and the margins earned by different channel members with the functions they perform and with the value of the consumers they bring in. Targeting algorithms allow granular opportunities for suppliers and individual channel members to achieve specific goals.

Some retailers that we have worked with offer suppliers the ability to target promotional offers to their loyalty program members (for a fee) based on past brand and category purchase behavior. Understandably, they don't allow targeting of competing brand users—recall that switching consumers from one brand to another doesn't benefit the retailer, unless of course there is a higher margin to be had. The two parties do find common ground, however. For example, P&G may not be able to target a Crest offer to a Colgate user at CVS, but they can target a "lapsed" user of Crest or a Crest toothpaste user with an Oral-B toothbrush offer.

Location-based mobile offers can be used to geo-fence (offers or notifications sent by a marketer when the consumer is in the vicinity

---

[2]Clearly, this is sustainable only when the supplier has efficient logistics in place and instances of OOS are exceptions, not the rule.

of a store that sells its products) or geo-conquest (offers or notifications sent by a marketer when the consumer is in the vicinity of a competing store). They can also be used to target based on what the local competition is. For example, an online offer may be different depending on whether the product is widely available in brick-and-mortar stores in the local market, or whether it is filling holes in distribution for a preference minority.[3] In all these cases, the opportunity exists for suppliers and their resellers to agree on the specific goals to be achieved at a given time with a given promotion.

Recall from Chapter 12 that as hotels free themselves from the very rate parity clauses they originally inserted in their contracts with OTAs, not only they but also OTAs can offer discounts to their members. If done in an untargeted way, this has the makings of what economists call the "prisoner's dilemma"—both parties do it though both would have been better off if they had refrained. Instead, targeted offers by hotels to their most valuable loyalty program members, and attractively priced bundles of flights, hotels, rentals—and even restaurant meals and other experiences—by OTAs to serve travelers who value the convenience of such services can leave both parties better off.

Finally, "retargeting" online (when an ad for that Zac Posen bag you were checking out on Nordstrom.com follows you around the web for several days) can be based not just on what the consumer bought or didn't buy in the past, but on what she looked at and presumably considered. Admittedly, the retargeting algorithm is often not smart enough, or rather does not have the data, to know that you bought the bag a couple of days ago. But that too is improving.

Connecting consumers' offline and online behavior is a difficult challenge. This is being met to some extent by the digital advertising giants Google and Facebook. Facebook's Offline Sales Measurement allows advertisers to connect their own customer databases to their Facebook accounts, using anonymized IDs to connect FB advertising exposures to offline behavior. But for suppliers who rely on independent channels for a substantial part of their business, their own customer database will have very limited coverage. They still need to convince their channel partners to share customer data, which is not easy when each party views their data as proprietary and as a source of leverage. Some companies are making progress on this front.

---

[3] Recall from Chapter 11 that a preference minority is a small segment in a geographical market whose preferences are different from the majority and are therefore less likely to be met by products stocked in local brick-and-mortar stores.

Natura registered over two million consumers who shopped at the company website or with an independent sales consultant via Natura Rede and in return provided data analytics support to boost consultant revenue. Another example we have heard of is Guarantee Mutual, a provider of voluntary employee insurance benefits, who brought all information technology functions in house.[xii] The human resource managers who are its end customers wanted a seamless experience no matter which channels they were interacting with, and channel members, who are independent brokers and agents, were not only willing but happy to hand over the IT functions (and therefore the customer data), to make their jobs simpler. Such instances may not be common, but the point is that channel members have to see a clear benefit to sharing data.

Google's Store Visit Conversions service uses Wi-Fi and GPS-based location data together with surveys of large consumer panels to connect (on an aggregate, anonymized level) online search with subsequent store visits. The company is also linking online behavior with credit and debit card data to get insight, again at an aggregate and anonymous level, about the offline purchases of consumers who searched for particular products or were exposed to particular advertisements on Google. And location data specialist Placed, which was recently acquired by Foursquare, connects exposure to advertising across various advertising platforms online to store visits, for an audience of more than 150 million consumers using its own location data and models that identify visits and assign them to places.

Just as targeted pricing and promotional offers can be used to reduce head-to-head price competition and conflict between channels, suppliers can use these services to quantify the impact of their digital advertising spending on visits and sales in their channel partners' brick-and-mortar stores. The evidence that the online advertising is also helping brick-and-mortar partners, not just the online channel, reduces the resentment they might otherwise feel.

15.5 CHALLENGES EVEN WHEN YOU CONTROL RETAIL PRICE DIRECTLY

Our focus is on the challenge of managing pricing and incentives to independent channel members when they, and not the supplier, determine prices, promotions, and selling effort to consumers. But pricing for digital and mobile distribution channels is no breeze even if you do get to set the price to consumers yourself.

15.5.1 Don't Erode Your Own Price to Get the Buy Box

Being a third-party (3P) supplier on a platform such as Amazon's or Walmart's marketplace allows you to set the price at which your product is sold to consumers.[4] Recall that was why Brooks wanted to be a 3P supplier. But the platform decides which seller gets the "buy box" for a specific product. On Amazon, for example, the buy box is the boxed section on the right-hand side of the page that provides details of a product that the consumer is looking at. Clicking in the box allows the consumer to add the product to their shopping cart or buy it instantly from the seller who won the buy box.

Figure 15.4 is a screen shot of the buy box when one of us looked at a Nespresso coffee machine in the summer of 2019—the winner is Amazon, which is usually the case if Amazon sells the product itself. And way down below the fold (we have deleted some intervening lines in the screen shot), after "Turn on one-click," "Add to List," "Add to Wedding Registry," and so on, is a link to other sellers. Because the odds of the consumer buying with a click on the buy box are so much higher than of scrolling down to buy from another seller, the buy box is highly coveted.

Amazon's (and Walmart's) buy box algorithms are kept private, but it is clear that the criteria include seller's price, inventory available, fulfilment performance, and customer satisfaction metrics, and it is also clear that price is a very important one.[xiii] Relying *only* on a low price is neither enough nor sustainable given the slippery slope of price erosion, but it is easy to see the pressure to do so. Our advice to suppliers is to resist the pressure that may cause you to lead reseller prices down, because other resellers will match your own lower retail prices. Instead, optimize fulfilment and customer service along with pricing in your efforts to win the buy box so that competition is not totally focused on price.

Of course, tight control over inventory and over who sells your products on 3P platforms will make the job of maintaining prices much easier. After all, if the only sellers on 3P are the supplier

---

[4] Around the 2017 holiday season, though, Amazon began to offer promotional discounts on some 3P products, funding the cost of those discounts itself and showing a "Discount Provided by Amazon" tag, so that pricing control may not be assured. See the article entitled "Amazon Cuts Third Party Prices" in the *Wall Street Journal* on November 6, 2017. We have also heard from some smaller sellers that Amazon has sometimes temporarily blocked their access to price setting and itself changed the price of the seller's product on the 3P marketplace to beat a lower price elsewhere.

Figure 15.4 The buy box on Amazon.

itself and/or a few of its most trusted resellers, competition for the buy box will be easier to focus mainly on non-price performance metrics. And a MAP policy will help further—witness Brooks and how it has navigated the Amazon marketplace.

15.5.2 Paywalls: When Information Wants to Be Free but Two-Sided Markets Fall Apart

In some cases, a revenue model that allowed prices to be low in one channel fails in another channel. The result is that pricing has to be different across channels even if they are all owned by the supplier and conflict among independent channel members is not the issue. As we discussed in Chapter 12, the digitization of media has made for a particularly challenging time for that industry, whose two-sided market model of readers/viewers and advertisers has been unraveling. It has become clear to publishers that advertising is no longer enough to sustain the digital channel to which consumers are shifting in droves, so they must rebalance their two-sided markets and make online readers pay more than they had become used to for the value they consume. "Information wants to be free," as tech visionary Stewart Brand famously said, but creating content costs money. And even though total expenditures on digital advertising now exceed that in traditional media, the lion's share of that digital advertising revenue—more than 60% in 2019—goes to Google, Facebook, and Amazon, leaving only a little for everyone else.

The *Times* of London made waves when it introduced a "paywall" in 2010—a system that prevents access to the newspaper's webpage content without a paid subscription. After several early experiments, The *New York Times* launched a "leaky" paywall in 2011, offering some free content on some devices but requiring a subscription for complete access. By 2012, circulation had overtaken advertising as the biggest source of revenue, and by 2014, there were almost a million digital subscribers. But advertising revenue continued to fall faster than subscription revenue grew, and the company continued to experiment. They tried limited free access on the NYT Now app to try to woo younger readers who are particularly prone to being driven away by paywalls,[xiv] and on the other hand, they tested a completely ad-free subscription. Both were ultimately discontinued, and perhaps with some help from growing demand since the 2016 U.S. presidential election, the company has been able to reduce the amount of free content it allows and continue to increase subscriptions.

With a few exceptions like the *Times'* ad-free subscription experiment and *Prevention* magazine's decision to cut out print advertising entirely and rely solely on subscription revenue, most try to strike a balance and the balance is increasingly shifting towards more fee than free. Time Inc. reduced the circulation and frequency of its magazines to reduce costs and survive with lower advertising but to a more targeted core audience. Other publishers are implementing paywalls that vary in their leakiness. Perhaps due to the pressure that it is under from competition authorities in the EU, and perhaps because it recognizes that the health of the publishing industry is important for the health of its search engine business, Google eliminated "first click free" which, as we noted in Chapter 12, required publishers to give the user free access to three articles per day in order to be listed in search results. Google also announced that it would build tools to help increase subscriptions and share user data with news organizations.[xv]

In making their pricing decisions across channels, media companies must quantify and creatively exploit (a) the interdependency in demand between advertisers and readers, the customers on the two sides of their market, (b) the preferences and behaviors of different consumer segments in each channel; and (c) the interdependency in demand between the channels. That is quite a formidable task!

Academic researchers have been tackling these issues and we point to a few recent articles as food for thought for the interested reader. One study examines the impact of the *New York Times* digital paywall not just on subscription revenue but also on reader engagement and print circulation.[xvi] It finds that reader engagement, as measured by number of visits and time spent on the website, decreased, but there is a positive spillover effect of the paywall on print subscriptions, and it discusses the implications of these results for advertising revenue.

Another study focuses on the digital channel and offers guidance on dynamically changing prices over time.[xvii] It offers the counterintuitive insight that online content should be offered free in periods of high demand and offered for a fee in periods of low demand—something the authors call "counter-cyclical offering." The authors' logic is that doing so balances subscription and advertising revenue by attracting high-value consumers who are willing to pay even in the off-season while not alienating the low-value consumers who are unwilling to pay for content but are much more likely to come in during the season if content is free, and contribute to advertising revenue at that time.

A third study illustrates how a newspaper or other media company can design and price a menu of multi-channel subscription plans for its readers using data that are relatively easy to obtain.[xviii] Consumers' willingness to pay for various multi-device plan configurations is obtained from surveys; the interrelated subscriber and advertiser demand and demand elasticities for each device are econometrically estimated from historical aggregate data; and an optimization tool then brings these inputs together to determine the profit-maximizing menu of multi-channel subscription plans across segments of consumers.

15.6 CONCLUSION

This brings to a close Part III of the book, in which we examined how suppliers can use their product line, pricing, trade promotions, and other channel incentives to manage the multiple channels they rely on once they have made the approximately right decisions about the type of channels and the intensity of their distribution breadth, and have the right metrics in place.

Suppliers with strong consumer pull, we've said more than once, have a lot of leverage in coordinating their channels. And while resellers don't want to be under the thumb of their suppliers, they do want the products they stock to sell, and sell easily. So they want suppliers to do their part in generating demand. All of which is a reminder of the importance of coordinating consumer pull along with reseller push. That is where we started with our organizing framework of Chapter 2 and it is where we return in the next, and final, chapter of our book.

Summary

- Channel incentives are needed to motivate resellers to stock, price, merchandise, and support products to consumers in the way the supplier would like and generate profitable sales in the market.

- The supplier must have clarity on both the sales and channel management goals of various incentives and also a clear-eyed view of the challenges in implementing them.

- The administrative challenges of monitoring reseller behavior, containing the bullwhip effect in the supply chain, preventing excess inventory from finding its way into unauthorized channels, dealing with balance sheet uncertainty, and ensuring that brand equity is being built, not eroded, are also part of managing channel incentives.

- Some suppliers may be able to differentiate product lines and retail prices across channels but others may decide that the same (or very similar) retail prices across channels is essential for the health of their brands and distribution.

- Keeping control of inventory and implementing a minimum advertised price policy can help when retail prices need to be coordinated.

- But equal prices across channels does not mean channel incentives to the different channels have to be the same. Quite the opposite. Incentives such as market development funds, administrative assistance, store-in-store funding, and location-based targeted advertising and promotional offers can be used to shore up high-value channels that may be getting "showroomed" or otherwise be under pricing pressure.

- Although suppliers have more control over pricing to consumers on 3P marketplaces than when they sell inventory to resellers, even that control is not complete. Pressure to win the buy box puts pressure on pricing, which is best controlled by limiting unauthorized 3P sellers, which, in turn, is best controlled by good forecasting and inventory control.

- Because consumers expect information to be free, pricing digitized products such as news and other media has its own challenges, even if that pricing is under the control of the supplier. Considering the interdependencies of demand between advertisers and readers/viewers and between digital and traditional channels is important.

APPENDIX: EXCERPTS FROM MIZUNO'S MAP POLICY[5]

Mizuno has unilaterally established this advertised price policy ("Policy") to protect and preserve the value, goodwill, premium image, reputation, and competitive standing of the Mizuno brand and to ensure that Mizuno products are displayed in a high-quality manner that enhances their market performance.

. . .

3. Product Advertising and New Product Pricing Charged to Consumers

   a. This Policy applies to all advertisements of Mizuno Products listed on the attached advertised price list ("List") in any and all media including, without limitation, flyers, posters, coupons, mailers, inserts, newspapers, magazines, catalogs, television, radio, and public signage, Internet sites, social media sites, apps, or any other electronic media, including without limitation a "click for price" notice, automated or pre-formatted emails (including bounce back pricing emails), and any other communication or device designed to evade or circumvent this Policy.

   b. For the time periods shown on the List, Reseller must not advertise new Mizuno Products on the List below the MAP set forth on the List, or advertise the new introductory Products below the NPIAP shown on the List, including any "dollar off," "percentage off," "rebate" or similar sales language which reflects or suggests a price below the listed MAP or NPIAP.

. . .

5. Policy Not Applicable to Sales Prices

   Each Reseller may sell Products at whatever price or prices such Reseller chooses. This Policy does not govern those sales prices. Rather, this Policy only governs prices that may be advertised.

. . .

---

[5]These excerpts are taken from the policy listed on Mizuno's website at https://www.mizunousa.com/category/customer+service/map+policy.do (accessed December 2019). The " . . . " indicates additional content in the policy.

7. Penalties and Termination

Mizuno may take the following actions, and others, for violations of this Policy:

   a. First Violation: Mizuno may require takedown or correction within 24 hours of notification.

   b. Second Violation: Mizuno may suspend all shipments, purchase orders and sales to the account for 30 days.

   c. Third Violation: Mizuno may suspend all shipments, purchase orders and sales to the account for 90 days.

   d. Fourth Violation: Mizuno may terminate the account for all Products.

ENDNOTES

i. Published research indicates that using trade promotions to smooth earnings is a common practice, but one that penalizes long-term average profits. For example, see: Chapman, C., and Steenburgh, T. (2008). An Investigation of Earnings Management Through Marketing Actions. *Management Science* 57 (1): iv–214.

ii. Stevens, L., and Bensinger, G. (2015). Amazon Seeks to Ease Ties With UPS. *Wall Street Journal* (22 December).

iii. Flint, J. (2015). Horror-Film Master Slashes Price for TV Shows. *Wall Street Journal* (13 January).

iv. FitzGerald, D. (2018). AT&T Unveils $15-a-Month Video Service. *Wall Street Journal* (22 June).

v. Chu, K. (2016). Changing Tastes Hit Luxury-Watch Dealers. *Wall Street Journal* (8 August), p. B3.

vi. Schaal, D. (2019). Marriott and Expedia Exclusive Agreement Will Retake Control of Wholesale Rates. (17 September). https://skift.com/2019/09/17/marriott-and-expedia-exclusive-agreement-will-retake-control-of-wholesale-rates/ (accessed 5 October 2019).

vii. Please see: Progressive Casualty Insurance Company (2019). Why Insurance Prices May Vary. https://www.progressive.com/shop/car-insurance-rates-differ/ (accessed 19 April 2019).

viii. Baker, W., BenMark, G., Chopra, M., and Kohli, S. (2018). Master the Challenges of Multichannel Pricing. *Sloan Management Review* (6 June).

ix. Israeli, A. (2018). Online MAP Enforcement: Evidence from a Quasi- Experiment. *Marketing Science* 37 (5): 685–853.

x. Gensler, S., Neslin, S., and Verhoef, P. (2017). The Showrooming Phenomenon: It's More Than Just Price. *Journal of Interactive Marketing* 38: 29–43.

xi. Crets, S. (2019). Brooks Running Launches Same-Day Delivery. DigitalCommerce360.com (6 September). https://www.digitalcommerce360.com/2019/09/06/brooks-running-launches-same-day-delivery/ (accessed December 2019).

xii. Coughlan, A. (2019). Omni, Multi, Channel, Consumer: When is an "Omni-Channel Strategy" a Good Idea? Presentation at Marketing Science Institute Trustee Meeting, Boston (5 April 2019).

xiii. This article by CPC Strategy provides a nice overview: Zeibak, L. (2018). 7 Steps to Winning the Amazon Buy Box in 2019. https://www.cpcstrategy.com/blog/2018/08/win-amazon-buy-box/ (accessed August 2019).

xiv. Chiou, L., and Tucker, C. (2013). Paywalls and the Demand for News. *Information Economics and Policy* 25 (2): 61–69.

xv. Nicas, J. (2017). Google Offers Hand to New Publishers. *Wall Street Journal* (2 October).

xvi. Pattabhiramaiah, S., and Manchanda, P. (2019). Paywalls: Monetizing Online Content. *Journal of Marketing* 83 (2): 19–36.

xvii. Lambrecht, A., and Mishra, K. (2017). Fee or Free: When Should Firms Charge for Online Content? *Management Science* 63 (4): 901–1269.

xviii. Kanuri, V., Mantrala, M., and Thorson, E. (2017). Optimizing a Menu of Multi-format Subscription Plans for Advertising-Supported Media Platforms: A Model and Application in the Daily Newspaper Industry. *Journal of Marketing* 81 (2): 45–63.

CHAPTER 16

Summary: Dashboards and Principles for Managing New Directions in Distribution

16.1 PULLING (AND PUSHING) IT ALL TOGETHER

"I believe that all good things taken to an extreme become self-destructive and that everything must evolve or die."
—Ray Dalio, quoted in the *Wall Street Journal*, April 25, 2019

We have written this book to provide insights into how marketers should evolve and manage their distribution channels during periods of significant change. Change typically means new channel options and accompanying conflicts with existing channel partners. Managing those conflicts while having the flexibility to adapt to a rapidly evolving—but still uncertain—future requires sound strategy executed with a marketing program that is both guided and evaluated by the right metrics.

For most people, the term "marketing program" or "marketing mix" has become synonymous with the 4 Ps (product, price, promotion, and place), thanks to Professor Edmund Jerome McCarthy's famous alliteration. Among the 4 Ps, product and price are usually preeminent and at least initially, distribution (or Place among the 4 Ps) choices are made so that they are consistent with product and price. Over the long term and in the face of the types of changes we noted in Chapter 1 and subsequently illustrated throughout the book, distribution choices begin to drive these other Ps. Examples you might recall from earlier chapters include Leather Italia creating a totally new price point for Costco.com; suppliers designing SKUs, packaging, and products to serve the needs of club stores, dollar stores, and Amazon; Ohio Art shifting production to China to satisfy Walmart's price requirements; Porsche's product line expansion for dealers; L'Oréal's brand portfolio for different channels; and media companies' investments in content and their pricing pressures for direct-to-consumer streaming channels.

Changes to a system that includes independent decision makers with their own priorities and goals will almost always have feedback or second-order effects—consequences that set in motion other changes that may have positive or negative effects. Anticipating and weighing these consequences is an important part of managing a distribution system. Feedback effects can nurture the system when the type of distribution channels and the intensity of their coverage are matched to demand and managed well with the other Ps. And those same feedback effects can damage the system if the root causes of conflict go unchecked. Again, examples you might recall from earlier chapters are the way suppliers like Burberry, Nike, and Brooks have contemplated whether and how to do business with Amazon; and the downward spiral of slipping price points, retail margins, distribution depth, and product quality that over-distribution sparked for Stainmaster and the Brooks of yore.

16.1.1 An Expanded View of the Push-Pull System

We introduced our perspective with the push, pull, and channel performance framework that we outlined in Chapter 2, and fleshed out in subsequent chapters. The distinction between push and pull only makes sense for a supplier selling through one or more independent channels, though it may also own a direct channel. The system of push-pull inputs and effects, which span the 4 Ps, recognizes that the upstream supplier is far from being the sole determinant of the system's behavior, performance, and evolution. Such a framework is needed to organize individual elements of the marketing program, its objectives and outcomes, and the relevant metrics in a way that yields a strategic picture of the firm's distribution channels.

In Part I, we examined what value distribution partners bring to the table, the consumer preference and loyalty that they generate for themselves in addition to the push they generate for the suppliers' products, and the resulting conflict and power dynamic between the two.

Then, in Part II, we zoomed in on downstream push effects and laid out a framework for measuring the breadth and depth of distribution push and matching it to demand so that there is a sustainable balance between the performance of suppliers and their channel partners. We presented metrics, tools, and processes for facilitating the matching of both the type and intensity of distribution coverage to demand. We paid special attention to the increasingly common expansion of distribution into new digital and direct-to-consumer channels.

In Part III, we provided guidance for using the product line, pricing, promotion, and other channel incentive programs to manage the channel for ongoing success.

We put it all together now in a somewhat expanded view of the push-pull system from Chapter 2. The shaded boxes in Figure 16.1

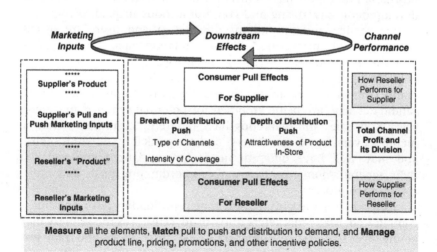

Figure 16.1 Expanded view of the push-pull system.

represent the expanded elements. They show both suppliers' and resellers' efforts to generate revenue and total channel profits and the tension as each party tries to get the consumer's search loyalty for itself and wants to know what the other party is doing to help its performance. The three Ms at the bottom of the figure summarize the approach we have proposed to get multi-channel distribution right: Measure, Match, and Manage. We believe the concepts in Figure 16.1 can be the foundation of an integrated, strategic view of distribution related decisions, intermediate metrics, and performance outcomes for suppliers and their channel partners.

16.1.2 A Note About Pull

This book is about distribution, so our emphasis throughout has naturally been on the push side. There is a large literature on different kinds of pull marketing inputs, how they work, and the importance of integrating the various pull (and push) elements in the marketing program so as to maximize their joint efficiency and effectiveness. We refer the interested reader to that literature for details.[i] But we do want to make a few points about the distinction between pull and push inputs and about how pull effects are generated.

Most companies with whom we have worked have separate organizations and, to some extent, career paths for sales and marketing, and that is probably a big part of the reason why the separation of push and pull inputs has endured. Brand management; new product development; advertising and communications in paid, owned, and earned media; and promotions directed at end users are usually the domain of "marketing." Channel relationships, the negotiation of trade promotions and other incentives, and execution at the point-of-purchase are often the responsibility of sales. Of course, many companies encourage alternating assignments, especially for candidates who are being groomed for potential senior management roles. Still, sales and marketing have different "customers" (channel members versus end-consumers) and are guided by different metrics and may well have different needs for specialized knowledge in their separate domains. This makes coordinating push and pull a complicated process.

But it is not the only reason that coordinating push and pull is complicated. Many marketers think of advertising as the primary marketing lever to create consumer pull. Sales force efforts and trade promotions/incentives are likewise typically seen as the primary way to generate distribution push. The potential second-order effects of pull inputs and effects on distribution push effects that we discussed earlier are also quite widely recognized—resellers are more willing to push products with strong consumer pull (by stocking a greater variety of SKUs, taking lower retail margins, and executing retail promotions). But there are also very important second-order effects from push to pull. Easy availability, visible in-store displays, and point-of-purchase advertising create consumer awareness, preference, trial, and repeat by what is sometimes called "activation" of the brand. Not only does distribution push have a much larger effect on sales than does advertising (recall the elasticities we discussed in Chapter 9), but it can have higher effects than advertising even on awareness of the advertising itself, and on brand consideration and liking.[ii]

Nor is all advertising created equal. Digital advertising elasticities, both display and search, are substantially bigger than traditional media advertising elasticities.[iii] But that shouldn't be a surprise. Consumers exposed to search or retargeted display ads have shown themselves to be further along the path-to-purchase than those who are just watching a TV program or browsing a magazine and happen to see an ad. We know, with quite some degree of confidence, that they are interested at least in the product category and may even be actively looking to buy a product, just as we might have that confidence if they looked for or visited a physical store. So should we think of search ads and even retargeted ads as a substitute for wide distribution or as advertising? Shoppable ads on Google, Instagram, and the like are even more akin to distribution. The question is about more than semantics. If we think of digital advertising as merely another form of advertising, we would fail to consider how search advertising and shoppable ads allow for easy findability of our online stocking outlets. We would also not appreciate how search advertising works with other types of traditional and social media advertising, sponsorships, and so on. Search is often the first stop along the way to a distribution outlet after being exposed to those other forms of communication.[iv] And, to the extent that retargeting ads are accompanied by some sort of special offer, marketers should factor these marketing efforts into assessments of the brand's overall promotion program. So the power of some digital advertising to drive substantial and often immediate sales increases derives from its ability to play all three roles: advertising, distribution, and promotion. The point is that marketers need to carefully consider effects of different parts of their marketing program, especially digital advertising, to determine what is pull and what is push, and how they can be substitutes, complements, or some of each.

Marketers focus a lot on measuring consumer pull effects in the form of various types of brand equity metrics. But our colleague

Professor John Deighton from Harvard Business School has good advice. "We can use the time spent measuring brand equity to investigate what really produces satisfied customers," he says, "such as product design that keeps ahead of competition, responsive customer service, healthy distributor relationships, and warranties that match claims." We agree. We would add that a quality product should be the star of the show and that clear goals are needed along with relevant metrics for *all* the elements of the system. This is crucial to coordinate push and pull, allocate funds and effort, monitor performance, and adapt to changing environments.

16.1.3 What Does It Mean to Coordinate Pull and Push?

Our short answer is that it is a balancing act to find a mix of marketing inputs that: (1) is efficient in driving sales, profit, and share for the supplier, (2) supports resellers to sustain shelf space and their selling effort, and (3) entails a total budget that is affordable for the foreseeable future. The first piece of this balancing act considers all marketing inputs for some given time frame that is relevant to management and optimizes the allocation of resources with respect to profits and other strategic goals, such as penetration or market share. Of course, that time frame can be quite different for shoestring start-ups versus well-funded strategic initiatives of large companies.

The second piece considers the reseller's view and the level of distribution push that will sustain the supplier's pull inputs. Retailers will not keep a product on the shelf that does not have the sales volume to justify the shelf space. And suppliers cannot continue to invest in advertising products that do not have enough breadth or depth of distribution to develop the required sales potential.

The third part of the balancing act is that the budget and especially some elements of the mix have to be sustained over the longer term. Some marketing inputs, like consumer and retail promotions and digital advertising, have an immediate effect, so they may pay out sooner than others. Product development, some brand-building communication programs, sales force expenses, and some channel support programs are slow to show results but their benefits can last a long time.

Suppliers have to decide when, and to what degree, pushing or pulling is the appropriate action. Coordinating the two certainly does not mean spending equal amounts on each. Marketers tend to worry about spending too much on push instead of pull, but adding up the dollars spent is not the only or even the most relevant metric. Indeed, as we noted in Chapter 8, many trade discounts are not permitted by accounting authorities to be classified as marketing "spend," but as deductions from revenue.[1]

Many successful brands have been created with little or no reliance on consumer pull inputs like traditional advertising. For example, how did Progressive Insurance become the fifth-largest auto insurance company in the U.S. that no one had ever heard of? By focusing on the nonstandard driver segment and putting all its marketing efforts into a large network of independent agents to whom that segment of drivers went for insurance. So even though it had no end-consumer pull, it "owned" the nonstandard segment in the minds of the independent agent channel.[2] In other cases, suppliers have generated consumer pull not through advertising but through prominent placement in key retail outlets, careful expansion of distribution to avoid losing momentum, and focus on package design and word of mouth (including the retailer's promotional efforts).

Good examples in the beverage market of using such "seeding" strategies to move from very limited to very broad distribution coverage include the energy drink Red Bull, which we discussed in earlier chapters. Arizona ready-to-drink iced tea became the volume leader in a market with heavily advertised and established brands from companies like Coca-Cola, PepsiCo, and Dr Pepper Snapple group. Chief Marketing Officer and co-owner Spencer Vultaggio is quoted as saying, "We've been 99 cents for more than 15 years now. It's a big part of our overall strategy, and our business model is such that we don't advertise for example, and we put those costs towards giving our consumer the value they want and expect... We feel like it's more important to spend money on something that our customer really cares about, instead of buying billboards or putting our cans in the hands of some celebrity for a few minutes."[v] Arizona used attractive packaging that appealed to consumers, differentiated SKUs for the take-home market in the supermarket (gallon jugs) from wide-mouth bottles and cans for convenience store and food truck channels, and used a very deliberate 99-cent price point. Early on, they also did a better job of focusing efforts on the high-potential SKUs and not overloading the channel with flavors.

---

[1] An interesting aside: ride-sharing companies Uber and Lyft deduct discounts to drivers from revenue but report discounts to riders as marketing expenses, arguing that drivers are its customers. This materially affects its net sales and gross profit numbers ("Do Ride-Sharing Customers Sit in the Front?" *Wall Street Journal*, April 29, 2019.

[2] Later, when the company expanded into the standard driver market and the direct-to-consumer channel, it did begin to advertise heavily.

16.1.4 Measure, Match, and Manage to Nurture Beneficial Feedback Loops

Many of the feedback effects in the push-pull system come from reseller actions and reactions, and they are difficult to identify in the short term. Still, knowing the likely feedback effects helps make better decisions. In Chapter 2, we described two prototypical examples of feedback loops, one desirable and one harmful. We briefly return to those now to reprise the guidance from the intervening chapters on how to foster the former and minimize the latter.

The first example of feedback loops was about coordinating push and pull inputs to get the right intensity of distribution coverage. This helps ensure that (1) consumers want to buy the product and can find it without too much effort, (2) resellers are motivated to keep their prices attractive and their merchandising sharp, and (3) there is enough channel profit to go around (i.e., to sustain the relationship and continue to fund the necessary push and pull inputs). The second example was about adding new (and often digital) channels that perform some functions well but tend to free-ride on existing (often physical) channels for others, and may sell at lower prices. As existing channels feel pressured to compete on price and see their margins shrinking, they cut back on distribution depth and other functions, which ends up harming the entire system. So what have we learned about how to nurture the desirable second-order effects and minimize the harmful ones?

First, *measure* everything—the inputs, the downstream push and pull effects, and how each party performs for the other. Depending on the types of channels, some push and performance metrics will be more relevant than others. For example, in addition to %ACV and %PCV, which are important measures of distribution coverage in any type of channels, findability online is also about top positions above the fold in search results for relevant keywords. And %PCSV (%Product Category Search Volume), which weights distribution outlets by the percentage of target consumers who search in those outlets, is particularly important when consumers channel hop, searching in one and buying in another. Depending on the type of brand and category, some performance metrics may be more useful than others. For example, in some cases the supplier may want to emphasize how fast their product turns over and the total dollar profit it generates per week and per square foot of shelf space. In other instances, higher margins will be more productive to emphasize. And in still others, it may be the basket size and profit of the product's buyers that is the most relevant. Similarly, in some cases the supplier may value cross-channel support, and in others the actual sales transacted in the channel. Relationships are important, but to repeat Jim Lecinski's maxim, "Data beats opinions."

Second, *match* the type and intensity of coverage to demand. To select the right types of channels and the right channel partners, understand which channels your target consumer visits and why, the functions performed by the channels, and the costs of serving them. A useful first step to accomplish this matching of type of distribution to demand is to compare the different channels' shares of category sales (and even more importantly, their share of target consumers' visits and purchases) with the share of the supplier's distribution and sales through each channel. Velocity graphs provide a way to identify sustainable combinations of market share and the intensity of distribution coverage within the selected channels so that resellers are neither too complacent to put in the necessary effort, nor too competitive and erode their margins. Also, when the brand portfolio and/or product line is large and differentiated enough, matching different brands and products to different channels is a viable option.

This type of matching is a strategic, longer-term decision. But there are still plenty of ongoing responsibilities. Suppliers need to *manage* their relationship with resellers; design and implement incentives tied to specific functions performed, distribution depth, and performance; and ensure that supply grows apace with forecasts of distribution and demand growth. Some new products may temporarily be offered exclusively to one channel, or the channel may get priority when supply is tight. Some channels may receive support in the form of special funds or privileges or sales opportunities because the value they provide in attracting profitable consumers is high even if those consumers buy, or repeat buy, elsewhere. And suppliers may stem price erosion with policies such as MAPs.

16.2 DISTRIBUTION DASHBOARDS

This process of *Measure*, *Match*, and *Manage* has to begin with a strong set of easily comprehensible and reasonably comprehensive metrics, and those metrics are most useful when assembled into a dashboard that displays current data and trends so that important changes in the push-pull system and channel performance can be monitored. Short-term uses of the dashboard may focus on showing changes from previous periods, identifying associated problems and opportunities, and modifying marketing tactics to address them. But strategic analysis of the data in dashboards is less about period-to-period changes and more about long-term trends. A push-pull dashboard can help identify and track feedback loops even when econometric models, which can handle only so much complexity, cease to be useful. We offer three illustrations in this section, increasing in level of complexity (and opportunity).

16.2.1 A Simple Illustration of the Insight from Push-Pull Dashboards

Ben's Brews, a (disguised) craft beer brand was faced with a decision on whether to expand distribution into a new geographic territory to serve a new set of retailers and consumers. However, the financial risk to the small company was significant. The expansion would require investments in distribution facilities, inventories, and receivables to support wholesalers and retailers whom they believed could be recruited to carry the brand. Slow turnover could also be a quality risk for a product that proudly advertised it contained no preservatives. Initial tests showed increases in sales shipments and reorders in the test areas. In balancing the risk and reward, consider two possible scenarios that might emerge from a simple "push-pull" dashboard underlying the same sales increase. The strategic picture represented by each is quite different.

Two Possible Test Area Scenarios	A	B
Brand Awareness	10%	90%
Brand Preference	5%	25%
% ACV	90%	30%
% ACV of Major Competitors	30%	90%
Share of Retail Inventory	30%	3%
Dollar Sales in Test	$18M	$18M

In our opinion, Scenario B represents a much safer bet for the expansion. One of the worst reasons for strong sales in the test would be that few other craft beers were competing for consumers in the same outlets, so consumers just bought the one that was stocked. That is likely to be the case in Scenario A, where consumer awareness and preference is low and Ben's Brews' investment in distribution gains could be very vulnerable to the inevitable future incursions of other craft beer brands.

16.2.2 A Distribution Dashboard for Pete and Gerry's Organic Eggs

Recall Pete and Gerry's Organic Eggs, the company we first introduced to the reader in Chapter 6. It markets free-range and organic eggs to consumers in partnership with over 120 family farms. From its origin in New Hampshire, it has been steadily expanding distribution, first in the Southeast, then in the Midwest, then on the West Coast, and now nationally. The company works mainly with brokers to get access to grocery, mass merchandise, warehouse club, and natural good chains, though senior executives directly negotiate shelf space, pricing, promotions, and so on with retail customers. The company also uses wholesalers to service independent grocers in some markets, especially in New England.

For many retail accounts, Pete and Gerry's uses the logistics infrastructure of large regional commodity egg producers to deliver its eggs to the store shelves. The reason for this is that many retailers rely on the Direct Store Delivery (DSD) infrastructure of the large regional producers who have historically provided all of the retailer's egg assortment. Many of these regional producers are franchisees of Eggland's Best, the largest egg brand in the country and the main competitor for Pete and Gerry's. So Pete and Gerry's must pay a fee of approximately 5–10% per case to utilize the regional producers' DSD network, which indirectly funds their competitor.

Beginning with one brand (Pete and Gerry's) and a handful of SKUs (a few pack sizes and egg sizes), the company added a second brand in the early 2000s, Nellie's. Nellie's is free range but not organic and, though it sells at a price point that is a dollar less per dozen than Pete and Gerry's, it is more profitable for the company because organic eggs are much more expensive to produce. In 2014 it also added liquid egg whites and in 2017 it launched a line of pre-peeled, ready-to-eat hard-boiled eggs. The company's pull marketing inputs consist of some broadcast and digital advertising, and targeted coupons to consumers using services such as Nielsen-owned Catalina. In addition to the fee for using the regional producers' DSD network, its push marketing inputs include broker fees, slotting allowances to get on the shelf, and trade promotions to fund retail promotions to consumers. As we noted in Chapter 6, Pete and Gerry's also supplies private-label eggs selectively to some retail clients, as long as they have ample supply and the retailer shares their commitment to humane farming practices and long-term partnerships with small family farms.

The company hopes to build brand awareness and preference and have wide enough distribution coverage so that consumers who want to buy their eggs find them in the stores where they customarily shop. But it also needs to make sure that the retailers who agree to carry their brand get enough revenue and profit per square foot of shelf space to continue to stock the brand and hopefully increase the number of SKUs and shelf space. They also need to monitor the store shelf to ensure their products are properly displayed and not out of stock, especially given that they rely on a competitor for delivery and stocking. Because the company spends the majority of its marketing budget on trade promotions, it needs to make sure that the incremental lift from the pass-through of those promotions to consumers is substantial and profitable and that those promotions can bring in new consumers, who will then continue to buy the company's products for at least part of their total egg needs.

In Figure 16.2, we have created a distribution dashboard for Pete and Gerry's that lists, for the year 2018, its main pull and push marketing inputs, and the downstream effects and performance metrics the company tracks. Above the dotted line in each box are the metrics for all retail formats and below the dotted line (in italics) are the metrics for the supermarket format in which the bulk of the company's products are sold. The numbers in parentheses are changes from the previous year.

Dashboards should be created such that they "roll up" across the supplier's brands, geographies, types of channels, and individual reseller accounts. Then the dashboard user can "click down" to different levels of granularity. The structure for rolling up (and therefore

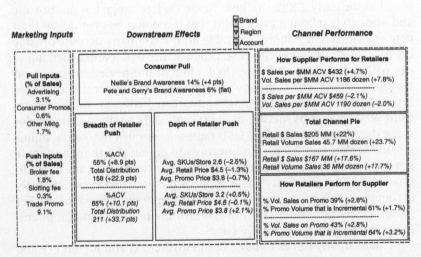

Figure 16.2 Pete and Gerry's Organic Eggs distribution dashboard.

clicking down) can be quite different for the different types of metrics in the dashboard. Metrics for push effects and performance are often disaggregated and monitored by brand, region, channel type, and individual retail account. Many pull metrics (awareness, consideration, preference, search loyalty), on the other hand, are disaggregated by region and brand, but not (at least not yet) by channel. The three "down arrows" at the top right of Figure 16.2 are intended to depict the ability to click down by brand, region, or retail account.

Total U.S. per capita consumption of eggs has grown at annual rates of 1–2% for the last 20 years and Pete and Gerry's market segments are growing even faster.[vi] Although they are small at the time of this writing (nationally, just over 3.2% of retail egg sales), market share and related metrics will become more important to monitor in the future, as producers and retailers emphasize cage-free eggs.[3]

The other metrics displayed in the dashboard are mostly very good news. Distribution, sales velocity, consumer awareness, promotion performance, and the number of items on the shelf are all growing or improving. Dashboards not only monitor market situations and raise warning flags, but they can also raise questions that are worth investigating further. We'll mention a few that come to our mind when reviewing the dashboard.

Nellie's awareness is higher and growing, while Pete and Gerry's is lower and flat. How much of that is due to marketing pull inputs like differential advertising for the two brands versus in-store presence at a lower price point? Drilling down to brand-level data reveals that Nellie's higher brand awareness is attributable to higher advertising spending. The company thinks the lower price point of Nellie's appeals to a wider audience, and the higher margin also justifies more advertising spend. Its national ACV distribution is almost half of Pete and Gerry's, and its volume market share is somewhat lower. And as you might expect, awareness levels for both brands are significantly higher in eastern regions of the U.S. than nationally.

As the company works to increase distribution of Nellie's, will it augment or replace the Pete and Gerry's brand on store shelves, especially in the larger (mass and warehouse club) retail formats with more price-sensitive consumers? Might that be responsible for the decline in SKUs per stocking store in those formats (versus supermarkets), even

---

[3]Walmart has pledged to transition its purchases of almost 9 billion eggs to cage free. Other retailers like Kroger and big egg buyers like McDonald's have made similar pledges. See, for example, https://www.fb.org/market-intel/cage-free-eggs-were-once-expected-to-dominate-the-egg-market.

though %ACV Brand and Total distribution are growing? Or is the decline simply a reflection of the fact that the mass and club formats carry a smaller number of SKUs in most categories than do supermarkets. Disaggregating the dashboard metrics to the individual brand and retail format can answer these questions.

The percentage of total sales on promotion is substantial and it has increased a bit year over year, but promotional price is not dipping. And importantly, the fraction of promotional volume that is incremental is more than 60% and growing. So regular Pete and Gerry's buyers are not increasingly lying in wait for deals. Additional metrics that would be helpful include penetration (the percentage of egg buyers who bought the company's brands at least once) and share of requirements (among those buyers, what percentage of their total egg purchases were Pete and Gerry's brands).

It would also be helpful to track distribution depth metrics such as number of facings and incidence of out-of-stock. These are important no matter what, but they may be particularly useful given that the company relies on competitors' logistics to deliver its eggs to the retail shelf in some accounts and has begun its own delivery to the retail warehouse in others. Differences in these depth metrics and performance metrics, such as sales velocity and GMROII, can help assess the benefit to the company and its retail partners of reducing dependence on competitors.

What this discussion illustrates is that many core metrics such as distribution coverage and sales velocity will always be relevant, while the importance of other metrics can be expected to wax or wane over the product life cycle or as competitive situations and channel dynamics evolve. Some metrics, such as promotion response in individual retail accounts, may be more relevant for short-term assessments of push and pull health, while others, such as share of category sales, volume sold on promotion, and incremental volume on promotion in different retail formats will reflect longer-term concerns.

16.2.3 A More Complicated Distribution Dashboard for Hotel Companies

Insightful as it is, the Pete and Gerry's dashboard is simpler than for companies who balance multiple physical and digital channels, not just different physical retail formats. We will briefly illustrate this with the hotel industry. Recall from Chapter 2 that most hotel companies are franchisors. Further, as we discussed at some length in Chapter 12, the distribution system in the hotel industry is in an uneasy balance

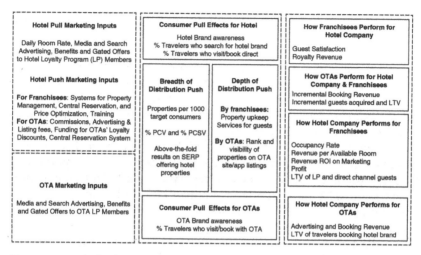

Figure 16.3 Distribution dashboard for a hotel company.

because hotel companies, especially the largest ones like Marriott, Choice, and Hilton, try to beef up their direct channels while also recognizing that they need their partnerships with online travel agents and meta-search sites. So a hotel company's distribution dashboard must cover three parties—the company itself, its franchisees, and its distribution channel partners. Figure 16.3 presents key metrics for such a dashboard.

The marketing inputs side of the dashboard is quite self-explanatory, but it is worth highlighting two points. First, recall that all the things that hotel companies do to make travelers aware of their brands and properties, and to entice them to keep coming back—advertising, in traditional broadcast media, search, and other online venues; loyalty program discounts, and other benefits like room upgrades and free stays—are paid for by the franchisees. So is all the push marketing support. Second, the OTAs also do all of the same things to entice travelers to their websites and apps and to keep them coming back, and they spend orders of magnitude more. For example, the annual advertising spending of one large hotel company we know is about $100 million to Booking Holding's spending of about $4 billion.

The hotel pull and push marketing inputs attract franchisees interested in owning/operating hotel branded properties, and they also build consumer awareness, preference, and maybe even loyalty to the hotel brand, and attract OTAs. But the OTAs' primary goal is to generate awareness, preference, and loyalty to their website or app. And, increasingly, hotel companies are using their marketing pull inputs to attract travelers not only to their hotels but also to their direct channel.

The distribution breadth and depth metrics in the middle of the dashboard also deserve a little explanation. The number and density of properties in a target market measure distribution coverage in terms of physical availability and the remaining metrics measure it in terms of findability. %PCSV weights the distribution outlets that offer the hotel brand by the percentage of travelers that search for hotels in those outlets. As far as findability metrics such as search results above the fold on the SERP are concerned, it is important to monitor them for branded versus category keywords. Hotel companies don't want OTAs to poach their branded keywords like "Marriott in Charlottesville" or "Hilton in Nashua" in sponsored searches, and similarly OTAs don't want hotels to poach their branded keywords like "Expedia hotels in Charlottesville" or "Travelocity hotels in Nashua." As we noted in Chapter 12, contract negotiations with OTAs include such search advertising protections for branded keywords.

The channel performance side of the dashboard is where the parties will find the most fodder for self-examination and adjustment. When it comes to the performance of its franchisees, a hotel company may care primarily about the royalties the franchisees generate for it and about guest satisfaction, which is important for the health of its brand. The franchisee, who incurs the fixed and variable costs of operating a property, assesses the hotel company with performance metrics such as occupancy rate, average revenue per available room (or RevPar, which is a combination of the average daily room rate and the occupancy rate, and is similar in concept to sales per square foot for a product retailer), and the profit it makes after paying all costs and franchise fees. The franchisee also wants to know what return it is getting on the marketing expenses it pays for. Consider the following situation. A hotel company recruits new franchisees into a market and increases its properties by 30%. Total revenues in the market grow only 10% because the new properties cannibalize significant sales from existing ones (recall distribution elasticities less than 1 from Chapter 9). The hotel company's royalty (which is a fixed percentage of total revenues) increases by 10% but the existing franchisees see their occupancy rates and RevPar shrink by 15%, cutting significantly into their profits. By paying attention to what the impact might be on those metrics before expanding franchisees, the hotel company can avoid setting in motion the harmful feedback from over-distribution.

The metrics are more complicated when it comes to the performance of the OTAs. To illustrate, let's consider a scenario in which a hotel company pays a 12% commission to the OTA—this is reportedly in the ballpark of the rate that large hotel companies like Marriott pay to OTAs. All else being equal, the direct channel is more profitable than the OTA channel by that 12%. But all else is rarely equal. For one, the hotel company spends a great deal on advertising, loyalty benefits, and gated discount offers to entice travelers to its direct channel. That needs to be accounted for. One hotel company we know estimated from its marketing mix models that, on average, a dollar of advertising brings incremental revenues (i.e., revenues it would not have earned if it had not advertised) of approximately $11 to the direct channel. That means approximately 10% of that revenue is being spent on acquiring it in the direct channel. Compare that with the 12% OTA commission spent on revenues that come through the OTA. In addition, the hotel company offers "members only" discounts and loyalty points in the direct channel. If those discounts are about 2%, the difference in acquisition costs between the two channels in this example may be wiped out.[4] However, travelers who are attracted to the direct channel are probably more engaged with and loyal to the hotel brand, so their LTV is likely to be higher than those who come through the OTA channel. These LTV metrics are therefore important for the hotel company to estimate and track.

On the other hand, there is probably a segment of OTA-loyal travelers who will not book direct, and another segment of "billboarding" travelers who book direct after first finding the hotel on an OTA site and who would have been lost to the hotel if it was not listed at the OTA. And if hotels are able to choose which rooms to release to OTAs and when, they may be able to make better use of their yield management systems to get bookings through the OTAs for room-nights that have a high probability of otherwise going un-booked. These segments and the revenues they bring are what we refer to in the dashboard as "Incremental Booking Revenue" and "Incremental Guests Acquired" from the OTAs. The segments would be valuable even if they don't have high LTV, because this is revenue that the hotel would otherwise not get at all. But the LTV doesn't have to be low. As we said in Chapter 12, hotels have the opportunity to engage with these guests once they come to the hotel property and try to retain them for future stays.

---

[4]The franchisees, who pay for everything, will have their own perspective depending on the total cost to them in each channel. They pay their usual advertising fee no matter what the channel and are always interested in the returns they receive from that advertising. In addition, they pay the commission in the OTA channel and a loyalty program and often a search marketing fee in the direct channel.

As is clear from the above illustration, a full evaluation of the economics of the different channels is a necessary though challenging endeavor. As with the Pete and Gerry's dashboard, the metrics in this dashboard can be used to actively manage push and pull over time and in individual markets and channels and also as a report card on whether there is a need to revisit fundamentals of the distribution strategy, such as the relative reliance on direct versus OTA channels.

16.3 THE MAGICAL NUMBER SEVEN PLUS OR MINUS TWO NUGGETS OF WISDOM

"Perhaps there is something deep and profound behind all these sevens, something just calling out for us to discover it. But I suspect that it is only a pernicious, Pythagorean coincidence."

—George Miller, *Psychological Review (1956)*

In closing, we want to also remind the reader of some qualitative principles to guide the management of multiple channels. Like most good management principles, they can sound a lot like common sense. But that should not detract from their usefulness as mental checks on whether a proposed change in channel strategy should be implemented. In 1956, psychologist George Miller wrote a famous article called "The Magical Number Seven, Plus or Minus Two: Some Limits on Our Capacity for Processing Information." Whether or not the limits on human capacity for processing information have anything to do with the number seven, we'll limit our reminders to seven points.

16.3.1 Consumer Search Loyalty Bestows Power and Can Create Conflict

Consumer search loyalty is the acid test of whether you have truly built consumer pull, and the ultimate source of power. Additional breadth and depth of distribution is the fastest way to grow, and brands with strong consumer search loyalty have an easier time getting distribution. Suppliers must cultivate search loyalty, and it is easier to measure in digital channels than it used to be in the physical world. But search loyalty reduces distribution elasticity and increases the potential for cannibalization among channels. Higher search loyalty makes it easier to overshoot the mark on distribution breadth. That, in turn, can backfire if it creates uncontrolled price competition, destroys reseller margins, and undercuts services that are vital to the long-term health of the business.

16.3.2 Prevent Power Outages: Power Is Precious and It's Easy to Use It Up

The power that comes from consumer search loyalty will enable the marketer to choose the best channel partners, enforce discipline, curtail free riding, and implement specific policies to ensure that resellers are building or at least not hurting the brand. Your relative power position will also determine the tactics you can reasonably and efficiently employ. More powerful channel "partners" can offer advice on category management, tempt with promotions that come with lots of strings attached, and make variously veiled threats to take their business elsewhere. Less powerful channel members may need to focus on how they contribute to partner profits, provide credible alternatives to strengthen negotiating positions, and be sure they are easy to do business with. Even the "temporarily powerful" can be easily tempted (perhaps unconsciously) to try to extract more than the other channel member's business model will bear (e.g., Costco permitting customers to return Leather Italia's well-worn or even abused furniture). Finally, although the end consumer is always a consideration, channel partners (suppliers and downstream resellers) are also your customer. Make every effort to realistically assess how far up or down the distribution channel your power and influence can extend before your reach exceeds your grasp.

16.3.3 Be the Expert on Where and Why Your Target Consumer Visits, (Re)Searches, and Buys

Consumers don't necessarily buy where they shop. Understanding where your target consumers search and where they buy, not just where your product category is purchased, is essential for prioritizing distribution coverage in different channels. For Brooks, it's not just the channels that sell a lot of running shoes, but the channels that dedicated runners visit to search for and/or buy their running shoes. Understanding why target consumers visit the channels they do is essential for prioritizing what functions to encourage and support in different channels. A 360-degree view of the end consumer may be infeasible for any given channel member but sharing path-to-purchase data (appropriately anonymized) with other channel partners is feasible if the owners of data are convinced that they will also benefit. Without such data, the role that some channel members play for your customers may not be fully recognized and many of the advantages of sophisticated marketing analytics can be lost. New technologies like blockchain facilitate data sharing, but data, and the insights gleaned from them, are a source of power that can be converted to profits. Sharing the profits will be essential to realizing the potential of new technologies. Better to share the data, power, and profits with your channel partners than hand it over to Facebook or Google.

16.3.4 Form Should Follow Function with Channel Pay and Incentives

Getting distribution right means consistently getting the right part of your product line in front of the target consumer at the right time and place, at the right price, and with the right type of service. Decide whether you want to differentiate or harmonize across multiple channels. If different consumer segments shop *and* buy in different channels, and you can align separate portions of a long product line and associated services for each channel, then go ahead and differentiate. If you are serving the same or similar consumer segments in different channels, and they use different channels at different stages of their path to purchase or at different purchase occasions, try to harmonize. Ideally, functions should be performed where they are most valued by the consumer and by the channel members who can perform them most efficiently. Remember that channel members earn their pay to perform functions, not only to make a sale. Design channel incentives and support programs that foster the desired behavior, minimize potential for opportunism by channel members, and are not too difficult to monitor. But also design programs in a way that does not run afoul of the law. Be particularly careful if you have a dominant market share, and avoid, as much as possible, making your own trade support contingent on the channel member's business with your competitors.

16.3.5 The Direct Approach Can Work, but You Really Have to Know What You're Doing

There are good reasons why independent channels are the rule, not the exception. Even if digital technology has made it easier to connect directly with end consumers, the aggregation of demand and supply is still not something most suppliers can accomplish on their own. Those lucky few who can are usually the most diversified suppliers or those with the most highly sought-after brands in high involvement categories. Which means you must decide whether the direct channel is a sales channel in full-on competition with independent channel partners; or a way to showcase the brand, conduct market research, and provide a benchmark for pricing and merchandising; or primarily an information channel to support consumers along the path-to-purchase and route them to channel partners. In each case, the costs, both fixed and variable, will be very different, and so will the metrics to measure success. Contribution margins may be higher in the direct channel (even that is not assured given the high costs of delivery and returns), but the costs of pull marketing are higher too, and the very substantial costs of expanding the product line to support the direct channel must figure in the equation. Also remember that if you want other channel partners to perform functions even if they don't get the sale, then you too should be willing to do that in your direct channel.

16.3.6   The Devil Is in the Details, and So Is the Profit

Take apart the resellers' business models, the specific target market access they can provide, the detailed functions they deliver, their resources, capabilities, and their cost structure. Also assess their willingness to reinvest for growth and in the health (not just the sales) of your brand.

It's not just whether you sell through digital intermediaries but what and how you sell through them. Should you sell to Amazon.com or sell on its 3P marketplace, and should you allow your retailers to be 3P sellers? Who sets the price? Which products are offered on which channels, when, and for how long? How much of your digital product should you provide to Google or Facebook or Spotify or Netflix and for how much payment? Who sets the cancellation and returns policy for your products and who pays for returns? Where does the transaction occur? Who gets the customer data? What happens when there are violations of MAP policies or of promotional agreements? The answers to any of these questions, even individually but certainly jointly, can make or break the distribution system.

16.3.7   Avoid Future Shock by Planning and Managing
the Rate of Change

The dilemma of changing or adopting new channels is mainly this: cannibalize your distribution channels too quickly and sales will be lost.

Move over to the new, growing channels too slowly and sales will be also lost. As we, and almost everyone else writing about channels, have noted, change is constant and it generally moves toward more efficient distribution systems. But getting the timing of adoption right is not easy. Neither is managing the transition. How do you talk to different audiences, sometimes out of both sides of your mouth, during the transition when uncertainty is apt to be greatest? If possible, time the opening of a new channel in periods of growth (think Apple stores). Allocate the product line among the different channels, prioritizing the newest or most desirable products for the more important channels (think Burberry or Nike). Take the same opportunity to prune less productive resellers and step up support for the ones you need (think Brooks or Progressive). Even so, transition periods are often rough seas to be navigated with care. Controlled growth in channels that represent the future, focused support for the traditional ones that will continue to be needed, and careful trimming of declining channels, are required to maintain the balance.

16.4 CONCLUSION: WHO WILL BE THE MASTERS OF MULTI-CHANNEL DISTRIBUTION?

It is easy to think about multi-channel distribution as mainly the adoption of digital technologies and online sales. We understand why selling over the web or on mobile dominates the conversation, but we hope we have convinced you that getting multi-channel distribution right is about much more than going digital. Within a given industry or market, will entrepreneurial, "born digital" competitors dominate brick-and-mortar based and other traditional incumbents? Which will prove to be the fittest in the still-evolving multi-channel distribution environment: Seventh Generation or the Honest Company? Netflix or Disney? Allbirds or Brooks? Levi's or Bonobos? The winners, we believe, will not be tied to how they started. They will build organizations that perform fundamental distribution functions sought by the end-consumer in the most efficient and sustainable ways. To that end, we hope our readers will benefit from the metrics, frameworks, and cases that we have endeavored to provide in this book, whether they are digital natives who realize they need to master physical channels, or traditional marketers who need to integrate digital and direct channels into the mix.

ENDNOTES

i. The following articles will give the interested reader a bird's-eye view of the types of issues researchers study in this domain: Batra, R., and Keller, K. (2016). Integrating Marketing Communications: New Findings, New Lessons, and New Ideas. *Journal of Marketing* 80: 122–145. Dost, F., Phieler, U., Haenlein, M., and Libai, B. (2018). Seeding as Part of the Marketing Mix: Word-of-Mouth Program Interactions for Fast-Moving Consumer Goods. *Journal of Marketing*, 80 (2): 62–81. Naik, P. (2007). Integrated Marketing Communications: Provenance, Practice and Principles. In: *The SAGE Handbook of Advertising* (ed. G.J. Tellis and T. Ambler), pp. 35–53. Thousand Oaks, CA: Sage Publications.

ii. See, for example: Srinivasan, S., Vanhuele, M., and Pauwels, K. (2010). Mind-Set Metrics in Market Response Models: An Integrative Approach. *Journal of Marketing Research*, 67: 672–684.

iii. Wiesel, T., Pauwels, K., and Arts, J. (2011). Practice Prize Paper: Marketing's Profit Impact: Quantifying Online and Off-line Funnel Progression. *Marketing Science* 30 (4): 565–756. Dinner, I., van Heerde, H., and Neslin, S. (2014). Driving Online and Offline Sales: The Cross-Channel Effects of Traditional, Online Display, and Paid Search Advertising. *Journal of Marketing Research* 51 (5): 527–545.

iv. See, for example: Du, R., Xu, L., and Wilbur, K. (2019). Immediate Responses of Online Brand Search and Price Search to TV Ads. *Journal of Marketing* 83 (4): 81–100.

v. Fulton, W. (2016). Why AriZona Iced Tea Is Cheaper Than Water. thrillist.com/drink/nation/arizona-iced-tea-price-don-vultaggio-interview (25 October), (accessed April 2018).

vi. American Egg Board (2019). Industry overview. https://www.aeb.org/farmers-and-marketers/industry-overview (accessed September 2019).

Author Index

Subject Index